THE WIDENING SCOPE OF SHAME

THE WIDENING SCOPE
OF SHAME

edited by
Melvin R. Lansky
and
Andrew P. Morrison

THE ANALYTIC PRESS

1997   Hillsdale, NJ   London

The following chapters appeared in earlier versions and are
adapted here by permission of their publishers: ch. 10, "A Common
Type of Marital Incompatibility" by S. Levin (*J. Amer. Psychoanal.
Assn.,* 17:421-436, 1969); ch. 11, "Further Comments on a
Common Type of Marital Incompatibility" by S. Levin (*J. Amer.
Psychoanal. Assn.,* 17:1097-1113, 1969); ch. 13, "Shame: The
Dark Shadow of Infertility" by C. A Munschauer (*Resolve National
Newsletter,* 18/2, 1993); ch. 18, "Shame, Humiliation, and Stigma"
by A. Lazare (in *The Medical Interview,* ed. Lipkin, Putnam, and.
Lazare. New York: Springer-Verlag, 1994); ch. 19, "Shame and the
Resistance to Jewish Renewal," by M. J. Bader (*Tikkun,* 9(6).

Published by The Analytic Press, Inc.
101 West Street, Hillsdale, NJ 07642

Typeset by Sally Zegarelli, Long Branch, NJ

Library of Congress Cataloging-in-Publication Data

The widening scope of shame / edited by Melvin R. Lansky,
  Andrew P. Morrison
    p. cm.
  Includes bibliographic references and index.
  ISBN 0-88163-169-8
  1. Shame. I. Lansky, Melvin R. II. Morrison, Andrew P., 1937-
  BF575.S45N49   1997
  152.4--dc21   97-11431
                                                           CIP

Printed in the United States of America
10 9 8 7 6 5 4 3 2 1

To Karen, Madeleine, and Joshua
M. R. L

To Rachel
A. P. M.

Contents

I. PSYCHOANALYTIC PERSPECTIVES

II. BIOLOGY, PSYCHOLOGY, PHILOSOPHY, SOCIAL THEORY

Contributors

HOWARD A. BACAL, M.D. is a Training and Supervising Analyst at the Institute of Contemporary Psychoanalyst and at the Southern California Psychoanalytic Institute. He is also a Supervising Analyst at the Institute for the Psychoanalytic Study of Subjectivity, New York City.

MICHAEL J. BADER, D.M.H. is a member of the San Francisco Psychoanalytic Institute and a Contributing Editor for *Tikkun Magazine.*

FRANCIS BROUCEK, M.D. is a member of the teaching Faculty, The Topeka Institute for Psychoanalysis and the Kansas City Psychoanalytic Institute. He has been in the private practice of psychiatry in the Kansans City area since 1979.

KAREN HANSON, Ph.D. is Professor of Philosophy, Indiana University.

JACK KATZ, J.D., Ph.D. is Professor of Sociology at the University of California, Los Angeles. He is currently completing *Mundane Metamorphoses: Emotions in the Practice of Everyday Life.*

BENJAMIN KILBORNE, Ph.D., previously on the faculties of the Sorbonne and the University of California, San Diego and Los Angeles, is currently on the faculties of the Los Angeles Psychoanalytic Institute, the Southern Californian Psychoanalytic Institute, and the Los Angeles Institute and Society for Psychoanalytic Studies, where he is also a Training and Supervising Analyst.

MELVIN R. LANSKY, M.D. (Editor) is Clinical Professor of Psychiatry, University of California.

AARON LAZARE, M.D. is Chancellor, University of Massachusetts Medical Center, and Dean and Professor of Psychiatry, University of Massachusetts Medical School.

ROBERT MICHELS, M.D. is Walsh McDermott Professor of Medicine University Professor of Psychiatry, Cornell University Medical College, and Training and Supervising Analyst, Columbia University Center for Psychoanalytic Training and Research.

ANDREW P. MORRISON, M.D. (Editor) is Associate Clinical Professor of Psychiatry at Harvard Medical School. He is on the faculties of the Boston Psychoanalytic Society and Institute and the Massachusetts Institute for Psychoanalysis.

CAROL A. MUNSCHAUER, Ph.D. is Clinical Assistant Professor of Psychiatry at the State University of New York at Buffalo School of Medicine. She is also a member of the Eastern Regional Division of the International Council for Psychoanalytic Self Psychology.

DONALD L. NATHANSON, M.D. is Executive Director of The Silvan S. Tomkins Institute and Clinical Professor of Psychiatry and Human Behavior, Jefferson Medical College, Philadelphia, PA.

SUZANNE M. RETZINGER, Ph.D. is a Mediator and Family Evaluator in the Ventura (CA) Superior Court. She is author of *A New Look at Countertransference: Shame and the Social Bond*, soon to be published.

THOMAS SCHEFF, Ph.D. is Professor Emeritus, Department of Sociology, University of California at Santa Barbara. He is the author of *Emotions, Social Bonds, and Human Reality: Part/Whole Analysis*.

ROBERT D. STOLOROW, Ph.D. is Faculty, Training and Supervising Analyst, Institute of Contemporary Psychoanalysis, Los Angeles; Faculty, Institute for the Psychoanalytic Study of Subjectivity; Clinical Professor of Psychiatry, UCLA School of Medicine.

LÉON WURMSER, M.D. is Training and Supervising Analyst, New York Freudian Society, and Clinical Professor of Psychiatry, University West Virginia, Charleston.

Preface

Why another book on shame? A significant number of first-rate contributions to the study of shame have appeared since the rediscovery of and expanded attention to shame began in 1971. Prior to that time, psychoanalytic interest in shame was marginal and fragmentary compared with the central position it had occupied in the very earliest psychoanalytic writings.

The year 1971 saw the publication of two major works that ushered in an era of psychoanalytic attention to shame and an explosion of investigation and writing on the subject. In that year, Helen Block Lewis's *Shame and Guilt in Neurosis* and Heinz Kohut's *The Analysis of the Self* were published. Lewis's work, combining sophisticated research methodology and nuanced therapeutic investigation, convincingly demonstrated the relationship of anger and impasse in the therapeutic situation to antecedent shame experiences that had not been acknowledged by either therapist or patient. Kohut's studies of lack of self cohesion and selfobject transferences in the narcissistic personality disorders not only ushered in the self psychology movement but also enhanced psychoanalytic understanding of affect in relation to self and that other used for the purpose of solidifying the sense of self. Shame, a major accompaniment to disorders of personality cohesion, came into sharp focus and increased prominence and remained an affect of major importance not only to those committed to self-psychology but also to mainstream psychoanalysts who acquired new-found appreciation of the nuances of affect in relation to self and object.

Important contributions to the study of shame followed. Leon Wurmser's (1981) *The Mask of Shame* remains a seminal and ground-breaking addition to the study of shame. Important collections of essays under the editorship of Helen Block Lewis (1987) and of Donald Nathanson (1987) put shame "on the map" of therapeutic attention. Influential single-authored books include those by Schneider (1977), Morrison (1989), Scheff (1990), Retzinger (1991), Lansky (1992), Broucek (1992), Nathanson (1992), and M. Lewis (1993).

Where does this book stand in relation to its predecessors? It is put forward not merely to repeat or update what has already been well done; its aim, rather, is to provide a broader perspective than can be found in any single existing volume intended for, but not limited to, clinicians. The book traces the evolution and current status not only of psychoanalytic thinking on shame but also that of biologic, social theoretical, philosophical, and research psychological contributions. It considers, as well, approaches centered on marriage and the family along with those drawn from general psychotherapeutic, medical, and religious contexts. Broad-based as it is, this book may profitably be read cover to cover, not used simply as a handbook or a reference work.

This collection necessarily reflects the outlook of its editors on the issue of shame. Although both editors are psychoanalysts heavily steeped in psychoanalytic discipline who draw from the entire range of psychoanalytic contributions, the work reflects a synthesis of a relatively mainstream position (MRL) with one closer to that of self psychology (APM). Despite these differences, which we hope will enhance the scope of the book, we share the following convictions:

1. That psychoanalytic thinking is, at its best, broad-based and integrated—an orchestra, as it were, and not a single instrument or type of instrument. Too much emphasis on any one paradigm or school of thought limits the application of psychoanalytic thinking to a narrow set of phenomena, explanatory concepts, and psychotherapeutic approaches. Both editors see the recognition of (often hidden) shame and shame-related phenomena as the key to an integrated psychoanalytic understanding of a very wide range of clinical phenomenology, often represented in the literature and in clinical practice by separate schools of thought in ways that are unintegrated, incomplete, and fragmentary.

2. The hidden nature of shame and of shame-related phenomena has tended to obscure the relationship of aspects of the clinical phenomenology to the clinical whole. We share the belief that the rediscovery and expanded understanding of shame and shame-related

phenomena is crucial to the attainment of a balanced and full psychoanalytic understanding that avoids pars pro toto theorizing. Often the hidden dimension, shame has been called the "veiled accompaniment" of clinical phenomena as widespread and divergent as narcissism, social phobia, envy, domestic violence, addiction, identity diffusion, post traumatic stress disorder, dissociation, masochism, and depression. Shame also provides important clues to the understanding of the instigation of dreams, nightmares, and impulsive action of all sorts.

3. The emphasis on shame, therefore, is neither limited to the consciously experienced emotion itself nor intended as a rival or replacement for any other affective phenomena (for example anger, anxiety, and guilt). A nuanced appreciation of shame adds to, rather than replaces, previous explanations of psychic or clinical phenomena. Indeed, simplified formulations that overemphasize the centrality of shame in clinical practice risk ignoring simultaneous competition, aggression, envy, and the guilt and anxiety that invariably accompany them (Lansky, in press).

4. Shame may be seen, therefore, not simply as the label for a specific emotion concomitant to social exposure of one as inadequate or unlovable. Shame, as we use the word, subsumes this narrow sense but also encompasses, more expansively, the entire spectrum of shame-related phenomena, among them: signal shame (a type of superego anxiety); shame as defense (characteristically seen as a reaction formation); and a constellation of feelings (embarrassment, humility, modesty, and the like) all aimed at obviating exposure and the consequent emotion of shame.

5. When its manifest and hidden aspects are understood, shame points, then, to the deepest levels of comprehension of the bond between self and others and the regulation of that bond by manifest affects signaling success or failure within that bond—pride or shame. Less visible, repressed aspects of the social bond also reflect shame. The understanding of shame unfolds pari passu with a deep understanding of the self in relation to others (not merely "objects" or "selfobjects"). Such an understanding is intimately related, therefore, to an understanding of social systems of every sort—from the internal world of internalized "objects"; to the family system; to the broader social order, large or small, in which shame and shame-related phenomena are key to the regulation of selfhood and esteem.

Our view of shame, then, is decidedly integrative, both clinically and theoretically. The book reflects this attitude.

Part I, begins with a lengthy essay by the editors on Freud's legacy on shame; traces Freud's brilliant discoveries as well as his conceptual inconsistencies and oversights in an historical context. Broucek's chapter on development and that by Morrison and Stolorow on narcissism are informed by self-psychological and intersubjective viewpoints. Commentaries by Bacal and Michels place these chapters in wider perspective. It is our aim in this section to present clinically pertinent perspectives on development and on narcissism. The chapters are not intended to serve as evenhanded reviews taking all contemporary positions into account.

Part II covers approaches to thinking about shame that are not psychoanalytic but are still useful to psychodynamically oriented therapists and psychoanalysts interested in a broader understanding of shame. The chapters include contributions on Helen Block Lewis, on Silvan Tompkins, two contributions on philosophy, and two on social theory. Karen Hanson's chapter traces the evolution of philosophical thinking on shame in two large sweeps. The first, from Aristotle to Kant, points to an expanding shame about shame. Hanson points to a quite different trend in the almost two centuries beginning with Hegel's (1807) *Phenomenology of Spirit.* This trend locates shame within "the human predicament." Wurmser's chapter on "Nietzsche's War on Shame" focuses on Nietzsche as the apotheosis of the more recent trend in philosophy. The two chapters on social theory by Scheff and by Katz highlight the evolution and current status of social, theoretical thinking about shame. Scheff's chapter draws attention to the 19th-century theoretical preeminence of shame, its disappearance early in this century with the ascendancy of role theory, and its subsequent reemergence in social theory in a time span very closely paralleling the early attention, disappearance, and reemergence of interest in shame in psychoanalytic thinking. A discussion of these six chapters by Benjamin Kilborne reminds us that, momentous as these theoretical and empirical trends in the study of shame are, they inevitably fail to capture the elusive human essence of shame. Kilborne emphasizes that great writers of fiction— Pirandello is a case in point—better capture the eternally elusive essence of the shame experience.

Part III turns to marriage and the family. The understanding of tension and distress in relationships among intimates is greatly enhanced by an understanding of shame. Two classic papers by Sidney Levin, an early psychoanalytic pioneer in the study of shame, point to shame's role in a particular type of marital incompatibility that will be recognized by all experienced clinicians. Carol Munschauer's contribution on infertility presents a self-psychological perspective on the psychological implications of this often overlooked challenge. Suzanne Retzinger's paper on shame and rage and marital quarrels draws on her sophisticated research, which was heavily influenced by Helen Block Lewis, into the relation of anger to unacknowledged shame and the relationship of reciprocal shaming to conflict escalation.

The final section offers contributions on the phenomenology of various clinical predicaments and other situations in which shame plays a prominent part. A chapter by Lansky on envy as process explores the multiple relationships between shame and envy. Nathanson's chapter on the compass of shame reflects his interest in the work of Silvan Tompkins and provides an introduction to the application of his own viewpoint to Attention Deficit Disorder. Wurmser's chapter on masochism synthesizes a vast body of theory and a penetrating clinical perspicuity on this complex and difficult topic. Aaron Lazare's chapter discusses the often overlooked features of shame and humiliation in the medical setting. Finally, Michael Bader explores the dynamics of shame in resistance to religious experience.

Our collaboration in the study of shame has been greatly enriched by the discussions of a group on shame dynamics that have been a regular part of meetings of the American Psychoanalytic Association twice yearly since 1991. Benjamin Kilborne, the group's founder and chairman, has been an erudite collaborator in our efforts to study shame. Leon Wurmser, a great pioneer in both theoretical and clinical understanding of shame, has been a regular attender. We are grateful to Drs. Kilborne and Wurmser and to others who have regularly or sporadically participated in the group and have enriched us with their participation, their perspective and their support.

Finally, we wish to thank the staff of The Analytic Press, Dr. Paul E. Stepansky and Eleanor Starke Kobrin especially, for their assistance, encouragement, and support for this project from inception to completion.

M. R. L.
A. P. M.

REFERENCES

Broucek, F. (1991), *Shame and the Self*. New York: Guilford.

Hegel, G. W. F. (1807), *The Phenomenology of Spirit*, trans. A. V. Miller. Oxford: Oxford University Press. 1977, pp. 111–119.

Kohut, H. (1971), *The Analysis of the Self*. New York: International Universities Press.

Lansky, M. (1992), *Fathers Who Fail*. Hillsdale, NJ: The Analytic Press.

———— (in press), Shame and the idea of a central affect. *Psychoanal. Inq.*

Lewis, H. B. (1971), *Shame and Guilt in Neuroses*. New York: International Universities Press.

———— ed. (1987), *The Role of Shame in Symptom Formation*. Hillsdale, NJ: Lawrence Erlbaum Associates.

Lewis, M. (1993), *Shame, The Exposed Self*. New York: Free Press.

Morrison, A. (1989), *Shame*. Hillsdale, NJ: The Analytic Press.

Nathanson, D., ed. (1992), *Shame and Pride*. New York: Norton.

Retzinger, S. (1991), *Violent Emotions*. Newbury Park: G. Sage.

Scheff, T. (1990), *Microsociology*. Chicago: University of Chicago Press.

Schneider, C. (1977), *Shame, Exposure, and Privacy*. Boston, MA: Beacon.

Wurmser, L. (1981), *The Mask of Shame*. Baltimore, MD: Johns Hopkins University Press.

I

PSYCHOANALYTIC
PERSPECTIVES

1

MELVIN R. LANSKY
ANDREW P. MORRISON

The Legacy of Freud's Writings on Shame

THE ECLIPSE AND REEMERGENCE
OF ATTENTION TO SHAME

The emphasis on shame in Freud's early formulations of conflict and defense was followed very abruptly by an almost complete eclipse of attention to shame after his turn to intrapsychic fantasy (Freud, 1905a). After that turn, we argue, the nature of shame and of shame conflicts was incompletely conceptualized and acknowledged mostly in relation to conflicts involving anality and exhibitionism. Interest in shame had a somewhat veiled reemergence in 1914 (see Freud, 1914a) with the unfolding appreciation of ideals and aspirations accompanying attention to narcissism and the ego ideal, but the relationship between shame and narcissism was never made explicit in Freud's subsequent writings. After a period of more than 70 years during which shame and shame dynamics were underemphasized in psychoanalytic writing, an explosion of interest in shame followed the appearance of major works by Heinz Kohut (1971) and Helen Block Lewis (1971) (see also Wurmser, 1981; Broucek, 1991; Nathanson, 1987; M. Lewis, 1991; Morrison, 1989; Lansky, 1992).

In this chapter, we provide both an outline of and a perspective on Freud's thinking on shame and its impact—thinking that is both explicit and implicit in his writings. Freud's explicit writings consider shame as an affective response to exposure and as a component of intrapsychic conflict. The implicit writings encompass the theory of dreams, narcissism, and the evolution of the psychoanalytic theories of conscience and of the psychoanalytic process.

We trace this history of Freud's writings on shame because of our conviction that a good deal of the polarization and dissension in psychoanalytic theory results from a lack of integration of theory with clinical observation and would be lessened if our basic concepts were expanded to take into account shame and shame dynamics—often hidden dimensions of complex clinical phenomena. To put the matter simply, we examine Freud's attention (as well as his inattention) to shame because this affect and modes of defense against it are salient, but often unrecognized, aspects of the psychoanalytic process as they are of human experience in general. The intimate relationship between shame and the integration of theory with observation is a complex one. In the course of developing our central themes, we hope to clarify this relationship and to illustrate the unifying effect of taking shame dynamics more fully into consideration.

We discuss in the next section three milestones in Freud's evolving view of conflict that specifically concern shame: shame as a *motive for defense* (that is, as an affective experience); shame as a *method of defense;* and shame in relation to *ideals and aspirations*. Next is a brief exploration of the shame dynamics in major dreams discussed in *The Interpretation of Dreams*. In the section on Conscience and that on the psychoanalytic process, we deal with some implications of our expanded understanding of shame, particularly as they bear on some basic psychoanalytic conceptualizations that, as originally formulated by Freud, are more implicit than explicit in their relationship to shame and that, on the surface, may even appear to be unrelated to shame. Since these concepts provide the basis of our daily clinical and theoretical psychoanalytic work, however, we believe there is a risk of forming inexact and downright incorrect formulations of the clinical significance of our work if the role of shame is not appreciated. While we emphasize the failure to recognize and appreciate the significance of shame, we wish also to avoid the other extreme of overemphasizing shame to the exclusion of balanced attention to other clinical phenomena.

The focus on shame is not simply an exercise in exchanging one affect for another, that is, shame for guilt. The longstanding failure to appreciate the role of shame had to do with a number of complex factors. First is an incomplete view of the nature of the social bond, attachment, and the centrality of relationships and relatedness to human experience, and the role of shame in regulating that bond/relationship. Second is the failure to realize the extent to which shame often exerts its dynamic influence in a veiled or hidden way—hiding, as it were, under more visible clinical phenomena such as anxiety, guilt, envy, contempt, and reaction to narcissistic injury.

Third is the silent pressure on analysts to avoid confronting their own shame in clinical encounters with the shame of patients, along with the mutual collusion between patient and therapist to avoid that confrontation, which often repeats the patient's lifelong predicament of having to protect the other from shame.

The same eclipse and reemergence of attention to shame has taken place in social theory (see chapter 8). Shame is the affect that signals the threat of danger to the social bond (Scheff, 1990) or to a sense of integrity and regard for the self. Shame as we now understand it results from any exposure that challenges the integrity of the self. Here the self is defined as a self before others or the sense of self that results from a self-evaluation derived from internalizing that actual or imagined view of oneself before others. At some point in development, shaming ceases to be an entirely social emotion and becomes internalized. The watchful eye making the shaming judgment becomes one's own, potentially independent of a sustaining relationship or the feared loss of social connection (Morrison, 1987). This source of shame becomes failure, a falling short of a cherished ideal (which may include, of course, the ideal of worthiness and sustenance in a loving relationship).

This view of the evolution of appearance of shame, then, is not just a matter of one emotional state's being emphasized over another—for example, shame over anxiety and guilt. It has philosophical roots (see chapter 7), harkening back to the central insight put forward by Hegel (1807) writing about self-consciousness. That is, that the self is a self only by virtue of being defined as such by the recognition conferred by the other. The sense of self, therefore, always remains at some risk for dissolution if the individual is rejected by significant persons in the social order.[1] The Hegelian insight into the relation of self to other highlights the importance of shame.

Shame signals danger to the self within the bond to the object. Shame, then, is inextricably linked to *what it is that one needs an object for*. Hence, the lack of conceptual integration that resulted

---

[1]Hegel's insight into the contingency of the experience of selfhood on the other represents a monumental link between philosophy and psychology and one that highlights the importance of self-consciousness and shame. The emphasis on the contingency of selfhood or recognition from the other, and on the ever-present risk of shame if this contingency is exposed, has been adapted to a wide variety of psychoanalytic points of view that differ in their views of the nature of that other in influencing the sense of self. For example, see the works of such diverse thinkers as Lacan (1977), Grunberger (1974), Stierlin (1959), Jacobson (1964), and Kohut (1971), to name a few.

from overlooking the role of shame and the unifying effect of taking it seriously in uniting the self-conscious individual psyche with the social order. It remained for later psychoanalytic work to develop a notion of shame that had an intrapsychic component that was independent of the actual presence of the other.

We are, of course, contending that the original psychoanalytic notions of self, object, and affect were too mechanistic to encompass a nuanced inquiry into the relationship of self to other. The other is not merely an object of an instinct; one does not need the other simply as an enabler of drive discharge.

The term object was used originally as one of the attributes of a drive or of desire. A *drive* had *source*, *aim*, and *object* (Freud, 1905a). "The object of an instinct is the thing in regard to which or through which the instinct is able to achieve its aim" (Freud, 1915, p. 122)). Freud's view of emotions did not take sufficiently into account regulation of the self as a social being both in fantasy and in actuality). Freud's original formulation of "the object" was made without concern for an understanding of the specific nature of the object (*of social bonding*), of relationship, or of sustaining function. We will return to these points after we trace briefly some highlights emphasizing the relationship of shame to the evolution of psychoanalytic theory generally and Freud's writing in particular.

The original connotation of "object" forecloses consideration of the (basically Hegelian) view that the self or sense of self develops not out of a psychology drive discharge at all, but out of response from and relationship with another. The sense of self emerges only gradually independently of that other as one learns eventually to distinguish one's subjective experiences and awareness of one's sensations as one's own. Kohut (1971), much more explicitly than any of his psychoanalytic predecessors, viewed this registration of feelings and sensations of one's own, in relationship with a confirming and soothing environment of selfobjects, as defining the experience of selfhood. We are emphasizing this contrast to underscore the role of the other in the sense of self as an essential and complex element in our understanding of shame.

The philosophical tradition beginning with Hegel has continued into 20th-century existential thought. Drawing from Hegel, Sartre (1945) put central emphasis on "the look" of the other that confers or denies selfhood to the self:

> Now shame as we noted is shame of *self*; it is the *recognition* of the fact that I *am* indeed that object which the other is looking at and judging. I can be ashamed only as my freedom escapes me in order

to become an object . . . beyond any knowledge which I can have,
I am this self which another knows [p. 350].

Sartre's point of view has elements in common with that of
Kohut, who saw the condition of selfhood unfolding in an affirming
environment of responsive selfobjects. Thus, affirmation from the
responsive selfobject providing the experience that nurtures the
developing self can, broadly, be compared to the conceptualization
of the watchful other conferring selfhood. Although differences
between the two viewpoints abound, there is certainly agreement
that the shaky, tentative, contingent sense of self attributed to people
with so-called self—or narcissistic—disorders is challenged or brought
into relief at times of relational dislodgement, rejection, or abandonment.

We turn now to a selective consideration of Freud's writings on
shame—explicitly in some of his basic notions of intrapsychic conflict
and implicitly in his basic notions of the conscience and of the
psychoanalytic process.

Shame in Freud's Early Theoretical
Writings on Intrapsychic Conflict

In this overview of shame in Freud's writings, we touch on three
important attitudes toward shame in relation to intrapsychic conflict
that remain important facets of psychoanalytic thinking: shame as the
painful affect underlying the need for repression; shame as a major
mode of reaction formation; and shame in relation to narcissism and
the ego ideal.

The Incompatible Idea: Shame
as a Motive for Defense

Shame occupied a surprisingly important position in Breuer's and
Freud's earliest prepsychoanalytic writings. In *Studies on Hysteria*,
Breuer and Freud (1893-95) conceptualized repression, the generic
term for defense, as protecting against awareness that would lead to
distressing affects, especially shame. They wrote:

*(B)y means of my psychical work, I have had to overcome a
psychical force in the patients which was opposed to the pathogenic ideas becoming conscious (being remembered)*. . . . From these

I recognized the universal characteristic of such ideas. They were all of a distressing nature, calculated to arouse the affects of shame, of self-reproach and of psychical pain and the feeling of being harmed; they were all of a kind that one would prefer not to have experienced, that one would rather forget. From all this, there arose, as it were, automatically the thought of *defense.* . . . The patient's ego had been approached by an idea which proved to be incompatible, which provoked on the part of the ego a repelling force of which the purpose was defense against this incompatible idea [pp. 268–269].

Here, quite clearly, defense is aimed at *awareness*. The reason for this defense is that the awareness in question would cause pain. The pain is specific, having to do with the anticipation of disapproval and rejection by others, a rejection that is internalized in the form of self-reproach. Such an anticipation involves not simply consciousness, but *self*-consciousness, that is, consciousness of the self as possessing attributes that are incompatible with the continued approval or acceptance of others (incompatible ideas). The pain defended against by the repression of incompatible ideas is, therefore, shame. Psychoanalytic attention to resistance takes cognizance of the distress generated by awareness of the incompatible idea—especially distress resulting from shame. This is the first of Freud's formulations relating self-consciousness to emotional pain. He did not, at this time or later, fully integrate self-consciousness into a psychoanalytic framework (see Broucek 1991; M. Lewis, 1992).

This very early, but astonishingly up-to-date, prepsychoanalytic formulation by Freud addressed the problem of consciousness and the problems of understanding the motives for banishing ideas from consciousness. Ideas, then, were subject to repression—the banning of such ideas from consciousness—if they were incompatible with requirements of acceptability and approval by self or others.

As an example of painful affect serving as a motive for repression, Freud linked shame with morality and discussed it as a cause of repression of sexuality in (Freud, 1895). This relationship, he suggested, is particularly strong for girls who are "seized by a *non*-neurotic *sexual* repugnance [which may account for] the flood of shame which overwhelms the female . . . " (p. 270). In Draft K, of this letter to Fleiss, Freud emphasized the social context of shame as an affect, with fear of revealing a repugnant secret to an observing audience. "I reproach myself on account of an event—I am afraid other people know about it—therefore, I feel ashamed in front of other people" (p. 225). In *The Interpretation of Dreams* Freud (1900) detailed embarrassing dreams of nakedness, and "a distressing feeling in the nature of shame and in the fact that one wishes to hide one's nakedness" (p. 242). Discussing problems of withheld information in the famous case of Dora, Freud (1905b) stated, "In the first place, patients consciously and intentionally keep back part of what they ought to tell—things that are perfectly well known to them — because they have not got over their feeling of timidity and shame" (p. 17). Finally, alluding to the displaced source of negative feelings about being in analysis, he stated, "He does not remember having been intensely ashamed of certain sexual activities and afraid of their being found out; but he makes it clear that he is ashamed of the treatment on which he is now embarked and tries to keep it a secret from everybody" (Freud, 1914c, p. 150). Shame and timidity are feelings to be gotten rid of, "worked through," allowing analysis to proceed fruitfully.

This phase of theory and inquiry did not concern itself with questions that arose fulminantly in the next phase, for example, what is the nature of *developmental forces* such that what unfolds ontogenetically and phylogenetically supersedes what came previously? The language of psychoanalysis went, in the short period between the *Studies on Hysteria* (Breuer and Freud, 1893–1895) to the *Three Essays on Sexuality* (Freud, 1905a) from a language emphasizing feelings, awareness, and meaning exclusively to a language that was preoccupied with forces—the drives and the forces opposing them. In this later context, shame was seen not only as an affect but also as a defense, a reaction formation against other instinctual tendencies.

Shame as Reaction Formation: Shame as Method of Defense

After Freud began to appreciate the role of unconscious fantasy and of sexual and aggressive wishes, he started to develop a model of the mind that pushed anxiety and guilt into theoretical preeminence. He relegated shame to matters connected with affects deployed by the psyche as "mental dams" to oppose maturationally emerging impulses toward anal erotism and exhibitionism.

Freud, in this phase of his writings, considered shame both as an affect and as a defense (Hazard, 1969).[2] Freud appreciated shame not only as an end stage of what we might now call narcissistic mortification (the affect), but also as that emotion the fear of which would safeguard us (i.e., provide mental dams or reaction formations) against certain uncivilized behaviors. Shame, in Freud's early writings expands from a *motive for defense*—avoidance of the affect of shame (*honte*)—to encompass a *method of defense*—the affect opposing instinctual "shamelessness" which keeps us on an ethical or civilized course (*pudeur*). This conceptualization of shame as not merely an emotion but as the fear of experiencing an emotion used to buttress morality—that is, to signal shame (Levin, 1967)—is actually an early formulation of the concept of signal anxiety that was developed in 1926.

This line of thinking has philosophical predecessors. In relegating shame to the status of a painful affect, the fear of which buttresses moral standards, Freud followed a line of thinking strikingly similar to the one found in Aristotle's *Nicomachean Ethics*:

> Shame . . . is defined . . . as a sort of fear of disrepute, and its expression is similar to that of fear of something terrifying; for a feeling of disgrace makes people blush, and fear of death makes them turn pale. Hence both [types of fear] appear to be in some ways bodily [reactions] which seem to be more characteristic of feelings than of states.
>
> Further, the feeling of shame is suitable for youth, not for every time of life. For we think it right for young people to be prone to shame, since they live by their feelings, and hence often go astray, but are restrained by shame; and hence we praise young people who are prone to shame. No one, by contrast, would praise an older person for readiness to feel disgrace, since we think it wrong for him to do any action that causes a feeling of disgrace [4.111–4.112; 1985, pp. 114–115, translator's brackets].

At this period of his thinking, Freud made assumptions about the relation of both shame and guilt to anxiety that would now strike us as questionable. Freud saw aggression as actual or fantasized *destructive acts* and hence as engendering guilt as a specific type of (what was later to be called) superego anxiety. He did not seem to

---

[2]In French there are two words for shame, and we would be well served by words that distinguish the affect from the defense. The French *honte* refers to the emotion itself; *pudeur* refers to something like modesty or comportment, that is, the defense, which would avoid shame.

take into account the aspect of aggression that exposes one's self-centeredness and loss of control and hence gives rise to *shame about the self, not simply guilt about the act.* That is to say, he seems to have emphasized the force of instinct and consciousness of destructive wish and to have lost sight of the earlier insights that took into account *self-consciousness* and the disapproval of or rejection by self or others. This peculiarity of focus favors guilt over shame.

Freud's intense preoccupation with development during this period also dominated his focus on that which would regulate progression through developmental stages, both phylogenetic and ontogenetic. He presumed that two phylogenetic developments tended to encourage conflict over tendencies to regress to superseded stages of development: upright posture, which put the genitals in view and perhaps in danger (Freud, 1930b); and the change in modes of sexual stimulation from predominantly olfactory to predominantly visual. In consequence, conflicts of exhibitionism over seeing and being seen came into phylogenetic ascendancy as did conflicts over odors, valued phylogenetically and ontogenetically at earlier stages but later experienced as disgusting and, therefore, shameful (Wurmser, 1981; Slavin, 1993). In both cases, reaction formations were necessary to construct constraints against returning to more archaic instinctual modes of functioning. "[T]hey consequently evoke opposing mental forces (reacting impulses) which, in order to suppress this unpleasure effectively, build up the mental dams I have already mentioned—disgust, shame, and morality" (Freud, 1905a, p. 178).

Fascinating though these developmental speculations be, they nonetheless give rise in practice to generalizations that have resulted in a delay in our appreciation of the role of shame in development, in the psyche generally and in human interactions, including the analytic situation. In emphasizing the role of reaction formations in defending against reversion to earlier states of development, Freud mechanized our conceptualization of shame by positing "mental dams" that oppose archaic instinctual forces and thus ignored the role of self-consciousness of our own affect-laden self-condemnations, our awareness of the reaction of the internalized or external other—in the understanding of shame. He also put forward a model that lends itself to the overgeneralization that, since shame *may* be a reaction formation, shame conflicts *in general originate from or are reducible to* conflicts in which shame serves as a reaction formation opposing archaic instinctual desires. This position was taken by subsequent ego psychologists (Nunberg, 1955; Hartmann and

Lowenstein, 1962), essentially restricting the scope of shame to zonal conflict.

The language of zonal conflict tends a priori to reduce each conflict once associated with a specific developmental zone to the status of being a "revised edition" of an earlier zonal conflict—that is, each new zonal conflict is seen as deriving from an earlier, phase-specific developmental conflict and hence is seen as reducible to it. The presumption that shame conflicts derive exclusively from antecedent repressed zonal conflicts systematically overlooks the role of shame as a response to failed aspirations and unsuccessful regulation of the relational components in all conflict. The concepts that have linked and limited shame to its role as instigator of reaction formations presume that a wide variety of developmental issues, for instance, so-called anal conflicts, are exclusively from conflicts involving anal erotism. While this view of zonal conflict is certainly clinically useful, it tends in many cases to be a mechanistic view of archaic conflicts and their derivatives. Such a viewpoint obviates an appreciation of shame as an affective response to loss of self-regard or lack of approval due to loss of control, for example, from rage, dirtiness, inner unlovability or emptiness, or from struggles with powerful persons for approval or autonomy. In consequence, many shame responses and conflicts over such loss of control, are presumed to be "anal" when, in fact, this designation reflects metaphorically a presupposition that all such responses and conflicts inevitably derive from and represent fixation at a zonal level of anal erotism.

Likewise, we find it questionable to presume that exhibitionism and voyeurism—conflicts over seeing and being seen—necessarily derive from archaic or unresolved wishes to exhibit or to see the genitals specifically. Such conflicts are indeed important in childhood and many do persist into adulthood; and many conflicts over seeing and being seen do concern sexuality generally and genitalia specifically. Nonetheless, it would be an error of considerable significance to assume that every exhibitionistic conflict derives from and is reducible to unresolved conflict concerning infantile genital exhibitionism or voyeurism. As is the case with "anality," such an assumption regarding exhibitionism and voyeurism presumes, without investigation, that current conflicts necessarily derive from childhood conflicts. Kohut's (1971) conceptualization of conflicts regarding the grandiose self is only one example of a shame conflict concerning exhibitionism that cannot be presumed to have arisen from infantile conflicts over exhibiting and seeing the genitals.

Aspirations and Ideals: Shame and Narcissism

After 1905, Freud's explicit theorizing on shame went underground for almost a decade, reappearing only indirectly when he advanced the concept of the ego ideal in "On Narcissism" (Freud, 1914a). The context of Freud's investigations at this time reflected awareness of the impact of severe pathology on successful analytic treatment. The original psychoanalytic treatment model, that of the transference neuroses, posited an intense attachment to the analyst (the nature of which was unacknowledged), which formed the basis of the emphasis on transference and the transference neurosis in psychoanalytic treatment. Freud became aware of clinical phenomena that seemed to reflect a retreat from attachment or an inability to attach. He began to investigate pathology that seemed to consist of a retreat from attachment to the other and movement, instead, to states of withdrawal, brooding, self-absorption, and preoccupation with self. Freud was ambiguous as to the degree to which such self-absorbed, self-loving, or self-protecting phenomena represented the primary state of affairs (i.e., primary narcissism) or were the results of a retreat from object love because of disappointment or rejection.

Either way, the focus of psychoanalytic inquiry was to change again. Insofar as self-absorption reflected a retreat from object love because of disappointment or rejection, the whole question of the nature of the bond between subject and object was reopened to study, including the question of the tentativeness of the social bond and of failure to meet aspirations and standards on which lovability and acceptance were presumed to be contingent.

The ego ideal is, of course, that part of the superego concerned with standards and aspirations. Self-conscious appraisals of ourselves that are discrepant with our aspirations, standards for lovability, and sense of competence, worthiness, and excellence generate shame—the signal of danger to social bonding (i.e., attachment) and to our own assessment of well-being with regard to our ideals. We are propelled to meet our standards in the actual, contemporary view of the other, in the internalized vision of that other, or, ultimately, with respect to our own gaze. Shame, then, is inextricably bound to narcissism—lovability, acceptability, selfhood—which depends on external or internal acceptability or recognition. Purely narcissistic conflicts are those which explicitly reflect conflicting aspirations and ideals of the self, for example, lovability as opposed to autonomy. Shame has been called the underside of narcissism (Morrison, 1989), and the veiled companion of narcissism (Wurmser, 1981).

Let us consider Freud's (1914a) essay on narcissism and contemplate a potential elaboration of shame that was never undertaken. We believe that "On Narcissism" introduced the several elements from which Freud might have considered shame in much greater depth and detail. We can touch only briefly on this important essay but the elements that seem to us most relevant to shame include the ego ideal, inferiority feelings, and self-regard or self-esteem.

Freud (1914a) explicitly derived his considerations of narcissism from libido theory: "The libido that has been withdrawn from the external world has been directed to the ego and thus gives rise to an attitude which may be called narcissism" (p. 75). From this proposal, Freud developed his notions of ego-libido and object-libido, primary narcissism, and reinvestment of libidinal cathexis in the idealized object. The "ideal ego" is invested with narcissism lost from the sense of original perfection emanating from the infantile ego and determines the subjective sense of self-regard (i.e., self-regard and self-esteem): "and when, as he grows up, he is disturbed by the admonition of others and by the awakening of his own critical judgment, so that he can no longer retain that perfection, he seeks to recover it in the new form of an ego ideal" (p. 94). Note here that Freud recognizes both "admonition of others" and "*awakening* of his *own* critical judgment" (italics added) as stimuli to regained perfection through construction of an ego ideal.

Freud then proceeded to his well-known formulation of the ego ideal and its relationship to what was to become the superego: "It would not surprise us if we were to find a special psychical agency which performs the task of seeing the narcissistic satisfaction from the ego ideal is ensured and which, with this end in view, constantly watches the actual ego and measures it by that ideal" (p. 95). Meeting the standards of the ego ideal defines the achievement of self-regard. Such an attainment harkens back to the earlier situation of the ego's success in loving or receiving love from an idealized object. An inability to love lowers self-regard, causing feelings of inferiority—further functions of the ego ideal. Freud ended his essay with a discussion of object love as a means of rediscovering lost narcissism through narcissistic idealization of, and investment in, the libidinal object. Liberation of homosexual libido is transformed into a sense of "guilt" out of a fear of loss of love of the parents, and, later, of the social group (pp. 101–102). Here, Freud equated guilt with loss of love, another example of his confounding shame with guilt.

Why did Freud concern himself with narcissism and ego ideal at this time in the evolution of his libido theory? We believe that he was struggling to deal with the major defections from psychoanalysis of Adler and Jung and that his narcissism paper represented, in part, an explicit attempt to refute their critiques of his theories of sexuality. In support of this contention, it should be noted that Freud (1914b) was writing *On the History of the Psychoanalytic Movement* in the same months of 1914 that he wrote "On Narcissism," with its extensive discussion of Adler's and Jung's views. In the *History*, he said of Adler, "Whatever in the nature of a masculine protest can be shown to exist is easily traceable to a disturbance in primary narcissism due to threats of castration or to the earliest interferences with sexual activity" (Freud, 1914b, p. 55). He also acknowledged, but did not further discuss, Adler's thoughts about the relationship of inferiority feelings to childhood and, implicitly, to smallness. Freud criticized Jung, whose new "movement" Freud (p. 60) considered to be the less important, for deleting the sexual from all developmental theory and substituting the "non-fulfillment of the life task" (p. 63). Jung's changes, he wrote, "flow from his intention to eliminate what is objectionable in the family complexes (i.e., sexuality), so as not to find it again in religion and ethics" (p. 62).

Freud's views on narcissism, then, rested on an inexplicit and incompletely developed notion of shame (see also chapter 3, this volume). We see narcissism, somewhat schematically, as shame-proneness accompanied by attempts to hide the inner experience of shame and disconnection from significant objects. This may be accomplished either by a retreat to self-absorption and imagined self-sufficiency or by grandiose aspirations that try to mitigate that shame in ways that may make intense demands on others so that one's real and ideal self become identical. This oscillation has been referred to by Morrison (1989) as the dialectic of narcissism.

We relate the nature of the narcissistic quest to the type of shame involved. We point to two fields of shame, predominating differently for specific groups of individuals. One group emphasizes the relational aspect, the bond of self to an object by which the self looks to the other for self-definition. Narcissism for this group consists of the yearning to be absolutely unique to the other. For the second group the more sharply differentiated self, relatively independent of feedback from the relational surround, nonetheless makes judgments about himself reflecting his performance or attainment of self-defined goals and ideals. For this group, narcissism consists of the quest to be the only; to be absolutely unique in the eyes of the important other. These categories approximate the field-dependent and field-independent groups delineated by Lewis (1971), except that we are suggesting that field independence does not represent protection against shame. For the first group, for whom the self continues to be *defined* by its bond to the object, the problem of shame is inextricably linked to the problem of *what it is that one needs an object for*. For the other, the problem of shame relates more to the nature of punitive self-judgment and inextricably harsh condemnations that are linked to matters of moral masochism, negative therapeutic reactions, and the like. The lack of conceptual integration in psychoanalytic theory and practice that results from overlooking the role of shame has led to gaps in uniting the self-conscious individual psyche within its relational matrix and the social order (that is, in perpetuating the one-person psychology of Freud's theorizing). Likewise, neglect of the role of shame has produced gaps in explaining the so-called loving functions of the superego and self-judgments regarding its ideals and aspirations. (Schafer, 1960; Lampl de-Groot, 1962.)

Freud's explicit attention to shame, then, dwindled from the preeminent and important position it had held in his very earliest writings to the role of affective accompaniment of a more limited, zonally circumscribed set of conflicts. Shame was also a component of the incompletely developed notion of signal anxiety, from the ego ideal, signal shame, presaging danger to self-regard or meaningful attachments because of deficiency in comparison with ideals that make the person lovable, acceptable, self-respecting, and worthy of bonding.

SHAME CONFLICTS IN FREUD'S DREAMS IN *THE INTERPRETATION OF DREAMS*

We turn to a brief examination of conflict in four of Freud's dreams used as illustrative material in *The Interpretation of Dreams*. The reader should keep in mind that each of these dreams is put forward by Freud to illustrate the specific point being made in the text and, therefore, is not intended as an example of a completely analyzed dream. We consider, in addition to the dream text, the day residue, Freud's associations, and conflicts to which the dream is a response.

The Irma Dream

The celebrated "specimen dream," (Freud, 1900, pp. 107–121) is intended to illustrate the application of the associative method to elements of the manifest dream to reach the latent dream thoughts.

In the day residue, Freud is preoccupied with his disgrace in the eyes of his colleagues because a case has gone badly. He says in the preamble:

One day I had a visit from a junior colleague, one of my oldest friends, who had been staying with my patient, Irma, and her family at their country resort. I asked how he had found her and he answered: "She's better, but not quite well." I was conscious that my friend Otto's words, or the tone in which he spoke them, annoyed me. I fancied I detected a reproof in them, such as to the effect that I had promised the patient too much; and, whether rightly or wrongly, I attributed the supposed fact of Otto's siding against me to the influence of my patient's relatives, who, as it seemed to me, had never looked with favor on the treatment. However, my disagreeable impression was not clear to me, and I gave no outward sign of it. The same evening I wrote out Irma's case history, with the idea of giving it to Dr. M (a common friend who was at that time the leading figure in our circle) in order to justify myself. That night . . . I had the following dream, which I noted down immediately [p. 106].

The manifest dream is as follows:

A large hall—numerous guests, whom we were receiving.—Among them was Irma. I at once took her on one side, as though to answer her letter and to reproach her for not having accepted my "solution" yet. I said to her: "If you still get pains, it's really only your fault." She replied: "If you only knew what pains I've got now in my throat and stomach and abdomen—it's choking me"—I was alarmed and looked at her. She looked pale and puffy. I thought to myself that after all I must be missing some organic trouble. I took her to the window and looked down her throat, and she showed signs of recalcitrance, like women with artificial dentures. I thought to myself that there was really no need for her to do that.—She then opened her mouth properly and on the right I found a big white patch; at another place I saw extensive whitish grey scabs upon some remarkable curly structures which were evidently modelled on the turbinal bones of the nose.—I at once called in Dr. M., and he repeated the examination and confirmed it. . . . Dr. M. looked quite different from usual; he was very pale, he walked with a limp and his chin was clean-shaven. . . . My friend Otto was now standing beside her as well, and my friend Leopold was percussing her through her bodice and saying: "She has a dull area low down on her left." He also indicated that a portion of the skin on the left shoulder was infiltrated. (I noticed this, just as he did, in spite of her dress.) . . . M. said: "There's no doubt it's an infection, but no

matter; dysentery will supervene and the toxin will be eliminated." . . . We were directly aware, too, of the origin of the infection.
Not long before, when she was feeling unwell, my friend Otto had
given her an injection of a preparation of propyl, propyls . . .
propionic acid. . . . trimethylamine (and I saw before me the
formula for this printed in heavy type). . . . Injections of that sort
ought not to be made so thoughtlessly. . . . And probably the
syringe had not been clean [p. 107]

Freud notes:

I smiled at the senseless idea of an injection of propionic acid and
at Dr. M's consoling reflections. [p. 108].

and then proceeds to his associations. He first tries to place the
blame for his failure on Irma:

It was my view at that time (though I have since recognized it as a
wrong one) that my task was fulfilled when I had informed a patient
of the hidden meaning of his symptoms. I considered that I was not
responsible for whether he accepted the solution or not, though
this is what success depended on. I owe it to this mistake, which I
have now, fortunately corrected, that my life was made easier at a
time when, in spite of all my inevitable ignorance, I was expected
to produce therapeutic successes [p. 108].

The accent here is on his sense of failure and probable disgrace, not
on Irma's suffering.

I was especially anxious not to be responsible for the pains which
she still had. If they were her fault, they could not be mine [p. 108-
109].

Then his thoughts turn to the possibility of having missed an organic
illness:

It occurred to me, in fact, that I was actually *wishing* that there had
been a wrong diagnosis; for if so, the blame for my lack of success
would also have been got rid of [p. 109].

His associations are followed in the text only as they lead to recent
and preconscious material. All of them lead to his wish for the
restoration of his professional status by placing the blame elsewhere.
He concludes:

The conclusion of the dream . . . was that I was not responsible for the persistence of Irma's pains, but that Otto was [p. 118].

His Uncle with the Yellow Beard

Freud explains in the preamble that he had been nominated for a prestigious appointment as professor extraordinarius. He learns, on the night before the dream, from a friend in a similar position, that his appointment may not proceed because of "denominational concerns," that is, because he is Jewish. The dream text is as follows:

I. My friend R. was my uncle.—I had a great feeling of affection for him.

II. I saw before me his face, somewhat changed. It was as though it had been drawn out lengthways. A yellow beard that surrounded it stood out especially clearly [p. 137].

Freud goes on to associate to his uncle's involvement in an illegal moneymaking scheme and his subsequent punishment. Freud recalls:

My father, whose hair turned grey from grief in a few days, used always to say that Uncle Josef was not a bad man but only a simpleton; those were his words. So that if my friend R. was my uncle Josef, what I was meaning to say was that R. was a simpleton [p. 138].

Associations to the yellow beard further linked R to the uncle. Freud concludes:

My uncle Josef represented my two colleagues who had not been appointed to professorships—the one as a simpleton and the other as a criminal. I now saw too why they were represented in this light. If the appointment of my friends R and N had been postponed for "denominational" reasons, my own appointment was open to doubt; if, however, I could attribute the rejection of my two friends for other reasons, which did not apply to me, my hopes would remain untouched [p. 139].

The dream thoughts, by underscoring his uncle's failure as the result of his flawed character, allow for the possibility of a reversal of Freud's humiliated status by providing another explanation for the failure of other Jews denied advancement. The uncle's failure is on grounds other than religious intolerance ("denominational considerations"). The wish, then, is to have this obstacle to the advancement in his professional status (i.e., his humiliation suffered because he was Jewish) removed and the pathway to his professional recognition (his restored pride) opened.

The Dream of the Botanical Monograph

This dream, presented twice (pp. 169–176, pp. 282–284), illustrates how Freud's preoccupation with one monograph (the monograph on Cyclamen) has displaced his preoccupation with a monograph on cocaine. The manifest dream is:

> I had written a monograph on a certain plant. The book lay before me and I was at the moment turning over a folded coloured plate. Bound up in each copy there was a dried specimen of the plant, as though it had been taken from a herbarium [p. 169].

Freud's associations go from the botanical monograph to the monograph on cocaine, a *Festschrift* honoring a colleague in which Freud's contributions on cocaine were passed over. This shame in the face of a humiliating slight from his colleagues was the instigation of the dream:

> All the trains of thought starting from the dream—the thoughts about my wife's and my own favorite flowers, about cocaine, about the awkwardness of medical treatment among colleagues, about my preferences for studying monographs and about my neglect of certain branches of science such as botany—all of these trains of thought, when they were further pursued, led ultimately to one or another of the many ramifications of my conversation with Dr. Konigstein. Once again the dream, . . . turns out to have been in the nature of a self justification, a plea on behalf of my own rights. . . . Even the apparently indifferent form in which the dream was couched turns out to have significance. What was meant was: "After all, I'm the man who wrote the valuable and memorable paper (on cocaine)," just as in the earlier [Irma] dream I had said on my behalf: "I'm a conscientious and hard working student." [p. 173].

Here Freud notices that the dream work has transformed his shame at being forgotten in the cocaine monograph to his guilt at having forgotten to bring his wife her favorite flower, Cyclamen.

Count Thun

This dream (pp. 208–218) is one of the most brilliantly and complete-ly analyzed in all the psychoanalytic literature. The stimulus to the dream, detailed in a long preamble, is Freud's reaction to seeing the handsome and powerful Hungarian Count confidently board a train and dismiss a questioning porter with a wave of his hand. Freud was embarrassed to catch himself humming part of Figaro's aria in *The Marriage of Figaro* in which the barber-turned-valet, on learning of Count Almaviva's sexual designs on Suzanna, vows to outwit the philandering count. Freud then finds out that his own reservation for a first-class train cabin with a urinal has not been honored.

The manifest dream is as follows:

A crowd of people, a meeting of students. A count (Thun or Taafe) was speaking. He was challenged to say something about the Germans, and declared with a contemptuous gesture that their favourite flower was colt's foot, and put some sort of dilapidated leaf—or rather the crumpled skeleton of a leaf—into his buttonhole. I fired up—so I fired up though I was surprised at my taking such an attitude.

(Becoming indistinct again) . . . It was as though the second problem was to get out of town, just as the first one had been to get out of the house. I was driving in a cab and ordered the driver to drive me to a station. "I can't drive with you along the railway-line itself," I said, after he had raised some objection, as though I had overtired him. It was as if I had already driven with him for some of the distance one normally travels by train. The stations were cordoned off. I wondered whether to go to Krems or Znaim, but reflected that the Court would be in residence there, so I decided in favour of Graz, or some such place. I was now sitting in the compartment, which was like a carriage on the Stadtbahn [the suburban railway]; and in my buttonhole I had a peculiar plaited, long-shaped object, and beside it some violet-brown violets made of a stiff material. This greatly struck people. (At this point the scene broke off.)

Once more I was in front of the station, but this time in the company of an elderly gentleman. I thought of a plan for remaining unrecognized; and then saw that this plan had already been put into effect. It was as though thinking and experiencing were one and the same thing. He appeared to be blind, at all events with one eye, and I handed him a male glass urinal (which we had to buy or had bought in town). So I was a sick-nurse and had to give him the urinal because he was blind. If the ticket-collector were to see us like that, he would be certain to let us get away without noticing us. Here the man's attitude and his micturating penis appeared in plastic form. (This was the point at which I awoke, feeling a need to micturate.) [pp. 209–211].

Freud traced his associations to a childhood experience of interrupting parental intercourse by bursting into the parents' bedroom and urinating on the floor. The dream, then, with its reference to the old man's micturating penis, can be seen as a turning of the tables on paternal phallic prowess. It demonstrates a bit of Freud's competitive neurosis in reaction to Count Thun's self-assuredness, a reaction that was activated by his humiliation when his reservation of a cabin with a urinal was not honored.

In each of these cases, the instigator of the dream is a clear-cut shame experience in the dream day. Each dream can be seen as a response to the experience of shame and an attempt to undo the humiliating situation.

Freud, to be sure, is revealed as a ferocious and ambitious competitor, and it may be presumed that it is not just the thoroughly analyzed Count Thun dream that evokes association to childhood sexual competitiveness. Nonetheless, all these dreams deal with a loss or withholding of status among contemporaries that evokes shame in the dream day. The contemporaneous experience of shame in the day residue clearly seems to be the instigator of the dream, and the wish in the latent dream thoughts is aimed at correction of this shame experience. Freud's reading of the predicament in the dream day as sexual competition is a manifestation of his (perhaps neurotic) processing of the instigatory experiences, not of the instigating conflicts themselves. Those current conflicts are all concerned with the restoration of lost status—not with the winning of an object of sexual desire.

We have taken pains to emphasize in great detail the clear-cut and pervasive presence of shame conflicts in these dreams because Freud's sensitivity to shame underscores the conspicuous omission of shame in his theoretical conclusions. He concludes that *fantasied action*, competitive wishes in the dreams, represented as fulfilled, are the instigators of the dreams. But the data suggest that it is the experience of shame (resonating with similar childhood shame experiences) that instigates the competitive wish. Theoretical implications of the omission are enormous. Neglect of the shame dynamics gives rise to an unfortunate lack of theoretical integration and to the sense that the unconscious is composed of more or less unchanging infantile wishes, "capitalists," as it were, in search of an "entrepreneur." This oversight amounts to a devaluation, not only of shame conflicts, but of the nature of the instigation of dreams and of the relation of present to past conflict.

SHAME IMPLICIT IN THE PSYCHOANALYTIC CONCEPTUALIZATION OF THE CONSCIENCE

A number of central concepts that pertain to the psychoanalytic theory of conscience and of self-regulation, which are not generally thought of as shame phenomena, actually involve shame to a much greater extent than is usually appreciated. We explore briefly the relationships of some of these implicit conceptualizations to what, we contend, are fundamental shame phenomena. Our focus on shortcomings implicit in the basic model of conscience in Freud's writing is not intended to be merely another oversimplified critique that posits a reified model of "classical" thinking and then refutes it in a dismissive way. We are not constructing a theoretical "straw man." Rather, it is our intent to show, by deconstructing the evolving Freudian model of the conscience, that the basic psychoanalytic model requires expansion in ways foreshadowed, but not completely developed, by Freud. Such an expansion of the psychoanalytic model of conscience must take into account a nuanced appreciation of the relation of self to affect and object; a sense of self-consciousness and self-evaluation mindful of the felt appraisal of the self as a self among others as well as in one's own eye; and an awareness of clinical phenomena related to conscience that are the more visible accompaniments of masked shame.

The Regulator

Self-regulation and conscience, conceptualized psychoanalytically, center, of course, on the notion of the superego. But the superego in Freud's work is an imperfect and incomplete model of conscience. There is an ambiguity in his use of the word superego. In its original sense (Freud 1914a, 1923) the *uber-ich* referred to the self-observing, self-conscious, self-evaluative part of the ego. Superego is used in one sense to mean conscience generally. This definition covers not only prohibitions, that is to say, fears of retribution for forbidden desire and hate (of which guilt is the signal of danger). It also denotes evaluative views of the self in comparison with which certain aspirations and ideals regarding accomplishments, comportment, and standing among others may be compatible or incompatible.

In the writings from "On Narcissism" (Freud, 1914a) to "The Ego and the Id" (Freud, 1923), Freud deals with a reconceptualization of the psyche culminating in the 1923 structural theory. He is concerned with expanding theory to account for the clinical phenomena of self-consciousness and *self-absorption.* Calling this self-absorption narcissism, he sees it as a direct result of detachment of interest from other to self owing to disappointment in object love. His theorizing about instincts takes this into account: Eros represents binding and attachment; Thanatos, unbinding and detachment; and narcissistic phenomena are formulated as phenomena of self-preoccupation resulting from disappointment (i.e., rejection and humiliation) in object love and subsequent detachment and self-absorption. Thanatos, in this earlier period, refers to *the unbinding from object ties without conscious decision to do so*—not to aggression per se. Regarding Eros and Thanatos, Freud (1940) writes: "The aim of the first of these basic instincts is to establish even greater unities and to preserve them thus—in short, to bind together; the aim of the second is, on the contrary, to undo connections and so to destroy things" (p. 148). Though the relationship between such detachment and the antecedent shame resulting from rejection or humiliation by self-conscious comparison (see the discussion of Freud, 1916) is obvious, Freud, who, at this time, is not theorizing at this clinical level at all, does not make this relationship an explicit part of his theorizing.

Freud's writings following "The Ego and the Id" (Freud, 1923) tend to use a more constricted sense of the superego, that referring to prohibitions based on fear of retaliation (castration) for forbidden desire (incestuous attachment in the oedipal period) (Freud 1924a, 1930a). From 1924 onward, the superego is the seat of prohibitions, the heir to the Oedipus complex, and the locus of guilt. Self-consciousness, comparison with ideals, and shame or narcissistic wounding are ignored in these writings. At this period in his thinking, Freud is preoccupied theoretically with the problem of aggression as seen clinically, developmentally, and societally. Aggression is considered more or less a primary phenomenon, and although some of his earlier writings point to the relationship of anger to antecedent shame, his preoccupation in writings after "The Ego and the Id" is on anger, conscious or unconscious, and consequent guilt, conscious or unconscious (Freud, 1930b), often with a focus on the relation of these factors to the resolution of oedipal conflicts in childhood (Freud, 1924a, 1930a).

In this period, the destructive instinct is to a degree recon-ceptualized. Instead of being the instinct that undoes connections and destroys the bonds of relationships, Thanatos becomes essentially *the aggressive instinct*. For the first time in Freud's writings, aggression is considered as an instinctual derivative (Freud, 1930b, pp. 129–130; Stepansky, 1977), without attention to the antecedents of anger and destruction. Furthermore, the problems of narcissism and of aspirations in relation to self-conscious comparisons has been put aside. The confusion resulting from this particular conceptual reformulation is significant. The "superego" ambiguously refers both to prohibitions exclusively and to conscience in its entirety. This persistent conceptual ambiguity has allowed us to sidestep problems related to self-consciousness and to shame in conscience generally and has caused us to overlook issues involving shame as a type of superego anxiety that cannot be explained by paradigms using the anticipation of external punishment as a model for conscience. The ambiguity of the word superego, then, by giving primacy to conflicts over aggression and guilt, avoids the problems of self-consciousness and the full implications of the fear of disapproval by self or other that would represent failure to attain ideals and goals.

Freud (1914a) recognized the importance of the problem of self-consciousness for the concept of conscience but never developed the notion completely or satisfactorily. He never fully conceptualized the self as defined by the regard—external or internal—of the other or of one's own tenacious eye so that shame could be taken into account. Instead, he bypassed the problem or tried to solve it mechanically by confusing shame with a more easily conceptualized variant of guilt. For example, he states, "And the sense of guilt (as well as the sense of inferiority) can also be understood as an expression of tension between the ego and ego ideal" (Freud, 1921, p. 131). Freud oversimplified that tension by viewing it as an internal-ized fear of punishment along the lines of the castration complex and by subsuming problems of the superego under the category of identification—a problem far too intricate to be treated in the scope of this discussion.

The same failure to distinguish between shame and guilt typifies the work of the post-World War II ego psychologists. Hartmann and Lowenstein (1962), for example, wrote, "In terms of psychoanalytic theory, we are reluctant to overemphasize the separateness of the ego ideal from the other parts of the superego, and it is, partly, the question of separateness on which the structural opposition of guilt and shame hinges" (p. 67). Later Lowenstein (1966) confused shame with guilt in the following passage:

Remembering the wrathful face or eyes of an idealized person is a
reflection of guilt feeling. Imagining the victim of one's aggression,
particularly his suffering expression or his reproachful gaze, can
intensify remorse. In some people, however, the guilt may be quite
tolerable so long as they do not actually see the victim of their
aggression. A patient of mine once remarked that he would not
commit a hostile act against a friend because he would have to look
him in the eye. Whereas he might well act in that particular way if
he were sure of never seeing the friend again [p. 311–312].

Hartmann and Lowenstein, in their theoretical preoccupation
with the development of psychic structure, take a line of reasoning
that privileges stable, postoedipal, depersonified structure as the
essence, indeed the totality, of conscience. Such a bias constitutes a
pars pro toto argument that privileges prohibition at the expense of
aspirations, the postoedipal superego at the expense of the ego ideal,
and guilt at the expense of shame. Their continuation of the narrow
focus pursued by Freud after 1923 theorizes abstractly using Freud's
later writings as a paradigm. This narrowed focus comes at the
expense of an accurate and useful theory that arises from a nuanced
consideration of the phenomenology of conscience. (For post-
Freudian views on the ego ideal, see Reich, 1954; Schafer, 1960;
Lampl de-Groot, 1962; Blos, 1974; Chasseguet-Smirgel 1985.)

The Signaling System

Signal anxiety, the revised concept put forward by Freud (1926), not
only marks a reworking of Freud's concept of neurotic anxiety per
se, but also reflects a recognition of "anxiety" as the regulatory affect
signaling danger to the equilibrium of the psyche generally.[3]
Accordingly, "signal anxiety" covers a much wider range of affective
phenomena than does the limited concept of consciously experienced neurotic anxiety. Signal anxiety, then, is a term covering not
only the conscious affects of anxiety, guilt, and shame, but also a
wide range of entirely unconscious signals of danger to the psyche.
Freud saw the formulation of signal anxiety as a major reformulation
of his theory of anxiety. Theoretical emphasis shifted from affect per
se to the problem of regulation and affect as signal. One aspect of
this shift, of course, is the signaling of danger to the relationship of

---

[3]Note our earlier discussion of reaction formation as an early formulation
of signal anxiety.

the self to the social order or to its own regard, or the loss of poise (Rangell, 1954) or composure before others. Accordingly, much of what Freud classifies as an aspect of "signal anxiety" actually is the specific type of superego anxiety concerning fear of rejection or exposure as disappointing, uncontrolled, weak, inferior, defective, dirty, or unlovable, that is, what we might just as justifiably call signal shame. Shame, here, is not only the emotion that signals the end result of exposure of the self as defective or unlovable, but also the superego anxiety that signals a threat to one's standing or esteem in one's own eyes or before others.

This subsuming of shame (signal shame) under the superordinate concept of signal anxiety does, indeed, have the theoretical advantage of developing psychoanalytic notions of conscience and of regulation (see Levin 1967, 1971). But in practice, because shame was essentially ignored by Freud after 1914, the effect of the 1926 theory has been to subordinate and mechanize the phenomena of shame, self-consciousness, and the need for recognition to the point that for 45 years specific attention to shame was almost entirely absent from the writings of ego psychologists (see, for example, Rapaport, 1957; Hartmann and Lowenstein, 1962).

The Danger Situations: Castration and Separation

The term castration may be applied either to the propensities to attack or retaliate in ways that *deprive, in actuality or in fantasy, either men or women of status given to sexual men* or to the anxieties of a man who is excessively or neurotically intrepid but who puts himself forward as a powerful, competitive, sexual male. Often this word is used without apparent awareness that, in speaking of castration, one is talking more metaphorically about personal and social humiliation and not about an actual physical attack on the genitals. As applied to intrapsychic conflict in adults, castration anxiety refers to sexual humiliation—or fear of it—which may or may not be a repetition and a direct derivative of infantile castration conflicts, that is, fears of actual retaliatory genital injury. Though we affirm the psychoanalytic emphasis on viewing manifest conflict as derivative of significant conflicts in the past, we do not assume that conflicts involving humiliation as a sexual being are easily reducible to infantile precursors in any simple way. We note with surprise that castration anxiety is seldom discussed as a variation of shame even though castration anxiety always involves shame dynamics. For example, the substantial shame elements in the oedipal myth and situation are seldom considered. In common usage, castration tends to be subsumed under the dynamics of guilt; that is to say, unacknowledged sexual or aggressive wishes carry with them an internalized anticipation of punishment (guilt) deriving from archaic fears of genital injury. That punishment is castration along the lines of that which is discussed in the case of Little Hans (Freud, 1909). We are concerned that the desire-retaliatory castration threat conceptualization lends itself to an oversimplified and inaccurate emphasis on the developmental anlage of adult conflict in ways that short circuit full appreciation of the role of shame in conflicts (oedipal or otherwise) in the adult clinical situation.

"Separation anxiety," also, is a concept that has attained general psychoanalytic usage in the absence of a specific formulation of what it is that distresses adult patients facing separation. We find it important to distinguish separation and reactions to it from loss per se. For example, when the analyst leaves on vacation, the patient's reaction reflects not a loss but *exposure of the person facing the separation as one who is unable to function without the sense that the analyst is present or nearby*. The patient becomes acutely aware of being much more needy and much less autonomous than he or she would like to see himself or herself. This predicament has to do with the person's sense of self-worth and sense of integrity and partakes much more of shame dynamics than of the dynamics of fear of loss. Separations give rise to shame (acknowledged or not) because they uncover something about the way we are constituted: we need an "object" to maintain our poise and our sense of self. Many errors have been made in considering separation anxiety simply as fear of loss rather than fear of loss of cohesion, poise, or composure, and the exposure of neediness and fear of inability to function without the other that gives rise to shame.

A danger situation not subsumed under the anticipation of castration or separation is that of loss or fragmentation of the sense of self or loss of meaningful attachment to the social order. Kohut (1971) was the first to appreciate the type of signal anxiety that threatens the loss of self, that is, "fragmentation anxiety." Kohut's original notion of shame was very closely tied, however, to his conceptualizations of "narcissistic libido" and the "grandiose self." More nuanced, contemporary views of shame underscore the role of (signal) shame as the specific type of signal anxiety that reflects the danger of loss of self-respect, of poise, of the selfobject tie and the sense of self.

Responses to Self-Conscious Comparison

Freud's (1914a) early work on narcissism had to do with the clinical problems posed by relentless self-involvement (in the narcissistic neuroses) reflecting either fixation at the level of primary narcissism or avoidance of involvement with the other. Such self-involvement he called narcissism and related it ultimately to frustration in object love. It was at this point that Freud paved the way for a more complex notion of conscience than had previously been understood from his formulations of dream censorship or of defenses that kept repressed material from consciousness. In positing the ego ideal, he, in effect, expanded the psychoanalytic notion of conscience to include *self-conscious comparisons with ideals, aspirations, and standards in regard to which one might feel ashamed*. Thus, he moved beyond a simple notion of conscience as a set of prohibitions by virtue of which one might be found guilty and punished for transgressions or for omissions. It is but a short step, yet one often not taken, to realize that reactions to narcissistic wounding or narcissistic injury are, in fact, acute shame states.

Some of Freud's most penetrating insights on shame in relation to self-conscious comparison are contained in his 1916 paper "Some Character Types Met with in Psychoanalytic Work." This astonishing paper does not specifically mention shame at all. Using a wealth of literary discussions on Shakespeare (Richard III, the "exception"; Lady Macbeth, "wrecked by success"), on Ibsen's *Rosmersholm*, and on Nietzsche ("criminals from a sense of guilt"), Freud puts forward brilliant observations on what would now be called three types of clinically significant superego phenomena. The latter two deal with guilt; the "exceptions," with shame.

In the brief section on the "exceptions," Freud points to character types characterized by a sense of personal defect, in response to which they carry a sense of having been cheated and not being able to deal with life as others do; hence they feel entitled to be "exceptions," that is, exempt from the rules that others follow. We are assuming that Freud's formulation has bypassed recognition of the fact that the experience of having been cheated involves not only a perception of one's defects, but also a self-conscious comparison with others who are felt not to have been cheated. Only within the contest of such an (unacknowledged) experience of shame can the vengeful feeling of entitlement to even the score occur. Freud notes explicitly. There is in such persons no apparent moral sensitivity to the impact of their claims for justice and specialness on the larger moral order. Freud (1916) writes:

> Now it is no doubt true that everyone would like to consider himself an "exception" and claim privileges over others. But precisely because of this there must be a particular reason, and one not universally present, if someone actually proclaims himself an exception and behaves as such. This reason may be of more than one kind; in the cases I investigated I succeeded in discovering a common peculiarity in the earlier experiences of these patients' lives. Their neuroses were connected with some experience or suffering to which they had been subjected in their earliest childhood, one of which they knew themselves to be guiltless, and which they could look upon as an unjust disadvantage imposed on them. The privileges that they claimed as a result of this injustice, and the rebelliousness it engendered, had contributed not a little to intensifying the conflicts leading to the outbreak of their neurosis [p. 313].

His major example is not clinical, but literary, the opening soliloquy of Shakespeare's *Richard III*, in which the hunchback Gloucester, later King Richard III, justifies his plots and treacheries following the end of the recent war:

> But I, that am not shaped for sportive tricks,
> Nor made to court an amorous looking-glass;
> I that am rudely stamp'd, and want Love's majesty
> To strut before a wanton ambling nymph;
> I, that am curtail'd of this fair proportion,
> Cheated of Feature by dissembling Nature,
> Deform'd, unfinished; Sent before my time
> Into this breathing world, scarce half made up,
> And that so lamely and unfashionable,
> That dogs bark at me as I halt by them;
> * * * * * * * * * * * * * * * * * * *
> And therefore, since I cannot prove a lover,
> To entertain these fair well-spoken days,
> I am determined to prove a villain,
> And note the idle pleasures of these days.
> [*Richard III* I, i, 14-23; 29-32; selection of quoted lines, Freud's]

Freud clearly points to the enduring self-conscious sense of defect without assuming explicitly (as we do) that this sense of narcissistic injury—the awareness of defect in regard to one's own aspirations of perfection or comparison with others—gives rise to shame. In reaction to that shame arise the sense of injustice, of having been cheated, and of being entitled to claim that one is an exception, that is to say, the sense of entitlement justifying the narcissistic rage following the sense of shame. What we are highlighting, although Freud does not state it explicitly in his discussion of the "exceptions," is the intimate relation of anger and destruction to antecedent shame. That these "exceptions" (perhaps everyone in conscious and unconscious fantasies of revenge and of triumph over adversaries) feel entitled to act outside of and oblivious to the moral order—and often do so—is a profound observation on the relation of narcissistic rage to conscience.

In addition, this brilliant little paper, with its far-reaching implications, seems to have been written as though it were simply a literary aside, split off from the mainstream of Freud's theoretical preoccupations at the time, i.e., contemporaneous metapsychological papers. The insights into the "exceptions" are not integrated with Freud's (1914) theory of narcissism. In his recognition of self-conscious comparison or self-judgment that gives rise (we are presuming from Freud's explicit formulations of the ego ideal) to, we assume, the shame and states of narcissistic rage that give rise to discontinuities in conscience in the "exceptions," Freud (1916) moves far ahead of the mainstream of his own theoretical work. In fact, the observations in these few pages were never consolidated into an explicit discussion of the implications of Richard's soliloquies. Richard's sense of defect and of having been cheated result from self-conscious comparisons with others and give rise to an unacknowledged shame experience, to narcissistic rage, and the sense of being exempted, as an "exception," from the usual rules of comportment. The splitting off of these clinically brilliant literary observations from the mainstream of psychoanalytic theorizing came at the expense of Freud's understanding the full implications of the phenomena of narcissistic injury, that is, the connection between self-conscious awareness or comparison, shame, and ensuing compensatory narcissistic entitlement and narcissistic rage. The result in Freud's work is an incomplete development of the notion of conscience that failed to take these factors fully into account.

Another and, we believe, similar response to self-conscious comparison is envy. We view envy as, in large part, a response to a shame experience and an attempt to deal with that shame experience. We are in strong agreement with the Kleinian expansion of Freud's thinking on envy, that is, that it is a much more general trait than that covered by the concept of penis envy. Though she does not use the language of shame, Klein (1957) also used the word "envy" in a sense that is much closer to the generic one we propose for the concept: *destructive hate that follows shame resulting from self-conscious comparison with the other* (see Morrison, 1989, pp. 127–128). Envy is not merely covetousness. One commits a serious conceptual error to, say, confuse penis envy with the wish for a penis; it may be accompanied by that, but the wish is not the essence of envy. Rather, penis includes envy of that which is male, as symbolized by the phallus. Moreover, Klein's (1946) expansion of envy to encompass envy of the breast and envy in general is one of the major constructive theoretical turns in the history of psychoanalysis.

We do not agree, however, with Klein's notion that envy is a manifestation of either the death instinct or primary aggressivity. Instead, we think that envy, like shame, is a self-conscious emotion following from an instigatory shame experience that results from seeing oneself as deficient or inferior as compared with the other. Where someone else is seen as being or possessing better, insofar as one experiences envy, one feels oneself lesser by comparison and thereby feels ashamed. Envy is the visible concomitant to unacknowledged or unconscious shame and, in fact, always follows self-conscious comparison and shame. The ensuing rage and attack come from the shame, which is bypassed or unacknowledged (Lewis, 1971). We view envy, therefore, as an antecedent to or a variant of narcissistic rage. Conceptualizing envy as always "downstream" from self-consciousness and shame, no matter how rapidly or subliminally this transformation occurs, tends to balance any clinical focus in which envy is prominent, so that it includes exploration of the patient's sense of shame and does not limit the purview of envy to the phenomena of sadistic control and destructive rage aimed at the powerful, large, or proud other.

The Paradigmatic Conflict of Neurotic Disturbance

The Oedipus complex has been put forward as the paradigmatic conflict of neurotic disturbance. Nonetheless, there seems to us to be a good deal of ambiguity about what the Oedipus complex actually is. Common psychoanalytic usage presumes the inference of associations of an original constellation of a family romance with a sexual attachment to the opposite-sex parent and consequent competitive feelings toward the other parent and fear of retaliation by that parent, especially if the bond with the same-sex parent is otherwise ambivalent or pathological. When we use the phrase Oedipus complex, we infer from the patient's associations—that is to say, his or her "complexes"—a *replay of that infantile family romance situation*. This, in our opinion, is a methodological error. We do not believe that adult oedipal conflicts are exact or even modified replays of the original family romance or that what we see clinically is merely a regression that follows fear of retaliation (i.e., the castration complex, not the full Oedipus complex). This interpretation simply reduces our basic concepts to fall in line with a guilt dynamic (typified by *the castration complex)*. It omits attention to, and proper conceptualization of, the pertinent shame conflicts, for example, those related to comparisons of oneself with an internal model of oneself as a sexually attractive, desirable, and adequate sexual partner—to name one of many possible ego-ideal conflicts that derive from "oedipal" conflicts in the adult. In a true oedipal conflict, we have a well-made play, not a neurosis. In a neurosis, there is not only a *regression from* these dangers of sexual competition, but also a *fixation* to a primarily nonsexual relationship; that is to say, an *overattachment to* a parent—an attachment that becomes both sexualized and a source of shame as a result of an adult conflict over *need*—not merely a replay of an infantile one. Often, overemphasis on the regression (i.e., castration only, the fear of retaliation) results in our overlooking the shame arising from the fixation—the infantile attachment or bond to a dominant other which is a source of intense shame because of dependency, perceived smallness, and inadequacy.

Central to the notion of the paradigmatic conflict is the warding off of punishment for forbidden desire and sexual competition by giving up the (desired) opposite sex parent and identifying with the (feared) same-sex parent (Freud, 1924a). Thus, what was seen prior to the formation of the superego as an external danger evolves, after the dissolution of the Oedipus complex, into guilt that emanates from the internal structure, superego.

This paradigm, however, neglects shame in the oedipal situation. Shame occurs with awareness of one's smallness, both genitally and totally, compared with the same-sex parent. "Castration anxiety" includes not only fear of actual dismemberment (and its derivatives), but also fear of humiliation as a sexual competitor. The oedipal situation is further complicated if the same-sex parent was held in contempt by the opposite-sex parent and the resultant identification is also accompanied by a profound sense of shame and a struggle against that identification (Greenson, 1954).

We speculate that Freud's privileging of guilt dynamics over those involving shame may have resulted from his reliance on his own self-analysis as the basis for his theorizing. We know clinically that the fear of shame tends to keep material out of consciousness, and it may be that Freud's overweighing fear and guilt in the oedipal conflicts resulted from his own inability to focus on his shame conflicts specifically. The obvious relationship of "castration" to fear of social humiliation rather than fear of actual dismemberment—at times, at least—is a telling case in point.

SHAME AND THE PSYCHOANALYTIC PROCESS

In considering central Freudian ideas that have important but often inexplicit relationships to shame, we turn now to some of Freud's notions about the psychoanalytic process: transference, resistance, countertransference, and interpretation. We hope that even our very brief consideration of these concepts from the point of view of shame dynamics enhances understanding of their depth, their clinical accuracy, and their relationship to the analytic process.

Consideration of the concept of *transference*, of course, takes into account everything that we have said about the object and the other. The concept of the transference expands *pari passu* with the idea of what persons need an object for. As the notion of object *qua* object of an instinct expands to include the object (selfobject, perhaps) that confers selfhood on the self, that confers regard (internalized as self-regard), that offers safety, selfhood, esteem and security, so the appreciation of the transference expands likewise. Shame enters in powerfully. Because many of the hitherto unrecognized needs for an object evoke shame—not guilt—they have to do with selfhood, esteem, bonding, and lovability, not with sexual and aggressive acts per se.

That the psychoanalytic situation favors the projecting of the superego onto the analyst as leader or parental figure (Strachey, 1934; Freud, 1921) makes that situation one in which the relatively stable system superego, projected onto the analyst and reintrojected in modified form, is subject to change. This possibility for change involves not only the analysand's sense of prohibitions and fears of retaliation that give rise to guilt, but also the aspirations and attendant anxieties about failing to meet them—which give rise to fear of rejection and exposure as dirty, inadequate, needy, uncontrolled, or disappointing, that is, to shame.

Countertransference is a bit more complex. Freud saw counter-transference simply as the analyst's transferences onto the patient. More recent writings (see Kernberg, 1975; Greenberg, 1991; Jacobs, 1991; McLaughlin, 1991), emphasizing reactions in the analyst or therapist to the patient's transferences, imply that such "countertrans-ferences," far from being simple neurotic artifacts, may be useful and even essential data guiding the treatment. (One may, of course, acknowledge this and still understand them to be colored by the therapist's or analyst's transferences.) We contend that there is a systematic problem that has limited our understanding of counter-transference, in written work especially. That problem has to do with the fact that discussions of countertransference are systematically limited by the material that the analyst chooses to disclose. Further, the reason that this state of affairs continues may have to do with the analyst's or therapist's fear of exposure and risk of being shamed (Retzinger, unpublished). We believe that many aspects of counter-transference are best studied in situations in which clinical material is gathered and recorded by audio or videotape and is not governed by the selection of the analyst and therefore is not limited by that person's fear of exposure and shaming. Only then will we be able to approach a systematic approach to the study of countertransfer-ence.[4] Such studies would disclose, we predict, what we have observed clinically in supervision and in examination of our own therapeutic work. That is, as shame is experienced by our patients, so too do themes and experiences of shame reverberate in our own reactions, which frequently lead to countertransference enactments with our patients. Such enactments include our tendency and collusion to avoid dealing with shame—in our patients, as in our-selves.

In conceptualizing *resistance*, we agree with Freud's (1900) formulation that anything interrupting the progress of the analytic work may be seen as a resistance. Resistance is of such importance because what underlies it also underlies self-sabotaging and self-defeating maneuvers in the patient's life that operate outside of his or her own awareness. Resistance, then, ought to be seen not as resistance to the analyst, but as resistance to the patient's own (psychoanalytic) project of expanding self-awareness, with its inevitable consequence of encountering painful affects, especially the

---

[4]Even this method, of course, does not capture countertransference responses that are silent or that do not show up clearly in explicit transac-tions between analyst and patient.

shame that has driven mental contents out of consciousness. Resistance is of such central clinical importance because recognition of its manifestations may be the only avenue to the clarification of fears of exposure, disgrace, disintegration, retraumatization, and consequent shame. We have thus come full circle, back to Breuer and Freud's (1893–1895) original formulations involving incompatible ideas and shame quoted earlier.

Finally, we turn to two basic concepts that refer to what the analyst does or refrains from doing in the context of the analytic situation: maintenance of analytic neutrality and interpretation.

Analytic neutrality, an attitude with which we wholeheartedly agree, refers to the efforts of the analyst to abstain as much as possible from taking one side or another in the patient's conflicts. Analytic neutrality has been confused by some as the advocacy of a stance of abstemiousness and lack of participation—usually with the rationale that a more participatory stance risks gratification of infantile wishes that thereby sidesteps analytic scrutiny with the net result of perpetuating rather than favorably modifying the disturbance. Our appreciation of shame in no way obviates these considerations, but it does add to them another level of complexity: to many patients, an abstemious, nonparticipatory stance is decidedly not neutral. The failure of optimal responsiveness is, to some, emotional desertion, retraumatization, and outright humiliation—not just an imagined slight in grandiose or infantile fantasy, but an actual deprivation of a sustaining object whose absence may generate intense shame. This dimension of analytic "neutrality" expands rather than replaces the original precept.

In the strict sense, *interpretation* implies that something means something else. As we use the word clinically, however, we mean to say that *manifest means latent*, that *something on the surface has an underlying meaning*. That which is manifest may be a dream or a theme, or it may be an affect (anger often "means" anxiety of some sort; anxiety often "means" something to do with aggression, etc.). An understanding of shame powerfully broadens our notions of interpretation, if one assumes that an overriding anxiety people have in the analytic situation is that *they are ashamed that they are not as other people are*. When one *interprets*, one *points out an underlying struggle*.

Let us emphasize at this point that we do not believe that interpretation and empathy are ever at odds; interpretation always requires empathy, and empathy always requires some means to communicate it, which speaks to something (whether word, act, or affect) below the surface. Accordingly, when a therapist of any persuasion correctly communicates that he or she *sees beneath the surface and imagines what it is like to be the patient*, what is conveyed, along with other specifics, is a clear affirmation that *you are understandable, you are as other people are*. The very act of conveying such an understanding, no matter what else it does, also mitigates the sense of shame that people in treatment invariably have. On the other hand, an interpretation freely given without empathic awareness may be experienced as an assault or accusation, and thus a further stimulus to shame. Thus, mitigation or instigation of shame reactions may be seen many times in every session, not just occasionally.

CONCLUSION

It is a tribute to Freud's genius that all his many contributions to the understanding of shame have proved to be of enduring value both clinically and theoretically. We have traced the essentials of his contributions, both explicit and implicit, with the intent of providing perspectives from the point of view of a century of evolving psychoanalytic understanding, from comparisons with social and philosophical theory (developed more fully in the chapters that follow), and from contemporary views on affect in relation to self and object. The last perspective is considerably more elaborated and nuanced than was the original, one-person model of the psyche put forward at the beginning of psychoanalytic theorizing.

We hope that these perspectives help the reader to a critical understanding both of Freud's monumental contributions to our understanding of shame and of the historical development of our evolving psychoanalytic appreciation of shame in relation to the entire scope of psychoanalytic understanding.

REFERENCES

Aristotle (n.d.), *Nicomachaen Ethics*, trans. T. Irwin. Indianapolis, IN: Hackett, 1985.
Blos, P. (1974), The genealogy of the ego ideal. *The Psychoanalytic Study of the Child*, 29:43–88. New Haven, CT: Yale.
Breuer, J. & Freud, S. (1893–1895), *Studies on Hysteria. Standard Edition*, 2. London: Hogarth Press, 1955.

Broucek, F. (1991, *Shame and the Self*. New York: Guilford Press.

Chasseguet-Smirgel, J. (1985), *The Ego Ideal*. New York: Norton.

Freud, S. (1892–1899), Extracts from the Fliess papers.*Standard Edition*, I. London: Hogarth Press, 1966.

——— (1900), *The Interpretation of Dreams. Standard Edition*, 4 & 5. London: Hogarth Press, 1966.

——— (1905a), Three essays on sexuality. *Standard Edition*, 7:130–243. London: Hogarth Press, 1953.

——— (1905b), Fragment of an analysis of a case of hysteria. *Standard Edition*, 7:7–120. London: Hogarth Press, 1953.

——— (1909), Analysis of a phobia in a five-year-old boy. *Standard Edition*, 10:5–149. London: Hogarth Press, 1955.

——— (1914a), On narcissism. An introduction. *Standard Edition*, 14:73–102. London: Hogarth Press, 1957.

——— (1914b), On the history of the psychoanalytic movement. *Standard Edition*, 14:7–66. London: Hogarth Press, 1957.

——— (1914c), Remembering, repeating, and working-through. *Standard Edition*, 12:145–156. London: Hogarth Press.

——— (1915), Instincts and their vicissitudes. *Standard Edition*, 14:117–140. London: Hogarth Press, 1957.

——— (1915), Some character types met with in psychoanalytic work. *Standard Edition*, 14:311–333. London: Hogarth Press, 1957.

——— (1921), Group psychology and the analysis of the ego. *Standard Edition*, 18:69–143. London: Hogarth Press, 1955.

——— (1923), The ego and the id. *Standard Edition*, 19:12–66. London: Hogarth Press, 1961.

——— (1924a), The dissolution of the Oedipus complex. *Standard Edition*, 19:173–179. London: Hogarth Press, 1961.

——— (1924b), Some psychical consequences of the anatomical distinction between the sexes. *Standard Edition*, 19:248–258. London: Hogarth Press, 1961.

——— (1926), Inhibitions, symptoms and anxiety. *Standard Edition*, 20:87–175. London: Hogarth Press, 1959.

——— (1930a), The economic problem of masochism. *Standard Edition*, 19:157–170. London: Hogarth Press, 1961.

——— (1930b), Civilization and its discontents. *Standard Edition*, 21:64–145. London: Hogarth Press, 1961.

——— (1940), An outline of psychoanalysis. *Standard Edition*, 23:144–207. London: Hogarth Press, 1964.

Greenberg, J. (1991), *Oedipus and Beyond*. Cambridge, MA: Harvard University Press.

Grunberger, B. (1979), *Narcissism*, New York: International Universities Press.

Hartmann, H. & Lowenstein,R. (1962), Notes on the superego. *The Psychoanalytic Study of the Child*, 17:42-81. New York: International Universities Press.

Hazard, P. (1969), Freud's teaching on shame. *Laval Theologique et Philosophique*, 25:234-267.

Hegel, G. W. F. (1807), *The Phenomenology of Spirit*, trans. A. V. Miller. Oxford, U.K.: Oxford University Press, 1979.

Jacobs, T. (1991), *The Use of the Self*, Madison, CT: International Universities Press.

Jacobson, E. (1964), *The Self and the Object World*, New York: International Universities Press.

Kernberg, O. (1975), *Borderline Conditions and Pathological Narcissism*, New York: Aronson.

Klein, M. (1946), Notes on some schizoid mechanisms. *Internat. J. Psycho-Anal.*, 27:99-110.

———— (1957), *Envy and Gratitude*. London: Tavistock.

Kohut, H. (1971), *The Analysis of the Self*. New York: International Universities Press.

Lacan, J. (1966), *Ecrits,* trans. A. Sheridan. New York: Norton.

Lampl-de Groot, J. (1982), The ego ideal and the superego. *The Psychoanalytic Study of the Child*, 18:95-106. New York: International Universities Press.

Lansky, M. R. (1992), *Fathers Who Fail*. Hillsdale, NJ: The Analytic Press.

Levin, S. (1967), Some metapsychological considerations on the differentiation between shame and guild. *Internat. J. Psycho-Anal.*, 48:267-276.

———— (1971). The psychoanalysis of shame. *Internat. J. Psycho-Anal.*, 52:355-362.

Lewis, H. B. (1971), *Shame and Guilt in Neurosis*. New York: Free Press.

Lowenstein, R. M. (1966), The theory of the superego: A discussion. In: *Psychoanalysis*, ed. R. M. Lowenstein, L. M. Newman, M. Schur & A. J. Solnit. New York: International Universities Press, pp. 29 8-314.

McLaughlin, J. (1971), Clinical and theoretical aspects of enactment. *J. Amer. Psychoanal. Assn.*. 39:595-614.

Morrison, A. P. (1987), The eye turned inward. In: *The Many Faces of Shame,* ed. D. Nathanson. New York: Guilford Press, pp. 271-291.

———— (1989), *Shame*. Hillsdale, NJ: The Analytic Press.

Nathanson, D., ed. (1987), *The Many Faces of Shame*. New York:Guilford Press.

Nunberg, H. (1955), *Principles of Psychoanalysis*. New York: International Universities Press.

Rangell, L. (1954), The psychology of poise, with a special elaboration on the psychic significance of the snout or perioral region. *Internat. J. Psycho-Anal.*, 35:313-332.

Rapaport, D. (1957), A theoretical analysis of the superego concept. In: *Collected Papers of David Rapaport*, ed. M. Gill. New York: Basic Books, 1967.

Reich, A. (1954), Early identifications as archaic elements in the superego. *J. Amer. Psychoanal. Assn.*, 2:218-238.

Sartre, J. P. (1945), *Being and Nothingness*, trans. H. Barnes. New York: Washington Square Press, 1966.

Schafer, R. (1960), The loving and beloved superego in Freud's structural theory. *The Psychoanalytic Study of the Child*, 15:163-188. New York: International Universities Press.

Scheff, T. (1990), *Microsociology*. Chicago: University of Chicago Press.

Slavin, M. (1992), *The Adaptive Design of the Human Psyche*, New York: Guilford Press.

Stepansky, P. (1977), A History of Aggression in Freud. New York: International Universities Press.

Stierlin, H. (1959), The adaptation to the stronger person's reality. *Psychiat.*, 27:143-152.

Strachey, J. (1934), The therapeutic action of psychoanalysis. *Internat. J. Psycho-Anal.*, 15:127-159.

Wurmser, L. (1981), *The Mask of Shame*. Baltimore, MD: Johns Hopkins University Press.

2

FRANCIS J. BROUCEK

Shame: Early Developmental Issues

In the history of philosophy the existence of a real external world has been far more frequently denied than the existence of other selves: and this though no one has denied our ability to perceive Nature while practically everybody has disputed our power of perceiving mental life in others. The reason for this is that *our conviction of the existence of other minds is earlier and deeper than our belief in the existence of nature* [Scheler, 1913 p. 259].

Emotions are not part of the mental processes of isolated subjects as such [Trevarthen, 1984, p. 137].

SOME GENERAL CONSIDERATIONS ABOUT EMOTION AND CONSCIOUSNESS

In subsequent sections of this chapter I attempt to integrate my ideas about the development of shame experience with certain general ideas about consciousness and the function of emotions put forward by infant researcher Trevarthen (1974, 1979, 1984). But first it is necessary to present those ideas in a summary form. According to Trevarthen (1979), there are three inseparable aspects to consciousness: 1) intentionality, knowing what one is doing and why; 2) awareness of the here-and-now reality, that is, knowing what is being seen, heard, touched; and 3) the sharing of knowledge and personal feelings, having intimacy with the consciousness of others and an awareness of affectional and moral responsibility to them. Although the first and third are of great importance in every free manifestation of human life, empiricists, says Trevarthen, have consistently ignored those factors in favor of the second, even though these three aspects of consciousness are not only inseparable but functionally interdependent. The infant makes "sense" out of sense data only to the extent that such data are functionally correlated with intentionality and shared consciousness. The third aspect of consciousness, having intimacy with the consciousness of others and awareness of our affectional and moral responsibility to them, is based on our species-general, innate understanding of the affective code that makes others' mental states observable from infancy on.

Hobson (1993), using terms introduced by Martin Buber, describes two distinct lines of cognitive development, the I-It line and I-Thou line. I-It cognitive development involves transactions with the impersonal world of inanimate objects and includes such things as visuospatial pattern recognition, understanding simple means–end relations, awareness of object permanence, and so on. Piaget's work tends to focus on this I-It line of development. The I-Thou line of cognitive development takes place within the intersubjective realm and makes possible the acquisition of language skills and the capacity to symbolize. Trevarthen (1974) concludes from his studies that "the endowment of the human infant for intersubjective functions is greater than that for the transactions of consciousness with the physical nonliving world and [we] would ascribe great theoretical significance to this fact" (p. 185). He maintains that the original and key function of human emotions is to regulate interpersonal contacts and the development of consciousness. As Trevarthen sees it, emotions define a person in relationship to other persons and are inseparable from contacts or relationships between persons. If humans also react with affect to impersonal objective events, it is because much of their early mastery of objects takes place in the context of cooperative (or oppositional) interaction with persons. The acquisition of language and other culturally significant skills also occurs in the context of cooperative exchange with persons and is thus also regulated by patterns of affective interaction. Language does not simply refer to things, *it refers the other's mind to things.* Our conviction of the existence of other minds, as Scheler (1913) observed, *is earlier and deeper than our belief in the existence of nature,* and this early intimacy with the consciousness of others is affectively mediated. We know that autistic children have serious language-acquisition problems based, most likely, on the autistic child's impaired capacity for intersubjectivity, what Hobson (1993) calls a "relatedness deficit." Such a deficit may stem from an impaired ability to "read" the affective code and engage in patterned affective interaction with others. It is also significant that autistic children do not show shame reactions in situations where normal children would (Hobson, 1993).

Not only does Trevarthen maintain that the primary function of the emotional processes in infancy is to set up and regulate interpersonal engagements and the development of human consciousness, but he rejects the currently fashionable effort to understand emotions too mechanistically in terms of neural processes. Trevarthan (1984) maintains that

> other less psychological correlates of emotion can easily be separated from the interpersonal. Thus, physiological regulation either of cerebral arousal or blood circulation, release of hormones and breathing, are coupled with emotional states simply because the brain and body are necessarily involved in behaviors that accompany interpersonal contacts. Emotions are not to be identified with or reduced to such brain and body states at any stage of development [p. 154].

Trevarthen also finds Darwin's effort to account for the adaptive function of emotion seriously lacking in that it fails to account for the relationship between emotions and the psychological processes that represent persons and relationships and thus fails to grasp the essential adaptive function of emotions in human life, which is to set up and regulate interpersonal engagements and mental cooperation (intersubjectivity).

The infant comes into the world with an inherent understanding of the primary affective code, says Trevarthen, and this understanding suggests an innate sensitivity to rhythmic patterns in movement and a receptivity to the forms of emotion along with a transmodal capacity to detect specific affect expressions in another and motorically reproduce those expressions. Meltzoff and Moore (1983) demonstrated the capacity of neonates to imitate adult facial expressions. These studies and those of Field et al. (1982) suggest that neonates can grasp the equivalence between facial patterns of movement they see and pattern of movement they make on their own. Infants can recognize correspondences across perceptual modalities innately, but how this is accomplished is something of a mystery. Meltzoff (1985) stated, "Because neonates can recognize the equivalences between the acts they themselves perform and those performed by the adults, they have a mechanism by which to begin to identify with other human beings, to recognize them as 'like me'" (p. 29). Why should an ability be translated as a "mechanism"? Couldn't one simply say that it is the innate ability of the infant to identify and identify *with* a nonspecific, the innate, preverbal, preconceptual knowledge that "we are alike" that founds these transmodal abilities?

Hobson (1993) argues that

> the very concept of "persons" with minds is founded upon precon-
> ceptual forms of awareness that people are different from things in
> affording intersubjective contact. The thesis is that infants are
> biologically "prewired" to relate to people in ways that are special
> to people, and that it is *through the experience of reciprocal,
> affectively patterned interpersonal contact* that a young child
> comes to apprehend and eventually to conceptualise the nature of
> persons with mental life [p. 104, italics added].

THE INTERSUBJECTIVE ROOTS OF SHAME EXPERIENCE

In my view, shame is closely linked with intentionality and intersub-jectivity. As Lichtenberg (1982) says, "the infant is an accomplished action initiator and responder before he can achieve psychic representation of the purpose of the action or of himself as the originator of the action" (p. 717). Competence and efficacy motiva-tions seem to be involved in these early efforts (Brazelton and Als, 1979; Broucek, 1979). These initiating and responding actions take place in the intersubjective field and are possible only by virtue of the infants' innate understanding of the affective code. In previous work (Broucek, 1982, 1991), I proposed that the earliest develop-mental trigger for shame is a sense of inefficacy (a perceived failure that in infancy is prototypically a failure to initiate, maintain, or extend a desired emotional engagement with a caretaker). Implied in that model is the alternative notion that the disruption in the "flow" of affective exchange could be looked upon as the trigger for shame by a slight shift of emphasis.[1] This sudden disruption of affective flow would bring about what Kaufman (1985) called the rupture of the interpersonal bridge. The interpersonal bridge is established through good-enough affective attunement on the part of caretakers so that an affective dialogue can take place between infant and caregiver based on a reciprocity and complementarity in affective exchange (flow) that promotes the development of the sense of self.

---

[1] I am grateful to Robert Stolorow (personal communication) for helping me clarify this point.

I use the term sense of self to refer to self-awareness of an immediate, preconceptual, and nonimagistic type; it is the basis of our most profound identification with our body, and it is what provides us with the experience of "indwelling," the experience of the "lived body" rather than body as part of the object world.

What I refer to as the sense of self or subjective self may be similar to what Emde (1983) has called "the prerepresentational self," which he sees as forming around an affective core that guarantees our continuity of experience despite developmental change. I consider that "affective core" to comprise the established patterns of intersubjective affective relatedness. Emde notes the paradox that, although the basic affective core is species general, it is also the foundation of our sense of ourselves as individuals. Our affective core not only guarantees the continuity of our experience over time but also insures that we are able to understand others "because our affective core touches upon those aspects of experience which are most important to us as individuals, it also allows us to get in touch with the uniqueness of our own (and others') experience" (p. 180).

To understand better how my views on shame differ from the efforts of others to conceptualize the nature of the shame experience, it may be useful to review some of those efforts. We might start by reviewing the ideas of the affect theorist Silvan Tomkins (1963, 1981). Tomkins identified nine innate basic affects: two positive affects, interest-excitement and enjoyment-joy; six negative affects, anger, fear, distress, shame, disgust, dissmell (the affective response to obnoxious odors); and one resetting affect, surprise. Tomkins's affect theory seeks to explain the "mechanism" of affective experience. It is a theory that asserts that qualitative states, affects, are triggered by quantitative differences in density of neural firing (the frequency of neural firing over time). Tomkins (1981) accounts for differences in affect activation by three variants of the density principle: stimulation increase, stimulation level, and stimulation decrease.

> Thus any stimulus with a relatively sudden onset and a steep increase in the rate of neural firing will innately activate a startle response. . . . If the rate of neural firing increases less rapidly, fear is activated, and if still less rapidly, interest is innately activated. In contrast, any sustained increase in the level of neural firing, as with a continuing loud noise, would innately activate the cry of distress. If it were sustained and still louder, it would innately activate the anger response. Finally any sudden decrease in stimulation that reduced the rate of neural firing, as in the sudden reduction of

excessive noise, would innately activate the rewarding smile of
enjoyment [p. 317].

Tomkins's efforts to explain qualitative experiences of affect in
terms of quantitative considerations are in the reductionist tradition
of Western science and are modeled after earlier scientific explanations of qualitative sensory experiences (e.g., color and sound).
Shame recognized by Tomkins (as by Darwin before him) as an
innate affect also somehow had to be accounted for in terms of
quantitative considerations about density of neural firing. Tomkins
attempted to fit shame into this schema by postulating that shame
was triggered by an incomplete reduction of the affects of interest-
excitement or enjoyment -joy. It was an affect auxiliary to the two
innate positive affects in a way analogous to the auxiliary functions
of disgust and dissmell with respect to the hunger drive.

There are unfortunately several problems with Tomkins's
explanation of the mechanism of activation of shame. First, developmental researcher Michael Lewis (personal communication) reports
that in his laboratory he has failed to elicit shame reactions through
interruptions of activities of joyful or excited children. Second, it is
not too difficult to think of numerous instances in which the formula
(that shame results from the incomplete reduction of positive affects)
fails to hold. For example, one is watching, with great interest and
excitement, a sporting event on TV when a technical problem
severely compromises the quality of the picture. One may feel
distressed or enraged about this turn of events—but ashamed? Or
imagine yourself enjoying a delicious meal when your dinner
companion shares some disconcerting information that dampens your
enjoyment of the meal. Neither introspection nor observation of
others confirms that shame is ordinarily activated in such situations,
but according to Tomkins's theory it ought to be. Third, many
experiences of shame are preceded not by affective states of interest-
excitement or enjoyment-joy but rather by negative affect states. A
public speaker who is in a state of considerable anxiety and
consequently stumbles through his presentation may move from
anxiety into shame. A man who feels intimidated in an argument
with another, more aggressive man may move from fear into shame
if being afraid in that situation is viewed by him as an unacceptable
personal weakness. Loss of control over anger such as might occur
when rage is triggered may be followed by shame. Clearly, there is
no invariant relationship between the positive affects and shame as
Tomkins's theory would require. Clinical experience convinces me
that the shame experience is more frequent and pervasive in those

persons whose affective states are prevailingly negative. Tomkins was not unaware of these problems in his efforts to fit shame into his general scheme of affect activation involving density of neural firing and he (personal communication) acknowledged feeling much less confident about this aspect of his theory than he did about the rest of ft. Nevertheless, he stuck by his explanation, and I think that the reason he did so was that he realized that, if shame is an innate affect and yet cannot be satisfactorily explained in terms of quantitative considerations about density of neural firing (or as an affect-auxiliary to the basic positive affects), it posed a possible challenge to his whole effort to understand affects in these terms.

Nathanson's (1987, 1992) efforts to formulate a developmental model of shame experience, based as they are on Tomkins's mechanistic formulations, are open to the same basic objections.

While I believe that Tomkins's attempt to explain the "mechanism" of shame does not stand up to critical scrutiny, his writings on shame reflect a great sensitivity and understanding of the intersubjective context in which shame is apt to occur. One of my favorite passages from Tomkins's (1963) magnum opus, *Affect, Imagery, Consciousness* poetically illustrates his sensitivity to the interpersonal sources of shame:

> If I wish to touch you but you do not wish to be touched, I may feel ashamed. If I wish to look at you but you do not wish me to, I may feel ashamed. If I wish you to look at me but you do not, I may feel ashamed. If I wish to look at you and at the same time wish that you look at me, I can be shamed. If I wish to be close to you but you move away, I am ashamed. If I wish to suck or bite your body and you are reluctant, I can become ashamed. If I wish to hug you or you hug me or we hug each other and you do not reciprocate my wishes, I feel ashamed. If I wish to have sexual intercourse with you but you do not, I am ashamed.
>
> If I wish to hear your voice but you will not speak to me, I can feel shame. If I wish to speak to you but you will not listen, I am ashamed. If I would like us to have a conversation but you do not wish to converse, I can be shamed. If I would like to share my ideas, aspirations or my values with you but you do not reciprocate, I am ashamed. If I wish to talk and you wish to talk at the same time, I can become ashamed. If I want to tell you my ideas but you wish to tell me yours, I can become ashamed.
>
> If I want to share my experiences with you but you wish to tell me your philosophy of life, I can become ashamed. If I wish to speak of personal feelings but you wish to speak about science, I will feel ashamed. If you wish to talk about the past and I wish to dream about the future, I can become ashamed [p. 192].

In the interpersonal situations that Tomkins lists, shame is clearly elicited by an intersubjective disjunction based on absent complementarity or reciprocity that results in a sense of rejected desire and rejected affectivity, failed intentionality, and inefficacy. Morrison (1994) has espoused a similar view framed in the language of self psychology. He expresses it in this way:

> Shame is, I believe one of our principal responses to selfobject misattunement and nonresponsiveness confounding the expectations of the self ready for, or hoping to receive, affirmation and mirroring, participation with, the idealized selfobject, or share humanity and alikeness with the alter ego (twinship) selfobject [p. 24].

WHEN DOES SHAME APPEAR IN DEVELOPMENT?

This is a controversial issue. If one maintains, as Tomkins and Nathanson do, that shame results from any sudden decrement in interest-excitement and enjoyment joy, then there is no reason why shame should not appear quite early—as early as the first few months of life. And indeed certain infant observational reports do suggest that shame may appear that early (see Broucek, 1982, 1991; Nathanson, 1987). If, on the other hand, one maintains that self-consciousness or objective self-awareness is a precondition for shame experience, as Michael Lewis maintains, then shame experience is not possible before 18 months. Another theoretical model that tries to place shame at a specific developmental stage was recently introduced by Schore (1991, 1994), who tries to tie the earliest experiences of shame to Mahler's practicing subphase of separation-individuation (12–18 months) and sees the function of shame as an inhibitor of hyperaroused states. Schore's prototypical shame reaction occurs when a practicing toddler, in an expansive, grandiose, hyperstimulated state of arousal, reunites with the caregiver expecting shared excitement and affective attunement but experiences instead a misattunement. Schore tries to synthesize the views of Freud, Mahler, Kohut, and Tomkins, the recent literature on shame, and the neurobiological developmental literature in a way that although extremely ambitious in its integrative intent, seems ultimately confusing, a polyglot pastiche of neurobiological, developmental, and psychoanalytic concepts. It is not clear (to me at least) why Schore wants to link the appearance of shame to a period later than some theorists suggest and earlier than others suggest unless perhaps out of his apparently strong attachment to the theories of Margaret Mahler.

Let us return to the problem of when it makes sense to talk about the developmental appearance of shame experience? Let us look at the "still face" experiments of Tronick et al. (1978). In those experiments interchanges between infants and their mothers were filmed under two different conditions In the first phase of the experiment, mother was told to interact with her three-month old infant as she normally would in a face-to-face exchange. Next she was instructed to leave the room for a few minutes and upon her return to make eye contact with her infant but not to engage in affective or verbal interaction. When presented with the still-faced mother, for a while the infants would attempt to engage the mother in their usual mode of interaction. When this failed, the infants exhibited one of two characteristic behaviors: some cried in distress, and others slumped in their seats with sudden loss of body tonus, turning the head downward and to the side, averting their gaze from the mother's face. Nathanson (1987) cited a discussion by Demos of these experiments in which she expressed the view that this latter group of children was exhibiting a primitive shame reaction. If so, this would seem to be consistent with Tomkins's ideas about the activation of shame as a result of disrupted interest-excitement. It would also be consistent with my view that shame is elicited by an intersubjective disjunction based on inefficacy and absent affective complementarity or reciprocity, in Kaufman's (1985) terms, "the rupture of the interpersonal bridge."

The developmental researcher Michael Lewis believes that shame is not possible before the development of objective self-awareness around 18–24 months. Although I also believe that objective self awareness is a watershed in the development of shame and that objective self-awareness brings about certain very important changes in the nature of shame experience (to be discussed), I believe that prototypical shame experiences may occur much earlier in development. According to Lewis (1989), "Shame is the product of two sets of cognitive activities: the person's evaluation of his or her action, thought, or behavior as failure, and a global self-evaluation" (p. 55). The first set of cognitive processes has to do with standards, rules, and goals and the evaluation of one's behavior in terms of these standards, rules, and goals (SRGs) (p. 51). The second cognitive activity is a global self-evaluation of a negative kind, Lewis takes the position that the development of objective self-awareness is essential for the two sets of cognitive activities.

Let's look at one of Lewis's examples of early shame, "Angry Donald," in the light of his formulations and assess the degree of fit. A mother is playing with her two-year-old child, and she has been asked to play a particular game.

> We observe her showing the child how to do the task. "Look," she says, "take this donut and move it from here to there." The child complies. "Very good. You are a good boy. Now," she says, "take the second donut and put it on this one." In this way she slowly goes through how to solve the task, the child watches her intently as she both explains and shows the child how it is done. She occasionally smiles but her face is serious. She often praises the child with such comments as "Good boy," "you are really clever," "Smart lad." Now she rearranges the problem, and presents it to the child. The child takes the first piece and puts it on the wrong shaft. The child smiles and looks up at the mother. The mother looks at the child and hollers, "No, no, no! What is wrong with you?" Our cameras close in on her face. The expression is one in which the nose is raised, nostrils flared, and we know that we will later score it as a contempt/disgust look. The child looks up at the mother confused and turns back to the task. However, his body is now hunched over, his smile is gone, and he no longer appears interested in what is happening. The mother insists that the child go on. The child reaches for the ring and, rather than placing it on the shaft, throws it across the room [p. 46].

Lewis comments that "the mother's disgusted face has shamed the child" (p. 46), an observation with which I would agree. The question is why, then, in the case of angry Donald and similar cases, is it necessary to posit an intervening cognitive process in which the child compared his behavior with some internalized set of standards, rules, and goals, evaluated himself as failing, and then made a negative global self-attribution?[2] In this example it seems that the

---

[2]There has been a running debate in the psychological literature of the last decade between "the cognitive imperialists," as Silvan Tomkins (personal communication) called them, and those, like Tomkins and Zajonc (1980), who espouse the primacy of affects. The former tend to see affect as invariably postcognitive, the result of evaluative processes of various kinds, while the latter see affect and cognition as relatively independent subsystems and maintain that the directionality is not exclusively from cognition to affect but may also be from affect to cognition. Lewis's (1992) explication of shame is too "cognitive" in my view. He believes that "all stimulus events elicit emotion through some cognitive process" (p. 117). Rather than line up on one side of the argument or the other, we can reject the whole effort to

child had no clear conception of what action would have constituted a successful compliance with the rules of the game, and hence an attribution of failure based on cognitive activity alone seems unlikely. It is clearly the mother's affective response to Donald's attempt to solve the problem that has shamed the child, as Lewis acknowledges. This example supports what we said earlier about shame, that is, that in early development it is elicited by an intersubjective disjunction based on absent affective complementarity or reciprocity that results in a sense of inefficacy, failed intentionality, and rejected affectivity. I would press the point even further by suggesting that the cognitive activity that Lewis describes as *producing* shame may instead be the *effect* of being shamed by the affective response of the other. In other words, the acquisition of SRGs and self-evaluation, as well as the acquisition of objective self-awareness (given a certain state of maturation of the central nervous system) may be stimulated and reinforced by the need to avoid the painful shame experiences growing out of disrupted affective attunement and failed inten-tionality. Lewis (1992), discussing the emergence of objective self-awareness, refers to the claim of Duval and Wickland that three conditions need to be met if the child is to develop objective self awareness:

> (1) There must be an entity who has a different point of view than the child; (2) the two different points of view must concern the same object; and (3) the child must be aware of these two different opinions simultaneously. They [Duval and Wickland, 1992] base their position on their belief that the objective self becomes differentiated from the subjective self. To begin with, the infant acts, perceives, and thinks but does not turn his attention on himself. The turning of attention on the self requires a conflict between the child's action and the action of others. This conflict enables the child to objectify his actions, thoughts, and feelings, and thus to develop objective self-awareness [p. 57].

So, when Angry Donald's pleasure, excitement, and anticipation of having that pleasure and excitement shared by mother is disrupted by mother's shaming disgust look and verbal disapproval, Duval and Wicklund's criteria are fulfilled. Thus one could make the claim that experiences of shame may serve as an important stimulus to the

---

view affect or cognition as having some invariable cause-and-effect relation-ship, It is more likely that in most situations we perceive, feel, and think simultaneously in a coordinated, nonlinear way.

acquisition of objective self-awareness in the child who is maturationally ready for this type of awareness.

Lewis and some other developmental researchers seem to believe
that the self comes into existence only when the infant acquires
objective self-awareness around the middle of the second year of life.
Lewis sees the infant's early capacities as reflexive in nature,
automatic social response patterns, and takes issue with Stern's
(1985) ideas about an emerging self, core self, and subjective self, all
of which, according to Stern develop in the first year of life and thus
predate the acquisition of objective self-awareness. As far as intersubjectivity is concerned, Lewis (1992) says,

> intersubjectivity becomes simply a set of complex behavior pattern
> that are triggered by other behaviors. Intersubjectivity is less
> controlled by complex cognitions and more by simple rules, such
> as circular reactions. It is not based on intention in terms of
> complex means-ends representation, but is more like automatic
> social responses [p. 229].

Lewis's denial of the infants' capacities for complex cognitions and
complex means–end relationships is contradicted by other developmental studies. The "switching on" experiments of Papousek and
Papousek (1975), although they do not deal specifically with
intersubjectivty, demonstrate the skills that infants bring to the
intersubjective encounter. The four-month-old infants in the
Papouseks' study had to find out by themselves and by chance that
rotating the head at least 30 degrees to a predetermined side three
times in succession would activate a multicolored light display.
Before the experiments, the light display was attractive to the infants,
but after several repetitions habituation occurred and they would
show less interest in the display. When the light display was
contingent on the infants' activities and the infants grasped that fact,
their behavior changed dramatically. They insatiably repeated the
behavior "with such joyful affect in . . . gestures and vocalization that
it seemed more like attachment than habituation" (p. 252). Lest we
dismiss this as a simple form of operant learning, the Papouseks
invite us to imagine ourselves as the experimental subject. "How easy
is it," they ask, "to discover that 'reinforcement' is contingent on
head movements, or that head movement has to be performed three
times successively in a given time interval, with rotations of at least
30 degrees each time?" (p. 252). If this doesn't involve complex
means–end relationships and complex cognitions, it's hard to imagine
what more one could ask of an infant. It is also important to note
that the "visual reward" in these experiments had no sustained

reward value per se; only the intentional or "willed" consequence of actions and effects has reward value. Such a psychological phenomenon can be described in stimulus–response terms only artificially and superficially. Is it too adultomorphic to suggest that the infant's intoxication with being the cause reveals a rudimentary self that has discovered that "I cause and I intend, Therefore I am?" I don!t think, so nor do I think that the self emerges full blown, like Athena from the head of Zeus, with the advent of objective self-awareness.

To return to the question of when shame first appears in the development of child, I think it a mistake to get too invested in trying to pin down exactly when it is that the child develops the capacity to experience shame. One could say that significant shame experiences may occur at any stage of development if one accepts the idea that such experiences are triggered by a breakdown in what Kaufman (1985) calls the interpersonal bridge, an idea I have tried to reformulate in the language of intersubjectivity.

SHAME AND OBJECTIVE SELF-AWARENESS

In a previous work (Broucek, 1991) I defined objective self-awareness (OSA) as "an awareness of oneself as an object for others and through the mirroring of the observing others, taking oneself as an object of reflection (objectifying oneself)" (p. 37). The acquisition of OSA appears to be the result of the interplay of developmental maturation of the central nervous system and social contextual factors such as conflicting points of view (as Duval and Wicklund suggest) and disjunctive affectivity.

Notwithstanding my belief that infants may experience the emotion of shame prior to the acquisition of OSA, early shame experience will not involve ideation about the self as it will after the appearance of OSA. Lewis (1992) sees OSA as a "prerequisite" for shame experience which allows for shame to be triggered by a global attribution of failure with regard to standards, rules, and goals (SRGs). In my view OSA not only is a prerequisite for more developed forms of shame experience but also is a source of shame in its own right. "Self-conscious" is a term often used as a synonym for embarrassment or milder forms of shame experience. OSA in and of itself may produce painful self-consciousness. Empirical support for the idea that developing OSA is a trigger for shame comes from the studies of young children's reactions to their mirror images when they first recognize those images as of themselves. Amsterdam (1972), in her study of mirror self-image reactions in infants and toddlers before age two, concluded that "every subject who showed recognition behavior also manifested either avoidance or self- consciousness or all three" (p. 304). The avoidance and self-consciousness these children exhibited point to a shame experience.

Lewis would probably say that these children were embarrassed rather than ashamed. Although he hedges on this point, Lewis is inclined to see embarrassment as a different emotion than shame. Embarrassment, he says, can be induced simply by a situation of unwanted exposure whereas shame involves a global attribution of failure As a demonstration that embarrassment can be elicited just by exposure, Lewis (1992) might simply point to a student in one of his classes. He observes, "My pointing invariably elicits embarrassment in the student pointed at" (p. 82). This embarrassment cannot be a form of shame, insists Lewis, because shame is produced by a negative evaluation of the self. How does he know that? *Because that is how he has defined shame.* Setting aside the fact that pointing a finger at someone is apt to be perceived as an accusatory gesture, there is a clear circularity in this type of reasoning. If embarrassment *is* a form of shame and yet is not the result of negative self-evalua- tion, then Lewis's definition of shame is faulty or incomplete. Claiming that embarrassment and shame are different affects strikes me as analogous to saying that anxiety and fear are different affects because in the case of fear there is some specific object of that fear that is cognitively apprehended, whereas with anxiety this is not the case. Here I follow Tomkins (1981), who maintains that basic affects can be "coassembled" with variable cognitive content, and every variation in cognitive content is not necessarily a different affect.

Whereas Lewis sees the development of OSA as essential for the appearance of shame, I see it as a development that greatly magnifies the potential for a shame experience and changes the nature of that experience: Prior to the development of OSA, the infant exists in a state that I have called *primary communion* as contrasted with earlier psychoanalytic notions of primary narcissism. The concept of primary narcissism presupposes an initially unrelated infant driven only by the need to relieve drive tension and who only gradually and reluctantly differentiates self from other. In the light of infancy studies of the last two decades, which reveal the infant's coming into the world equipped for social interaction from the outset, the infant's supposed lack of self- and other differentiation is no longer tenable. Stern (1985) and Lichtenberg (1982) have been the most vocal and persuasive critics of these venerable psychoanalytic assumptions about the infant's earliest mental states. In contrast to primary narcissism, the term primary communion presupposes an infant fundamentally related to a primary caretaking other by way of an innate understanding of the affective code and the utilization of that understanding to bring about mutual affective attunement with the caretaker.

The appearance of OSA means the end of primary communion.[3] At the time of acquisition of OSA, the self becomes split into the immediate "I" and the mediated, objectified "me"; and the self's experience of the other also becomes split into the other, who relates herself to myself in an attuned way so as to maintain my subjective sense of self and the other who objectifies me and thus becomes a potential source of shame. A child may experience being looked at in a way that supports her affective initiatives and responses, or she may experience being looked at in a way that objectifies her and activates shame.

OSA brings about a potential alienation from one's subjective sense of self, a *primary dissociation* that I consider to be the prototype of all later dissociative events. Dissociative experiences typically involve a sense of viewing oneself from a position outside the body with a loss of the subjective indwelling sense of self. With the advent of OSA, the child no longer experiences herself as centered in the way she previously felt herself to be or grounded in the previously taken for granted intersubjectivity. Many of the behaviors that Mahler, Pine, and Bergman (1975) described as characteristic of the individuating child during the rapprochement subphase of separation-individuation may reflect the shame and ontological insecurity associated with the acquisition of OSA.

OSA makes possible the formation of a self-image, and later, with increasing cognitive maturation, a self-concept. At this point standards, rules, and goals (SRGs) begin to become increasingly important, as Lewis (1992) notes, since failure with respect to SRGs may not only bring about an affective disjunction in the interpersonal field (in the form of verbal disapproval, a frown, or a contempt/disgust look on the part of the caretaker) but failure also makes it harder to form and maintain a favorable self-image. It may be helpful to think of the earliest self- representation as a representation of a relationship, a representation more affective than conceptual in nature, which once firmly installed in the unconscious may be very resistant to change.

---

[3]In the Genesis myth the acquisition of OSA is represented as "The Fall." God recognizes that Adam and Eve have eaten from the forbidden fruit tree because they are suddenly objectively self-aware—they realize that they are naked and try to hide from Him.

The formation of an ideal self-image is also made possible by OSA. When a child learns to objectify herself, she simultaneously acquires the ability to compare herself with others and thus becomes sensitive to her relative smallness, weakness, and lack of competence as compared with parents, older siblings, and most other people. The ideal self-image that she will construct will be an imaginative product purged of these inferiorities and purged of the negative affects (principally shame and fear) that go with these perceived inadequacies. Kohut's, 1977, idealized selfobject is needed as a phase-appropriate substitute for the unrealized ideal self-image and is as well a model for its subsequent development. The idealized selfobject rescues the post-OSA child from the shame of her recognized inferiority and strengthens her in pursuit of her ideal self. One of the paradoxical aspects of the ideal self is that although its formation owes much to the need to escape from shameful feelings of inferiority vis-á-vis others, later failure to live up to that image may become the dominant source of shame for many people (Piers and Singer, 1953; Morrison, 1989). It is one of those many instances, with which clinicians are all too familiar, in which the attempted solution becomes the problem.

The interplay of pre- and post-OSA developments can lead to certain forms of psychopathology, particularly those which we bring together under the label of narcissistic disorders. OSA draws the child away from the more immediate unselfconscious state of indwelling and directs her toward what she sees and imagines herself to be. In earlier work (Broucek, 1982) I proposed that when the child acquires OSA the oscillation between the subjective sense of self (as indwelling) and OSA (as an outside, looking-on experience) will become gradually regulated into a pattern unique to that individual. A pre-OSA weakened sense of self coupled with strong shame propensities may tip the balance toward the later dominance of OSA over the subjective sense of self. The immediate "I" is "confiscated" by the visible, objectified "me." Lichtenstein (1963) proposed that the dilemma of human identity is that the experience of the actuality of being and self-objectification are mutually incompatible experiences; in gaining one we lose the other. The more one's consciousness is dominated by OSA, the more one begins to live a spectral existence as an image until. in extreme cases, image becomes everything and the authentic self, the I-being, is lost. I believe that it is possible to understand narcissism in a way that is faithful to the myth of Narcissus, a youth who became totally absorbed with his own reflection at the expense of interest in others and the world. Narcissus became entranced not by his self but by his image, his reflection. It really doesn't matter much whether Narcissus loved or hated his reflected image; what matters is that he was captured and dominated by that reflected image and his psychic life reflected that domination. He became an "imagologue," to borrow a neologism coined by Milan Kundera (1991) in his novel *Immortality*.

If the child's I-being (Stern's core self, Winnicott's true self) is over time not responded to in a tender, empathically attuned way that aims and strengthens her core sense' of self, when OSA is acquired the weakened sense of self (depleted by shame) may be more easily drawn away from the indwelling first-person position (I-being) into an objectified third-person position, more and more frequently. It is as though the I-being has a gravitational force that under normal developmental conditions is sufficiently strong to keep the sense of self from being pulled away by the gravitational force of the objectified self-image but under pathological conditions is not strong enough to prevent that from happening. The child discovers that her parents have a certain image of what they want her to be, and conforming to that image may become more important (if she wants love and approval) than her own innate inclinations, which may be at variance with parental expectations. This situation produces a shame experience for the child. How she appears to the parents becomes more and more her dominant, anxiety-laden concern. As development proceeds, her psychic life thus becomes taken over by considerations of how she appears to others and a false self (Winnicott) or spectral self is created. The major function of the false self is to protect from shame.

Since the "imagologue" is engaged in projecting a certain image that she tries to pass off as herself, she is of necessity bound to deal with others more as images rather than as persons. Because of this situation, exhibition must masquerade as communication since communication is a capacity of persons but not of Images. All one has to do to witness exhibition masquerading as communication is watch the late night television talk shows, where "imagologues" are generously represented among the celebrity population (movie stars, sports heroes, rock stars, politicians).

SOME BRIEF REMARKS ON
THE SOCIALIZATION OF SHAME

Lewis (1992) has called our attention to the extensive use that parents and educators make of the child's susceptibility to shame in their socialization efforts. He notes that

Parents use a variety of socializing techniques. If a parent fails to use reasoning and finds it inappropriate or inadmissible to yell or punish, the use of the disgusted/contemptuous face is an ideal solution. It is ideal because it serves to inhibit the action that the parent does not wish the child to perform. It is all the more effective because it is secretive. The disgusted face is made very quickly, and parents can deny that they made it; or if they admit to it, they can deny that it was detected by the child. Parents are often unaware that they are producing these faces. When I have pointed out their use of the disgusted face, they often are shocked to discover this action. Even more important, parents are usually unaware that their use of the disgusted face is a shaming device [p. 111].

Lewis's observations of parents and children in normal circumstances revealed that 40% of codable parental facial expressions were of the disgust/ contempt variety. He notes that parents, teachers, and peers all use the the disgust/contempt face to induce feelings of shame and humiliation in children.

Other ways in which parents, teachers, and peers deliberately induce shame in children include power assertion, overt verbal expressions of disgust or contempt, sadistic "teasing," various forms of ostracism such as "the silent treatment," and, last but not least, love withdrawal. Lewis believes that if there is any stimulus for shame that is prototypical the most likely candidate is love withdrawal; in his view it is most likely to elicit a global self-evaluation of failure. It is also the most painful form of severance of the interpersonal bridge.

We live in a time when various forms of child abuse have received a great deal of attention in the professional literature and in the popular media, particularly focused on the more dramatic forms of physical and sexual abuse. Consequently, there is frequently a failure to recognize that these more dramatic forms of abuse have something in common with other, less dramatic but still very damaging forms of abuse, that is, the infliction of heavy doses of shame and humiliation on children. I believe that the path from childhood abuse to psychopathology invariably goes through the realm of shame and shame-rage.

Since a great part of childhood is spent in an educational environment, it is important to look at how shame and shame anxiety either facilitate or derail the learning process in childhood and how schools and teachers make use of the power of shame. Pride and shame are closely connected with issues of competence, efficacy, the successful meeting of standards and rules, and achievement of goals,

(SRGs). Whether a child's educational experience is more a source of pride or of shame depends on a number of variables, not the least important of which is whether the teachers he comes in contact with are prone to use shaming as a pedagogical device. The famed Swedish film director Ingmar Bergman (1970) recalled a childhood filled with humiliation: "Isn't it a fact children are always feeling deeply humiliated in their relationships with grownups and each other? . . . our whole education is just one long humiliation, and it was even more so when I was a child" (p. 00).

One is particularly vulnerable to shame whenever one enters a learning situation To learn, one has to accept the shame of ignorance or incompetence and tolerate it in order to reach the pleasure and satisfaction that learning brings. In a large group of equally ignorant peers the camaraderie of shared ignorance may diminish the shame of that ignorance to a minimal and tolerable level. Once the learning process begins, however, students advance at different rates and the situation is no longer so egalitarian. Comparisons are made in the form of grades and teacher comments, and, as we all know, shame thrives on invidious comparisons.

With regard to the issues of SRGs, the child may have to deal with several sets of SRGs—his parents, his teachers, and his own—and these may be either congruent or conflicting. For example, Lewis (1992) reminds us that some families value academic performance more than others and that in these families, children's academic failure is more likely to lead to shame than it is for the children of families that do not value a high degree of academic excellence. Or, to take a different case, little Tommy may be given the message by his parents that they consider him slow and don't expect of him more than passing performance. Tommy may find himself having to deal with a teacher who considers him bright and expects good classroom performance. Tommy himself may prefer to obtain average grades so as to feel comfortably placed with his peer group—neither looked down upon as inferior nor envied and possibly disliked for superior performance. If he does indeed obtain average grades, he may feel slightly ashamed with respect to his teacher, proud when he takes his grades home to his parents, and quietly self-satisfied with his peers.

Whether failure with respect to SRGs in the school situation will evoke shame or not also depends, as Lewis (1992) points out, on the type of attribution the subject makes in case of failure. If the self-attribution of failure is specific to a certain action of the self or set of actions and does not involve a global devaluation of the total self, shame may be averted; and in that case, according to Lewis, guilt is more likely to be the affective response. Although I do not share Lewis's belief that the essential distinction between guilt and shame rests on whether a specific or global self-attribution of failure is involved (guilt is about transgression, not failure), I do share his view that shame usually (but not always) involves a global attribution of failure involving the total self.

Shame in adolescence deserves extensive treatment on its own, which this essay can not begin to address.

SUMMARY

I have attempted to integrate my ideas on the nature of shame into a developmental theory of intersubjectivity developed by Trevarthen and coworkers and most recently extended by Hobson (I 993). In so doing, I have retained my earlier emphasis on the infant's sense of inefficacy and failed intentionality vis-á-vis the caretaking other but have added emphasis on the disruption of affective "flow," a flow that depends on reciprocity and complementarity in the affective exchange between caregiver and child.

Controversies about the developmental timing of shame capacity have been explored but not resolved. Competing theories have been examined in an admittedly partisan fashion. The importance of objective self-awareness for the development of more advanced types of shame experience has been discussed at some length. Finally some thoughts about the socialization of shame have been advanced.

REFERENCES

Amsterdam, B. (1972), Mirror self-images before age two. *Develop. Psychobiol.,* 5:297–305.
Bergman, I. (1970), *Bergman on Bergman* (interviews with Ingmar Bergman by S. Bjorkman, T. Manns & J. Sima). New York: Simon & Shuster.
Brazelton, T. & Als, H. (1979), Four early stages in the development of mother-infant interaction. *The Psychoanalytic Study of the Child,* 34: 349–371. New Haven, CT: Yale University Press.
Broucek, F. (1979), Efficacy in infancy: A review of some experimental studies and their possible implications for clinical theory. *Internat. J. Psycho-Anal.,* 60:311–316.
———— (1982), Shame and its relationship to early narcissistic developments. *Internat. J. Psycho-Anal.,* 63:369–378.

_____ (1991) *Shame and the Self.* New York: Guilford Press.

Emde, R. (1983), The prerepresentational self and its affective core. *The Psychoanalytic Study of the Child,* 38:165-192. New Haven, CT: Yale University Press.

Field, T., Woodson. R., Greenberg, R. & Cohen, D. (1982), Discrimination and imitation of facial expression by neonates. *Science,* 218:179-181.

Hobson, P. (1993), *Autism and the Development of Mind.* Hillsdale, NJ: Lawrence Erlbaum Associates.

Kaufman, G. (1985), *Shame: The Power of Caring.* Cambridge, MA: Schenkman.

Kohut, H. (1977), *The Restoration of the Self.* New York: International Universities Press.

Kundera, M. (1991), *Immortality.* New York: Grove Weidenfield.

Lewis, M. (1991), Self-conscious emotions and the development of the self. *J. Amer. Psychoanal. Assn.,* 39:49-73.

_____ (1992), *Shame: The Exposed Self.* New York: The Free Press.

Lichtenberg, J. (1982), Reflections on the first year of life. *Psychoanal. Inq.,* 1:695-727.

Lichtenstein, H. (1963), The dilemma of human identity. *J. Amer. Psychoanal. Assn.,* 11:173-223.

Mahler, M. Pine, F. & Bergman, A. (1975), *The Psychological Birth of the Human Infant.* New York: Basic Books.

Meltzoff, A. (1985), The roots of social and cognitive development: models of man's original nature. In: *Social Perception in Infants,* T. Field & N. Fox, ed. Norwood NJ: Ablex, pp. 1-30.

_____ & Moore, M. (1983), Newborn infants imitate adult facial patterns. *Child Devel.,* 54:702-709.

Morrison, A. (1989), *Shame.* Hillsdale, NJ: The Analytic Press.

_____ (1994), The breadth and boundaries of a self-psychological immersion in shame: A one-and-a-half person psychology. *Psychoanal. Dial.,* 4:19-35.

Nathanson, D. (1987), A timetable for shame. In: *The Many Faces of Shame,* ed. D. Nathanson. New York: Guilford Press

_____ (1992), *Shame and Pride.* New York: Norton.

Papousek, H. & Papousek. M. (1975), Cognitive aspects of preverbal social interaction between human infants and adults. Ciba Foundation Symposium. In: *Parent-Infant Interaction.* New York: Association of Scientific Publishers.

Piers, G. & Singer, M. (1953), *Shame and Guilt.* Springfield,IL: Thomas.

Scheler, M. (1913), *The Nature of Sympathy.* Hamden, CT: Archon Books, 1970.

Schore, A. (1991), Early superego development: The emergence of shame and narcissistic affect regulation in the practicing period. *Psychoanal. Contemp. Thought.*, 14:187–250.

———— (1994), *Affect Regulation and the Origin of the Self.* Hillsdale, NJ: Lawrence Erlbaum Associates.

Stern, D. (1985), *The Interpersonal World of the Infant.* New York: Basic Books.

Tomkins, S. (1963), *Affect, Imagery, Consciousness, Vol 2.* New York: Springer.

———— (1981), The quest for primary motives: Biography and autobiography of an idea. *J. Personal. & Soc. Psychol.*, 41:306–329.

Trevarthen, C. (1974), Intersubjectivity and imitation in infants. *Bull. British Psycholog. Soc.*, 27:180–187.

———— (1979), The tasks of consciousness: How could the brain do them? *Ciba Foundation Symposium*, 69:187–215.

———— (1984), Emotions in infancy: Regulators of contact and relationships with persons. In: *Approaches to Emotion*, ed. K. Scherer & P. Eckman. Hillsdale, NJ: Lawrence Erlbaum Associates, pp. 129–157.

Tronick, E., Als, H., Adamson, L., Wise, S. & Brazelton, T. (1978), The infant's response to entrapment between contradictory messages in face-to-face interaction. *J. Child Psychiat.*, 17:1–13.

Zajonc, R. (1980), Feeling and thinking: Preferences need no inferences. *Amer. Psychol.*, 35:151–175.

3

ANDREW P. MORRISON
ROBERT D. STOLOROW

Shame, Narcissism, and Intersubjectivity

Narcissism has been variously defined as a form of pathology, a developmental stage, or a type of primitive object relationship (Pulver, 1970; Sandler, Person, and Fonagy, 1991). Kohut viewed narcissism as an age-appropriate concern with one's sense of stability, cohesion, worthiness, and well-being (Stolorow, 1975). In this chapter, we consider narcissism in its broader context, as a reflection of all aspects of self-experience, including the experience of oneself as expansive, grand, independent, and autonomously sufficient; or as contracted, small, vulnerable, and weak (Morrison, 1989, pp. 64–66). We suggest that the archaic motivational core of narcissism is a yearning for absolute uniqueness in the eyes of a designated, idealized "other," a yearning to be the one that matters most to that designated "other" (Morrison, 1986).

Here we note the intersection of "self" and "other" in the experience of narcissism—a quest in each of us to be taken as special or exceptional to a person special in our particular galaxy. Such a view, with its emphasis on a two-person (intersubjective) field, redresses an emphasis that evolved from some of the initial vagueness of Freud's (1914) "On Narcissism." Narcissism initially was viewed as a retreat, resulting from traumatizing disappointments in love, from object attachments to self-absorption. From the perspective of object love as exemplified by oedipal longings—ascribed primary significance as a developmental task/achievement—narcissism was seen as regression away from mature relationships to a more primitive state. For a long time in the history of psychoanalysis, this observation was taken as self-evident, leading to a value judgment that privileged object love over concerns about self and subjective experience. Taken to its extreme, this view of narcissism as pathology suggested that narcissistic patients were unable to form transferences to the analyst (because of fixation on self) and thus were unanalyzable. In this context, psychosis and schizophrenia were called "the narcissistic neuroses."

This early perspective on narcissism certainly corrected the absence of attention to self-experience that had dominated early psychoanalysis; but, we suggest, it went too far in eliminating the importance of, and connection to, that important "other" in the person's life. It too severely limited our appreciation of the rich and ubiquitous tapestry of narcissistic manifestations, particularly with regard to the relationship of the sense of self to the other. Narcissism represents self-experience, but in connection with that matrix of significant others who constitute the particular environment special to each of us.

The individual quest to be found unique is *not* unusual or pathological in and of itself but, rather, represents an early, infantile expectation to be treated as special or singular by the parent/ caregiver. The expectation of being the special, "only" one is analogous to Kohut's (1977) designation of a developmental need for mirroring. Like the infant's need for mirroring, the archaic expectation to be appreciated for one's uniqueness is age appropriate and nonpathological and represents the wish for the parent's "glow of pride and joy" (p. 236).

When met, the need to be seen as special—that is, to be valued by parents as a total, unique individual (rather than admired exclusively for some particular attribute like looks, intelligence, etc.)—leads, in general, to contentment, stability, and a feeling of self-cohesion. When that need is repeatedly not responded to, however, disappointment in the quest to be viewed as unique (including affirmation of particular affects—see section on intersubjectivity, this chapter) leads to exquisite narcissistic vulnerability and shame sensitivity. We feel ordinary, insignificant, worthless, or pathetic for our unrecognized need—the very attributes that constitute a "language of shame" (Morrison, 1996). It is the early, severe, and humiliating thwarting of this quest that leads to the defensive grandiosity constituting the so-called narcissistic personality disorder.

The desire to be experienced as special, "the only," is, we repeat, a yearning common to each of us that contributes to the sense of oneself as bounded and distinct from the other. Each of us is, in our own integument and our own eyes, unique and separate. Insofar as we experience ourselves in flow and at one with our human environment, this motivational push toward affirmation of uniqueness can remain quiescently in the background. If a person becomes self-consciously aware of difference, separateness, or inferiority, however, the demand to be viewed as special surges to the forefront as a potential balm for the rude experience of insignificance (see sections on Broucek and on intersubjectivity, this chapter). Here we enter the realm of pathological narcissism, where demands reflecting envious attack, contempt, paranoid mistrust, and excessive competetiveness become self-sabotaging and alienating. These demands can be viewed as attempts to defend against weakness and overwhelming shame. As one patient put it, "I am just a grain of sand on the beach, and I can't stand it."

Whether smoothly integrated into the warp of self-experience or mockingly ridiculed, the desire to be treated as special and unique is, we suggest, the core expectation of narcissistic phenomena and provides, as well, a link to the other (who values us) in the sense of self. When this quest for acceptance and recognition of our attributes by the caregiver is significantly fulfilled in infancy, a healthy core of self-love and self-acceptance results. When it is thwarted, self-hatred or defensive grandiosity (or both) emerge as an expression of pathological narcissism in later years. That is, one's insistent clamoring to be "the only" to another frequently reflects a demand geared to make up for early parental failure to provide the needed recognition. As a particularly needy patient put it to his wife, "I have a right to your love." This demanding sense of entitlement can be differentiated from the quiet expectation of two people in love, who may marvel at the experience and good fortune of having found each other.

Our view of narcissism as a reflection of the range of self-experience is essentially phenomenological and broad. The suggestion that shame is the affect lying at the very core of derailed narcissistic experience should come as no surprise; many writers have observed that shame is the painful feeling relating to the sense of self-as-a-whole (Lewis, 1971; Kohut, 1971, 1972; Wurmser, 1981) and hence consitutes the principal source of pain in narcissistic states (Bursten, 1973; Broucek, 1982, 1991; Kinston, 1983; Morrison, 1983, 1989). In what follows we try to weave historical antecedents into a tapestry illustrating the relationship between shame and narcissism; to underscore some specific perspectives on that relationship in more recent writings, particularly those of Kohut and of writers influenced by Kohut and self psychology; and finally to introduce an intersubjective viewpoint into the matrix of shame and narcissism.

EVOLVING VIEWS ON NARCISSISM

Freud's 1914 essay "On Narcissism"—written in part in response to issues raised by the defections of Adler and Jung from the psychoanalytic movement—had in place those elements which might have enabled him to address the relevance of shame to the psychoanalytic corpus. Freud's earlier writings had ambiguously characterized shame as affective experience, as defense (i.e., reaction formation against an exhibitionistic drive), and as symptom (see Chapter One, this volume). "On Narcissism" introduced the concepts of the ego ideal, self-regard, and the idealized other, which together might have led to further elaboration of shame had Freud chosen to do so. He did not, turning his subsequent attention to creation of the structural theory, where ego, id, and superego conflicted with each other, leading to guilt and anxiety. While "On Narcissism" never explicitly identified shame in relation to narcissism, neither did Alfred Adler in his writings deal directly with shame, although his concerns readily lent themselves to a consideration of the distresses of humiliation. Adler (1907) wrote of organ inferiority and inferiority feelings in general, with their accompanying passivity. According to Adler, these feelings in turn generated the reaction of masculine protest, or aggressive hostility and rage. Adler was also concerned with what he called psychic hermaphrodism, or bisexuality, which might also have been considered in its capacity to generate shame, although he did not explicitly make that connection.

Neither Freud nor his early psychoanalytic adversaries moved beyond their interest in narcissism or in feelings of inferiority to the underlying affective response of shame. Little attention was paid to shame or narcissism for the next several decades (with the exception of Piers and Singer 1953), until Hartmann (1950) moved from an emphasis on ego by stating that narcissism is "libidinal cathexis not of the ego but of the self" (p. 85) and, later, Hartmann and Lowenstein (1962) stated that "the ego ideal can be considered a rescue operation for narcissism" (p. 61).

Narcissism, the sense of self, and their relationship to the ego ideal became "appropriate" foci of interest within ego psychology in the 1960s, and with attention to these elements came a potential awareness of the role of shame. Seen in relationship to the superego, the ego ideal was of particular concern to Reich (1960), Jacobson (1964), and Murray (1964), who viewed it primarily in terms of its primitive archaic moorings. This view of narcissism focused on its pathology and early developmental roots, variously emphasizing primitiveness and archaic sources, rigidity, or selfishness and "entitlement"—that is, *fixation* at a prerelational developmental level. A primitive, archaic ego ideal caused wide swings between idealization and wish for merger with an omnipotent other and concomitant feelings of worthlessness, or fantasies of self-aggrandizement and omnipotence resulting in disdain and devaluation of the other. Thus self-experience oscillates between feelings of worthlessness and smallness (narcissistic vulnerability) and expansive grandiosity. These swings in self-assessment determine as well the value and necessity of the other, in whose eyes the person yearns to shine. Narcissism and the ego ideal were viewed fundamentally from a pathological perspective, with "pathological" narcissism and "primitive" ego ideal reflecting early injuries and humiliations, leading to feelings of failure, inferiority, and shame.

At the same time, others were observing in their patients that ideals originate not in the distant, abstract "ego ideal" but in a subjectively experienced "ideal self" (Sandler, Holder, and Meers, 1963; Schafer, 1967). Their emphasis was on the shape of the ideal self—the person that we want to be—compared with that of the "actual self"—the person we perceive ourselves to be at any particular time. The greater the sensed discrepancy or gap between ideal and actual selves, the greater the propensity for shame and for narcissistic insult. In a similar vein, at this time narcissism was being connected with the development of personal identity (Erikson, 1950; Lichtenstein, 1964).

We have traced, then, the disappearance of Freud's initial interest in shame in his 1914 contribution on narcissism as he turned instead to structural conflict and its theoretical elaborations; the subsequent hiatus in interest both in shame and narcissism until Hartmann (1950) distinguished between ego cathexis and self-cathexis and reintroduced the ego ideal and narcissism in the 1950s; and subsequent work on "pathological" narcissism and archaic ego ideal manifestations, with a developmental view of shame and narcissism as being primitive, to be relinquished as one aspires to more mature, oedipal concerns.

Also during the 1960s and 70s others were taking a more clinical view of ideals, failure, and shame through the clinically derived concept of the ideal self. Attention had not yet explicitly been focused on the relationship between shame and narcissism, however. Bela Grunberger in France was exploring narcissism from the perspective of what he called the "monad." Grunberger (1979) distinguished between instinctual conflict and narcissism, which he viewed as memory traces of, and longing to return to, the prenatal bliss of absolute merger with the mother and her body. This longing he viewed as primitive, an archaic remnant that must be modified or relinquished in favor of the paternal reality principle that "inevitably" follows from development and maturity. Shame represents recognition of the failure to move beyond yearnings for the state of the monad toward the "paternal," the real.

Piers and Singer (1953) explicitly considered the relationship of shame to narcissism by examining the role of the ego ideal. They wrote about "a core of narcissistic omnipotence" as the first quality of the ego ideal, emphasizing again the pathological in terms of "overinflated, grandiose, or perfectionistic ideals that put the ego under unbearable tensions" (p. 26). Others, too, touched on shame's relationship to narcissism but inevitably emphasized the primitive, pathological essence of both (Lynd, 1958) or were ambiguous about which of the two entities—shame or narcissism—caused the other. Levin (1967, 1982), for instance, suggested that shame caused narcissistic disequilibrium and the "disruption of 'narcissistic injury',' while the previous authors saw it the other way around, with narcissistic vulnerability and injury (e.g., failure with regard to the ideal self) leading to shame (Piers and Singer, 1953; Sandler et al., 1963).

In the 1970s and 80s, psychoanalytic attention to narcissism truly came into its own and, in fact, tended to dominate the theoretical and clinical landscape. Much of this interest was initiated by the contributions of Kohut. But other factors, political and social, played their role in this burgeoning opening to narcissism. The dominance of ego psychology within American psychoanalysis was being contested by newly minted analysts who wanted consideration of their own perspectives (existential, interpersonal, relational). The nature of patients coming for analytic treatment seemed, to analysts, to be changing, moving from those with traditional neurotic problems that reflected oedipal conflicts to those with problems of identity, self-definition, and isolation. Some (Lasch, 1978) suggest that changes in the social fabric of families and communities have led to the altered nature of those patients seeking treatment and the clinical scene's becoming dominated by the individual needs of people cut off from supportive social structures, people at sea in their quest for personal values and identity and emotionally or physically isolated from family and caregivers. Thus, in place of the conflicts generated by the "overcrowding" of personal space and competing feelings toward too many people in the personal surround, the dominant experience in current society had shifted to that of isolation, the anomie described by Durkheim (1897) that leads to preoccupation with and vulnerability of the sense of self (Lasch, 1978).

Besides Kohut, certainly one of the major articulators of this new emphasis on narcissism and shame was Helen Block Lewis (1971), who wrote from a phenomenological perspective about shame in relation to the sense of self (see chapter 5, this volume). For Lewis, shame was about oneself and thus, inevitably, involved narcissism. Her view of narcissism was, however, intimately connected with attachment to others in the social surround, since she viewed the person as essentially social/relational. Lewis (1981) saw shame fundamentally in terms of its function to protect the individual's relationship to significant others. Both shame and guilt are affects that "function to maintain and repair lost affectional bonds" (p. 261) rather than to control drives. Shame represents one's "relation . . . to another person in unrequited love" (p. 244) and maintains a sense of separate identity, protecting against loss of self-boundaries. On the other hand, Lewis believed that the searing experience of shame leads to what she called an "'implosion' or momentary destruction of the self; narcissism is love of [one]self" (p. 248).

Lewis was vague in her description of what she meant by "momentary destruction" of selfhood, but clearly her view of narcissism was unidirectional and limited, reflecting only self-love. Lewis's writings on shame did not explicitly acknowledge the place of vulnerability in narcissistic states. Probably as a result of her own emphasis on shame experiences rather than theoretical constructs, she relegated narcissism to a subspecies, a part, of shame. Narcissism's function was to help maintain affectionate ties and to deal with shame. Shame sensitivity was related to what Lewis identified as "field-dependency," in which a person relies heavily on feedback from the environment for self-esteem and to feel competent and attached. According to Lewis, field-dependent persons tend to be women, who are shame prone and given to depression.

One of Lewis's major contributions is her emphasis on what she called "bypassed" (or unconscious) shame and its role in negative therapeutic reactions and failed treatments. She was particularly sensitive to the potential shaming elements of psychotherapy and provided strong clinical examples of the intrusion of shame into the therapeutic encounter. The sense of self shrivels and recoils in the face of shame, especially if shame is bypassed and not recognized. Calling attention to the importance of transference shame, Lewis emphasized how unconscious shame can destroy a therapeutic relationship. Her therapeutic goal was to help patients recognize and accept shame and to deal directly with its consequences.

Erikson (1950) had contributed to the emerging interest in narcissism by emphasizing development and diffusion of identity. According to Erikson, the individual strives to define himself, to attain a cohesive and clear sense of who he is, in relation to others and to the surrounding environment. Erikson described stages of social development, evolving from a primary stage of basic trust to one where the infant either achieves autonomy or is cast into shame and doubt. Thus, Erikson viewed shame and doubt as a reflection of early failure in attaining self-respect, self-control, and competence in defining self-boundaries. His observation about the development and relevance of shame anticipated by several decades the perspective relating shame to failure in attaining ideals. The relationship of identity to the experience of selfhood for Erikson seems clear.

As Erikson's developmental system emphasized independence and autonomy as the alternative to shame, others viewed narcissism from a different perspective, that is, from the vantage point of worthiness for merger or reunion with an idealized (often paren-tified) "other." From this perspective, one strives to become part of the all-powerful parent, and narcissism represents cosmic together-ness rather than *splendid isolation* (as Freud, 1892–99, described his period of sequestered self-analysis). This view of narcissism is similar to Grunberger's (1979) concept of the monad and, according to Bursten (1973), a lifelong task for the person with a narcissistic personality is to rid himself of shame so as to make himself worthy of a fantasied reunion with the idealized other.

Janine Chasseguet-Smirgel (1985), who differentiated the ego ideal from the superego, delineated the ego ideal as heir to primary narcissism. The ego ideal represents an attempt to regain the lost, primordial state of bliss when there "was no unsatisfaction, no desire, no loss . . . an example of perfect, unending contentment" (p. 5). With recognition of separateness from, and dependence on, the other comes an end to this blissful state and a projection of perfection onto the other, who becomes the ego ideal. Narcissism is thenceforth defined by the quest to bridge the gulf between oneself and one's ego ideal through fantasied fusion with the idealized other.

Shame fits into this perspective, as it does for Bursten's (1973), as a reflection of the sense of narcissistic injury and absolute futility resulting from the conviction that one is unworthy of love from the idealized other (the projected ego ideal). The unending quest for worthiness of that love (i.e., attempted fusion with the lost ideal) is defined by Chasseguet-Smirgel (1985) as "the malady of the ideal," which she sees as the principal source of human unhappiness and misery throughout life. That is, we are perpetually cursed to seek that state of self-perfection guaranteed to justify and provide for the fantasied love that remains forever out of reach. Failure is inevitable, and with it pain and shame, the "malady." In addition, she views the narcissistic search for fusion to be always regressive. Indeed, attempts to regain the ideal state of oneness become themselves another source of shame, a position consistent with that of ego psychology. That is, shame evolves from need and dependency (Erikson, 1950), as well as from a sense of unworthiness.

While it seems clear that there is an intimate relationship between shame and narcissistic vulnerability, our examination of that relationship raises some interesting questions. Is there any place in our conceptualization for the idea of primary narcissism, or must narcissism always be considered in relation to significant others? Does narcissistic vulnerability lead to shame because of failure to attain complete independence and autonomy in one's identity formation, or does shame come from failure to attain worthiness for merger or relationship with the idealized other? That is, to what degree is shame determined by *need* itself (conceptualized as dependence, regressive longings for closeness, etc.), as compared with an ideal of fantasied absolute self-sufficiency? If, as suggested at the beginning of this chapter, narcissism has to do with a yearning to be absolutely unique, the "only," to a significant other, where do we put the emphasis—on the "unique," the "only," or the "significant (idealized) other"?

These questions can be brought together in the formulation of a *dialectic of narcissism* (Morrison, 1989), postulating a dynamic tension betweeen the expansive and contracted elements or poles of self-experience. Thus, narcissism (seen as the sense of self at a given moment) is expressed through expansiveness, specialness, exhibition-ism, and haughtiness at some moments, for some people; and for others through contractedness, smallness, feelings of insignificance and omnipotent idealization of the other. Both poles are present for most of us—one in the foreground, the other background—at any given moment. The tension between these poles is fundamental to the dialectic of narcissism, and shame can be attached to either pole. Broucek (1982) has designated these same elements of narcissism as *egotistic* and *dissociative*.

The tension between the goals of narcissism—between reunion and merger with the idealized other and autonomy, identity, and uniqueness—is also part of the dialectic, allowing us to view these goals as alternating in a figure–ground relationship rather than standing necessarily as antithetical one to the other. Shame enters the dialectic as the affective response to failure in attaining either goal (i.e., reunion or autonomy) and thus serves as a gnawing reminder of imperfection. Which comes first? Is shame about standing alone, in isolation, or is it always in relationship to the highly regarded other? Is shame the *result* of imperfection and smallness? Is the shame about failure and insignificance so painful that it *generates* instead as a defensive response the familiar grandiose expression of narcissism? Thus, the relationship itself between shame and narcissism enters the dialectic of narcissism as a tension between cause and effect, foreground and background, at any particular moment. This dialectic is further elaborated later, in the section on intersubjectivity, in our reformulation of Kohut's concepts of vertical and horizontal splits.

NARCISSISM, SHAME, AND SELF PSYCHOLOGY

Kohut's contributions to the psychology of narcissism represent a radical departure from those perspectives that we have considered so far. Fundamentally, Kohut moved from a view of narcissism that judged self-concerns to be "bad" or "primitive," less worthy than a selfless involvement with, or love of, others. Kohut (1966) proposed that narcissistic development is itself a legitimate focus for psychoanalytic attention and is not inevitably pathological and that narcissism can best be understood and studied in a developmental line independent of that for love of others. From his assumptions about the significance of self-experience, and his clinical attempt to remain empathically close to the patient's feelings, Kohut derived a clinical system differing from the dominant metapsychology of American psychoanalysis at the time, whose emphasis was on drive theory, the centrality of oedipal conflict, and the inevitability of love for a cherished "other."

By now familiar to most psychotherapists working intensively with patients, Kohut's writings emphasize the central role of *empathy* as an observational means of acquiring data about the patient's experience; the emergence, understanding, and working through of the *selfobject functions* of mirroring, idealization, and twinning within the transference relationship; the inevitability of *selfobject failure* experienced by the patient within the bond with the therapist and the importance of attending to these experiences in successful therapy; and the complex tension between a person's experience of cohesion and continuity and his lifelong need for embeddedness in a matrix of responsive others. Where, we wonder, does shame fit into this sketchy overview of self psychology and narcissism?

More than previous psychoanalysts, Kohut paid close attention to shame and its role in narcissistic vulnerability. He viewed shame as a response of the person overwhelmed with grandiosity and unable to discharge exhibitionistic demands. In this way, Kohut's view of shame was still essentially wedded to a vision of libido and drive (in this instance, that of exhibitionism). Later, after moving away from a drive model of motivation, Kohut had little more to say about shame. In 1971, however, he viewed shame-prone persons as ambitious and success driven, responding to moral or external failures with shame. Later, likening shame with narcisstic rage, Kohut (1972) emphasized the absence of available selfobject functions in the generation of both shame and rage, in addition to shame's source in disequilibrium from overwhelming grandiosity. In his 1977 book, Kohut spoke of shame only once, but here powerfully as he described the lethargy, "guiltless despair," and depression of those who feel that they cannot remedy lifelong failures that confront them: "The suicides of this period are not the expression of a punitive superego, but a remedial act—the wish to wipe out the unbearable sense of mortification and nameless shame imposed by the ultimate recognition of a failure of all-encompassing magnititude" (p. 241).

While Kohut did not explicitly elaborate the place of shame in self-experience, his 1977 work is replete with shame-related phrases, including "mortification," "disturbed self-acceptance," and "dejection." His sensitivity to shame experiences in narcissistically vulnerable patients suggests that shame is the core affective experience of Kohut's "Tragic Man."

Strikingly missing from Kohut's explanation of shame is the role of the self-ideal or of strong ideals themselves. He was quite explicit on this point, stating that shame "is due to a flooding of the ego with unneutralized exhibitionism and not to a relative ego weakness vis-à-vis an overly strong system of ideals" (Kohut, 1971, p. 181n). Kohut's position here is particularly arresting in the light of compelling clinical evidence of shame's relationship to failure to attain goals and ideals or to live up to an image of an ideal self (what Sandler et al. [1963] refer to as the "shape of the ideal self").

Kohut's omission becomes less surprising, however, when we consider the operant forces within psychoanalysis at the time and the theoretical relationship that the ego ideal bore to some of these forces. Kohut understood the ego ideal fundamentally to be a structure of drive control, and as he moved progressively away from the drives until, in 1977, he rejected their relevance altogether, the ego ideal became commensurately extraneous. Also, for Kohut the ego ideal represented the embodiment of an object relations perspective as an internalization of the idealized parental love-object. His understanding of shame was based on the judgment that object love had been overemphasized in psychoanalysis at the expense of self (narcissistic) development. Object relations lie "on the psychological surface that can easily be translated into behavioral terms," and thus constitute mere "social psychology" (Kohut, 1966). Since, from this particular viewpoint, the ego ideal is the product of object relations it has no place in a truly depth-psychological understanding of shame.

Clinical observation dictates, however, that failure with regard to ideals be incorporated into a self=psychological appreciation of shame. By his exclusive attention to overwhelming grandiosity at the expense of failure to realize ideals in the generation of shame, Kohut had a limited perspective on the shame experience. Kohut did, however, note the importance of selfobject failure in the generation of shame, and, of course, the revival of the idealized parental imago is one of the principal selfobject transferences to emerge in treatment. This transference experience provides a sense of participation in the omnipotence and tension regulating qualities of the idealized other, leading to a feeling of protection and calm. Stolorow (1986), writing about the "dimensions" of experiencing another, has compared the selfobject with the conflictual/relational dimension. The idealizing selfobject experience has of necessity some conflictual/relational features, potentially linking it to the "love object" of traditional theory. Shame (and ultimately shame sensitivity) can result from faulty responsiveness of the idealized other, leading as well to the feelings of emptiness and depletion described by Kohut (1977) as resulting from inadequate tension regulation (Morrison, 1989). Similarly, the absence of adequate affirmation or mirroring can lead to experiences of humiliation, fragmentation, and shame, as well as to related fears of abandonment over unmet exhibitionistic needs.

We can elaborate, then, on Kohut's view of shame by emphasizing early failures in responsiveness as formative in the development of shame proneness. With regard to the idealized other, Kohut (1977) spoke of *compensatory* structure, particularly in the form of ideals, aimed at overcoming deficits and thus, we suggest, counteracting shame. When the quest to attain a compensatory ideal fails, especially becuase of lack of response from the idealized other, the person is jettisoned back into a state of shame (Morrison, 1989, p. 78). Kohut (1977) equated shame with "guiltless despair," thus pointing to the close relationship between shame and depression. In essence, shame may be considered the hallmark of the defeated person in a state of self-depletion, a person who has fallen shamefully short of his goals (Morrison, 1989, p. 81).

The selfobject dimension of a human relationship is ever- present, whether in the forefront or functioning silently in the background (Stolorow and Lachmann, 1984–85). Shame predominates at moments of breach in the selfobject dimension of relationship, which confronts one with one's need for selfobject functions and one's corresponding lack of worthiness or total self-sufficiency. Out of this need, and in order to restore the bond that heals shame, we each participate in selecting, imagining, or creating our own selfobject experiences (Morrison, 1994). When this process works—either through our own creative process or in the context of successful psychotherapy—we are in a position to attain that self-acceptance functioning as an antitdote to shame.

Following Kohut, considerations about narcissism and its relationship to shame multiplied. Broucek (1982) emphasized the importance of self-conscious experience ("objective self-awareness") as a necessary precurser to shame, which he connected with the parents' failure to respond to the infant's gestures and pleasure (see chapter 2, this volume). This environmental failure contributes to the infant's experience of incompetence, inefficacy, and the "inability to influence, predict, or comprehend an event which the infant expected . . . to be able to control or understand" (p. 370), generating vulnerability to shame. Broucek contrasted the views of Kohut and Kernberg about "grandiosity" and "the grandiose self," which Kohut saw as a healthy part of age-appropriate development and Kernberg viewed as a "pathological" defense against the developing infant's anguish. According to Kernberg, the grandiose fantasy is meant to ward off conflicts over dependency and aggression through the creation of the ideal self. Here Kernberg considers the ideal self to be a pathological grandiose structure serving to protect against feelings of weakness and rage. Broucek (1982) suggested that shame follows from this grandiose construction because of the disparity between the exalted ideal self and the "objectively derived self-observation." He also notes that Kernberg does not actually use the word shame in his writings about narcissism, but that his phrases (like Kohut's) are shame variants—"haughty grandiosity," "shyness," and "feelings of inferiority." While Kernberg has written extensively about narcissism, his is exclusively a theory of pathological narcissism, and therefore his comments do not readily relate to the more general theory of narcissism offered in this essay.

Broucek (1982) proposed that shame plays a double role in the grandose self (which he tended to see, along with Kernberg, as pathological). It can serve as a *stimulus* to reactive self-aggrandizement, but also as a *response* to the realization of excessive grandiosity (as in Kohut's view of shame as a response to overwhelming exhibitionism). Broucek also differentiated *egotistical* narcissism (with contemptuous devaluation of the other and haughty self-aggrandizement) from *dissociative* narcissism (with underlying feelings of unworthiness, inferiority, and self-scorn, and a projection of grandiosity onto the idealized, omnipotent other). The relationship of this perspective to Reich's (1960) notion of oscillating self-esteem and to Morrison's (1989) dialectic of narcissism is clear.

In his discussion of analysts' reactions to the selfobject transferences of their patients, Kohut (1971) examined the interplay of analysts' narcissistic vulnerabilities with those of the patients. Regarding patients' idealizations, Kohut spoke of the analysts' need to prevent stimulation of their own grandiosity and their tendency to defend against this stimulation by negating or aborting idealization and treating it as a defense against hostility. Similarly, Kohut underscored the tendency of analysts to be oblivious to the idealizing love that often underlies patients' expressions of anger.

In a similar vein, some writers have noted the strong tendency of a patient's shame to stimulate (or resonate with) shame experiences of the analyst, often leading to a collusion between the two to avoid articulation and exploration of this emotion because of its painful consequences to *both* of them (Levin, 1971; Wurmser, 1981; Morrison, 1989; Broucek, 1991). One reason, we believe, that shame was for so long ignored by psychoanalysts had to do with their need to avoid considering their own shame as it inevitably reverberated with that of patients. This evasion of shame began with Freud, who, as we have seen, turned from shame to guilt, intrapsychic conflict, and the structural model, perhaps in part to conceal his own shame sensitivity (Wurmser, 1981; Lansky and Morrison, this volume).

As narcissism claimed the attention of analytic thinkers in the 1960s and later, an opening to consideration of shame and its consequences became inevitable. Similarly, with renewed attention to countertransference phenomena and enactments in recent psychoanalytic thought, the possibility of analysts' facing their own shame within the treatment relationship has become more palatable. These feelings can serve as opportunities for greater understanding of patient–therapist interactions, making the feelings more "permissible" as tbey become incorporated into the armamentarium of psychotherapeutic practice. Subtleties of the therapeutic interaction permeate contemporary analytic thinking (Gill, 1982; Greenberg and Mitchell, 1983; Hoffman, 1983; Schwaber, 1983; Aron, 1996), enhancing recent attention to such mutual feelings as shame between patient and therapist. Finally, the evolution of an intersubjective approach to the treatment relationship (Stolorow and Atwood, 1992; Benjamin, 1990; and others) allows for further elaboration of shame's place in the shared experience between the participants in therapy. Since Kohut, the ubiquity of shame experiences for each of us seems more acceptable.

In summary, Kohut's contributions on narcissism represented a radical change in how narcissism was viewed within psychoanalysis. Narcissistic phenomena had their own developmental process, and were always present in one way or another for each of us. Previous developmental, pathological, and relational views of narcissism were radically revised, with regard to excessive pathologizing of narcissism and over-privileging of object attachment. Concomitantly, the companion affect of shame came to light along with its sibling, guilt. The *intensity* and *pervasiveness* of shame varies according the salience of narcissistic vulnerability for given patients at moments in time, but, following Kohut, the ubiquity of shame experiences for each of us seemed more likely and acceptable.

We have seen, however, that the *nature* of shame feelings varies with particular manifestations of self-experience. Shame may reflect self-consciousness or awareness of need for the other (e.g., selfobject need). Shame may speak to feelings of defectiveness, inferiority, unworthiness, or weakness, experienced alone or in relationship to another. It may represent dialectical tension between the yearning to be absolutely unique and to be worthy of reunion and merger with the idealized other. Thus, with shame as with narcissism, there lurks always the shadow of others in relation to oneself, varying from that background matrix of indistinct presences who sustain and affirm our existence, to the sharply etched configuration of the lover, who helps to create meaning and purpose by responding reciprocally to our expressions of affection. It may be that Kohut focused too exclusively on the development of self-experience and less than adequately attended to the interactive other—an emphasis that current contributors are attempting to redress (e.g., Bacal, 1985; Stolorow et al., 1987; Fosshage, 1995). Particular theoretical orientations tend to dictate an emphasis on subject or object in the intersubjective equation, but each must play a role in our reflections on shame and narcissism.

Also, questions regarding the primacy of deficit versus conflict states in narcissistic phenomena need to be addressed. The interpretations of Freud's concept of primary narcissism as an inability to form object ties imply an incapacity, a developmental deficit. As we have seen, however, contemporary thinking acknowledges the importance of the other in defining narcissistic states, whether through denial of need for that other (e.g., self-sufficiency) or through efforts at worthiness for merger with her (e.g., dependency). The tension in this dialectic is clearly that of internal conflict, though not, perhaps, the intersystemic conflict of traditional theory. This distinction is elaborated in the following section.

We turn, then, to a more detailed consideration of this intersubjective interpenetration of our own experience with that of the other in the genesis of shame. Elsewhere, Atwood and Stolorow (1984) have emphasized that "patient and analyst together form an indissoluble psychological system, and it is this system that constitutes the domain of psychoanalytic inquiry" (p. 64). Within the context of the patient–therapist dyad, shame and sensitivity to shame may form a reverberating affective signal, frequently excluded from exploration in our patients because of the therapist's personal vulnerabilities to the chilling impact of his own shame experiences.

THE INTERSUBJECTIVE CONTEXTS OF SHAME

A consistent focus on the vicissitudes of self-experience leads inexorably to a recognition of the motivational primacy of affect, since affect, as the infant researchers have amply demonstrated (e.g., Demos, 1984; Stern, 1985; Cohn and Beebe, 1990) is the prime organizer of self-experience within the developmental system. A shift from drive to affectivity as the central motivational construct for psychoanalysis represents a shift from an intrapsychic to an intersubjective paradigm (see Stolorow and Atwood, 1992, for a full development of this idea). From birth onward, affective experience is regulated, or misregulated, within intersubjective systems of reciprocal mutual influence (Beebe, Jaffe, and Lachmann, 1992). In a chapter written in collaboration with Daphne Stolorow, Stolorow (Stolorow, Brandchaft, and Atwood, 1987) stated:

> Affects can be seen as organizers of self-experience throughout development, if met with the requisite affirming, accepting, differentiating, synthesizing, and containing responses from caregivers. An absence of steady, attuned responsiveness to the child's affect states leads to . . . significant derailments of optimal affect integration and to a propensity to dissociate or disavow affective reactions . . . [p. 67].

It is in such derailments of the process of affect integration, we contend, that the intersubjective roots of shame can be found.

A basic idea of intersubjectivity theory is that recurring patterns of intersubjective transaction within the developmental system result in the establishment of invariant principles that unconsciously organize the child's subsequent experiences (Stolorow and Atwood, 1992). It is these unconscious ordering principles, forged within the crucible of the child–caregiver system, that form the basic building blocks of personality development. Increasingly, we have found that those principles which unconsciously organize the experience of affect are developmentally central in building and shaping the personality and are of greatest clinical import. From early, recurring experiences of malattunement, the child acquires the unconscious conviction that unmet developmental yearnings and reactive feeling states are manifestations of a loathsome defect or of an inherent inner badness. A defensive self-ideal is established, representing a self-image purified of the offending affect states that were perceived to be intolerable to the early surround. Living up to this affectively purified ideal becomes a central requirement for maintaining harmonious ties to caregivers and for upholding self-esteem. Thereafter, the emergence of prohibited affect is experienced as a failure to embody the required ideal, an exposure of the underlying essential defectiveness or badness, and is accompanied by feelings of isolation, shame, and self-loathing.

Broucek (1991) has offered an account of the intersubjective origins of shame that emphasizes the caregiver's failure to respond supportively to the child's experiences of efficacy and intentionality, resulting in the child's acquiring a painful sense of being viewed as an object rather than as a subject. In our language, Broucek understands shame to originate in malattunement to affect states that have in common elements of excitement, pride, and pleasure in one's own functioning. We believe that shame can, in fact, derive from malattunement to *any* significant aspect of the child's affectivity, including both the joyful affective experiences that accompany developmental progress and the painful reactive affect states evoked by injuries and disruptions (e.g., anxiety, sadness, longing, and despair).

To illustrate the theoretical and clinical advantages of conceptualizing both narcissistic disturbance and shame in terms of the fate of affect within an intersubjective system, we turn to a reconsideration of the dissociative processes that Kohut (1971) believed were pathognomonic in certain narcissistic personality disorders. Kohut theorized that, when the child's archaic grandiosity encounters massive, traumatic deflations, then the grandiosity and the child's longings for the caregiver's mirroring participation in it undergo repression in order to prevent retraumatization. The consequences of this experiential sequestering of archaic grandiosity beneath a repression barrier--what Kohut called a "horizontal split in the psyche"--are symptoms of narcissistic depletion, such as feelings of emptiness, deadness, and worthlessness. In the most common type of narcissistic personality, Kohut believed, the depletion symptoms alternate in experience with states of conscious, noisy, imperious grandiosity. The noisily grandiose and depleted states are separated from one another by a "vertical split"--by disavowal rather than repression.

As useful as Kohut's formulation may have been, it was seriously marred by his use of the same term, "grandiose self," to refer both to what is traumatically deflated and repressed and to what is being imperiously expressed. In so doing, Kohut conflated two organizations of experience that have distinctly different origins and meanings. We believe that what is deflated and sequestered under a horizontal split is best termed *archaic expansiveness*, a phrase referring to the broad range of joyful affective experiences that accompany developmental progress. The imperiousness, arrogance, entitlement, and contempt segregated on one side of the vertical split, by contrast, are best captured by the term *defensive grandiosity*. It is defensive in at least three senses.

First, as Kohut noted, it represents an accommodation to a caregiver's narcissistic use of the child's qualities and performance. As Bacal and Newman (1990) have pointed out, this attempt to maintain a bond through compliance with the caregiver's emotional requirements is analogous to Winnicott's (1960) concept of the "false self" (see also Brandchaft, 1993), akin to the defensive self-ideal discussed earlier.

Second, insofar as the defensive grandiosity contains elements of "splendid isolation," omnipotent self-sufficiency, and devaluation of others, it buttresses repression of the horizontally split-off developmental longings for connection—in this instance, longings for mirroring affirmation of the deflated archaic expansiveness.

It must be remembered that caregivers who repeatedly deflate a child's expansiveness are unlikely to respond with attunement and understanding to the child's painful emotional reactions to these deflations. The child, therefore, is likely to perceive that his painful reactive affect states are unwelcome or damaging to the caregivers and therefore must be sacrificed in order to maintain the needed ties.

Thus the third, and perhaps most important, defensive function of the noisy grandiosity is that it serves to disavow the affective pain on the other side of the vertical split, feelings that are perceived to be unacceptable to the surround, manifestations of a loathsome defect (such as worthlessness, inadequacy, weakness, or smallness) that had to be eliminated.

Intense shame reactions can be evoked along either of these two splits. The breakthrough of archaic expansiveness into conscious experience is usually accompanied by anticipatory shame, not, as Kohut (1972) claimed, because of a "psychoeconomic imbalance," but because the person expects to encounter the same traumatic deflations that the expansivensss originally received from caregivers. Challenges to or puncturings of the defensive grandiosity generally also produce shame, because they threaten to expose the disavowed vulnerability and pain that have come to be organized as irrefutable evidence of an underlying immutable flaw. It is here that narcissistic rage and destructiveness are readily called into play in a desperate attempt to restore the defensive grandiosity and rid one's self-experience of the unbearable shame (Kohut, 1972; Stolorow, 1984; Morrison, 1989).

The most deleterious clinical consequence of Kohut's failure to distinguish conceptually between archaic expansiveness and defensive grandiosity is that it has led to the mistaken belief that it is therapeutically beneficial to "mirror" defensive grandiosity, which is tantamount to colluding with the defense and can lead to addiction to the therapist's "responsiveness." In our experience, the most effective approach to defensive grandiosity is neither to mirror nor to puncture it, but to wait for *openings* in it–that is, for opportunities to make contact with the painful affect walled off on the other side of the vertical split. Such efforts invariably evoke intense shame in the transference, as the patient feels convinced that the analyst can only react with secret revulsion and contempt to the defectiveness that has been exposed. The investigation, interpretation, and working through of this shame, and of the organizing principles from which it derives, are crucial in the establishment of a therapeutic bond in which the disavowed affective pain can be integrated and the defensive grandiosity become less necessary. With the formation of an expectation that painful emotional reactions to injuries and disruptions can evoke acceptance and understanding rather than disdain, an expanding zone of safety is created wherein the patient can dare to bring primary developmental longings out of repression and expose them to the analyst.

The intersubjective implication of this perspective on archaic expansiveness and defensive grandiosity is that these factors pertain not only to patients but to their therapists as well. Our own repressed expansiveness or disavowed conviction of defect is inevitably engaged in the intense relationship we coconstruct with our patients. At times we recognize attributes in ourselves, enlisted in contact or combat with our patients, that generate shame in our sense of self-as-therapist, equivalent to feelings that accrue in psychotherapy within our "other" in his or her role as patient. Bacal and Thompson (1996) have written about shame in connection with "the selfobject needs of the analyst"; in response to a construct of a "one-and-a-half person psychology" (Morrison, 1994), Stolorow (personal communication) posited a "three-person psychology"—what pertains for the patient is there as well for the therapist. Defensive grandiosity may be relevant in the experience of both therapist and patient, and emergent shame is then an affective theme in the intersubjective system that we call psychotherapy.

CONCLUSION

Shame can seep into the very core of our experience of ourselves and thus constitutes the essential pain, the fundamental disquieting judgment that we make about ourselves as failing, flawed, inferior to someone else, unworthy of the praise or love of another, or falling short of a cherished ideal. Because shame is so centrally a feeling about ourselves—about our subjective essence—we are here suggesting that it lies at the very affective core of disquieting narcissistic phenomena. Having defined narcissism broadly, as that aspect of psychology which relates to the subjective experience of selfhood, we suggest that shame and narcissism are inextricably intertwined. Writers have differed about which phenomena relate to narcissism and which to shame. Further, shame generates defenses, and often it is difficult to locate the shame behind rage, contempt, or despair. Narcissism itself may be delineated by either its expansive or its contracted poles, with shame intersecting the sense of self as too grandiose, or as small and diminished.

Following Freud's early descriptions of shame as affect and as defense, and his bold foray into narcissism, both were relegated to the back burner as he elaborated the structural hypothesis, with guilt at its center. Shame and narcissism were not to be considered again until the 1960s (with the exception of earlier works by Piers and Singer, 1953, Alexander, 1938, and Erikson, 1950), when each tended to be viewed as primitive, fixated, preoedipal manifestations of undifferentiated development. These views are inherent in Grunberger's (1979) "monad," Reich's (1960) primitive ego ideal, and Jacobson's (1964) archaic identifications. With Kohut came a different view of narcissism as a normal developmental line parallel with, and independent of, object love. Shame played a greater part in his perspective, but it still reflected a failure of integrated selfhood (i.e., the overwhelming grandiosity from the vertical or horizontal splits). With subsequent description of the aspirations for an ideal self, narcissism and shame over failure to attain the ideal, and the defenses generated to protect against the pain of such failure, became a more clinically rooted way of thinking about self-experience.

From this overview of narcissism and shame, we move from one person to two, from the patient's sense of reality to the intersubjective creation of relationship, in which both participants inform each other's experience. We have posited affect as the essence of cocreated experience between therapist and patient, with that common thread evoking specific memories and reveries for each participant. One major example of this affective resonance between participants in the treatment relationship is shame, potentially a shared experience between therapist and patient. In particular, we suggest that shame is frequently the intersubjective affective experience of disjunctive narcissistic elements within the treatment setting. This shared affective experience potentially facilitates understanding by the therapist of the patient's quandaries through the creative use of countertransference awareness as an entry point into the patient's affective world.

Interpretations of narcissism following Freud tended to emphasize its developmentally primitive, pathological nature, with Kohut's perspective opening the way to fuller psychoanalytic engagement with persons suffering from narcissistic disturbances while simultaneously minimizing those problematic aspects of grandiosity described in this essay. Kohut's use of the global term "grandiose self" to cover multiple narcissistic conditions tended to conflate developmentally expectable with arrogant, more patholgical narcissism. We have suggested the term "archaic expansiveness" to refer to the narcissism of developmental progress, represented in Kohut's "horizontal split"; for more pathological, disavowing, "vertically split" narcissism, we argue that "defensive grandiosity" is the best descriptor. Shame enters in response to perturbations of either of these narcissistic elements within an intersubjective system. The archaic yearning for absolute uniqueness in the eyes of an idealized other, the developmental core of narcissism, becomes defensive and pathological when its components are relied upon to disavow unbearable affective pain that is felt to be unacceptable and inimical to the maintainance of needed ties.

Psychoanalysis has not until recent times usefully grappled with the problems posed by shame to its theories of narcissism, of the relationship between self and other, of conflict and deficit, and of interactions between transference and countertransference. In this essay, we hope to have shed some light on these issues.

REFERENCES

Adler, A. (1907), *Study of Organ Inferiority and Its Psychical Compensation*, trans. S. E. Jellife. New York: Nervous & Mental Disease Monograph Series, No. 24, 1917.
Alexander, F. (1938), Remarks about the relation of inferiority feelings to guilt feelings. *Internat. J. Psycho-Anal.,* 19:41–49.
Aron, L. (1996), *A Meeting of Minds*. Hillsdale, NJ: The Analytic Press.
Atwood, G. & Stolorow, R. D. (1984), *Structures of Subjectivity*. Hillsdale, NJ: The Analytic Press.
Bacal, H. (1985), Optimal responsiveness and the therapeutic process. In: *Progress in Self Psychology, Vol. 1*, ed. A. Goldberg. New York: Guilford Press, pp. 202–227.
——— & Newman, K. (1990), *Theories of Object Relations*. New York: Columbia University Press.
——— & Thompson, P. (1996), The psychoanalyst's selfobject needs and the effect of their frustration on the treatment: A new view of countertransference. In: *Basic Ideas Reconsidered: Progress in Self Psychology, Vol. 12*, ed. A. Goldberg, pp. 17–35.
Beebe, B., Jaffe, J. & Lachmann, F. (1992), A dyadic systems view of communication. In: *Relational Perspectives in Psychoanalysis*, N. Skolnick & S. Warshaw. Hillsdale, NJ: The Analytic Press, pp. 61–81.
Benjamin, J. (1996), An outline of intersubjectivity: the development of recognition. *Psychoanal. Psychol.*, 7, Suppl.:33–46.
Brandchaft, B. (1993), To free the spirit from its shell. In: *The Intersubjective Perspective*, ed. R. Stolorow, G. Atwood & B. Brandchaft. Northvale, NJ: Aronson, 1994; pp. 57–76.
Broucek, F. J. (1982), Shame and its relationship to early narcissistic developments. *Internat. J. Psycho-Anal.,* 63:369 378.
——— (1991), *Shame and the Self*. New York: Guilford.

Bursten, B. (1973), Some narcissistic personality types. *Internat. J. Psycho-Anal.*, 54:287-300.

Chasseguet-Smirgel, J. (1985), *The Ego Ideal.* New York: Norton.

Cohn, J. & Beebe, B. (1990), Sampling interval affects time-series regression estimates of mother–infant influence. *Infant Behav. & Develop.*, 13:317.

Demos, V. (1984), Empathy and affect: Reflections on infant experience. In: *Empathy, Vol. 2*, ed. J. Lichtenberg, M. Bornstein & D. Silver. Hillsdale, NJ: The Analytic Press.

Durkheim, E. (1897), *Le Suicide*. Paris: F. Alcan.

Erikson, E. H. (1950), *Childhood and Society*. New York: Norton.

Fosshage, J. (1995), Countertransference as the analyst's experience of the analysand: influence of listening perspectives. *Psychoanal. Psychol.*. 12:375-391.

Freud, S. (1892-99), Extracts from the Fliess papers. *Standard Edition*, 1:175-280. London: Hogarth Press, 1966.

————— (1914), On narcissism: An introduction. *Standard Edition*, 14:67-102. London: Hogarth Press, 1957.

Gill, M. (1982), *Analysis of Transference, Vol. 1.* New York: International Universities Press.

Greenberg, J. & Mitchell, S. (1983), *Object Relations in Psychoanalytic Theory*. Cambridge, MA: Harvard University Press.

Grunberger, B. (1979), *Narcissism.* New York: International Universities Press.

Hartmann, H. (1950), Comments on the psychoanalytic theory of the ego. *The Psychoanalytic Study of the Child*, 5:74-96. New York: International Universities Press.

————— & Lowenstein, R. (1962), Notes on the superego. *The Psychoanalytic Study of the Child*, 17:42-81. New York: International Universities Press;

Hoffman, I. Z. (1983), The patient as interpreter of the analyst's experience. *Contemporary Psychoanalysis.* 19:389-422.

Jacobson, E. (1964), *The Self and the Object World*. New York: International Universities Press.

Kinston, W. (1983), A theoretical context for shame. *Internat. J. Psycho-Anal.* 64:213-226.

Kohut, H. (1966), Forms and transformations of narcissism. *J. Amer. Psychoanal. Assn.*, 14:243-272.

————— (1971), *The Analysis of the Self*. New York: International Universities Press.

————— (1972), Thoughts on narcissism and narcissistic rage. *The Psychoanalytic Study of the Child*, 27:360-399. New Haven, CT: Yale University Press.

_____ (1977), *Restoration of the Self*. New York: International Universities Press.

Lasch, C. (1978), *The Culture of Narcissism*. New York: Norton.

Levin, S. (1967), Some metapsychological considerations on the differentiation between shame and guilt., *Internat. J. Psycho-Anal*. 48:267–276.

_____ (1971), The psychoanalysis of shame. *Internat. J. Psycho-Anal*. 52:355–362.

_____ (1982), The Psychoanalysis of Shame. Unpublished.

Lewis, H. B. (1971), *Shame and Guilt in Neurosis*. New York: International Universities Press.

_____ (1981), Shame and guilt in human nature. In: *Object and Self*, ed. S. Tuttman, C. Kaye & M. Zimmerman. New York: International Universities Press.

Lichtenstein, H. (1964), Narcissism in emergence and maintenance of primary identity. *Internat. J. Psycho-Anal.*, 45:49–56.

Lynd, H. M. (1958), *On Shame and the Search for Identity*. New York: Harcourt, Brace & World.

Morrison, A. P. (1983), Shame, the ideal self, and narcissism. *Contemp. Psychoanal.*, 19:295–318.

_____ (1986), *Essential Papers on Narcissism*. New York: New York University Press.

_____ (1989), *Shame*. Hillsdale, NJ: The Analytic Press.

_____ (1994), The breadth and boundaries of a self-psychological immersion in shame: A one-and-a-half person perspective. *Psychoanal. Dial.*, 4:19–35.

_____ (1996), *The Culture of Shame*. New York: Ballantine.

Murray, J. (1964), Narcissism and the ego ideal. *J. Amer. Psychoanal. Assn.*, 12:477–511.

Piers, G. & Singer, M. (1953), *Shame and Guilt*. New York: Norton.

Pulver, S. (1970), Narcissism: The term and concept. *J. Amer. Psychoanal. Assn.*, 18:319–341.

Reich, A. (1960), Pathologic forms of self-esteem regulation. *The Psychoanalytic Study of the Child*, 15:215–232. New York: International Universities Press.

Sandler, J. Holder, A. & Meers, D. (1963), The ego ideal and the ideal self. *The Psychoanalytic Study of the Child*, 18:139–158. New York: International Universities Press.

_____ Person E. & Fonagy, P., ed., (1991), Freud's "On Narcissism: An Introduction." New Haven, CT: Yale University Press.

Schafer, R. (1967), Ideals, the ego ideal, and the ideal self. In: *Motives and Thought*, ed. R. R. Holt, *Psychological Issues*,

Monogr. 18/19. New York: International Universities Press, pp. 131–174.

Schwaber, E. (1984), Psychoanalytic listening and psychic reality. *Internat. Rev. Psycho-Anal.*, 10:379–392.

Stern, D. (1985), *The Interpersonal World of the Infant*. New York: Basic.

Stolorow, R. D. (1975), Toward a functional definition of narcissism. *Internat. J. Psycho-Anal.*, 56:179–85.

———— (1984), Aggression in the psychoanalytic situation. In: *The Intersubjective Perspective*, ed. R. Stolorow, G. Atwood & B. Brandchaft. Northvale, NJ: Aronson, 1994, pp. 113–119.

———— (1986), On experiencing an object: A multidimensional perspective. In: *Progress in Self Psychology, Vol. 2*, ed. A. Goldberg. New York: Guilford, pp. 273–279.

———— & Atwood, G. (1992), *Contexts of Being*. Hillsdale, NJ: The Analytic Press.

———— Brandchaft, B. & Atwood, G. (1987), *Psychoanalytic Treatment*. Hillsdale, NJ: The Analytic Press.

———— & Lachmann, F. M. (1984–85), Transference: The future of an illusion. *Annual of Psychoanalysis*, 12–13:19–37. New York: International Universities Press.

Winnicott, D. W. (1960), Ego distortion in terms of true and false self. In: *The Maturational Processes and the Facilitating Environment*. Madison, CT: International Universities Press, 1965, pp. 140–152.

Wurmser, L. (1981), *The Mask of Shame*. Baltimore, MD: Johns Hopkins University Press.

ROBERT MICHELS

Rethinking Shame: Commentary on Chapters 1, 2, and 3

Lansky and Morrison, along with Broucek and Stolorow, believe that shame has been inappropriately ignored both in psychoanalytic theory and in clinical psychoanalysis. They believe that the data— clinical and developmental—speak for themselves, but that nevertheless, after the initial prominence of shame in Freud's earliest formulations, later theoretical preoccupations and overly narrow conceptualization distracted him and his followers from recognizing its central role.

There is much to be said for their view and also something that might be said about it. First, to speak on its behalf, psychoanalysis went through a phase of striving to be a positivist natural science of the mind, with instinct, energy, and drive as core concepts, and a tendency to relegate man's inherent social nature to a derivative of the organismic requirements of drive gratification. Within this model affects were at first seen as secondary to drive tension and discharge, and later as signals among the several structures of the mind. Complex affects that involve social relatedness—and, for that matter, everything that involved social relatedness—were largely outside the domain of discourse. In this phase of psychoanalytic history, shame became a mere footnote, although, as Lansky and Morrison point out, a recurring and intriguing one.

Psychoanalysis, however, is a dynamic, evolving discipline. Its philosophic underpinnings are increasingly seen as hermeneutic, constructivist, and relativistic as well as positivist. Its theories have become "two person" as well as "one person." It has reformulated its core issues, and, as a result, object relations, the self, and the therapeutic process have joined drives as central themes. Its developmental interests have broadened to encompass both earlier and later periods than the oedipal. Above all, it is less concerned with metapsychology and more concerned with clinical process; less likely to look to evolutionary or neurobiology for its concepts and more comfortable with developmental psychology and the humanities as a source of guidelines for interpretation; and less likely to see psychoanalysis as a school of psychology and more likely to see it as a method of inquiry and of psychotherapy. Almost every one of these changes has increased its interest in affects and emotions, or, perhaps more accurately, has diminished the artificial barriers of an earlier era that interfered with recognizing their clinical centrality. We no longer need to be ashamed of shame and can recognize, study, and discuss it without being constrained by our own theories.

Lansky and Morrison point out that shame and the notions associated with it are more likely to come to mind when we think of a person attached to, or in relationship with, others. The first fully articulated psychoanalytic theory—with its organismic, mechanistic, one-person psychology—could ignore shame without noticing its absence. Before this, in prepsychoanalytic clinical observations, the role of shame had been prominent, but as the focus of attention shifted from clinical process to psychologic theory, shame receded into the background. If we study the mind in relation to the body, rather than in relation to other minds, shame is a less essential concept.

As psychoanalytic theory evolved from its initial preoccupation with drives and biological roots to a concern with the enduring structures of the mind, the origins of these structures in social relationships became clear. Objects were no longer simply essential for drive gratification, they were also the substrate for the development of the self and were active contributors to psychological growth. Interest in the relation of the self to objects led to a reawakening of interest in shame, as, in Lansky and Morrison's terms, "the signal of danger to social bonding" and danger to our assessment of our relationship to our (originally social) ideals. It also opened the possibility of alternative emphases: are shame and guilt minor variations of the same basic state or distinct categories; Are superego and ego ideal facets of a single structure, or are they separate structures? Are preoedipal dynamics subsumed in postoedipal structures, or do they persist alongside them?

Lansky and Morrison repeatedly answer these questions in ways that will keep shame central, and they criticize the alternative answers as wrong or biased. I believe that they make a better case for their having a reasonable alternative rather than for their answer's being the preferred one. They can formulate dreams or clinical material in the language of shame as well as others have in the language of guilt, just as these phenomena can be formulated in the language of drives, or objects, or conflicts. Their reformulation is helpful, as long as they do not go too far and argue that their version is better, preferred, more faithful to the data, or more inclusive. This claim has been made by advocates of each of the other formulations, and one can always identify a case or vignette that seems to support each of those views. The problem is not whether any of these views provides a useful perspective (they all clearly do) or whether any one can organize the data (they all clearly can), but whether there is any basis for selecting one as superior to the competing alternative views that can do the same. In individual cases shame may be a valuable organizer; there are always patients or analysts for whom a given word or concept or dynamic may be a best fit. But this depends on the meaning of that word or concept to the specific patient or analyst, not on its general theoretical advantages or conceptual superiority. Most theorists are unhappy that their theory cannot be demonstrated to be superior, but the history of the field is a history of repeated retellings, rediscoveries of lost concepts and reformulations, each of which expands our horizons but none of which, in spite of the claims of its advocates, replaces its predecessors or diminishes their continuing value. There are fashions, to be sure, but they seem to be just that, fashions, rather than truly progressive advances in our understanding. There are many ways to tell a tale, and perhaps the more the better, but claiming that one way is best has repeatedly turned out itself to be just another tale. This claim and the arguments against it tell us something important about the role of concepts and theories in psychoanalysis, but more of this later.

The issue of whether there is a single best theory is raised by their discussion of castration and separation anxiety, guilt and shame. They construct useful alternative formulations, but go on to suggest that they are more than alternatives, they are preferable substitutes (e.g., "when the analyst leaves on vacation, the patient's reaction reflects not a loss—but the exposure of the person facing the separation as one who is unable to function without the sense that the analyst is present or nearby, and hence the patient becomes acutely aware of being much more needy and much less autonomous than he or she would like to see himself or herself. This predicament has to do with the subject's sense of self-worth and of integrity and partakes much more of shame dynamics than the dynamics of fear of loss." Perhaps for some separations in some analyses of some patients, but I have seen patients for whom the traditional formulation was far more in tune. I emphasize the point because there is more at question than which formulation is preferable—the basic nature of the psychoanalytic enterprise is involved. Lansky and Morrison have the same overconfidence in their alternative formulation of envy as "always resulting from self-conscious comparison and shame" and in their suggested reformulation of the Oedipus complex. The effect of taking these statements seriously would be to narrow, not broaden, our repertory of interpretations—not the outcome that the authors seem to desire.

The word shame has many meanings. It is both a noun and a verb (one can feel shame, and one can also shame another). The noun refers to an emotion but is also used for the acts that precede that emotion (one can do shame) and the objective state of disgrace that follows such acts (a state of shame). As an emotion it is complex, with important cognitive aspects and an emphasis on self-awareness. I see the view mentioned by Broucek—that shame may appear in the first few months of life—as the destruction of common sense by a theoretical abstraction. If there are sudden decrements in interest-excitement and enjoyment-joy in the first few months of life (and I believe there are) this suggests to me that these features alone are not sufficient to define what the rest of us mean by shame, not that shame appears that early in life. Shame is a developmentally advanced complex emotion, whose boundaries with other emotions, whether precursors or contemporary neighbors, are blurred and to some extent arbitrary, heavily influenced by cultural context and linguistic convention, in contrast to the more strongly biologically shaped emotions that appear earlier in development. One of the problems in tracing a concept such as shame through a century of psychoanalytic thinking is to distinguish the many meanings of the term and the changing fashions of language and to differentiate these from fundamental changes in the ways in which psychoanalysts have considered the underlying phenomena.

Broucek introduces his discussion of early developmental issues with a quotation from Trevarthen: "Emotions are not part of the mental processes of isolated subjects as such." It is not clear to me what this sentence means. In one sense, no subject is ever isolated. The infant must have real others, and by the time it is biologically possible to survive without them, it is no longer psychologically possible to be without internal objects. But this would mean that Trevarthen's statement refers to a null class. If we do think of subjects as isolated, we might consider infants before they are capable of the psychological recognition of others, or adults who are separated from others and have only their internal objects, or possibly those who are dreaming—but of course each of these does have emotions! If we restrict our discussion to the emotion at hand, most would argue that shame only has meaning in some actual or internal social field, that infants are not born with the capacity for shame, but that it is a developmental achievement based on some social awareness integrated with more "primitive" earlier undifferentiated presocial emotional precursors. This complex developmental origin reminds us once again that we have choices to make in whether to label a state "shame" or to dissect it further into its dynamic or earlier developmental components, and that the decision among these alternative choices cannot be based on one being "right" or "true" while the others are "false" or "wrong." In dealing with the world of subjective human emotional experiences, we have many possibilities and no single truth. Broucek's discussion of the relationship between shame and embarrassment again makes clear that we are dealing with constructions, artificial categories, not natural entities, and that "shame" means what we want it to mean. We cannot discover its "true" meaning.

The result is that our developmental knowledge reaffirms our descriptive and clinical position—shame is a useful concept that provides one way, but not a unique or preferred way, of organizing developmental as well as descriptive and clinical information. Theories that limit its availability as a concept impoverish the field. Theories that insist that it is regularly central also impoverish the field.

In their discussion of shame, narcissism and intersubjectivity, Morrison and Stolorow make clear that the meaning of "shame" depends on the theoretical structure in which it is embedded. They discuss classical psychoanalytic models, self psychology, and intersubjectivity. They seem to see these as a progressive series leading to ever-greater understanding and theoretical refinement; once again, I see an interesting and enriching array of alternative formulations, each able to organize the data, and perhaps each preferable in one or another situation, but none having replaced the others. Morrison and Stolorow believe that there has been a winner in the race among these competing theories. I think that the notion of competition is only one of the metaphors that can describe the dialogue among these several theories, a metaphor that incidentally, each of the theories would have no difficulty interpreting. It is clear that none of these schools have convinced the others, and the accusations among them of stupidity or stubbornness are the least interesting explanation for this important fact. I think a preferable metaphor is that psychoanalysts are involved in constructing accounts, narratives, portrayals of their patients' lives and their experiences in treatment. Any concepts that help in that process are welcome, but such constructions do not have imperatives that must be followed. Constructs may center on drives, conflicts, objects, affects, anxiety, defense, guilt, shame, narcissism, tragedy, or many other themes. Each of these, along with their theoretical accompaniments, is a pigment on the palette of the working therapist/artist. One may have a favorite set of pigments, or one may be handicapped by having too few, but there are many ways to construct an image, and it is hard to imagine why one might want to discard a hue one has employed successfully in the past even when adding an attractive alternative.

My own idea of psychoanalysis is that it is a therapy involving an attempt to review, reframe, reformulate, and restructure an individual's inner world—wishes, fears, thoughts, feelings, and all else. There are no "correct" or "natural" categories for conducting this process. Patients and analysts each have their own concepts and theories, and the several concepts and theories of psychoanalysis offer more alternatives for the analysts. Each individual develops a personal set of categories, and the clinical process goes best when the analyst's categories are close enough, but not too close, to the patient's—close enough for understanding and comfort, not too close to preclude discovery and enlightenment. These general comments relate to the language and concepts of affects as well as other mental phenomena. Shame refers to a complex, developmentally relatively late-appearing affect; and therefore, while the term may be immensely useful for some, it may be virtually irrelevant for others, who deal with the phenomena that might be encompassed by shame either by related affects (guilt or embarrassment) or by dynamic formulations that deal with the infrastructure of shame (fear of loss of approval by family and peer group) or most likely some combination of these. Whether it is useful to view shame as an emergent concept, or preferable to dissolve and dissect it into adjacent categories and component elements, depends on the analyst, the patient, their culture, and the alternative concepts and models available. It is often a valuable addition, but no single mental concept is essential for our work. There is no pigment without which we cannot paint a rich portrait of human experience, the activity that is central to our discipline.

Finally, a few specific comments—my footnotes to these three chapters.

Lansky and Morrison offer an interesting gloss on Freud's discussion of Richard III, someone who claims privilege because of an "unjust disadvantage imposed on [him]." They do not notice that, in Freud's views at that time, this dynamic would apply to every woman, each (in Freud's view) unjustly deprived by biology.

Morrison and Stolorow see the desire to be treated as special and unique as a central theme in development. This is certainly true for many, perhaps most. The authors fail to notice, though, that, if a child is, in fact, special and unique, but unfortunately so because of disease, defect, or social stigma, there is a far more powerful wish—namely, to be the same as everyone else. It is only those who are secure in their recognition that they are the same who can afford to wish to be different.

In that same discussion Morrison and Stolorow repeat Kohut's methodologic error and remind us of Freud's analogous error of the last century. A patient's clinical account of earlier parental empathic failures tells us about the patient but does not allow us to make inferences about the actual parenting behavior. Freud discovered (and we are today rediscovering) that memories of sexual abuse are not always veridical. Kohut failed to recognize (and Morrison and Stolorow do not correct his failure) that memories of unempathic parenting are also not always veridical.

Finally, shame is an intensely social phenomenon, more dependent on cultural context than most other affects or dynamics are. Many writers have suggested, for example, that there are cultures based on shame in the same way that Western cultures, at least in the past, have been based on guilt. Piers and Singer explore this at length, and Singer as a cultural anthropologist discusses the role of shame in several cultures. These chapters, however, privilege development above culture. Once again, a choice among alternatives—neither is right or wrong—but, in view of our current knowledge of infancy and of culture, we might learn more about shame from observing and studying its role in several cultures than from speculating about its psychological origins in infancy.

REFERENCES

Piers, G. & Singer, M. (1953), *Shame and Guilt.* Springfield,IL: Thomas.

HOWARD A. BACAL

Shame–The Affect of Discrepancy: Commentary on Chapters 1, 2, and 3

PROLOGUE AND PROCESS

I approach the task of responding to these three chapters with some hesitation. I am invited to offer not a detailed critique of the articles, but to write about the thoughts they evoke in me. For some while, I believe I have nothing to add to what the authors have written in these fine, comprehensive, and scholarly essays. It takes but a moment of self-scrutiny to realize that not only am I a little anxious about the task before me, but also my procrastination is due to signal shame. Thus far, I am validating the authors' views through my own experience. Since I cannot think of anything to say myself, however, I reflect on the disruptive feelings occasioned by my apparently undoable assignment. Gradually it dawns on me that my feelings constitute a gateway to ideas that could enrich the views of Broucek, Lansky, Morrison and Stolorow on the essential nature and development of the shame experience, with whose perspectives I basically agree. But I am a little ahead of my subjective process. I am still not sure at this point that I can do this.

I am aware that the experiences I am describing certainly arise from the threat of exposure to others, and to myself; that I will be unable to meet the authors' and their readers' expectations, as well as my own. The shaming judgment of inadequacy or failure would come from both within and without. At this point, I realize I have added but a small nuance to what the authors have amply stated. So, I still feel a little shaky about whether I can contribute anything that would justify the requested submission of even "10 to 15 pages (double spaced)." Have they not said it all?

As I temporize and torment myself with the specter of possible
failure, I realize that I am especially interested in—as well as troubled
by—a particular aspect of my experience, a distressing sense of
discrepancy between what I feel I can do and what I and the authors
expect of me. I begin to feel a bit better since I have, in effect,
reduced the discrepancy a little by discovering that I may have
something to say after all. I think my experience of distress reflects
a threat to the integrity of my self that arises from the possibility that
I may be unable to bridge the *gap*[1] between what, at this moment,
I feel I can do and what I and they require of me—the discrepancy
between who I feel I am at this moment and what I and they would
like me to look like in print (ultimately, the "narcissistic image" of
who I am as a thinker and author)—when my words are printed or,
worse still perhaps, when I have no words at all to submit for
printing. Yet this dynamic, too, I sadly reflect, has also been at least
partly enunciated in one way or another by the authors and by
others. At the same time, I am comforted by the discovery that I am
on to something, since a reread of the three chapters yields innumer-
able examples in which experiences of discrepancy of one sort of
another are associated with shame experience. I decide I need some
help.

I consult a respected colleague about my plight, and I share with
him some theoretical ideas that support my contention that a central
underpinning of the shame experience lies in the felt inability to do
away with painful experiences of discrepancy. Not only does he aver
that he has a similar view, but also he is sure that I will be able to
develop my ideas into a good commentary. He also adds to the
theoretical model that I have been thinking about that would give
substance to our shared view. I feel quite a bit better now. I reflect
that I have received an abundantly optimal response from my
colleague. I have not only been mirrored, twinned, shared with, and
materially confirmed by a respected other. I have also been responded to in such a way as to narrow the gap between what I felt I was
(a nonauthor in this context) and how I needed to experience myself

[1] I have elsewhere suggested that the *experience* of an unbridgeable gap
between the self and the other may be the essence of the generation of the
affect of envy (Bacal and Newman, 1990). The sequence of fear about the
inability to bridge a gap—associated with the affect of shame—preceding the
experience of the unbridgeable gap that is associated with envy accords with
Lansky and Morrison's contention that envy is always "downstream" from
shame.

in order to try to create something worthwhile. In other words, I have got a bit of therapy for my persistent and paralyzing signal shame. After one last delay in which I drive to a shop to purchase a new cartridge for my printer, I am ready to write. Now that the discrepancy between what I would like to accomplish and what I feel I can achieve is substantially decreased, I realize that there is so much to respond to in these beautiful essays that I only regret that I must restrict my comments, on this occasion, to this single theme.

THEORETICAL PERSPECTIVES ON DISCREPANCY AS IT RELATES TO THE SHAME EXPERIENCE

Some of the theory I propose that is relevant to the perspective on shame that I am emphasizing has been mentioned by the authors of these three papers. For example, Lansky and Morrison (chapter 7) point out that

> self-conscious appraisals of ourselves that are *discrepant* with our aspirations, standards for lovability, and sense of competence, worthiness, and excellence generate shame, . . . shame, then, is inextricably bound to the problem of narcissism—lovability, acceptability, selfhood—which depends on external or internal acceptability or recognition (italics added).

And, as they point out, Freud (with Breuer) and in other early works, implied a remarkably up-to-date formulation of shame as a defense against awareness of pain and of exposure associated with anticipation of disapproval and rejection both in the eyes of the self and of others.

Morrison and Stolorow also suggest that shame is frequently the affective experience in narcissistically *disjunctive* intersubjective interactions in the treatment situation. The difference (disjunction?) between me and the authors is that I would place discrepancy, or disjunction, at the center of my theoretical perspective on the shame experience.

I especially wish to draw attention to Broucek's questioning the validity of Freud's theory of primary narcissism, whose validity is also cast in doubt by Morrison and Stolorow. Instead of "an initially unrelated infant driven only by the need to relieve drive tension and who only gradually and reluctantly differentiates self from other," Broucek posits that the infant exists in a state of fundamental relatedness to a primary caretaking other by way of an innate

understanding of the affective code and the utilization of that
understanding to bring about mutual affective attunement with the
caretaker. He calls this state *primary communion* and posits that the
infant exists in this state prior to the development of objective self-
awareness (OSA), which he defines as "an awareness of oneself as an
object for others and through the mirroring of the observing others,
taking oneself as an object of reflection (objectifying oneself)." His
view is that OSA "is not only a prerequisite for more developed forms
of shame experience but is a source of shame in its own right" (p.
23). He observes that the acquisition of OSA appears to result from
the interplay of the maturation of the central nervous system,
conflicting viewpoints, and disjunctive affectivity.

I find it interesting and useful in the present context to observe
that Broucek, in identifying the earliest experience as one of
"primary communion"—communion is defined (by the American
Heritage Dictionary) as "*the act or an instance of sharing, as of
thoughts or feelings*"—affirms in essence Balint's (1937, 1968)
original, extensive conceptualization of the infant's quality of
relatedness to its early environment; and that Broucek also describes
how certain aspects of "the acquisition of OSA"—especially the
occurrence of "conflicting viewpoints" and "disjunctive affectivity"—
has a striking correspondence to the determinant of the "basic fault,"
described by Balint (1968) as the disruption of concordant relatedness between the infant and his primary caretaker. Broucek states:
"The appearance of OSA means the end of primary communion,"

Balint (1968) repudiated Freud's theory of primary narcissism. He
argued that the experience of birth, when the baby must breathe,
disrupts a state of relatedness that the fetus has with its intrauterine
environment, which he called a "harmonious interpenetrating
mixup." (This idea has points of contact with Grunberger's "monad,"
which Morrison and Stolorow describe.) Balint contends that aspects
of the early extrauterine environment also normally become primary
substances or objects that the infant can take for granted. The air
surrounding him, with which he will have a new interpenetrating
mix-up—that is, where the boundary between the air that is part of
him and that which is not cannot be delineated with certainty—and
certain objects, beginning with the mothering figure, assume for the
infant varying degrees of the quality of such primary substances in
the early stages of postnatal life. Balint posits that, in this situation,
the wishes of this primary object are felt by the infant to be identical
to his own; for example, the mother is experienced as wishing to
love and satisfy the infant just as much as he wishes this from her.
Balint called this state of relatedness with primary objects primary

love, or primary object relationship. Winnicott's (1958) concept of "ego-relatedness" has analogous meaning. Whether we call this primary love, the monad, ego relatedness, primary communion, archaic selfobject relationship (Kohut) or (my preference) primary relatedness—a designation that I think more accurately reflects contemporary perspectives and that Broucek actually comes within a hair's breadth of using—it identifies the earliest situation not as "narcissistic" (in the sense of the infant's being self-preoccupied)[2] but as *relational*. That is, the earliest situation is not one of primary narcissism but is, rather, relational in the particular respect that it is characterized not only by mutual affective attunement but also—and perhaps at least as significantly—by affective sharing, that is, important experiences of a lack of discrepancy between the infant and the mothering figure.

I believe that experiences of this state of relatedness sufficient to enable their integration into the fabric of the self are essential for the establishment of the child's basic, quiet sense of entitlement to, and therefore expectation of, selfobject responsiveness. Balint (1968) theorized that traumatic disruptions of these states of primary love— what I am calling primary relatedness—leave a wound in the psyche that he called the "basic fault." The notion of "fault" arose not only from its metaphoric association with the geological term but, more importantly, from the way so many patients described it.

> The patient says that he feels there is a fault within him that needs to be put right . . . there is a feeling that the cause of this fault is that someone has either failed the patient or defaulted on him, and . . . a great anxiety invariably surrounds this area, usually expressed as a desperate demand that this time the analyst should not—in fact must not—fail him [p. 21].

What Balint unfortunately leaves out, in this otherwise vivid description of the patient's experience of the basic fault—which is analogous, as I have observed elsewhere (Bacal & Newman, 1990), to Kohut's (1977) understanding that the primary defect in the self

---

[2]The *American Heritage Dictionary* defines narcissism as the excessive love or admiration of oneself.

is consequent to disruption of an archaic selfobject relationship[3]—is
that it is invariably associated with profound *shame*. What I am
drawing attention to here is that the basic fault—this defect in the self
with which such shame is associated—is brought about by a significant *discrepancy* between the selfobject needs of the individual and
the capacity of those in his environment to respond to them. In the
idiom of Stolorow, Brandchaft, and Atwood (1987, 1983), we may
speak of archaic intersubjective disjunction. We must, of course,
recognize that there are other reactions to the awareness of the
interruption of primary relatedness which may have profound
implications for our understanding not only of the individual but also
of the relationship between the individual and the group and of the
relationship between groups. Consideration of this reaction is beyond
the scope of my discussion; I will just mention that this awareness
may produce not only painful feelings of discrepancy but also
experiences of separateness and difference that may or may not
become involved in conflict and that may or may not evoke shame.
That is, we eternally and variously seek both a sense of togetherness
and a sense of separateness, both a sense of identity with others and
a sense of distinctiveness in relation to others, each of which may
become problematic under certain circumstances. Interestingly,
probably the most prevalent circumstance in which they are inclined
to become problematic is in situations of discrepancy, or intersubjective disjunction.

Balint (1968) further suggested that inevitable disruption in the
experience of primary relatedness produced two reactions[4] in the

---

[3]Kohut's view of a primary defect in the self and the situation that
determines it—the disruption of archaic states of selfobject relatedness—is
remarkably analogous to Balint's conceptualization of the basic fault as
resulting from disruption of states of primary love. In other words, Kohut's
retention of the theory of primary narcissism was inconsistent with his
theory of self psychology.

[4]Balint (1959) also coined the terms *ocnophilia* and *philobatism* to
denote more-or-less normal characterological types that express more
organized reactions to the disturbance of the primary object-relationship. The
ocnophil clings to his object as a vital support without whom he experiences
intense anxiety. The philobat tends to shun objects, which he experiences
as either indifferent, unreliable, or even dangerous and prefers the "friendly
expanses" between them, which the ocnophil regards as "horrid empty
spaces." Both, however, are seeking, although by very different routes, to
recapture the early harmonious relationship with their environment (see
Bacal and Newman, 1990, p. 127).

infant in the attempt to reinstate it. One reaction is the detour of "narcissism," through which the child attempts to give to himself what he previously experienced in relation to the primary other. The second is through the route of active object-love[5] through which the child attempts to please the other so as to be satisfied in return.

Here, parenthetically, but importantly, we must recognize that the definition of narcissism as love of self is inaccurate. Narcissism should, rather, be defined as inordinate self-preoccupation. This self-preoccupation may manifest self-love or protest self-admiration; but its latent content is self-loathing, and it is replete with intense needs for certain kinds of relatedness, as both Balint (1968) and Kohut (1971, 1977) have described. "Narcissistic" reactions to painful, shameful discrepancy constitute attempts to avoid shame by shunning threatening experiences of mutual relatedness. When rudely ejected from the garden of Eden, we yearn for but are intensely wary about and exquisitely sensitive to offers of blissful togetherness that might reawaken our longing for paradise but may also result in re-injury to wounds that have not yet healed.

Morrison and Stolorow depict these issues vividly in their description of Kohut's idea of the vertical split, to which they offer important conceptual corrections, as well as useful advice about the optimal response to what they call *defensive grandiosity*. In keeping with my line of theorizing, I propose that we use the term *defensive narcissism* rather than *defensive grandiosity*. Narcissism, as Morrison notes, may be expansive or contracted; but it is always a reaction to the threat or experience of failure of the deeply yearned-for but even more deeply feared primary relatedness, a longing that hides beneath the "horizontal split." That is, narcissism, as Balint argued, is always secondary, that is, defensive; and shame is the affect that motivates narcissistic avoidance of genuine and trusting human relatedness. It is the affect of discrepancy in relation to the "other"—whether this discrepancy centers on a wish to be admired or a wish to be loved—from within or from without. The task of reducing these experiences of debilitating discrepancy constitutes one of the most important

---

[5]Today, we might reformulate—or add to—this the self-psychological view that the child attempts to provide not only "love" but also selfobject responsiveness for the caretaker. It is also important to consider to what extent these provisions entail false-self accommodation (Winnicott, 1960) to the requirements of the other, which not only may compromise the sense of self but also may fail to achieve the aim of reducing painful experiences of discrepancy in relation to the other.

challenges to the optimal responsiveness of the therapist (see Bacal, 1985, in press).

REFERENCES

Bacal, H. A. (1985), Optimal responsiveness and the therapeutic process. In: *Progress in Self Psychology, Vol. 1,* ed. A. Goldberg, Hillsdale, NJ: The Analytic Press, 1995, pp. 202–226.

———— ed. (in press), *Optimal Responsiveness.* Norwood, NJ: Aronson.

———— & Newman, K. M. (1990), *Theories of Object Relations.* New York: Columbia University Press.

Balint, M. (1937), Early developmental states of the ego: Primary object-love. In *Primary Love and Psycho-Analytic Technique*, London: Tavistock, 1965.

———— (1959), *Thrills and Regressions.* London: Tavistock

———— (1968), *The Basic Fault.* London: Tavistock

Kohut, H. (1971), *The Analysis of the Self.* New York: International Universities Press.

———— (1977), *The Restoration of the Self.* New York: International Universities Press.

Stolorow, R. D., Brandchaft, B. & Atwood, G. (1983), Intersubjectivity in psychoanalytic treatment, with special reference to archaic states. *Bull. Menninger Clin.* 47:117–28.

———— (1987), *Psychoanalytic Treatment.* Hillsdale, NJ: The Analytic Press.

Winnicott, D. W. (1958), The capacity to be alone. In: Winnicott, *The Maturational Processes and the Facilitating Environment*, pp. 29–36. London: Hogarth Press.

———— (1960), Ego distortion in terms of true and false self. In: *The Maturational Processes and the Facilitating Environment*, London, Hogarth Press, pp. 142–153.

II

BIOLOGY,
PSYCHOLOGY,
PHILOSOPHY,
SOCIAL THEORY

4

DONALD L. NATHANSON

Shame and the Affect Theory of Silvan Tomkins

If distress is the affect of suffering, shame is the affect of indignity, of defeat, of transgression and of alienation. Though terror speaks to life and death and distress makes of the world a vale of tears, yet shame strikes deepest into the heart of man. While terror and distress hurt, they are wounds inflicted from outside which penetrate the smooth surface of the ego; but shame is felt as an inner torment, a sickness of the soul. It does not matter whether the humiliated one has been shamed by derisive laughter or whether he mocks himself. In any event he feels himself naked, defeated, alienated, lacking in dignity or worth [Tomkins, 1963a, p. 118].

With these words, Silvan Tomkins introduced the 462-page section on shame in his four-volume masterwork, *Affect Imagery Consciousness*. His writing on shame ranges from observations about infants and children to the shared world of the adult and the larger field of society as well as the deepest inner layers of the soul. It contains some of the most trenchant statements about shame ever made and offers important suggestions for clinical work. Couched in nearly impenetrable prose and based in a theory that was destined to be ignored until our present era, it has, for more than 30 years, been skimmed by every serious student of shame, all of whom agree that this is a major contribution but have then gone on to ignore it completely.

The major innovators are rarely kind to their readers; they do not provide links between their own ideas and the belief systems they replace. Even though I have lived through this final two-thirds of the 20th century taking for granted Einstein's theory of relativity, no drawing, equation, or lecture has ever allowed me to understand in any useful way what is meant by the statement that gravity occurs because the fabric of spacetime is warped by mass. Events occurring at the subatomic level take place so far from my field of observation that, although I can memorize and reduplicate what I have been taught, this realm of data exists in a compartment of my mind quite separate from day-to-day reality. I live in a world dominated by my unshakable faith that none of us is thrown off our spinning planet because we are held here by gravity, a force that operates to accelerate a dropped object at 32 feet per second per second of real time.

So it is for Tomkins and the realm of affect theory, which states that everything we understand and accept about our own emotions is based on a similarly attractive, intuitive, and primitive hypothesis. Given a slice of birthday cake, it is doubtful that any chemist or biologist would be able to determine the life cycle of the wheat, cows, chickens, or cane that supplied the raw materials from which cake is assembled. In the process of baking, too much has happened to the flour, milk, eggs, and sugar—too much molecular rearrangement—for the history of these substances to be apprehended fully. Where Freud relied on adults to provide verbal descriptions of their emotional experience (from which he might speculate about the sequences that led to them), Tomkins asserted that, by the time we are capable of describing our emotions in words, too much has happened to the raw materials from which these emotions were assembled for us to trust words. Freud was at heart an archaeologist who sought to visit the past through study of the artifacts left to us by history. Tomkins was an Einstein who asked us to study emotion in an entirely different manner. The 20th century belongs to Freud, whose work fits our predilection to see children as small adults and to assign what we do not understand to the realm of untestable and otherwise incomprehensible invisible forces. If, as I believe, the next era of our field will be dominated by the concepts offered by Tomkins, some review of them must precede and accompany this series of excerpts from his writing on shame.

Freud grew up in the last half of a 19th century that had seen an industrial revolution based on the applications of the hydraulic forces provided by steam engines. Electricity, the new force of his era, was then explained in terms of pressure, flow, and resistance; the concepts of Ohm, Ampère, and Watt were essentially hydraulic. So attractive was the idea that the mysteries of life could be explained simply that with the beginning of the 20th century came a burst of grand unifying theories. Einstein sought (vainly) to subsume all of matter and energy under one "unified field theory," while Osler (only seven years older than Freud) asked us to assign to one diagnosis all the signs and symptoms offered by a patient. So much are the healing arts still under the influence of Osler that even today clinicians seem surprised that more than one illness may afflict a patient at the same time; special attention is given to the concept of "dual diagnosis." Freud's concept of a drive mechanism is an attempt to explain a wide range of phenomena from the standpoint of a grand unifying theory. His drives are predominantly hydraulic, their energy powering sexual activity (with its attendant "normal" excitement) when allowed full expression and negative affect when sexuality is somehow thwarted. For Freud, everything comes out of the interconvertibility of matter and energy; everything that makes for personality derives from one primordial substance. Even though it is now the fashion for contemporary psychoanalytic theorists to maintain that the psyche is developed in an interpersonal or relational context rather than the solitary model favored by Freud, the forces contained and modulated by these relational events are subsets of drive energy.

Tomkins, on the other hand, was a contemporary of von Neumann and the other mathematicians whose work was to produce the computer revolution. In June 1962 he organized a conference called "The Computer Simulation of Personality: Frontier of Psychological Theory." What follows are excerpts from his lead presentation at that meeting as published a year later (Tomkins, 1963b):

> Many years ago, in the late 1930's, I was seized with the fantasy of a machine, fearfully and wonderfully made in the image of man. He was to be no less human than auto-mated, so I called him the humanomaton. Could one design a truly humanoid machine? This would either expose the ignorance or reveal the self-consciousness of his creator or both [p. 3].

> Computer simulation has attracted and will continue to attract strange bedfellows. . . . The computer offers not only much promise but also many different promises.
> It enables one to deal with organized complexity, and so it recommends itself to all who object to the varieties of impoverishment of science which have been recommended in the name of method, cleanliness, rigor, and empiricism. It is a complexity amplifier as the microscope was a space amplifier. Its increment of transformability of concepts is of the same order of magnitude as that of arabic numerals over Roman numerals [p. 7].

Needed for the study of emotion, Tomkins is saying, must be some novel way of analyzing complexity. The smooth, homogeneous surface of the skin is a mass of crevasses and outcroppings when its spaces are amplified by a simple magnifying glass; another world of cells, membranes, and nuclei when space is amplified by the light microscope; and yet another realm of molecules and atoms when space is amplified by the electron microscope and its newer descendants. With its ability to process millions of simple mathematical calculations each second, the computer allows us to study events by increasing the complexity of the data under consideration while making accessible but separate each realm of that complexity. A computer analogy not only allows but actually requires us to separate what Freud unified. To Tomkins, affect and drive involve completely different biological systems.

> How should such a computer be built and how programmed if it is to bear a reasonable resemblance to the critical characteristics of a human being? . . . We conceive of the human being as governed by a set of mechanisms which are from moment to moment not only in competition with each other, but are also relatively independent of each other, as well as somewhat dependent on each other. Such organized programs as are inherited govern at best only small sectors, in fits and starts. The whole human being seems at the outset more fearfully than wonderfully made. Indeed, were it not for the concern of his parents, the neonate would not be viable. It is difficult to exaggerate his incompetence . . . [pp. 10–11].

Yet how does the neonate communicate to its hovering parents what it needs them to do? How is it that so many complex actions are organized by a life form too primitive to "know" what it is doing? Tomkins conceives of the drives as a group of mechanisms that provide information about "time, of place, and of response—where and when to do what when the body does not know how to otherwise help itself. When the drive signal is activated it tells a very specific story—that the 'problem' is in the mouth in the case of hunger, farther back in the throat in thirst, . . . in the nose and throat and chest if it is an oxygen drive, in the urethra if it is the urination drive, at the anal sphincter if it is the defecation drive" (p. 15). We get hungry because the level of some nutrient has dropped below a critical set point; triggered next is a sequence of food-gathering behaviors that bring the needed substance toward the mouth, which is already moving in such a way as to maximize the possibility of intake. When the breast is near, the hunger drive works perfectly to allow feeding.

Complex as this drive mechanism must be to detect a need and instrument its satisfaction, it contains none of the compelling force Freud knew was necessary to make such a mechanism effective. It is an information transducer but not a motivator.

It is the affects rather than the drives which are the primary human motives. First, the affects constitute the primary motivational system not only because the drives necessarily require amplification from the affects, but because the affects are sufficient motivators in the absence of the drives. One may be sexually excited. Indeed, one must be excited to enjoy the sexual drive, but one need not be sexually aroused to be excited. Second, in contrast to the specificity of space-time information of the drive system, the affect system has those more general properties which permit it to assume a central position in the motivation of man. Thus, the affect system has generality of time rather than the rhythmic specificity of the drive system. Because the drive system is essentially a transport system, taking material in and out of the body, it must impose its specific temporal rhythms. But the affect system is under no such constraint. One can be anxious for just a moment or for half an hour, or for a day, or for a month, or for a year, or a decade, or a lifetime, or *never*, or only occasionally now though much more frequently some time ago, in childhood, but not as an adult, or conversely. The affect system permits generality not only of time, but of intensity. I can feel strongly about this and weakly about that. It also permits generality of density of affect investment. I can feel strongly about something for a little while, or less intensely for a longer while, or very intensely all my life. Thus, affects are capable of both insatiability and finickiness as well as extreme lability.

Feedback and affect are two distinct mechanisms which may operate independent of each other. The infant passively enjoys or suffers the experience of his own affective responses long before he is capable of employing a feedback mechanism in instrumental behavior. He does not know "why" he is crying, that it might be stopped, or how to stop it. Even many years later he will sometimes experience passively, without knowledge of why or thought of remedial action, deep and intense objectless despair. Without initial awareness that there might be a specific cause that turns affect on and a specific condition which might turn it off, there is only a remote probability of using his primitive capacities to search for and find these causal conditions. The affect system will remain independent of the feedback system until the infant discovers that something can be done about such vital matters. Even after he has made this discovery it will be some time before he has achieved any degree of control over the appearance and disappearance of his affective responses. Indeed, most humans never attain great precision of control of their affects. The individual may or may not correctly identify the "cause" of his fear or joy and may or may not learn to reduce his fear, or maintain or recapture his joy.

We have stressed the ambiguity and blindness of this primary motivational system to accentuate what we take to be the necessary price which must be paid by any system which is to spend its major energies in a sea of risk, learning by making errors. The achievement of cognitive power and precision requires a motivational system no less plastic. Cognitive strides are limited by the motives which urge them. Cognitive error can be made only by one capable of committing motivational error, i.e., begin wrong about his own wishes—their causes and outcomes.

The creation of a humanomaton would require an affect system. What does this mean in terms of a specific program? The have self-rewarding and self-punishing characteristics. This means that these responses are inherently acceptable or inherently unacceptable . . . [pp. 16–18].

Recasting work begun a century earlier by Darwin, Tomkins suggested that the primary site of action for the affect system was the face. In a review of his theory published 25 years later, Tomkins (1987) stated:

What are the major affects, these primarily facial responses? I have distinguished nine innate affects, and separated them into two groups, positive affects and negative affects.

The positive affects are as follows: first, *interest* or *excitement*, in which we observe that the eyebrows are down and the stare tracking an object or fixed on it; second, *enjoyment* or *joy*, the smiling response; third, *surprise* or *startle*, with eyebrows raised and eyes blinking.

The negative affects are the following: first, *distress* or *anguish*, the crying response; second, *fear* or *terror*, in which the eyes may be frozen open in a fixed stare or moving away from the dreaded object to the side, the skin pale, cold, sweating, and trembling, and the hair erect; third, *shame* or *humiliation*, with the eyes and head lowered; fourth, *dissmell*, with the upper lip raised; fifth, *disgust*, with the lower lip lowered and protruded; sixth, *anger* or *rage*, with a frown, clenched jaw, and red face.

If these are innately patterned responses, are there also innate activators of each affect? Consider the nature of the problem. Such a hypothesis must include the drives as innate but not exclusive activators. The neonate, for example, must respond with innate fear to any difficulty in breathing but must also be capable of being afraid of other objects. Each affect has to be capable of being activated by a *variety* of unlearned stimuli. The child must be able to cry at hunger or at loud sounds as well as at a diaper pin stuck in his or her flesh.

It must therefore be intrinsic to this system that each affect be activated by some general characteristic of neural stimulation, a characteristic common to both internal and external stimuli, and not too stimulus-specific (like a releaser). Next, the activator has to be correlated with biologically useful information. The young child must fear what is dangerous and smile at what is safe. The activator has to "know the address" of the subcortical center at which the appropriate affect program is stored—not unlike the problem of how the ear responds correctly to each tone.

Next, some of the activators must be capable of habituation, and others not; else a painful stimulus might too soon cease to be distressing and an exciting stimulus never be let go—such as a deer caught by a bright light. These are some of the characteristics to be built in to the activation sensitivity of the affect mechanism. It would seem most economical to search for commonalities among the innate activators of each affect. This I have done, and I believe it is possible to account for the major phenomena with a few relatively simple assumptions about the general characteristics of the stimuli that innately activate affect.

I would account for the differences in affect activation by three general variants of a single principle—the density of neural firing or stimulation. By density, I mean the number of neural firings per unit of time. My theory posits three discrete classes of activators of affect, each of which further amplifies the sources that activate them. These are *stimulation increase, stimulation level,* and *stimulation decrease.* Thus, there is a provision for three distinct classes of motives: affects about stimulation that is on the increase, about stimulation that is level, and about stimulation that is on the decrease.

With respect to density of neural firing or stimulation, then, the human being is equipped for affective arousal for every major contingency. If internal or external sources of neural firing suddenly increase, s/he will startle or become afraid, or become interested, depending on the suddenness of the increase in stimulation. If internal or external sources of neural firing reach and maintain a high, constant level of stimulation, which deviates in excess of an optimal level of neural firing, s/he will respond with anger or distress, depending on the level of stimulation. If internal or external sources of neural firing suddenly decrease, s/he will laugh or smile with enjoyment, depending on the suddenness of the decrease in stimulation.

The general advantages of a system that allows affective arousal to such a broad spectrum of levels (and changes of level) of neural firing is to make the individual care about quite different states of affairs in quite different ways.

Such a neural theory must be able to account for how "meaning" in such neural messages operates without the benefit of a

homunculus who "appraises" each message before instructing the
individual to become interested or afraid. (It is clear that any theory
of affect activation must be capable of accounting for affect that is
triggered in either an unlearned or a learned fashion.) Certainly the
infant who emits his or her birth cry on exit from the birth canal
had not "appraised" the new environment as a vale of tears before
s/he cries. It is equally certain that s/he will later learn to cry on
receiving communications telling of the death of a beloved person;
this does depend on meaning and its appraisal. I would argue that
learned information *can* activate affects only through the general
neural profiles I have postulated.

Thus, for a joke to "work," the novelty of information adequate
to trigger interest, and the final laughter depend on the *rate of
acceleration of information* in the first case and on the *rate of
deceleration* in the second case. If we hear the same information a
second time, there is a sense in which it may be appraised as
essentially a repetition, but, because we now "see it coming," there
is neither interest or enjoyment because the gradients of neural
firing are now much flatter (because compressed) than when the
information was first received.

Similarly, with the startle response, a pistol shot is adequate as
an unlearned activator, but so is the sudden appearance of a man
with two heads. In such a case I would suggest that the rate of
neural firing from the conjoint muscular responses of the double-
take and the very rapid recruitment of information from memory to
check the nature of the apparent message also have the requisite
square wave profile of neural firing called for in my model. In short,
"meaning" operates through the very general profiles of acceleration, deceleration, or level of neural firing as these are produced by
either cognitive, memorial, perceptual, or motor responses. Any
such responses singly or in concert can, through their correlation
between meaning and the profiles of neural firing, "innately" fire
innate affect programs by stimuli or responses that are themselves
learned.

The conjoint characteristics of urgency, abstractness, generality
and modularity together produce both match and (in varying
degrees) mismatch between affect and other mechanisms, making
it seem sometimes blind and inert, other times intuitive and flexible;
sometimes brief and transient, other times enduring and committing; sometimes primarily biological, other times largely psychological, social, cultural or historical; sometimes aesthetic, other times
instrumental; sometimes private and solipsistic, other times
communicative and expressive; sometimes explosive, other times
overcontrolled and backed up [pp. 139-142].

Stimulus density, square waves, levels of neural firing—what kind
of psychology is this? The affect system, this pattern Tomkins has

discerned as figure from the ground of human life, is the bridge between biology and psychology. Innate affect is a biological phenomenon, each affect another highly distinct way the *body* is taken over by programs responsive to the categories of stimulation he has described. Certain levels, or variations in the level, of stimulus density activate one or another of the six basic affect protocols, after which something happens in the musculature and the microcirculation of the face, something so recurrent and reliable and predictable that we come to recognize as a separate gestalt each of these six ways that the face responds. On the basis of her meticulous observations of infants studied with the aid of videotape, Demos (1988) has pointed out that an affect converts what is essentially a quantitative occurrence (these meaning-free shifts in brain physiology) into the kind of qualitative experience we call a feeling. Affect, says Tomkins, makes good things better and bad things worse; it makes us care about different kinds of things in different ways.

Tomkins is therefore the first investigator to claim for emotion a role of this magnitude. Freud (1915) saw affect as the result of drive forces gone astray, and emotionality itself a sign of libido unbound. Sartre (1948) called emotion the sign that the mind has shifted from healthy, adult neocortical cognition to the type of thinking more typical of primitive beings. Jung (Hillman, 1961) suggested that affect occurs when the forces of the conscious and the forces of the unconscious mind meet and explode with a special kind of energy much like that postulated by the physics of his day for matter and antimatter. But Tomkins asks us to understand that the drives are navigators and affect the engine that moves us, that nothing can be important or urgent unless it is amplified by affect. There is no obligatory link between any affect and any triggering source—normal sexual excitement is a coassembly of sexual arousal (the scripts telling the organism what to do) and the affect interest-excitement (the mechanism that makes it an action worth doing), which means that anything capable of interfering with the affect turns the drive into a paper tiger. The sex drive can be amplified by any affect to produce the wide range of sexual experience, and the affect interest-excitement can make anything the subject of attention as long as it provides a steadily increasing stimulus gradient of just the right slope.

So now Tomkins has described affect as something that has evolved to amplify or make urgent and important stimuli that conform to any of the six categories of stimulus increase, stimulus level, or stimulus decrease by making something happen on the face, something that we learn to interpret because it is a compelling program that, from infancy through senescence, literally takes over the body. As Basch (1988) has said so eloquently, the human brain is a comparator, a comparison engine. We have evolved to compare what we experience in the present with our stored memories of previous experience, just as we analyze any pattern on the basis of previously encountered similar patterns. Basch (1976) suggests that we use the term affect for any of these purely biological events; our *awareness* that an affect has been triggered is then called a "feeling," just as we speak of any sensory experience as a feeling. In the formal language through which Basch has introduced affect theory into psychoanalysis, the term emotion is reserved for the further combination of an affect with our memory of any previous experience of that affect. If affect is biology, then I suggest that emotion be understood as biography.

Nothing may be said to be the subject of our attention unless it has been brought into focus by an affect. There are nine innate affects, and therefore we are born with nine quite different ways of paying attention. Consciousness itself (always the great mystery of psychology and now the subject of intense interest by physicists who know nothing about affect) is defined by Tomkins as a special channel of neocortical activity made available only by affect. Experience teaches an unbiased observer that it is not the drives that bring needs into conscious awareness—no one is hungry when involved in a compelling activity; even a competent source of sexual arousal will not be noticed when attention is held by another source of affect. Nothing can be conscious unless amplified by affect, just as nothing can enter the dynamic unconscious unless it first triggers one of the affects, then is found to be unacceptable to our psychology, and next is shunted away from consciousness by another affective mechanism, usually shame.

Finally, another old horse of classical psychology must be put out to pasture, for there is in humans no such thing as "stimulus-response (S-R) pairs" (Mowrer, 1939). No stimulus brings forth a response unless that stimulus triggers an affect, and it is to the combination of stimulus and affect that we respond. Each of us has the same palate of innate affect mechanisms, even though the vast differences in our individual experience must lead us to create radically different personal libraries of stimulus-affect-response sequences. It is these "S-A-R triplets," grouped by their similarity, that we come to know and name as our emotions.

A working theory of emotion must take into account all possible instances of emotion, including those biological disorders characterized by powerful and relatively inflexible affective experiences operating without the normal freedom and plasticity of the affect system as described by Tomkins. Panic disorder, mania, "classical" depression, and "atypical" depression are clinical constellations characterized by the apparent presence of one or another innate affect triggered by mechanisms unrelated to the normal innate triggers. It was for this reason that I extended Tomkins's idea of the computer simulation needed to produce a humanomaton and introduced the desktop computer model for all emotion (Nathanson, 1988, 1992). The biological substrata (central nervous system, neurochemistry, facial musculature, and microcirculation) may be regarded as *hardware*, the affects and drives a form of *firmware* (the sort of program now placed on a ROM or "read only memory" chip), while the gestalt of individual experiences leading to upregulation and downregulation of each affect are a form of *software* (each family in any era and every different neighborhood requires at least slightly different patterns of affect modulation). The affects are built-in programs that are set in motion normally when their stimulus requirements are met, but they are also capable of being simulated when the sites of action from which we deduce the presence of an affect are activated by other neurochemical mechanisms. In each of the 30 years I have practiced outpatient psychiatry, one or more adults have visited my office for treatment of nearly crippling "anxiety" easily traced to the adrenergic effects of pseudoephedrine, a commonly available medication swallowed by millions in hope of relieving the nasal congestion due to the common cold. Persistent emotionality of any sort (including shame) may be due to problems of hardware or software and will usually be misinterpreted as otherwise normal manifestations of the firmware.

Where, then, does shame fit into the concept of human emotion provided by the affect theory of Silvan Tomkins? If shame is an innate affect, it must have an activator capable of triggering a highly specific mechanism, and this combination of stimulus and innate affect mechanism must produce the wide variety of responses we know as what Wurmser (1981) has described as the "shame family of emotions." The members of this family include embarrassment, humiliation, mortification, shame, the experience of being put down or treated with contempt, the shame-rage or "humiliation fury" described by Lewis (1971), deference, awe, masochism, sadism, narcissism, guilt, and many of the clinical conditions lumped as "depression." Each of them will turn out to be a specific coassembly within which the innate affect Tomkins calls shame-humiliation is triggered by one or more sources and linked with various systems of response. All of them are shame. Let us pick up the thread of Tomkins's narrative from the 1987 summary:

I regard shame as an affect auxiliary, and as a theoretical construct, rather than an entity unambiguously defined by the word "shame." Our languages of communication are rough-hewn devices, sometimes coarse and sometimes marvelously subtle, reflecting insights and purposes of past cultures, which in part continue to be vital to the present, but in part alien and irrelevant.

If one were to trace the varying meanings of the word "shame" over the past few thousand years, one would illuminate the rich textures of cultural *mentalité* rather than find this primary human feeling to be a fundamental invariant. A word in ordinary language may or may not confer the precision necessary for a scientific language. Thus, to write "salt" is not the same as to write "NaCl" or "sodium chloride," especially since both sodium and chloride may be combined with other elements to make compounds for which the word "salt" might be as useful a name. Nonetheless "salt" may do as a rough equivalent of sodium chloride so long as one does not insist that potassium chloride *is* "salt" or is *entirely different* from table salt.

Similarly, the common word "shame" will be adequate for my needs as a rough equivalent of the theoretical entity referring to a specific affect auxiliary. It is important for one to understand that the *word* shame (today) refers more to feelings of inferiority than feelings of guilt, and therefore more to responses of proving oneself "good" (in the sense of being superior) than to responses of proving oneself "good" in the moral sense. As for the *theoretical construct* shame, however, I will argue that these are *not* differences in shame, but rather differences in objects and sources, and differences in responses to both sources and affects. Therefore, strictly speaking one can be "ashamed" of *either* being inferior or being immoral and of striving either to overcome inferiority or immorality.

The reader at this point will have serious reservations that it does not "feel" the same to have failed and to have hurt someone, nor therefore to try to succeed or to make restitution. Nonetheless, I will argue that though the *total* complex of affect, source, and response may feel quite different in these two cases (and indeed prompting the invention of the word "guilt" to distinguish shame from guilt) that the component affect is nonetheless identical in both cases, could one abstract the elements from each of these complexes.

A comparison with other affects may be helpful. Consider Freud's distinction between fear and anxiety. In fear one "knows" what one is afraid of. In anxiety one does not. A phobia will prompt one to avoid a quite specific object. An anxiety attack will not. There is a nontrivial sense in which these "feel" to be very different experiences. Nonetheless I argue that the affect (whether one calls it fear, terror, or anxiety) is identical. It is extremely improbable that such a fundamental motivating mechanism could be split and differentiated into several mechanisms every time its trigger varied in source. Similarly, when the response to fear varies, the "feel" is also quite different, but no less misleading about the underlying affect mechanism. Thus in anorexia one starves for fear of eating, whereas in bulimia one eats compulsively for fear of starvation or emptiness. Different as these complexes are, I believe the affect of fear is identical in these otherwise opposed complexes of responses.

The differences in complexes of source, affect and response and the identity of affects must be preserved because the varieties of such differences are without limit and the difference between shame and guilt is but *one* of *many* possible variants of shame which we will examine later.

In order to understand the nature of shame as an affect mechanism, let us first examine the nature of the affect mechanism. The affect mechanism is *not* identical with our concepts of motivation, which latter refers to a much more unitary, compact, and reasonable phenomenon than does the construct of affect. . . . It is in many ways similar to the set of complex relationships between an alphabet, words, grammar, and semantic rules. An alphabet is *not* a word, but words require an alphabet. Grammar is not semantics, but semantics require a grammar. Any system requires the property of modularity, or varying combinatorial capacity, to generate complexity. The affect mechanism is one mechanism among many that together enable us to feel and act as "motivated." It is, in my view, the single most important component in motivation, but nonetheless partial and incomplete as a "motive" in our ordinary use of that term [pp. 134–137].

The conjoint characteristics of urgency, abstractness, generality and modularity together produce both match and mismatch and (in varying degrees) mismatch between affect and other mechanisms, making it seem sometimes blind and inert, other times intuitive and flexible; sometimes brief and transient, other times enduring and committing; sometimes primarily biological, other times largely psychological, social, cultural or historical; sometimes aesthetic, other times instrumental; sometimes private and solipsistic, other times communicative and expressive; sometimes explosive, other times overcontrolled and backed up.

If the objects of affects are abstract and depend for their particularity on supplemental information from perception, memory, and cognition then clearly the "same" affect is rarely *experienced* in entirely the same way. My experiences of excitement at sexuality, poetry, mathematics, or at another's face can never be described as entirely identical "feelings," despite the identity of the triggered affects. Further, any impediment to such excitement evokes unequal varieties of "shame," with respect to experience, despite identity of the affect of shame.

This is complicated by the fact that shame is not a primary affect as I conceive it, but rather an affect auxiliary. In our consideration of the nature of auxiliary mechanisms, let us first study drive auxiliaries.

Dissmell and disgust are innate defensive response, which are auxiliary to the hunger, thirst and oxygen drives. Their function is clear. If the food about to be ingested activates dissmell, the upper lip and nose are raised and the head is drawn away from the offending odor. If the food has been taken into the mouth, it may, if disgusting, be spit out. If it has been swallowed and is toxic, it may produce nausea and be vomited out, either through the nose or nostrils. The early warning response via the nose is dissmell; the next level of response, from mouth or stomach, is disgust.

If dissmell and disgust were limited to these functions, we should not define them as affects but rather as auxiliary drive mechanisms. However, their status is somewhat unique in that dissmell, disgust, and nausea also function as signals and motives to others, as well as to the self, of feelings of rejection. They readily accompany a wide spectrum of entities that need not be tasted, smelled, or ingested. Dissmell and disgust appear to be evolving from the status of drive-reducing acts to those that have as well a more general motivating and signal function, both to the individual who emits this signal and to the one who receives it.

Just as dissmell and disgust are drive auxiliary acts, I posit shame as an innate affect auxiliary response and a specific inhibitor of continuing interest and enjoyment. As disgust operates only after something has been taken in, shame operates only after interest or enjoyment has been activated; it inhibits one, or the other, or both [pp. 142–143].

Here is the critical point, the fulcrum around which this new theory of shame pivots. Tomkins has defined the innate affects as analogic amplifiers of whatever has triggered them—an affect is a mechanism that makes a situation more noticeable on the basis of one, and only one, of its qualities. Something (anything) that produces data too rapidly will be made salient as a fearful stimulus, *but it will be salient only because of this situation of* stimulus increase, *and it is the amplification of this rate of rise in data acquisition that makes it salient*. Nothing else about the stimulus, no "quality" of the stimulus apart from the rate at which it enters some moiety of the central nervous system, is responsible for its registration within consciousness as a fearful stimulus. Something (anything) that produces data at an optimal rate of rise (and this can occur over a wide range of possible rates) will trigger the affect interest-excitement. Nothing else about the stimulus, no "quality" of the stimulus apart from the rate at which it enters some module of the central nervous system, is responsible for its registration within consciousness as an interesting or exciting stimulus. Similarly, whenever any stimulus wanes or produces information at a decreasing rate, it triggers the pleasant affective experience Tomkins calls enjoyment-joy; we know this affect as contentment when the rate of stimulus decrease is slow, and laughter when it is rapid or sudden.

The algebra of affect theory is simple and compelling. It is Newtonian in concept and as easy to understand as the idea that acceleration is defined as the *increase* in rate seen during a specific period of time, regardless of what object is moving at what speed. The six basic affects (interest-excitement, enjoyment-joy, surprise-startle, fear-terror, distress-anguish, and anger-rage) represent all the possible responses to conditions of stimulus increase, stimulus decrease, and stimulus level. Each of these six affects bears a two-word group name, the first indicating the mildest presentation of the affect and the second defining the upper reach of its intensity. Dissmell and disgust bear single names, for Tomkins (personal communication) wanted to emphasize that they evolved as responses to specific noxious substances and involve neurological mechanisms entirely different from the innate affects. These two food-centered, drive-based mechanisms take on powerful emotional significance as the organism grows to maturity and learns to use them as analogues for the concepts of distancing and rejection. Even though dissmell and disgust are experienced by us as affects, and are included in the list of nine innate mechanisms, in the most precise language they are understood as auxiliaries to a drive rather than analogic amplifiers of the rate of rise or fall, or the level and density of stimulation.

It is when Tomkins shifts our attention to shame that the idea of an analogic amplifier seems much more complex and daunting. Go back to Newton for a moment. The shift from algebra to calculus involved no more than the understanding that acceleration itself can vary. If acceleration is defined as the increase in speed noted in a specific period of time, then our experience at the wheel of an automobile confirms that it is easy to vary the acceleration of the car by slight changes in pressure on the gas pedal. The pedal acts as a transducer of our instructions, transforming minute variations created by our leg and foot muscles into powerful and highly meaningful alterations in vehicular speed. Mathematical analysis of these variations in acceleration involves what is called the "first derivative" of the formula for acceleration, and it is with this concept that the field of calculus was introduced.

The analogy to shame is perfect. Interest-excitement and enjoyment-joy are highly pleasant first-order responses to acceleration and deceleration, analogues of rates of stimulus acquisition that happen to be optimal for the organism. But just as variations in acceleration are matters of calculus, *any decrease in the rate at which these pleasant stimuli enter the central nervous system*, the variation itself, is a competent stimulus for another neurologic mechanism. This second-order neurologic mechanism is therefore an analogic amplification of any impediment to the appreciation of whatever was, only a moment ago, a competent trigger for positive affect. The affect Tomkins calls shame-humiliation not only is an analogue of the impediment to the flow of information, but also makes this impediment salient (the entire focus of our attention) by amplifying it. Instantly, when shame affect is triggered, it turns down the rapt interest or good humor only a moment ago in progress, thus making us all the more aware that something has impeded the flow of the immediately preceding event. It does not matter what has created this impediment—again, content is of no importance here— only that there has been an impediment and that this impediment is now urgent and important.

From an evolutionary standpoint, it seems logical to assume that dissmell and disgust evolved long after the hunger drive; as auxiliaries to the drive they protect the organism by limiting hunger and keeping us away from noxious food. Similarly, shame-humiliation, the auxiliary to the innate affects of interest-excitement and enjoyment-joy, is likely to have evolved much later than the mechanisms it assists. Unlike the moth that is consumed by the flame toward which it is drawn by tropisms unprotected by such auxiliaries, shame confers increased safety to higher organisms that are capable of interest in so many sources of data.

One final point before returning to Tomkins: the basic theorem of his system states that each affect is an analogic amplifier of whatever has triggered it. No matter what affect we consider, that particular affect is itself an analogue of the stimulus increase, stimulus decrease, or stimulus level condition that preceded it and is now amplified by it. As an analogue of its stimulus, the affect itself possesses exactly the same qualities of stimulation of that original stimulus. *Each affect is therefore a compelling stimulus for the production of more of that same affect.* Excitement makes us more excited; contentment brings on more contentment. And shame, which is triggered by this second-order variation in stimulus acquisition that we experience as an impediment to interest-excitement or enjoyment-joy, itself becomes a powerful impediment to further positive affect. The shame mechanism is both the response to impediment and an ongoing trigger to more impediment. The clinical implications of such a mechanism loom increasingly large as one begins to appreciate the difference between an innate affect and the adult experience of emotion:

> The innate activator of shame is the incomplete reduction of interest or joy. Such a barrier might arise because one is suddenly looked at by another who is strange; or because one wishes to look at, or commune with, another person but suddenly cannot because s/he is strange; or one expected him to be familiar but he suddenly appears unfamiliar; or one started to smile but found one was smiling at a stranger. It might also arise as a consequence of discouragement after having tried and failed, and then lowered one's head in apparent "defeat." The response of shame includes lowering the eyelid, decreasing the tonus of all facial muscles, lowering the head via a reduction in tonus of the neck muscles, or a tilting of the head in one direction.
>
> Discouragement, shyness, shame, and guilt are identical as affects, although not so experienced because of differential coassembly of perceived causes and consequences. Shyness is about strangeness of the other; guilt is about moral transgression; shame is about inferiority; discouragement is about temporary defeat; but the core affect in all four is identical, although the coassembled perceptions, cognitions, and intentions may be vastly different.
>
> Biologically, disgust and dissmell are drive auxiliary responses that have evolved to protect the human being from coming too close to noxious-smelling objects and to regurgitate these if they have been ingested. Through learning, these responses have come to be emitted to biologically neutral stimuli, including, for example, disgusting and dirty thoughts. Shame, in contrast, is an affect auxiliary to the affects of interest-excitement and enjoyment-joy.
>
> Any perceived barrier to positive affect with the other will evoke lowering of the eyelids and a loss of tonus in the face and neck muscles, producing a head hung in shame. The child who is burning with excitement to explore the face of the stranger is nonetheless vulnerable to shame just because the other is perceived as strange. Characteristically, however, intimacy with the good and exciting other is eventually consummated. In contrast, the disgusting other is to be kept at a safe distance permanently [Tomkins, 1987, pp. 143–144].

There is a hierarchy of the negative affects. Rage and terror are the most punishing of the basic affective experiences; anguish, more tolerable. When it is experienced as an affect, dissmell keeps others at a distance and prevents any sampling or testing of a potential relationship. Disgust motivates us to keep away from whatever or whoever once made us feel good, but as anyone who has ever seen a couple go through the hell of divorce and later reconcile, it can be overcome. Shame is the least toxic of the negative affects, for it operates in the context of positive affect and always carries the hope that the impeded good scene may return and, with it, the positive affect associated with it. Only when disgust and dissmell have been coassembled with shame affect does reconciliation with the shaming other become problematic. Tomkins (personal communication) once commented that people whose characters seem imbued with chronic shame are the most deeply loving in our society because they will not relinquish hope for the return of the happy relationship. Few in our society are as difficult to treat and as defended against intimacy as those who have relinquished hope because they are convinced that positive affect can only lead to shame, self-disgust, and self-dissmell.

> If shame is activated by the incomplete reduction of interest or joy, then the varieties of these circumstances depend first on what are either the innate or learned sources of positive affect, and second on what are either the innate or learned sources of the incomplete reduction of positive affect. Such sources go far beyond the questions of inferiority and guilt which have dominated the discussion of shame versus guilt. In effect, this implicates all the positive values of human beings *and* all the problems that interfere with these values, but not to the extent of *complete* and *enduring* interference.
>
> In shame the individual wishes to resume his or her commerce with the exciting state of affairs, to reconnect with the other, to recapture the relationship that existed before the situation turned problematic. In this respect shame is radically different from the drive auxiliary responses of disgust and dissmell. In disgust the bad other is spit out, or vomited forth. In dissmell the bad other is kept at a distance because of an offensive smell. No one wishes to eat again the food that disgusts, or to come close to the smell that repels. The food is both rejected now and rejected for all time to come, as are the symbolic objects of dissmell and disgust, as are untouchables in a caste society. Disgust and dissmell are responses appropriate to a hierarchically ordered society [pp. 144].

> If shame is an affect attenuation of excitement and enjoyment it is essentially *impunitive* rather than extrapunitive or intropunitive compared with disgust and dissmell. This is not to say that it does not hurt and sting, but rather that it is *less* malignant than are the drive auxiliaries of disgust and dissmell.
>
> I have stressed the partial and temporary nature of shame. The reader may wonder about those who experience frequent and enduring mortification by shame. Can this be anything but malignant?

I would distinguish in this case between shame as affect amplification and shame as affect magnification. Any affect may be radically increased in toxicity by undue magnification. Even excitement, rewarding as it may be, can become malignant if its density is unduly magnified in frequency, duration, and intensity.

Similarly, shame, if magnified in frequency, duration, and intensity such that the head is in a permanent posture of depression, can become malignant in the extreme. But this is a consequence of the magnification of affect, rather than its nature as an amplifier. Analogous would be the lesser inherent toxicity of distress compared with terror. Nonetheless a continuing intense distress would be toxic in the extreme as would any negative affect if it became greatly magnified. Yet chronic distress over a period of months, as in infant "colic," can be tolerated both biologically and psychologically better than could a chronic intense state of terror. Even a chronic state of intense shame nurtures the hope and wish to resume the state of full excitement or enjoyment partially reduced in shame and by shame. This is why even intense shame or shame as guilt is not only compatible with continuing sexual excitement but may by contrast heighten such conflicted sexual excitement [Tomkins, 1987, pp. 150–151].

We clinicians are always drawn up sharply by Tomkins's apparent equation of shame and guilt. There seems to be no evidence for the existence of a predecessor emotion specifically linked to guilt in the way shame affect, as an innate reducer of interest-excitement and enjoyment-joy, operates for shame. Indeed, there is no predecessor mechanism that would allow the definitive separation, at all levels of infant development, of these two emotions, which appear so different in the adult. The adult emotion of guilt and the adult range of shame are related "molecules" built of similar atoms; the major difference is that guilt requires the coassembly of fear at a very early stage in development. In guilt, it is this addition of fear-terror (as in fear of retribution or punishment) that blanches the red cheek of shame and gives guilt its peculiar and highly individual character. Intuition alone would lead us to speculate that shame, easily visible in the neonate, does not fuse with fear to make guilt until the organism is old enough to understand the nature of an action, the possibility that such an action may cause harm to another, and the existence of a set of rules for behavior that, when violated, may trigger a response from more powerful others. Only after such fusion can the new entity, which we call guilt, then travel the highway of individual development as a separate, known, and labeled emotion. There is no guilt without the presence of shame affect, even though there is shame aplenty without guilt.

Further, the experience of shame may be made malignant by excessive recruitment of other affect with which it is then combined, as in that severe combination of shame, and distress or fear, and reduction in the nonspecific reticular amplification, that together constitute "depression."

The experience of shame itself characteristically recruits secondary and tertiary positive or negative affects toward shame. Thus one may develop secondary excitement at the sequence excitement-shame, as in awaiting the response of an audience to a play one has written, or in which one acts, or in awaiting the beginning of an adversarial contest as player or as audience, or in awaiting a sexual encounter. Thus some fighters, speakers, or lovers who cannot generate secondary excitement at the excitement-shame sequence report that they are in such cases incapable of adequate performance because the *absence* of shame or fear attenuates both primary and anticipatory excitement [Tomkins, 1987, pp. 151].

Shame is a great teacher because of the intensity at which we will work to avoid humiliation. Here, Tomkins has given new meaning to the concept of overconfidence, an attitude that reduces the vitality of our performance by blocking access to the scripts for the excitement and fear that power our intent to prevent shame.

Similarly one may have fear of such anticipated sequences of excitement-shame as stage fright, which typically is dissipated by pure excitement or joy after the play (dramatic or adversarial) begins. Fear may also be generated prior to an uncertain sexual encounter which promises not only excitement but also possible shame as distancing, or as guilt.

Next one may recruit anger at the excitement-shame sequence, either afterward or as anticipatory anger. The increased amplification of the conjunction of excitement followed by shame may deeply anger the self at its victimization, or direct such anger at the other, or at the dyad for being equally "inhibited" either in the expression of excitement or of shame or of sexuality, as incompetence or as guilt, or as shyness, or as discouragement. Thus one may become furious at one's victimization by guilt, which is experienced as ego-alien.

Such victimization by shame or by shame as guilt may also recruit dense distress, in which one celebrates one's impotence to free a self that wishes to liberate itself but does not know how.

Excitement-shame may, as we have noted before, also recruit secondary shame at this sequence, so that the individual becomes ashamed of shame itself. I may, however, recruit disgust or dissmell rather than shame. In such a case we have the paradox of one part of the self performing psychic surgery on another part of the itself, so that the self which feels ashamed is totally and permanently split off and rejected by a judging self that has no tolerance for its more humble and hesitant self. If disgust is recruited, there is a lingering acknowledgment that the offending self was once better but is now offensive. If it is dissmell, the other part of the self is represented as completely and enduringly offensive. Such disapprobation may be united with anger against both the fear and the shame of death, as in the poet's protest not to go "gently" into the night but to rage and rage.

Magnification of shame occurs not only by combining multiple affects about the same scene, as when a rape victim may experience not only shame, but disgust, dissmell, anger, and distress as well as terror, but also by combining multiple sources of *shame* about the same scene. Thus an impotent failure of sexuality may generate multiple feelings of deep shame such that the individual not only feels the shame of sexual inferiority, but of a totally inferior self, along with shyness, along with discouragement, guilt, defeat, and alienation. These are *all* the same affect of shame but to different aspects of the same scene.

"Consider a classic shame scene such as toilet training by a mother who taunts her child as "baby" on the occasion of loss of control of anal or urethral function. Such a child may feel multiple sources of shame as well as multiple other negative affects. S/he has lost love, and lost respect from the mother, evoked too much attention and control from her, and also too much turning away in disgust and dissmell. The child has not only done something "wrong" as immoral but also wrong as incompetent. S/he not only failed in this act but the competence of the self may have also been called into question. The distance now between the child and his mother is experienced as shyness. The difficulty of controlling himself or herself and maintaining the mother's love and respect is experienced as discouragement as well as defeat and indignity. Added to multiple sources of shame may be anger at the impatient mother, disgust at her disgust, dissmell at her dissmell, terror at his own affects as well as at her, and distress at the loss of what was once mutually enjoyed. Such a scene's magnification implicates all varieties of violations of values: moral—"soiling is wrong"; aesthetic—"soiling is ugly"; truth—"you promised to control yourself"; instrumental—"you have no skill"; and they are all "shameful."

Let us now examine more closely some of the varieties of shame, those sources of positive affect that may suffer partial and temporary attenuation which it is *hoped* will not become either permanent or complete.

First of all shame is in no way limited to the self, to the other, or to society. A once beautiful place, where one lived, and which is now ugly, for whatever reason, may cause the head to bow in regret and shame on being revisited in hope of recapturing idealized memories. But, as is characteristic of shame, one may also bow one's head in awe and shame at the unexpected grandeur and beauty of a sudden view of an ocean or mountain, never before encountered, that overwhelms by its beauty rather than by its ugliness. In such cases there is often an invidious comparison to the self as unequal to such beauty and grandeur, as in the confrontation with parents or parent surrogates who make the self feel small and unworthy by comparison.

Again, shame may be felt at the vicissitudes of fate, particularly in the face of death, when the self reluctantly acknowledges the fragility of cherished relationships. The head is bowed at a cemetery because one does not wish to give up the beloved but is required to do so. Shame is also experienced as a less permanent defeat in discouragement, following great effort that has so far come to naught. One bows one's head in acknowledgment of defeat for the time being but with the hope that it may one day be raised in pride.

Shame is experienced as shyness when one wishes to be intimate with the other but also feels some impediment to *immediate* intimacy. That impediment may be located either in the self, the other, or in the dyad, or in a third party who intrudes.

Shame is experienced as inferiority when discouragement is located in the self as an inability of the self to do what the self wishes to do. This is experienced differently than is the same phenomenon as discouragement, which stresses the failure of great effort, rather than the incapacity of the self.

Shame is experienced as guilt when positive affect is attenuated by virtue of moral normative sanctions experienced as conflicting with what is exciting or enjoyable. As in the case of any shame, such guilt requires a continuing interest or enjoyment which is only partially or temporarily attenuated. This is in contrast to moral outrage, moral disgust, or moral dissmell. In the extreme case immorality may be judged "beneath contempt," "inhuman," or "animalistic." All such feelings and evaluations differ from shame as "guilt" in totally and forever condemning what is judged immoral, whether by the self against another, or by the self against the self, as in "I can never forgive myself for what I did." In this case the self splits itself into two, a good self and totally bad self.

Feelings of shame or of shame as guilt may be experienced either as coming from without or from within. The common distinction between shame and guilt as resting on the locus of evaluation is in error since I may feel inferior or guilty because someone so regards me, *or* because I so regard myself. Further, I may feel ashamed because *you* should feel ashamed or guilty but do not. I may feel ashamed or guilty because you feel ashamed or guilty but *should not*, as in the case of my sanctioning slavery reluctantly.

To the extent to which I have conflicting values or wishes I may feel ashamed or guilty for opposite reasons at the same time.

Thus I may feel ashamed of my wish to exhibit myself and of my wish not to exhibit myself, and of my wish that you exhibit yourself and of my wish that you not exhibit yourself.

To the extent that any primary affect is conflicted I may be shamed equally by feeling it and by not feeling it. Thus I may feel shame at being distressed at the plight of the self or the other, as well as shame at *not* feeling distress at the plight of self or other. I may feel shame at my own fear and also at my own fearlessness to the extent that I have been socialized by one parent to be fearless and by another parent to be cautious.

In contrast to conflict and ambivalence as a source of shame, is a *narrow optimal bandwidth* for excitement or enjoyment and therefore for freedom from shame at partial reduction of the sources of positive affect. Thus, I may define acceptable intimacy by a restricted zone of optimal closeness. In such a case, if the other is too close s/he is experienced as shaming by intrusion, but if the other is too distant s/he is also experienced as shaming by not being close enough.

The experience of shame itself may become a further source of shame whenever there is a narrow optimal zone of shame as acceptable. Thus if I am *too* shamed or too shameless I may experience *either* as shaming.

The same dynamic may be experienced at the experience of *any* affect that violates a narrow optimal bandwidth. I may wish to be less excitable than I am, less prone to become angry or distressed or disgusted or dissmelling, or fearful. This is to be distinguished from shame at affect *conflict*, as described above. In this case there is no conflict about specific affects, but rather a strict set of criteria for the variety, frequency of sources of affect, or for the affect's intensity, duration, or density, or about its translation into action.

Shame may be evoked by a *complete* rejection of *any* affect (including shame). It is not that there is a narrow bandwidth of acceptable sources, affect density, or responses to affect but rather a total intolerance of specific affects, sources and actions in response. The affect is simply condemned, so that whenever it appears it is capable of shaming the individual who wishes it had not appeared. Any affect may be condemned for one of a variety of reasons other than conflict. It may be condemned as unaesthetic and ugly, as engulfing the individual, as immoral, as typical of a lower class, as offensive to a beloved, as exaggerating and illusory, as too costly to one's commitments. These varieties may in turn generate varieties of shame [pp. 151–155].

Notice that Tomkins shifts back and forth between the innate trigger for shame (incomplete reduction of interest or joy) and the learned triggers for the affect. It is important to realize that none of these learned triggers could produce shame affect unless it involved the duplication from memory of the innate trigger. As long as I

remember that when I am angry someone may humiliate me, anger
can trigger shame in the absence of whoever taught us to forge that
link. Tomkins referred to such learned assemblages as "affect-shame
binds," a term in no way related to the theory of "double binds" in
schizophrenia popular in our field during the 1960s. Shame, the
mechanism that has evolved to amplify impediment to positive affect
in such a way that it becomes an even more powerful impediment,
can therefore bind or impede literally any psychological function.

> The experience of shame is inevitable for any human being insofar
> as desire outruns fulfillment sufficiently to attenuate interest without
> destroying it. "I want, but. . ." is the essential condition for the
> activation of shame. Clearly not any barrier will evoke shame since
> many barriers either completely reduce interest so that the object
> is renounced, or heighten excitement so that the barrier is removed
> or overcome. If shame is dependent on barriers to excitement and
> enjoyment then the pluralism of desires must be matched by a
> pluralism of shame. One person's source of shame can always be
> another person's fulfillment, satiety, or indifference [p. 155].

In the preceding paragraph, Tomkins presents a model that offers
a clear distinction between affect theory and classical psychoanalytic
theories for oedipal guilt and shame. As I have explained in detail
elsewhere (Nathanson, 1992), sexual desire, or "need," as it is
sometimes expressed, is a drive mechanism that owes its power not
to the nature of the system for arousal, but to the fact that arousal
occurs at an optimal acceleration that therefore triggers interest-
excitement. No drive-based need can achieve salience unless it is
amplified by an affect. It is not the sexual part of oedipal longing that
(when thwarted) produces shame, but the amplifying affect of
interest-excitement.

> Insofar as human beings are excited by or enjoy their work, other
> human beings, their bodies, selves, and the surrounding inanimate
> world, they are vulnerable to a variety of vicissitudes in the form of
> barriers, lacks, losses, accidents, imperfections, conflicts, and
> ambiguities that will impoverish, attenuate, impair, or otherwise
> prevent total pursuit and enjoyment of work, of others, of sexuality
> and other drive satisfactions, and of the surrounding physical and
> social world [pp. 155–156].

So shame, a genetically programmed auxiliary to two of the six
primary affects, is an inevitable experience with which each of us
must come to terms. The affect itself will be triggered whenever
anything interferes with either of the two positive affects, interest-

excitement or enjoyment-joy, as long as there remains adequate stimulus for the continuation of that positive affect. Shame affect is not recruited when our rapt involvement in a television show is terminated by an electrical failure simply because there is no more television show to trigger positive affect. But if your mother catches you watching a show when you should have been doing homework, there is shame aplenty as she provides a temporary barrier to your affect-mediated involvement in a show that remains both available and a competent trigger for interest.

THE COMPASS OF SHAME

Acceptance of Tomkins's idea of a physiological mechanism, an innate affect functioning as the nidus of a wide variety of emotional experiences, does not help us as clinicians. There is too much information here. Is shame merely an amplified impediment to the experiences of excitement or contentment? Can we always identify the sequences of stimulus, affect, and response that form each of the common presentation of shame? How can this new approach to human emotion illuminate our understanding of shame and enhance our efforts as therapists? After much discussion of these matters with Professor Tomkins, I reorganized his data in a form more accessible to modern clinicians. The following analysis of shame may be considered an extension from his affect theory into script theory, the final development of his work on human emotion.

Crisp and sharp as the facial expression of innate affect may be in infants, it is soon muted by the action of those adults who act as the external modulators of infantile affect display. By the age of three years, children are expected to hold in check their affective display so that it does not take over a public space. Earlier, I mentioned that our old concept of "stimulus-response pairs" must give way to the more logical sequence of "stimulus-affect-response," for no stimulus can bring on a psychological response unless it first triggers an affect. Tomkins asks us to use the word *scene* to indicate any such sequence of triggering source, affect, and eventual response.

From the earliest stirrings of affective life, an infant groups scenes on the basis of their similarity. Stern (1985) referred to such groups or families of scenes as "Representations of Interactions that have been Generalized" (pp. 97–99), for which he coined the acronym RIGS. Through these RIGS the infant assembles a set of rules about the nature of life. Such internal formulations allow it to know what to expect in situations that resemble but are not precisely identical to those in which they were deduced. A RIG is not a specific remembered experience but the summation and integration of a host of experiences—that from which we can make assumptions about a new but related experience.

Yet more is going on here than the mere coalescence into a family of scenes of situations that resemble each other on the basis of their sequences of source, affect, and response. Whenever the organism is able to form such groupings, the group itself becomes an entity that is now capable of triggering affect. Imagine the following scene: A newspaper advertisement sends you scurrying to the neighborhood market to take advantage of a special bargain on your favorite dessert, only to be rewarded by an apology from the store manager, who informs you that it had just sold out. Should this sequence of excited anticipation and disappointment recur more than once, it is likely that you would respond to similar advertisements with something other than excited anticipation. Tomkins suggests that the family of scenes (the new entity produced when we link similar scenes into a group) itself triggers an affect, and that this affect *magnifies* everything within the group. If we have become disgusted by the apparent lies promulgated in the advertisement, disgust affect will permeate our every involvement with that store and its advertising even in situations apparently unrelated to the original scene. This action, of affect acting to magnify the components of the scenes within a group, produces what Tomkins calls a *script*, and it is through such scripts that all adult life is managed. It is to my grouping of the range of possible scripts associated with shame affect that I wish to call your attention.

In the life of an infant or small child there is a limited range of situations in which shame affect can be triggered (see Table 1). The way each of us travels through these eight categories of experience gives rise to the characteristic thoughts listed with each. By the time we are adults, shame affect is triggered by a wide range of individual and interpersonal stimuli. Often these involve such scenes as the revelation of something we would have preferred kept hidden, or betrayal, or any sudden reduction in self-esteem. In all these situations, we suddenly see ourselves as less than our usual self-image. For example, the shame affect triggered when our sexual partner seems bored despite the degree of our arousal may be experienced as a poorly defined, wrenching feeling in the gut. Most experiences of affect occur without earning an emotion label; most of what we call "hurt feelings" are sequences involving shame affect. Only the most frequently repeated sequences of triggering source and physiological affect achieve the recognition of a name.

Table 1.

THE COGNITIVE PHASE OF SHAME

Search of memory for previous similar experiences.
Layered associations to

A. **Matters of personal size, strength, ability, skill**
("I am weak, incompetent, stupid.")

B. **Dependence/independence**
(Sense of helplessness.)

C. **Competition**
("I am a loser.")

D. **Sense of self**
("I am unique only to the extent that I am defective.")

E. **Personal attractiveness**
("I am ugly or deformed. The blush stains my features and
makes me even more of a target of contempt.")

F. **Sexuality**
("There is something wrong with me sexually.")

G. **Issues of seeing and being seen**
The urge to escape from the eyes before which we have been exposed.
The wish for a hole to open and swallow me.

H. **Wishes and fears about closeness**
The sense of being shorn from all humanity. A feeling that one is
unlovable. The wish to be left alone forever.

Source: Nathanson, 1992.

Regardless of what triggers shame or how it is eventually explained, the trigger launches a program for the physiological affect mechanism with its stigmata of blush, slump, averted gaze, and loss of attention to whatever pleasant stimulus only a moment ago occupied the individual. Perhaps the vasodilatation responsible for the blush even affects the brain itself, for nobody can think clearly in the moment of shame. But it is not necessary to postulate so direct a physiological mechanism, for if normal attention is the type of cognition amplified by interest-excitement, and if shame affect is the built-in attenuator for interest, then shame (by turning off the mechanism that produced the specific type of consciousness in operation up to that moment) turns off interest-based consciousness and turns on shame-based consciousness and shameful attention.

Within a moment—for no innate affect lasts more than a moment—we begin to recover our ability to think clearly, and then scroll through our past experiences of shame. This, of course, is the biographical sequencing defined by Basch (1976) as the formal difference between an affect and an emotion; it is during this cognitive phase of the shame experience that we review the list in Table 1 and are flooded with the thoughts associated with past episodes of shame affect.

More must happen, however, before this emotional experience can be completed—the definition given us by Basch (1976) must be adjusted to include our *responses* to the newly formed combination of affect and memory. Immediately on reviewing these past experiences we must make some sort of decision about the new self revealed during the moment of shame. Our choice is simple: accept the new information (I am less than I might have wished) or defend against it. Most of the time we defend against the experience of shame affect by choosing one of the patterns of behavior I have described as the Compass of Shame (Figure 1). Each pole is a library that contains such material as the carefully learned and practiced form of script that may represent a subroutine—a bit of business that

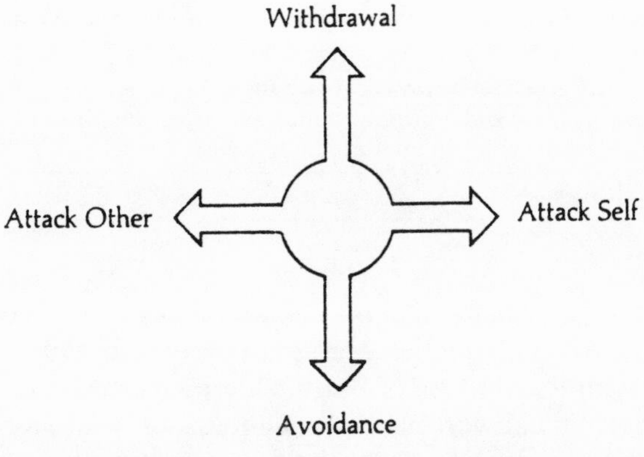

Figure 1. COMPASS OF SHAME   Source: Nathanson, 1992, p. 312.

we might adopt for one or another specific situation—or others that may become a defining character style.

Whenever we let the affect take its course, we tend to withdraw and hide. The most benign behaviors of the *withdrawal* pole of the compass involve such gestures as putting hand to lips as if to prevent or retract whatever has just been said, or placing hand to forehead in a miniaturized version of hiding. At the pathological end of the spectrum lie all the ways we hide from those who represent no harm; the withdrawal of depression is often drawn from this pattern of response. Since it is the affect interest-excitement that makes sexual arousal salient, and shame-humiliation that acts to amplify any impediment to excitement, shame turns off sexual arousal. In men, shame therefore prevents the turgor needed to produce an erection and causes impotence. In women, sexual arousal produces turgor and pelvic heat when unimpeded, whereas shame produces "frigidity" when the accompanying excitement is turned off. In an extensive review of sex therapy manuals written before this recent explosion of interest in shame theory, I found none that mentioned shame as a cause of sexual dysfunction, despite my own observation of its nearly universal importance in this cohort.

Yet there are those among us for whom this moment of affect-born isolation is far too redolent of dangerous personal isolation and abandonment. Shame, which for others produces a welcome moment of hiding, offers them an even greater punishment. For those to whom the aloneness of shame affect is too painful, some guarantee of safety must be achieved. This may be accomplished by reducing one's self-esteem in the presence of a more powerful other or by administering a public put-down to oneself in order to make the listener feel bigger. By this mechanism of *attack self* behavior, we accept a reduced sense of self that does not interfere with the enhanced sense of safety from the isolation of shame that it confers. At the healthy end of the spectrum this may be expressed as normal deference to authority, whereas the pathological realm is expressed as self-abnegation and masochism over a wide range of severity. There is no instance of masochism other than that produced in the name of shame; no treatment of masochistic behavior can be successful unless it addresses shame as a primary concern. Since it is dissmell and disgust that makes people shy away from us, it is likely that an *attack self* script will contain liberal quantities of self-dissmell and self-disgust ("How could you want to be with someone as horrible as me?")

There are also those moments (for some of us all of the time, for all of us some of the time) when we simply cannot abide the feeling of shame and will do anything to avoid it. The *avoidance* pole of the compass of shame represents the ways we prevent the experience of shame by calling attention to whatever brings us pride, or the ways we block the physiological experience with drugs, alcohol, or hedonism. Everything we have learned to consider as narcissism falls into this category; narcissism is nothing more than a group of scripts through which we try to avoid shame. What Freud (1914) described as the "stone wall of narcissism" may be understood as a way of preventing the incursion of new information about the self for a person to whom the significant fraction of information about the self has been a source of shame. Often, narcissism is a nonspecific barrier to information about the self made necessary because the history of that person has been characterized by so much empathic failure that it seems safest to remain immured. Shame is soluble in alcohol and boiled away by cocaine and the amphetamines; no treatment of substance abuse makes sense unless it addresses shame and these methods of its avoidance.

Sometimes the moment of shame is associated with a feeling of lowered self-worth that is simply unbearable. In such a situation, we are likely to reduce another person so that we can at least be better than someone else. By the systems of behavior collected as the *attack other* pole of the compass, we reduce, humiliate, abuse, and torture those who come into our path. Everything we have previously called sadomasochistic may be understood as behavior intended to manage shame. Table 2 shows these four categories of behavior and, in each case, the affects used to increase their power along with some of the ways we might treat patients in each category.

The crisp edges of innate affect, the pure mechanisms seen in the face of the infant, are blunted and smoothed by the waters of time. What appears so clearly on the display board of the face in early childhood is masked through the process of socialization and the accretion of scripted mechanisms for affect modulation. By the time we reach adulthood, the innate affect shame-humiliation rarely if ever appears by itself, for so thoroughly has it become admixed with self-

Table 2.

PATTERNS OF RESPONSE TO SHAME AFFECT: THE COMPASS OF SHAME

Point of Compass	Style of Operation	Range of Action	Sexuality	Auxiliary Affects	Treatment
Withdrawal	Shame affect as such	Hiding to depression	Impotence; frigidity	Distress; fear	Identify affect
Attack self	Avoid helplessness	Deference to masochism	Masochism	Distress self-disgust; self-dissmell	Define; support; replace
Avoidance	Prevent the affect	Cover-up to drugs	Machismo	Excitement: anger	Define; support; identify
Attack other	Avoid inferiority	Put-down to sadism	Sadism	Anger; dissmell; disgust	Support; define; replace

Source: Nathanson, 1994b.

dissmell and self-disgust, the other affects of rejection, that for all practical purposes they are fused into one complex amalgam.

There really is no simple, discrete emotional experience we can call "shame." The range of situations made salient by the action of the physiological program Tomkins has defined as the innate affect shame-humiliation is far too wide to be understood as one "emotion." In reality, there are four clusters of shame-related affective experience, differing from each other on the basis of source, previous life experience, and scripted response. The poles of the compass of shame are script libraries responsible for emotionality of four quite different types; within each pole lie the scripts for behaviors and emotional experiences that are benign and quite "normal," as well as some of the most devastatingly pathological ways of life available to the human. To complicate matters still more, each of these scripts may be brought into play when shame affect is triggered or simulated by disorders of biology—the sort of malfunctions now treated with the selective serotonin reuptake inhibitor antidepressants fluoxetine, paroxetine, and sertraline. Even the quaint old term "depression" takes on new meaning when one recognizes that the more-or-less constant experience of any negative affect is "depressing" (Nathanson, 1994c).

The affect theory of Silvan Tomkins provides the link between the biology of the brain and the emotional experiences we study as clinicians. Shame, the built-in inhibitor of positive affect, as an analogue of that impediment can come to limit or interfere with the expression of any affect, any drive, any form of perception or method of synthesis. It is with this new theory that we enter the second century of scientific psychotherapy and hope to provide ever more sophisticated remedies for emotional discomfort.

REFERENCES

Basch, M. F. (1976), The concept of affect: A re-examination. *J. Amer. Psychoanal. Assn.*, 24:759–778.
——— (1988), *Understanding Psychotherapy*. New York: Basic Books.
Demos, V. (1988), Affect and the development of the self: A new frontier. In: *Frontiers in Self Psychology: Progress in Self Psychology, Vol. 3*, ed. A. Goldberg. Hillsdale, NJ: The Analytic Press, pp. 27–54.
Freud, S. (1914), On narcissism: An introduction. *Standard Edition*, 14:73–102. London: Hogarth Press, 1957.

———— (1915), Instincts and their vicissitudes. *Standard Edition*, 14:117–140. London: Hogarth Press, 1957.

Hillman, J. (1961), *Emotion*. Evanston, IL: Northwestern University Press.

Lewis, H. B. (1971), *Shame and Guilt in Neurosis*. New York: International Universities Press.

Mowrer, D. H. (1939), Stimulus response theory of anxiety. *Psycholog. Rev.*, 46:553–565.

Nathanson, D. L. (1983), Affect, affective resonance, and a new theory for hypnosis. *Psychopathol.*, 21:126–137.

———— (1992), *Shame and Pride*. New York: Norton.

———— (1994a), Shame transactions. *Transactional Anal. J.*, 24:121–129.

———— (1994b), Shame, compassion, and the "borderline" personality. *Psychiatric Clin. North Amer.*, 17:785–810.

———— (1994c), The case against depression. *Bull. Tomkins Inst.*, 1:9–11.

Sartre, J. P. (1948), *The Emotions*. New York: Philosophicl Library.

Stern, D. N. (1985), *The Interpersonal World of the Infant*. New York: Basic Books.

Tomkins, S. S. (1963a), *Affect Imagery Consciousness, Vol. 2*. New York: Springer.

———— (1963b), Simulation of personality: The interrelations between affect, memory, thinking, perception, and action. In: *Computer Simulation of Personality*. ed. S. Tomkins & S. Messick. New York: Wiley, pp. 3–57.

———— (1987), Shame. In: *The Many Faces of Shame*, ed. D. Nathanson. New York: Guilford, pp. 133–161.

Wurmser, L. (1981), *The Mask of Shame*. Baltimore, MD: Johns Hopkins University Press.

THOMAS J. SCHEFF
SUZANNE M. RETZINGER

5

Helen Block Lewis on Shame: Appreciation and Critique

In her pathbreaking study of sequences of emotions in psychotherapy sessions, Lewis (1971) discovered a microworld underlying even seemingly innocuous discourse. In this little world, shame is king. As a microscope reveals a jungle of flora and fauna in a drop of water, so Lewis found that human contact is haunted by hidden shame. She discovered a path through the jungle by coding cues to shame in verbatim transcripts of psychotherapy sessions. Although her work is not widely understood, it provides a unique entry into the world of shame.

Like most established shame scholars, Lewis considered shame to include many variants and cognates. Darwin (1872), Elias (1978), Tomkins (1963), and many others treated shame as a large and complex *family* of emotions, which they understood to include embarrassment, shyness, and humiliation. Schneider (1977) noted that all European languages except English have two versions of shame. One denotes disgrace (in German *schande*; in French *honte*). The other means modesty, shyness, or awe (in German *scham*: in French *pudeur*). The European usage is important for a broad approach, because disgrace-shame is visible only in crises, but, in its latter meaning, the shame of modesty and shyness is a part of everyday life.

The domain of shame as Lewis (1971) conceived it was especially large, including even guilt as a complex affect that involves a shame component. This orientation led her to detect and analyze the complex interaction between shame and guilt as they occur in verbatim transcripts of therapy sessions. The relationship between shame and guilt is one of the many sharply contested issues in the field.

Theories of emotion are seldom stated in a way that allows them to be tested, or even illustrated with examples. A useful general theory needs to specify *causal sequences,* which show the linkage between its concepts, and observable *markers.* Lewis's work implies a general theory of shame dynamics and is stated in a way that is amenable to testing and modification.

The most influential approach to human motivation is psychoanalytic theory, but as with most other general theories, its basic concepts are little more than metaphors. Central terms, such as the unconscious, repression, and the superego, are so vaguely defined that they remain hypothetical, even in discussions of case histories. The casual manner of the traditional psychoanalytic approach to theory and methods was in many ways ideal for beginning explorations of the nature of emotions. Had the tradition insisted on methodological rigor, Adler, Kohut, Lynd (1958), and other psychoanalysts might have been too inhibited to develop their far-ranging investigations. But for growth in knowledge to continue, more system and rigor is now required. Models of causal sequences are needed and internal states specified clearly enough so that their external manifestations can be detected in dialogue.

Psychoanalytic concepts have a hypothetical quality because they are not adequately defined. They represent internal states (such as anxiety), structures (such as the superego), and processes (such as repression) without specifying how we are to detect their manifestations in actual behavior. Lewis's work, especially her magnum opus *Shame and Guilt in Neurosis* (1971), suggests that detecting shame cues in verbatim texts may be an Ariadne's thread, guiding us through the labyrinth of the intra- and interpersonal world.

Lewis was in an ideal position to build on and extend the psychoanalytic tradition of exploring human emotions in great depth. She was trained as both psychoanalyst and research psychologist. Her background in systematic research methods enabled her to exploit the knowledge she gained in the practice of psychoanalysis, leading to her groundbreaking study of shame. What makes Lewis's work on shame and guilt so productive is that it is grounded in actual, concrete events. A comparison between Tomkins's idea of an *affect bind* (e.g., the shame-contempt bind) with Lewis's idea of a *feeling trap* illustrates this point. Since neither Tomkins nor Lewis clearly defined those ideas, as is characteristic of many discoverers, it might have been difficult if not impossible to be sure we know what they meant.

In this instance, Lewis's empiricism paid off; although she did not define a feeling trap, she showed many actual instances of it in the verbatim texts. What she meant from these instances is clear: a shame/anger feeling trap involves a long sequence of emotional reactions to emotional reactions. She showed that the affect of humiliated fury is produced by being angry that one is ashamed, and ashamed that one is angry, and so on. Such sequences can have a self-perpetuating quality, as we suggest later,

Tomkins may have meant something similar by his concept of an affect bind. But since he neither defined affect binds nor illustrated them with concrete examples, there may be no way of clarifying his intention.

When it comes to understanding human motivation, details are extraordinarily important. When qualitative (case history) and quantitative studies gloss over the details, as most of them do, it becomes almost impossible for the reader to learn from them. On the other hand, verbatim texts and transcripts empower the reader, who is able to interpret them anew, even if they have been interpreted in earlier studies. Verbatim texts preserve the voice of the subject for all eternity, even if it was muffled by earlier interpretations.

Unlike virtually any other researcher in the human sciences, Lewis is both *interpretive* (she made complex inferences about thoughts and feelings) and *systematic*, in that she used a standard coding procedure (Gottschalk, Wingert, and Gleser, 1969) for detecting hidden emotions in verbal texts. This combination turned out to be particularly appropriate for constructing a wide-ranging theory of shame in its interactional context.

Lewis's (1971) main discoveries can be summarized under five headings:

1. *Prevalence of Shame.* In the several hundred sessions she coded, shame was overwhelmingly the most prevalent emotion, far outranking anxiety, pride, love, anger, grief, and fear, the nearest competitors. Her work implies that shame dominates most psycho-therapeutic work. Typical patients are already having difficulty in managing shame in their life before they come to therapy. In therapy, a new burden of shame may be added: they are to tell their shameful secrets to a stranger. Unless the therapist is exquisitely sensitive to this issue, a patient's burden of shame may be increased rather than decreased by therapy.

Finding the overwhelming prevalence of shame in sessions was not a subjective judgment on Lewis's part. She used a coding system (Gottschalk et al., 1969) that includes the primary emotions: anger, shame, fear, grief, contempt, disgust. In her coding of the transcripts, shame was the only emotion she detected regularly and repeatedly in every transcript. Her major study demonstrated that shame is the dominant emotion in the sessions she studied.

2. *Unconscious Shame.* Lewis's study showed that important emotions occur outside the patient's awareness. In most writing about emotion, the opposite assumption is often made: no awareness, no emotion. In an attempt to bridge these two worlds, Lewis used an ambiguous phrase to described the type of emotion she discovered to be endemic in clinical transcripts: *unacknowledged* shame. This concept does not distinguish between shame experienced by the patients, but not expressed, and unconscious shame, which was neither experienced nor expressed. Lewis's actual findings suggest, however, that in the overwhelming majority of instances, the patient was unaware of her or his shame. One does not have to *feel* ashamed—be aware—to be in a state of shame.

Lewis found that unacknowledged shame could occur in two seemingly opposite formats: *overt, undifferentiated* shame and *bypassed* shame. In the case of overt shame, there is conscious awareness of emotional pain, usually accompanied by unwanted physical manifestations, such as blushing, rapid heart beat, or sweating. However, the emotion is *denied* through misnaming: shame is disguised through the use of codewords such as feeling "insecure," "uncomfortable," "weird," "hurt" (Gottschalk et al., 1969; Retzinger, 1991).

For example, instead of saying that one is embarrassed, one says, "It was an awkward moment for me." There are two kinds of misnaming involved in this sentence, denial of shame, and projecting from inside one's self to the outer world: "It was not *I* who was embarrassed; it was the *moment* that was awkward." Lewis (1971) called this kind of shame overt and undifferentiated (pp. 196-197). Shame affect is overt or available to consciousness but the person experiencing it either will not or cannot identify it. At the moment that the person himself says, "I am ashamed," shame affect is likely to be diminishing. An observer may identify that the other person is having a shame reaction, or the person himself may identify it as it is receding, but while shame is occurring the person is unable to communicate.

In the second type of unacknowledged shame, which Lewis called bypassed, there is little awareness of emotional pain. Except for a very brief wince or gasp, feelings are immediately blanked out. Emotional pain is hidden from self and others by thought, speech, or behavior that is rapid and fluent but has a quality of obsession and repetition. Persons who describe this state often report an absence of feeling, or feeling neutral, blank, hollow, numb, or "spaced out." Lewis (1971) described this state as follows: "The person is aware of the cognitive content of shame-connected events, but experiences only a 'wince,' 'blow,' or 'jolt.' . . . the person's experience proceeds smoothly, except for a peripheral, nonspecific disturbance in awareness, which serves mainly to note the shame potential in the circumstance. The ideation of bypassed shame involves doubt about the self's image from the 'other's' viewpoint" (p. 197). In bypassed shame, one does not allow the feeling of shame to develop. Instead, one wards it off by rapid mental, verbal, or behavioral moves.

Compulsive replaying of a scene in what Lewis called "the interior theater" of the mind is one of the most frequent defenses against bypassed shame. An example was recalled by a male student: "Walking across campus, I was gloating over how witty I had just been in a casual conversation with an acquaintance. But I groaned aloud when I realized that the woman I had made fun of was his ex-girlfriend and that they were still close. I kept thinking of what a fool I am, of what he must think of me, and of what I might have said instead. Come dinner and bedtime, I was still doing it." Bypassed shame refuses to subside. This type of shame, however, is not manifested as bodily feelings but, rather, as compulsive cognitive activity.

Lewis inferred shame states of these two types by noting a recurring *context* of shame, situations in which patients seemed to feel criticized or rejected, in many cases, by the therapist. In such contexts, she noted the two different patterns of reaction. That is, in all contexts involving unacknowledged shame, she saw either one or the other pattern.

It appears to us that the term *unconscious* would have been preferable to Lewis's term, unacknowledged. One learns, through long practice, to avoid the pain of feeling humiliated or unworthy, the feeling that the self is useless or disintegrating, by misnaming the feeling (overt shame) or by becoming hyperactive in thought, fantasy, speech, or action. In the obsessive (bypassed) defense against shame, one creates a project, real or imaginary, involving money, sex, power, fame, or some other attribute so involving that one is able to distract one's attention from the direct feeling of shame. After thousands of repetitions, especially in childhood, the project takes on a compulsive, automatic quality. One is obsessed.

3. *Feeling Traps.* In her careful coding of emotions in therapeutic dialogue, Lewis showed that they often occurred in rapid sequence. A normal shame episode seems to be very brief, a few seconds at most. (Ekman and Friesen, 1975, have suggested that all normal

emotions have short durations.) But in Lewis's study, many shame episodes were much longer.

These lengthy episodes seem to involve emotional reactions to one's emotional reactions, One can become angry about being ashamed, and then ashamed of being angry, and so on. Darwin (1872), like many others who have commented on shame, noted that shame is the most social and reflexive of emotions, when he explained how blushing itself can cause further blushing. Shame always involves viewing the self from the point of view of the other, which occurs in the internal theater as the self viewing itself. The potential for reflexive loops of shame, of runaway self-consciousness, is therefore high. This characteristic gives rise to the possibility of feedback loops reaching unlimited intensities and durations.

As already indicated, Tomkins (1963) noted the potential for loops of shame, with itself and with other emotions. His principle of *contagion* includes both internal and social loops (p. 296). Like most of his theory, however, this idea is treated only abstractly, without even hypothetical examples. Lewis's approach to the reflexiveness of shame, since it was tied to verbatim texts, implies an exact model of pathological emotions and social relationships.

At many points in the sessions she studied, Lewis (1971) found that when shame was evoked it developed into such lengthy sequences that she called them feeling traps. The most common loop that she noted was both intra- and interpersonal. The patient and the therapist would become entangled in an exchange that involved hostility on both sides, often followed by withdrawal or silence by the patient. For example, a patient might feel rejected or criticized by a comment or interpretation by the therapist. The patient would show brief indications of shame, then of anger. The anger would seldom be expressed directly, but indirectly and covertly as impatience, sarcasm, veiled criticism, withdrawal. This cycle, of shame→anger→aggression (or withdrawal) by one party, leading to a similar cycle in the other, and so on occurred in many of the sessions Lewis studied. (For a detailed analysis of a spiral between one patient and her therapist in Lewis's study that extended over many sessions, see Scheff, 1987). Lewis (1971) called the resulting affect shame-rage or humiliated fury: "Shame evokes retaliatory rage at the 'other' or at the witness, but since it is shame-rage, hostility is quickly directed back upon the self by guilt. In this characteristic pattern, hostility evoked in shame is trapped against the self both by the passivity of the self and by the person's value for the other" (p. 198).

The affect of helpless anger, important in Labov and Fanshel's (1976) analysis of a therapy session, may be a variant shame-anger sequence. In quarrels, the anger episodes in the cycle are overt. But anger can be disguised in the form of sarcasm, abruptness, or even pained resignation (Retzinger, 1991). This is the form that anger seems to take in helpless anger.

The most significant point of Lewis's analysis is that when shame is acknowledged it does not develop into endless spirals. One implication is that *irrational aggression is caused by unacknowledged shame*. (For preliminary support from an experimental study, see Tangney, 1992. Scheff's (1994) study of the origins of the two World Wars supports this hypothesis when applied to large-scale conflict.) This same sequence was discovered, independently of Lewis's work, in a study of the text of Shakespeare's *King Lear*. Zak (1984) demonstrated that the suffering and destruction of Lear and most of the other major characters was self-inflicted; Lear, Gloucester, Edmund, Edgar, and other major characters denied and disguised their own shame. Only Cordelia, the Fool, and, in part, Kent, acknowledged shame.

Zak's interpretation puts the play in an entirely new light, since historically it has usually been seen as implying a hostile and unforgiving universe. (In a widely known interpretation, Cavell, 1987, proposed that shame was central to the play, but he treats the failure of acknowledgment less directly than Zak does.)

4. *Shame and the Social Bond*.   Lewis's approach implies a basic social and psychological context for shame: the experience of being *disconnected* from self or others. This idea is the basic thesis of Lewis's (1977) discussion of male and female emotions. Similarly, pride signals, and is generated by, the feeling of being *connected* with self and others.

Disconnection can take two forms: the first is feeling excluded or invisible (for example, in a conversation with two friends, one notices that they look more often at each other than at oneself.) The second form is feeling exposed or invaded by the other(s), as if one is so worthless that the boundaries of oneself are under another's control rather than one's own control. This idea connects shame contexts with concepts of social relationships.

Lewis's work on shame illuminates current theories of family systems, particularly Bowen's (1978) conceptualization of undifferentiated relationships. He argued that pathological relationships involve either too much focus on the relationship or too little. What he called *fusion* (isolation) involves relationships in which participants give up their own points of view and needs to the relationship. In *cut-off* (engulfment), the participants are too little concerned with the relationship. These patterns are reported with great frequency in studies of family systems. Bowen's ideas can be directly related to the types of shame situations mentioned earlier: the shame of feeling invisible or rejected corresponds to an isolated relationship: the shame of feeling invaded or exposed, to an engulfed one.

Patterns of interaction in families often involve subtle issues that can be understood only by close attention to gestures, context and mood. Crucial patterns are embedded in the familial context, in a way that is difficult to fit into experimental or survey designs, or even conventional case studies. Lewis's approach to shame through discourse is sensitive to context and to the particular relationship that is formed between therapist and patient.

5. *Shame in Treatment Failure.* As outlined, Lewis's main findings were the vast prevalence of shame in psychotherapy sessions; that it almost always goes unacknowledged and can therefore can lead to interminable loops of shame and anger or to withdrawal; and, finally, that unacknowledged shame disrupts social bonds. These findings are the basis for her conclusion that unacknowledged shame may be the principal cause of treatment failure (Lewis, 1987).

Lewis's interest in shame as a cause of treatment failure was generated initially by her own work as a therapist. She reported that she had had many treatment failures as an orthodox psychoanalyst but that, when she began to analyze the patient's shame, her effectiveness increased dramatically. She has also indicated that the length of psychoanalysis could be drastically shortened by focusing on shame (personal communication). Understanding the importance of shame in her own work as analyst, she could document its centrality with her research. The pervasiveness of unacknowledged shame leads to feeling traps, which in turn result in quarrels or withdrawal. These developments prove to be profoundly threatening to or disruptive of the bond between therapist and patient. Without a secure bond, therapy falters or fails outright.

CRITIQUE

Lewis's findings have not been equally accessible to a large audience. The first idea, the possibility that shame dominates most psychotherapy sessions, is perhaps the mostly widely accepted. It has been explicitly proposed in treatises on shame by Wurmser (1981),

Broucek (1991), Goldberg (1991), M. Lewis (1992), Nathanson (1992) and in other recent works. Although only implied, Goffman's (1967) widely known work on impression management, back and front stages, and interaction ritual implies that shame (he calls it embarrassment) or the anticipation of shame dominates most human interaction of all types, not just psychotherapy (explicitly treated in his discussion of the social functions of embarrassment).

The second finding, that shame usually occurs outside of awareness, has been less discussed than the first. The idea of bypassed or unconscious shame is particularly counterintuitive. Since overt, undifferentiated shame corresponds in some ways to our usual understanding of this emotion as being intense and having highly visible manifestations such as blushing, sweating, heart palpitations, and the like, the idea that it is often mislabeled is one that many people are willing to consider.

The idea that shame can be completely unconscious seems to go against a widely held assumption about emotion: that it is always felt or experienced. Lewis, as already indicated, argued that one can be in a state of shame without feeling *ashamed*. It may be that resistance to this idea is responsible for the lack of widespread appreciation of Lewis's work. Certainly her fourth finding, that there is an intimate connection between shame and the social bond, has attracted little attention. The same can be said for the last finding listed here, that unacknowledged shame may account for most treatment failures, although there has been some interest in this idea among therapists.

The method that Lewis used in her basic study may also have made her work inaccessible. Her extremely detailed examination of transcripts, which would now would be called discourse analysis, seems to be off-putting to academics and clinicians alike. Her method is novel and is recognized by neither quantitative nor qualitative researchers. The design of her study is not systematic enough for one camp and is too systematic and detailed for the other. Clinicians react in a way similar to the qualitative researchers: they don't see the purpose of the precise detail.

Lewis's approach itself seems to be responsible for some of the difficulties. Since it was developed as she went along, there are gaps and flaws that make her findings and their implications less accessible than they might be. One problem is that, although Lewis's method was explicit and systematic, her theory was never stated explicitly. Without a clearly stated theoretical framework, the reader may become lost in the masses of detail. To make Lewis's work more accessible, all the key concepts should be defined: unacknowledged shame in its two forms, overt and bypassed; feeling traps; and the social bond (Retzinger, 1991; Scheff and Retzinger, 1991; Scheff, 1994). Additional attention needs to be given to several other features of Lewis's approach.

Acknowledgment of Shame

One clear implication of Tavuchis's (1991) work is that Lewis's treatment of the process of *acknowledgment* of emotions was greatly oversimplified. Although she might have known that to be acknowledged and discharged, emotions must be worked through along biologically, psychologically, and socially appropriate paths, this complexity does not come through in her writing. Tavuchis notes that a genuine apology is more than saying that one is sorry (the easy part); one must also *feel* sorry (the hard part). An effective apology also involves a complex coordination between self and other, the person to whom one apologizes. The apology must come at the right time and place and with the right timing and the right feelings on the part of the other. Acknowledging one's shame seems to involve a similar conjunction between verbal and nonverbal elements, between self and other.

Except for psychanalytic discussions of working through, which remain somewhat vague, there is little discussion of the conjunction of inner and outer, self and other elements anywhere in the literature, let alone careful studies. Lewis's descriptions of shame therapy are similarly vague. Although Lewis used her theory effectively as an analyst, she never wrote a clear description of shame therapy. (Perhaps the most detailed description to date is found in Goldberg, 1991.)

Shame Loops

Since Lewis nowhere discounts it, readers may get the idea that unacknowledged shame always leads to anger and hostility. The possibility of a second kind of self-perpetuating loop of shame (being ashamed of being ashamed, and on and on and on), leading to lengthy shame-shame cycles, is not mentioned by Lewis but is implied in the work of Elias (1978) on the history of manners in Europe. Analyzing verbatim excerpts from European etiquette manuals that ranged over hundreds of years, from the late Middle Ages until the end of the 19th century, his work suggests that shame was increasingly unacknowledged both in advice on behavior and, by implication, in behavior itself.

Elias's work implies that reflexive loops of shame may be much more prevalent than shame-anger. For example, in the European context, increasing shame about sexuality, and denial of that shame, might lead not only to anger but also to further shame. This conjecture may help to explain what appears to be a bifurcation of male and female sexuality in Western societies: a shame/anger feeling trap for men, a shame/shame feeling trap for women. Male bypassing of shame could lead to the machismo syndrome and sexual violence; female overt shame loops to late-blooming sexuality or, in more extreme form, passivity or withdrawal.

The idea of shame-shame loops also fits well with the distinction Adler (1956) made between two types of defenses against rejection: the inferiority complex (shame-shame loops as the dominant personality characteristic) and the drive for power (shame-anger as dominant).

Normal and Pathological Shame

Although the idea is implicit in her work, Lewis did not clearly distinguish between normal and pathological shame. Normal shame can be considered to be a brief but extremely important emotion. Although it is painful, it is an automatic, instantaneous warning signal of moral trespass or inappropriate *distance* from other(s).

The role of shame in regulating distance may be a key to understanding all social relationships. If one comes too close to us, we feel invaded or exposed—a shame state; if one stays too far from us, we feel rejected or invisible—another shame state. Embarrassment and shame signals help regulate social distance; they provide an instant and continuous readout of the "temperature" of a relationship, of the state of the bond. If shame signals are suppressed or ignored, we cannot tell where we stand with the other. Normal shame may be crucial in developing and maintaining understanding and trust, which are the ingredients of a secure bond. In this scheme, all social relationships depend on the expression and effective monitoring of normal shame.

In contrast to normal shame, pathological shame may be extremely long in duration and isolating or destructive in effect. It involves loops of emotional reactions to emotional reactions such as shame-anger, shame-shame, shame-fear (panic, anxiety attacks) or shame-grief (unresolved grief).

As already indicated, the importance of pathological shame is implicit in Adler's (1956) description of the relationship between the child's bonds to its family and later adult personality. He proposed that a child needs love (at least one secure bond) at critical points in its growth. If not, the child develops in one of two directions: an "inferiority" complex (chronic overt, undifferentiated shame) or "striving for power" (bypassed shame).

What is missing from Adler's scheme is a model that specifies causal links and external cues. The Lewis approach implies such a model. The child who lacks adequate familial bonds will not learn to cope with shame, which arises inevitably in social life from situations of rejection, error, and failure. For this reason, the child is likely to become shame prone and easily entangled in intra- and interpersonal shame loops. Lewis's approach suggests a model for the development of shame proneness and low self-esteem.

Pride and Shame Relation

Another problem with Lewis's treatment of shame is that, like most of the other authorities, she fails to pair it with its opposite, pride. Both shame and pride dynamics are needed for an understanding of levels of self-esteem. The omission of prideful contacts is particularly disastrous in Goffman's (1967) analyses, inasmuch as they ostensibly concern normal interaction. Since most of Lewis's research concerns psychotherapy sessions, we are free to imagine that, although such meetings are awash in shame, most social interaction is not. (For an explicit pairing of pride and shame, see Wurmser, 1981.) High self-esteem is not just the capable management of shame, it also implies the substantial presence of justifiable pride.

A glimpse of behavior that suggests high self-esteem is afforded by the therapist in the Labov and Fanshel (1977) study. In the beginning of the hour, the patient (Rhoda) delivers a minor insult by failing to greet her properly. The therapist simply ignores this behavior. Rhoda quickly follows up with a more complex and intense insult, implying that the therapist is incompetent. The therapist shows clear but brief signs of anger at this point. After only a few seconds, however, she simply reiterates her original question. Rhoda, who appears to have had no experience with authority figures other than with shame-anger loops, is clearly puzzled by an authority who does not retaliate in kind. Rhoda is jolted out of her usual interpersonal routines. The therapist's ability to sidestep Rhoda's insults may have been a key to the success of this particular session and to subsequent ones.

Another example of what seems to be high self-esteem is suggested by an episode on *Candid Camera* between the star Alan Funt and a young boy (he appears to be six or seven years old). Funt discovers that the boy, until this point enormously self-assured, cannot pronounce a word correctly; he says "pusgetti" instead of spaghetti. Funt proceeds to taunt the boy, producing the beginnings of fluster and embarrassment. The boy, however, very quickly recovers his poise by the use of a tactic that seems inspired. When it becomes clear that Funt will not leave his mispronunciation alone, the child simply smiles, leans forward toward Funt, repeating the mispronounced word so many times and with such emphasis that he (the boy) begins to laugh. He made his mistake into a game by exaggerating it. ("You want mistakes? I'll give you mistakes!") Tactics like this may be the hope of the world. Like Rhoda's therapist and like the Spaghetti Boy, we all may need to find devices that allow us, as individuals and as groups, to avoid or extricate ourselves from loops of shame.

Elsewhere, we (Scheff, 1990; Scheff and Retzinger, 1991; Retzinger, 1991; Scheff, 1994) have suggested that interminable conflict between individuals and between groups (destructive family conflicts, duels, feuds, and wars) are caused by the denial of interdependency and the denial of shame. In this reading, it is not simply alienation (lack of community) and shame that leads to conflict, but the denial of alienation and of shame.

Countertransference

Lewis (1971) discovered that "shame in the patient-therapist *relationship* was a special contributor to the negative therapeutic reaction" (p. 11, italics added). In part, her interest in shame "stemmed from the *discomforts* of the analyst in the patient-therapist relationship" (14, italics added). Lewis has shown that one unresolved aspect of transference is bypassed shame which is easily overlooked (bypassed shame is unconscious). This idea may apply equally to countertransference.

Shame can be used to unpack the concept of countertransference and provide a tool for treatment. Excessive shame (embarrassment, discomfort, etc.) in the therapeutic session may indicate that the bond is in need of repair. If the therapist can tolerate his or her own shame, as well as the patient's, growth can occur for both client and therapist; if a therapist cannot acknowledge his or her own shame and the patient's, the patient's shame experiences may be transformed into derogatory thoughts about the therapy and shameful images about the self as a patient (Lewis, 1971) and perhaps be viewed as resistance by the therapist. Resistance in itself is a misnomer for shame, as well as an expression of shame (Lewis, 1987).

Lewis began her work with the therapeutic relationship, but went on to analyze patient shame that occurred in the treatment of eight patients; four of whom were field independent and thus prone to guilt and four of whom were field dependent and thus prone to shame. Different symptoms emerged depending on cognitive style or proneness to shame or guilt; that is, depressive patients are more shame prone; obsessive-compulsive patients are more guilt prone. Lewis traces sequence of emotion from neurotic symptoms (often beginning with the patient's hostility) back to their source in unanalyzed shame.

Lewis falls short, however, in not providing an equal analysis of the therapist's feelings, that is, the effect of the patient on the therapist, which in turn affects the patient and the therapeutic relationship. The therapist's reactions can be a source of further shame for the patient (Scheff, 1987).

If shame is not acknowledged it disrupts behavior; both therapist and patient can go into a holding pattern, repeating routine responses rather than finding new responses to unique situations. Therapists can also have trouble maintaining neutrality when they find themselves caught in the throes of unacknowledged shame; patients may be either idealized or vilified, rather than seen as they are.

CONCLUSION

In this brief tribute to Helen Lewis, we have outlined some of the major implications of her pioneering work on shame and related emotions, such as guilt and embarrassment. We hope that this outline may at least hint that Lewis's approach and findings have major implications both for research and for clinical practice. It implies that verbatim transcripts of social interaction can provide a virtually untapped resource for studies of the role of emotion in human conduct. For the practice of psychotherapy and psychanalysis, Lewis's work suggests the need for a new approach focused on the role of pride and shame in the patient's life and in the therapeutic relationship.

REFERENCES

Adler, A. (1907-1936), *The Individual Psychology of Alfred Adler*. New York: Basic Books, 1956.

Bowen, M. (1978), *Family Therapy in Clinical Practice*. New York: Aronson.

Broucek, F. (1991), *Shame and the Self*. New York: Guilford.

Cavell, S. (1987), *Disowning Knowledge*. Cambridge: Cambridge University Press.

Darwin, C. (1872), *The Expression of Emotion in Men and Animals*. London: John Murray.

Ekman, P. & Friesen, W. (1975), *Unmasking the Face*. Englewood Cliffs, NJ: Prentice-Hall.

Elias, N. (1978), *The History of Manners*. New York: Pantheon.

Goffman, E. (1967), *Interaction Ritual*. New York: Anchor.

Goldberg, C. (1991), *Understanding Shame*. New York: Aronson.

Gottschalk, L., Wingert, C. & Gleser, G. (1969), *Manual of Instruction for Using the Gottschalk-Gleser Content Analysis Scales*. Berkeley: University of California Press.

Labov, W. & Fanshel, D. (1977), *Therapeutic Discourse*. New York: Academic Press.

Lewis, H. B. (1971). *Shame and Guilt in Neurosis*. New York: International Universities Press.

_____ (1976), *Psychic War in Men and Women*. New York: New York University Press.

_____ (1987), *The Role of Shame in Symptom Formation*. Hillsdale, NJ: Lawrence Erlbaum Associates.

Lewis, M. (1992), *Shame: The Exposed Self*. New York: Free Press.

Lynd, H. (1958), *On Shame and the Search for Identity*. New York: Harcourt.

Nathanson, D. (1992), *Shame and Pride*. New York: Norton.

Retzinger, S. (1991), *Violent Emotions*. Newbury Park, CA.: Sage.

_____ & Ryan, M. (1989), Crime, violence, and self-esteem. In: *The Social Importance of Self-Esteem*, ed. A. Mecca, N. Smelser & J. Vasconcellos. Berkeley: University of California Press, pp. 165–199.

Scheff, T. (1987), The shame-rage spiral: Case study of an interminable quarrel. In: *The Role of Shame in Symptom Formation*, ed. H. B. Lewis. Hillsdale, NJ: Lawrence Erlbaum Associates, pp. 109–149.

_____ (1990), *Microsociology*. Chicago: University of Chicago Press.

_____ (1994), *Bloody Revenge*. Boulder, CO: Westview Press.

_____ & Retzinger, S. (1991), *Emotions and Violence*. Lexington, MA: Lexington Books.

Schneider, C. (1977), *Shame, Exposure, and Privacy*. Boston: Beacon Press.

Tangney, J. (1992), Shamed into anger? The relation of shame and guilt to anger and self-reported aggression. *J. Personal & Social Psychol*, 62:669–675.

Tavuchis, N. (1991), *Mea Culpa: The Sociology of Apology and Other Remedial Actions*. Stanford, CA: Stanford University Press.

Tomkins, S. (1963), *Affect-Imagery-Consciousness, Vol. 2*. New York: Springer.

Wurmser, L. (1981), *The Mask of Shame*. Baltimore, MD: Johns Hopkins University Press.

Zak, W. (1984), *Sovereign Shame*. Lewisberg, PA: Bucknell University Press.

6

KAREN HANSON

Reasons for Shame, Shame Against Reason

Some philosophers are ashamed of shame. This position may be entered as a emancipatory strategy, as when Nietzsche (1974) ends Book Three of *The Gay Science* with this catechism:

Whom do you call bad?—Those who always want to put to shame. (#273)
What do you consider most humane?—To spare someone shame. (#274)
What is the seal of liberation?—No longer being ashamed in front of oneself [#275, p. 200].

Alternatively, the same conceptual pass may be reached by tying down more firmly the range of acceptable attitudes and behavior, as Aristotle (1984) does when he says that

[s]hame should not be described as an excellence; for it is more like a passion than a state. . . . [And this] passion is not becoming to every age, but only to youth. . . . [A]n older person no one would praise for being prone to the sense of disgrace, since we think he should not do anything that need cause this sense [p. 1781].

Other philosophers see shame as salutary. Descartes (1985), for example, claims that "[p]ride and shame have the same function, in that they move us to virtue, the one through hope and the other through anxiety" (p. 403). And even if virtue eludes us, some argue, it is still better, still becoming, even in maturity, to feel shame rather

155

than to feel none. So, while Spinoza (1955) would not exactly *praise* the older person feeling shame, he does say that

> shame, . . . though not a virtue, is yet good, in so far as it shows, that the feeler of shame is really imbued with the desire to live honourably; in the same way as suffering is good, as showing that the injured part is not mortified. Therefore, though a man who feels shame is sorrowful, he is yet more perfect than he, who is shameless, and has no desire to live honourably [p. 226].

It may be possible, thus, to take some pride in shame. A penultimate step along this route is almost taken by Pascal (1966), who in his tortured accounts of human nature—"What sort of freak then is man! How novel, how monstrous, how chaotic, how paradoxical, how prodigious! Judge of all things, feeble earthworm, repository of truth, sink of doubt and error, glory and refuse of the universe!" (p. 64)—begs us to look at ourselves and see our evident "disproportion" to the universe and the implications of our misfit: "If it is not true, there is no truth in man, and if it is true, he has good cause to feel humiliated; in either case he is obliged to humble himself" (p. 88) If we reflect honestly and reason properly, we are thoroughly humiliated; but that exercise in humiliation discloses our central claim to dignity: "Man's greatness comes from knowing he is wretched: a tree does not know it is wretched. Thus it is wretched to know that one is wretched, but there is greatness in knowing one is wretched" (p. 59).

If one moves further in this direction of thought and feeling, one can turn self-abnegation into self-assertion. Augustine (1961), for example, is sometimes accused of this, of revealing pride while confessing shame. In his boyhood and youth he was not just wretched but especially vile, particularly abominable: "I was blind to the whirlpool of debasement in which I had been plunged away from the sight of your eyes. For in your eyes nothing could be more debased than I was then. . . . " (p. 39). A fork in this path of pride seems to lead one strangely full circle, to an almost Nietzschean freedom, to an embrace of shame that amounts to shamelessness.

The prospect that one may be empowered by wholeheartedly owning, or owning up to, one's shame is, however, more than a bit opaque, and it deserves more careful scrutiny. John Rawls describes shame as "the feeling that someone has when he experiences an injury to his self-respect or suffers a blow to his self-esteem" (p. 442). Now, if this characterization is at all plausible, and if, as many moral philosophers claim, self-respect is a necessary condition for active participation in the moral life, for appropriate participation in social affairs, shame tends to harm, never to enhance, our vitality. As Rawls puts it, self-respect is a—perhaps the most important—"primary good," (p. 62) something every rational person is presumed to want, no matter what else he or she wants, no matter his or her interests, plans, or projects. According to Rawls, shame is painful precisely because it involves a loss of self-respect, and without self-respect "nothing may seem worth doing, or if some things have value for us, we lack the will to strive for them. All desire and activity becomes empty and vain, and we sink into apathy and cynicism" (p. 440).

Nietzsche, too, has profound doubts about the idea of pride purchased through humiliation, and many of his expressions of misgiving focus specifically on the thought of Pascal. The abjectness required by Pascal's religious faith is, according to Nietzsche (1972), in some way *thrilling*, but that faith also "resembles in a terrible fashion a protracted suicide of reason—of a tough, long-lived, wormlike reason which is not to be killed instantaneously with a single blow" (p. 47). If reason is kept alive, what does it say about shame? And if we in our lives are to retain or develop full vigor, how should we handle shame?

REASON AGAINST SHAME

Philosophers have often tried to use reason to evaluate shame—to judge its general character and its function and appropriateness in specific circumstances—and they have sometimes also sought to secure for reason a sphere of operations insulated from any threat of shame. Kant's moral philosophy might be understood as a signal case of this second aspiration, and his enormous influence has surely, if often covertly, helped shape many modern versions of the first agenda.[1]

The Kantian assurance that morality is founded on reason alone, not on passions, interests, or affections and certainly not on social reactions and conventions; the Kantian insistence that the only thing

---

[1]The poet Heine famously speaks of Kant's "world-destroying thought," but Immanuel Kant does more than sweep away preceding understandings of reason and the world and our situation within or in opposition to the world. Kant's work in metaphysics and morals is crucial for modern Western philosophy; it would be difficult to overestimate his influence. Lewis White Beck (1965) offers one summary of this influence by citing what he calls a philosophers' adage: "You can philosophize with Kant or against Kant, but you cannot philosophize without him" (p. 3).

unconditionally good is a good will; and the import of the Kantian claim that a good will is autonomous—these crucial elements of his thought produce an account of the moral life from which shame is simply banished. Insofar as one is moved to or restrained from action because of the feeling of shame, insofar as one is interested in acquiring or retaining a good reputation, insofar as one's behavior is shaped or controlled by thoughts of how others will view it, to that extent one does not yet, according to Kant, participate in morality. Kant's law of morality, the categorical imperative, is determined by a priori reason; and reason—not prudence or social interests or sensitivity—is the sole principle of the good will.[2] While some philosophers try to distinguish various kinds of shame and then seek to identify from among these types one sort that might count as a distinctively moral emotion, it seems that on the Kantian account there is no such thing as moral shame.

Kant's insistence that morality must be grounded in reason alone does not proceed from a position of utter naivete about the personal and social forces that may in fact operate in the practical affairs of

---

[2]Kant (1959) contrasts what he calls "hypothetical imperatives" with what he says is the law of morality, the categorical imperative, by describing the former as commanding various actions as "good to some purpose." Hypothetical imperatives "present the practical necessity of a possible action as a means to achieving something else which one desires (or which one may possibly desire)" (p. 31). Thus, "If you want to make money in the stock market, buy low and sell high" is a hypothetical imperative, and so is "If you want to be accepted in the best circles, mind your manners." Each commands an action, but only as a means to an end one might be presumed to want. Still, the first action is required only if one takes as one's purpose making money in the stock market, the second only if one aims to be accepted in the best circles. "If you do not want to bring shame upon yourself, do not make promises you cannot keep" is likewise a hypothetical imperative. The avoidance of shame may or may not be one's guiding purpose.

Moral laws are not, however, according to Kant, discovered through experience, and they do not depend on our individual predilections: "moral laws should hold for every rational being as such" (p. 28). Moral concepts thus "have their seat and origin entirely in a priori reason" (p. 28). "[D]uty is practical unconditional necessity of action" (p. 43); it does not depend on our feelings, inclinations, social proclivities or natural propensities. The objective necessity of the law of morality is given, Kant says, only in the categorical imperative: "Act only according to that maxim by which you can at the same time will that it should become a universal law" (p. 39).

life. For an act to have moral worth, according to Kant, it must be done out of duty; but, Kant (1959) admits, it is

> absolutely impossible by experience to discern with complete certainty a single case in which the maxim of an action, however much it may conform to duty, rested solely on moral grounds and on the conception of one's duty. It sometimes happens that in the most searching self-examination we can find nothing except the moral ground of duty which could have been powerful enough to move us to this or that good action and to such great sacrifice. . . . [B]ut even the strictest examination can never lead us entirely behind the secret incentives, for, when moral worth is in question, it is not a matter of actions which one sees but of their inner principles which one does not see [p. 23].

This difficulty about our experience and discernment suggests to Kant that our first question cannot be the empirical one, "Is there true virtue anywhere in the world?" The prior question, *obviously* prior, according to Kant, is, "What *is* virtue?"; and it is reason, not experience, that must be called upon to answer this question: "Our concern is with actions of which perhaps the world has never had an example, with actions whose feasibility might be seriously doubted by those who base everything on experience, and yet with actions inexorably commanded by reason" (p. 24). Kant then illustrates the reasonableness of his concern by offering a logical analysis of a social virtue: sincerity in friendship can be demanded of everyone, and this demand is not in the least diminished even if a completely sincere friend has never existed.

Kant acknowledges that the pure a priori philosophy of morals will have to be applied and that this application will require something he calls "anthropology." The empirical facts of our lives do not, however, soften or transform the requirements of morality. Practical rules are described as wholly derivable from moral principles, and the latter remain grounded in reason alone. The effect of the Kantian account is that morality is protected from the frailties and contingencies of our individual and communal lives. Reason stands firm as a buffer not only against a corrupt or confused social world and against corrosive or misguided emotions but also against, in the end, the social world and emotions *tout court*.

The idea that reason can thus block, in particular, the moral weight of shame is at least as old as Socrates, but this assurance has a different edge in some modern moral philosophy. When Crito begs the condemned Socrates to escape from prison, part of Crito's desperate appeal takes the form of arguing that Socrates' inaction will disgrace both Socrates and his friends. Crito is in fact already ashamed. First, he says, there was the embarrassment of these matters' having been brought to public trial; second, there was the conduct of the defense; and now there is the impending execution, which if carried out will reflect badly on all of them. Everyone knows that with a little courage and a few bribes, Socrates' friends could have helped, could still help him to escape. If they don't save him, if he doesn't agree to save himself, their friendship will seem worthless and they will seem cowards. Socrates says, in turn, that he appreciates Crito's warm feelings, but that he cannot "accept advice . . . unless reflection shows that it is the best course that reason offers" (Plato, p. 33). He reminds Crito of their shared conviction that only some opinions should be taken seriously, that "what we ought to consider is not so much what people in general will say about us but how we stand with the expert in right and wrong, the one authority, who represents the actual truth" (p. 23).

Reason here distinguishes opinions that matter from those that do not, and reason dismisses the force of ill-conceived public disapprobation, thus dissolving its sting. Reason and a clear perception of the truth are the ultimate arbiters, so external opinion really only matters at all insofar as it accords with the truth. But true opinion *does* still matter. Reason may show us that some feelings of shame are inappropriate, but it does not show us that shame is a morally inappropriate feeling.

Socrates is admired today, as he was over 2,000 year ago, as a model of reason and autonomy. Nonetheless, some modern conceptions of autonomy seem to go well beyond any notions represented in or articulated by the Socratic dialogues, and those conceptions may have an effect when contemporary philosophers offer their versions of the relation between shame and reason. The 20th-century American philosopher Arnold Isenberg may serve as an interesting, if extreme, case in point. He can, in fact, be used as a kind of stalking horse, both to follow traces of the Kantian legacy in modern moral philosophy and to capture a sense of the prodigality of philosophy's defenses against shame.

It is worth remarking at the outset that philosophers may find surprising the distinction Isenberg draws between pride and shame, and they may go on to find compelling or inadequate the grounds for his distinction. But it must be understood that philosophers will not find at all surprising Isenberg's insistence on subjecting all emotion to standards of reasonableness. There are first of all those who, like David Hume (1888), draw a sharp distinction between emotion and reason but who reverse what Hume himself calls his "extraordinary opinion," his judgment that "reason is and ought only to be a slave of the passions" (p. 415). Those who offer a more cognitive analysis of emotion, who emphasize connections between emotions, beliefs, and evaluations, will find other points of entry for a consideration of reasonableness. What becomes salient will vary: is reasonableness a question of the "object" of the emotion?—of there being no false beliefs or improper inferences at play in the emotion?—of the empirical link between the emotion and its practical context? The questions that seem pertinent will vary with one's understandings of both emotion and reason, and philosophers will be divided on these matters. But the basic premise underlying Isenberg's (1973) discussion—the idea that emotion may be assessed for its reasonableness—does not immediately isolate Isenberg from most of the Western tradition.

Isenberg (1973) takes both pride and shame to be natural feelings, but, in his view, pride can be reasonable and shame never is. "Reasonableness" is here understood to have immediate moral import: "pride should be proportioned to the real value of the things of which we are proud" (p. 360) and thus "reasonable pride . . . will depend on a comprehensive and just sense of values" (p. 358). Given a comprehensive and just set of values, however, why should we not equally allow for the idea of reasonable, proportionate shame?

Isenberg notes that the qualities and actions of which we are ashamed will vary according to our standards of value, and he asserts that such standards are largely derived from our social group and are impressed upon us by social sanctions. This is the extent of Socrates' *objection* to some feelings of shame—not all groups have standards he wants to take seriously—but it is not at all the ground for Isenberg's battle against shame. Quite the contrary: according to Isenberg, if a personal flaw, malady, or misdeed *truly* is an evil, it merely deepens, doubles the evil to heap on it the reflexive judgment of disgrace that is shame. Isenberg does agree with Socrates that some things that we take to be shameful will be seen not to be so once we bring to bear on them an accurate set of values. If we are ashamed of our poverty, it may be because we have misjudged the value of wealth. If we have been ashamed of our clumsiness, it may be because we have overestimated the importance of physical grace:

> [T]here are weaknesses which, since they are created by estimation will disappear when the estimation is corrected; and with the weakness goes the shame in the weakness. But there are other weaknesses that are not created by estimation: estimation must, on

the contrary, take account of them as real. Though we should not, in our feelings, *exaggerate* these weaknesses, yet they remain; and with them, it appears, a modicum of shame. . . . Yet it is as unreasonable to tolerate the sear of shame upon the spirit as it is to permit a wound to fester in the body. There is not such a thing as a right amount of shame, as there is a right kind and amount of pride. *Every* shame, however circumscribed, must go [p. 369].

How can reason insist upon this eviction? One possibility, according to Isenberg, is that it can effect a redirection of desires. A distinction is regularly drawn between what is desired and what is desirable, or what is, at any rate, considered desirable. Moralists often urge us to bring our desires in line with the truly desirable, and Isenberg, though he makes much of the idea that the alignment of standards and desires is a two-way process of adjustment, agrees with this as a general exhortation. The moral sentiment expressed in the notion of the desirable may require improvement as much as may our individual preferences and inclinations, but standard and desire must be coordinated. Otherwise, our actual interests will lack the sanction, the support, of our total judgment.

What if, however, our desire is hopeless? What if our interest, though in line with a true standard, is doomed, if it can never, in our particular circumstances, be fulfilled? Isenberg's presumably emblematic case is the longing of the humpback to be straight. Straightness *is* the standard; normality *is* desirable. One can imagine a denial of this claim, a querying or revaluation of the inherent worth or importance of one posture over another; but Isenberg would see this revaluation as the self-deception known since Aesop as "sour grapes." A proper philosophy should not ask the humpback to suffer, in addition to physical deformity, a distortion of perception or judgment. But it is also unreasonable, in Isenberg's view, that the humpback add to the misery of his condition the feeling of shame. The solution is "a total redirection of wish: privately and subjectively, normality must cease to be his standard." He can recognize the objective desirability of straightness, but cease to see it as *his* good, his desire. "And when you lack what you do not want, there is no shame" (p. 370).

All sorts of natural disadvantages are to be treated according to this scheme; and the natural shame connected with a true liability is to be expelled by reason. We are to see that special handicaps and misfortunes—though imposed from without—are not categorically different from the ordinary conditions of life, many of which are the result of our active choice, in that they imply certain limitations on our further possibilities and hence on our reasonable goals.[3]

Suppose I have a chance to learn either violin or ballet, but I have neither the time nor the opportunity for both. I choose the violin. Should I then be ashamed of my inability to dance ballet? Should I try to convince myself that dancing ballet is worthless? Neither one—I should recognize that it is an excellent thing to dance ballet, but my recognition of my present incapacity to achieve this particular excellence should provoke no feeling of shame. I should acknowledge that, as I wished to learn violin, I had to give up my desire to learn ballet. I should understand that, in the inevitable compromises of life, some options close when others are chosen, but the reasonable course is to desire what may still be attained. And so it is with unchosen misfortunes. They may close off some genuinely desirable possibilities, but the reasonable course is not to pine for those or to be ashamed of their absence; the reasonable course is to desire what may still be attained.

This line of thought has some plausibility, because it is certainly true that developing some of our capacities may entail letting others shrivel; pursuing some of our desires will require giving up entirely on others. This does not mean that what we have given up is not objectively desirable, that the talents we have not developed are not, when developed, genuine human excellences. But it is reasonable to accommodate ourselves to these losses and deficiencies and to feel no shame on account of them, because we realize that no one can be, do, or have everything. We recognize, as Isenberg does, that "[n]o matter who you are, there are more things you cannot do than you can: what Shakespeare and what Newton did not know and could not say filled volumes, even in their own times" (p. 371).

There is a problem, though, with this reasoned route to the abolition of shame. A kind of bridge can indeed be constructed on these structural correspondences, in order to show the similarities

---

[3]The idea should arouse suspicion that limitations imposed from without are, because *metaphysically* on a par with limitations that are chosen, therefore *morally* and *emotionally* on a par with the latter. Themes connected with this suspicion will surface again near the end of the paper. For now, it is worth noting that there is some tension, some irony, in a strategy of relief from shame that emphasizes the liberatory potential of autonomous desire but fails to find significance in the difference between limitations one freely chooses and limitations imposed upon one, limitations over which one has no control.

between special misfortunes and handicaps on one side and the ordinary conditions of human life—its restrictions and finitude—on the other. One thing that is left out of this construction, however, one thing that is ignored in the focus on individual choice and the redirection of desire, is the weight of social reaction, the real or imagined public opinion that is a crucial feature of shame.[4]

Isenberg (1973) rightly emphasizes the reflexive character of shame, but individual reflection and judgment are not here guided by reason alone. Without some thought of others' contempt, derision, disapproval, the empirical conditions for shame are not approached. Isenberg is not unaware of this fact, but he will not admit that the emotions engendered by the thought of others can wash away reason's bridge out of shame. Others recognize that the artist's devotion to painting has left no time for a career in mathematics, and hence they do not deride his incompetence with numbers. The scientist has been busy in the lab, and so she feels—society in general recognizes—no disgrace in her inability to perform great feats of gymnastics. There can be, it is true, circumstances in which her lack of athletic skill would be greeted with ridicule, people for whom her lack of athletic prowess would loom large, so that they would treat her with contempt. But these would not be the people with whom she identifies; these would not be circumstances she has to inhabit.

Even as a merely schematic illustration, however, Isenberg's humpback presents problems not shared by the artist ignorant of mathematics or the unathletic scientist. As Isenberg himself recognizes, the liability of the humpback's deformity "is not the pain alone, nor the pang of comparison, not the unwantedness, nor the fear of it, nor the sexual impasse, but all these" (p. 371), and he may well not have the option of avoiding others' aversion. And then, unfair and irrational as others may be in their ridicule or shunning, he is not unreasonable in being hurt by it. He may cease to care about this wider world's reactions and thus overcome his sense of shame. The first step in moving to this dispassionate stance may even be a consideration of the unreasonableness of the others' reactions. But it is not, in the end, his reasoned judgment that matters most here; what is decisive is his emotional reaction.

Furthermore, though we may in this sort of case long for a philosophic argument that will demonstrate the inappropriateness of shame—as here we do see misery unfairly heaped on undeserved misfortune—we must remember that not all public contempt is

---

[4]This may not, of course, be all that's left out. See footnote 3.

unjustified. There are acts and traits of character that any reasonable moral philosophy must condemn. If I have committed one of these reprehensible acts or displayed a weak or malicious character, can—should—reason then cut me loose from shame? Isenberg, putting a Kantian spin on Aristotle's view, claims that if I were perfectly reasonable I should not have erred in the first place. Given that I have erred, however, what is the next step of, or toward, reason?

Isenberg grants that moral improvement cannot be effected without reflection, that it is only when we notice, seriously contemplate, our faults and misdeeds that we have any chance of correcting them. Reflection upon our weaknesses and errors is a thus a reasonable moral requirement, but such reflection may well provoke shame. How is reason supposed to block this?

Isenberg's suggestion is that shame must be recognized as an ineffective and hence dispensable element in the operations of moral reflection and reconstruction. We must see our failures and imperfections and then consider what we might do to improve. Self-contemplation identifies the problems, but attention must then turn to the future, to purposes and resolutions. Shame helps not at all, does *no* good in this economy: "Shame and regret are literally helpless, for they are concentrated upon what we can do nothing about, on the past. Hence, they are 'passive,' incompatible with action" (p. 375).

In his haste to move on, to replace not just shame but also guilt and remorse by resolute action and improved conduct, Isenberg sees shame as in fact worse than useless. It is a compounding of our original error, a further sign of our weakness:

> It will never do to argue that just as pride of achievement encourages us toward further exertion, so to dwell upon our failures is to produce a revulsion toward good. . . . [T]here is no "law of effect" which operates in this manner; for if there were, it would follow that to *cultivate* the sense of guilt, to brood over our infirmities, would be tantamount to improvement; but this, on the contrary is morbidity. Despondency is *weakness*; it reduces the power to act; it confirms us only in despondency, in loathing of self; it indicates no direction in which effort may move . . . [p. 374].

A variety of objections could be produced against Isenberg's line of thought. If pride of achievement truly can encourage us toward further exertion, there is no reason to believe shame cannot produce a "revulsion toward good." It would *not* then follow that "to cultivate the sense of guilt, to brood over infirmities, would be tantamount to improvement": We can as easily—given the view that pride can encourage exertion—claim that to deepen or broaden our pride, to plume ourselves upon our achievements and to glory in our comparative excellences, would be tantamount to the renewal of our efforts; when, on the contrary, it would effect, or mark, complacency. Pride and shame seem symmetrical. The point in each case is not to become impaled by the feeling but to let it work as a spur.

And even if shame does not always work as a spur, even if it does become a permanent thorn in our side, this may not always be something reason should decry. If shame is felt on account of one's malice and misdeeds, then its pain might be thought *deserved*. Pain may be, in general, a bad thing; but the pain associated with an appropriate penalty is sometimes thought to contribute to, to be required for, the good of justice.

Kant (1959) sets the stage for this view when he says that "the sight of a being adorned with no feature of a pure and good will, yet enjoying uninterrupted prosperity, can never give pleasure to a rational impartial observer." Moral goodness—which the malicious miscreant lacks—"seems to constitute the indispensable condition even of worthiness to be happy" (p. 9). Isenberg insists that shame, because it is painful, is *inherently,* basically bad. Reason could endorse it only if shame led to something good, served a useful purpose, were a necessary element in a move toward personal improvement. A broadly Kantian rationality may be more stringent: some, by virtue of their deeds and character, are simply unworthy of happiness. Shame may entail suffering, but it is reasonable that the wicked should suffer, and we do not need to justify our sense of this justice in terms of socially useful consequences or the personal reformation of the wicked.

An objection of this sort, and the stalemate it suggests, may begin to provoke appropriate and important questions about the authority and the definitiveness of philosophy's characteristic appeal to reason. Those questions may have to be set aside on this occasion, however, because, in a direct address to them, problems about shame would become merely illustrative. There are specific questions about *shame*—its nature and operations—yet to be faced in this tangle of moral philosophy. We should query, in particular, Isenberg's assertion that shame is *passive*, "incompatible with action," "helpless," because "concentrated upon what we can do nothing about, on the past."

THE MORAL FORCE OF SHAME

Isenberg has a notion of shame avowedly akin to that articulated in Spinoza's (1955) definition: "*Shame* is pain accompanied by the idea of some action of our own, which we believe to be blamed by others" (p. 181). Isenberg (1973) takes care to mention his own allegiance to the idea of "autonomous conscience"–"a man may feel himself disgraced by something that is unworthy in his own eyes and apart from any judgment but his own" (p. 366)–though he claims this is only a terminological departure from the Spinozistic account. The terminology of autonomy is, of course, quite charged philosophically, so this turn may not be lightly made. Setting that issue aside for the moment, however, we must note this definition's focus on *action* evidently already *completed*. Indeed, Spinoza (1955) himself explicitly says that "[s]hame is the pain following the deed whereof we are ashamed" (p. 181).

There are certainly other notions of shame, however, where the object on which we focus is not a past deed. To survey these other notions, we can note first that we may be ashamed of all sorts of contemplated action, deeds we are tempted by or that we plan for the future, as well as deeds we recollect. This possibility in fact fits the language of Spinoza's formal definition, if sometimes our idea of our action is conveyed not by memory but by imagination. A more comprehensive conception of shame is also articulated by Aristotle, in the *Rhetoric*, where, in turn, the treatment of the idea is less censorious than in the *Nicomachean Ethics*. Once Aristotle (1984) says, "Shame may be defined as pain or disturbance in regard to bad things, whether present, past, or future, which seem likely to involve us in discredit" (p. 204), the way is cleared to see, as Descartes does, a virtuous force to shame.

For if we recognize that shame is not always concentrated on the past, we see immediately at least some ways in which shame could be far from "helpless"; it could be understood to spark or extinguish action. I am tempted to run from this fight, but I consider that I will then be thought cowardly, so I enter the battle. I hatch a plan to sabotage a rival, but I recognize how disgraceful my actions would seem, were they ever to come to light, so I refrain from the plan's execution. Shame that arises with the thought of, as Aristotle put it, "bad things [in the] future" is usually understood to have an inhibitory or preventive force. Thus Samuel Johnson (1953) claims that "[f]ew can review the days of their youth without recollecting temptations which shame rather than virtue enabled them to resist" (p. 114). And Spinoza (1955) notices something he calls "modesty"— "the fear or dread of shame, which restrains a man from committing a base action" (p, 181). Resistance and restraint may be in one sense negative, but they imply power, determinative force. And there is still the shame that is directly motivating, not inhibitory but propulsive: I act because I shall be ashamed if I do not.

Another reading of shame's positive potential is offered by Emerson (1972). Reflecting on the negative, preventive force of shame, he glimpses, as well, a positive dynamic, a way in which shame may have the capacity to *mix* helplessness and strength:

> —has any man asked himself what that is when in the petty act he meditates he suddenly comes full upon this great light in himself and flees before it and hides himself? Perhaps the most extraordinary fact in our experience is the deep joy that attends the stings of remorse—for it is the acknowledgment that this higher Judgment seat is also ours [p. 19].

Here, once again, shame is allied with pride. And as the *absence* of a sense of restraint—no inhibitions, no inclination to flee and hide oneself—is called "shamelessness," so the *presence* of shame, of inhibition and restraint, may entail not just pain and disturbance but also pleasure—for Emerson, "joy." There is in fact a territory of contemplated action where the questions, "Have you no shame?" and "Have you no pride?" cover the same ground.

This should remind us that our character and condition, as well as our deeds, are at stake in imputations of shame. This is so not merely because our personal traits and particular circumstances can be, reasonably or unreasonably, sources of shame; it is also because our reactions to our own deeds are personally telling. And this is not merely because they signal or reveal an underlying structure of character. Isenberg (1973) says that while he agrees with Spinoza that the feeling of shame "can *bear witness* to an uncorrupted conscience," so that the person who feels shame may be seen to be better than the one who is both wicked and shameless, it does not follow that the feeling should be reckoned good just because it testifies to something good (p. 374). But shame, like regret and remorse, can be understood not as an independent informant but as part of the very operation of the uncorrupted conscience. The person who is *ashamed* of a malicious act is a deeply different sort of person from the one who is not ashamed, the one who simply knows the act was wrong and who, coolly if sincerely, resolves never to repeat it.

Moreover, as the capacity for shame may constitute part of our character, feeling ashamed may not be, in yet another way, as wholly passive as Isenberg claims and as the language of suffering suggests. Even if we stick with Isenberg's focus on shame felt about past deeds, there are at least two dimensions in which the assumption of passivity requires reexamination. One has to do with time itself, or our existence in it. Isenberg sees shame's helplessness as a function of its "concentration upon what we can do nothing about, on the past" (p. 375); but we might see the past as exactly what we *can* do something about, what we sometimes *must* do something about. Of course we cannot, through shame or any means, undo the past, make it the case that it did not happen or that we did not commit the act we committed. But we can *do* something about the past—make reparations, try to atone, feel truly ashamed.

That we feel ashamed is just what others may demand of us—not always unfairly—as a condition of reconciliation. This demand will seem puzzling if we persist in construing shame as utterly passive. For how could others require of us a feeling, something we are either gripped by or not, something we cannot voluntarily *do* or bring about? Yet from their point of view, if we are not ashamed of a malicious act, if we merely cognize that the act was wrong, then we apparently do not feel the force of their blame and disapprobation, do not feel disturbed by being subject to their discredit. Now how can *they* help feeling estranged from us?

Shame may sometimes be a required element of atonement—becoming at one—because of the way in which feeling shame requires attention to and the *incorporation* of the viewpoints of others. The reflexivity of perception and judgment that is definitive of shame is one modulation of the general reflexivity of self-consciousness. And with some attention to the nature of self-consciousness, we can see the second way in which Isenberg's assumption of shame's passivity requires modification. Self-consciousness involves being both subject and object. It involves knowing or thinking about and being the object known, the thing thought about. It involves both activity and passivity.

SHAME AND THE METAPHYSICS OF THE SELF

How this is possible, how to describe and understand this reflexivity, is the crucial metaphysical question of the self. How can something be an object to itself? How can consciousness be directed upon the very self in which consciousness inheres? If consciousness grasps the self, what grasps the consciousness grasping the self? Answers to this vertiginous array of questions will invariably have ethical implications. One way to combat the philosophical dizziness of the metaphysical problem of self-consciousness is to widen the circle through which reflection spins. An adequate account of the self's reflexivity may require the identification of points outside the self from which perspectives on the self may be drawn. An adequate account of the self may require, that is, a recognition of others.

Hegel (1977) says that self-consciousness can exist only when and by the fact that it exists for another; "it exists in being acknowledged":

> Each is for the other the middle term, through which each mediates itself with itself and unites with itself; and each is for itself, and for the other, an immediate being on its own account, which at the same time is such only through this mediation. They *recognize* themselves as *mutually recognizing* one another [P. 111].

Self-consciousness is only secured, then, if recognition by the other is secured, and Hegel describes a paradoxical life-and-death struggle for this recognition.

To be assured of its own existence as an independent self-consciousness, each seeks to compel the other's acknowledgment. This amounts to seeking the death of the other, as an independent self-consciousness. If the other is destroyed, however, so is the possibility of acknowledgment, so seeking the other's death is at the same time staking one's own life. But risking one's own life is required, in any case, and from another direction, in order to demonstrate to the other one's own independence. This struggle is not exactly resolved, but it achieves a dynamic structure in the relationship Hegel calls "lordship and bondage" or "the master/slave." "Lord" (or "master)" is the name Hegel uses to speak of the independent consciousness, "bondsman" or ("slave") the name for the dependent consciousness; but each remains implicated in the other, dependent on the other for existence. And each suffers or achieves— through their relationship—reversals in the status of self-consciousness.

Sartre's view of the self is developed, in part, in opposition to Hegel, but he endorses and produces interesting refinements of the idea of the reciprocities of self-consciousness. And one of the primary vehicles he uses to carry his own account of the reciprocal relation between self and other is an analysis of shame:

> I have just made an awkward or vulgar gesture. This gesture clings
> to me; I neither judge it nor blame it. I simply live it. . . . But now
> suddenly I raise my head. Somebody was there and has seen me.
> Suddenly I realize the vulgarity of my gesture, and I am
> ashamed. . . . [T]he Other is the indispensable mediator between
> myself and me. I am ashamed of myself *as I appear* to the Other
> [pp. 221–222].

The other, Sartre says, *can* be for me a mere object. I may see a man
on a park bench as I see the bench—20 feet away from me, six feet
away from the chestnut tree, in the shadow of the trees' branches.
But if I recognize that *I* am seen by *him*, *he* becomes the subject and
I am objectified. Phenomenological support for this ontology is
elaborated in Sartre's striking dramatization of shame, the example of
"consciousness at a keyhole."

Suppose, he says, "moved by jealousy, curiosity, or vice," I am
listening at a door, looking through a keyhole. Alone in the hallway,
I grasp the spectacle on the other side of the door as "to be seen,"
the conversation as, "to be heard," and I am absorbed in the acts of
listening and looking. I am, as Sartre puts it, "a pure consciousness
of things." Suddenly, though, I hear footsteps in the hallway and
realize that someone is looking at *me*—seeing me stooped in the hall,
seeing me bent over at the door, seeing me looking through the
keyhole. I am now conscious of *myself*; I discover myself, I exist for
myself—in shame. Shame "reveals to me the Other's look and myself
at the end of that look"; shame "is the *recognition* of the fact that I
am indeed that object which the Other is looking at and judging"
(pp. 259–261).

Sartre's descriptions of self-consciousness have a dire confrontational edge, and in drawing out the implications of his view he
employs images nearly as extreme as Hegel's: "the *Other's look* as the
necessary condition of my objectivity is the destruction of all
objectivity for me" (p. 269). I regain my subjectivity, my freedom, by
seeing the Other as object; but "the Other-as-object is an explosive
instrument which I handle with care . . . ":

> my constant concern is to contain the Other within his objectivity,
> and my relations with the Other-as-object are essentially made up of
> ruses designed to make him remain an object. But one look on the
> part of the Other is sufficient to make all these schemes collapse
> and to make me experience once more the transfiguration of the
> Other. Thus I am referred from transfiguration to degradation and
> from degradation to transfiguration . . . [p. 297].

The metaphors that convey Hegel's understanding of self-consciousness are profoundly antagonistic, and Sartre's account of shame emphasizes the continuous opposition of self and other; but through this belligerent imagery both insist on the inherently *social* character of the self and its reflexive attitudes. Aristotle's (1984) calm, prosaic enumeration, in *The Rhetoric*, of the conditions under which, and the people before whom, we feel shame brings the soaring metaphysical point down to homely practical detail in the observation of the specific case:

> [S]ince shame is the imagination of disgrace, in which we shrink from the disgrace itself and not from its consequences, and we only care what opinion is held of us because of the people who form that opinion, it follows that the people before whom we feel shame are those whose opinion of us matters to us. Such persons are: those who admire us, those whom we admire, those by whom we wish to be admired, those with whom we are competing, and those whose opinion of us we respect . . . [p. 2205].

With characteristic thoroughness, Aristotle proceeds to subdivide and specify further these categories of persons—we admire those "who possess any good thing that is highly esteemed; or from whom we are very anxious to get something that they are able to give us . . . " (p.2205) and so on—and to add some categories—"those not open to the same imputation as ourselves; ... those who are likely to tell everybody . . . , those who have never yet known us come to grief . . . " and so on. The spelling out of these categories will vary with, and perhaps tell us about, various social structures: Aristotle says, for example, that those with whom we compete are "our equals" (p. 2205); we might agree, but we should notice that Aristotle, in patriarchal, slave-holding ancient Athens, would specify this group quite differently than we would—and we would variously—in late 20th-century America.

It is suggested by the form of Aristotle's account that we may feel no shame before those for whom we have contempt, but he is careful to remember that even these people may have ties to people whose opinion *does* count for us. (So, for example, he says that "we feel shame not merely in the presence of the persons mentioned but also of those who will tell them what we have done, such as their servants or friends" [p. 2206].) The logic of his account leaves space for the avoidance of shame, but when he tries to give concrete examples of those whose opinions will definitely not matter, all he mentions are animals and tiny children. We are stuck in a web of opinion, and, inappropriate as some of those opinions may seem if we have a different domain of admiration, a different range we respect, shame seems to work, for good or ill, as a social glue, binding us to one another.

We need not, of course, be fastened down to our present company or fixed by the prevailing opinions and values of our larger society. Even if it is not that we are shameless—we do reflect on our character and deeds and we do have a capacity for shame—we might remain utterly undisturbed when we see that our neighbors and countrymen think badly of us. This does not mean that the "other" is not crucial to self-consciousness. We need not endorse the particular details of either Hegel's or Sartre's analysis, but any philosophic description of self-consciousness must make an account of how one can be an other, an object, to oneself (as subject) or how one can take the view of another toward oneself (as object). Still, the other whose reproving stare elicits our sense of shame can be, in the end, an abstraction, a generalization, a long-dead parent, or an idealized friend, an imagined league of worthy associates.

Our capacity to become unhinged from, or to willfully, thoughtfully ignore, immediate social circumstances encourages moral philosophers in their endorsements of autonomous thought and action. But the notion of autonomy, while genuinely important in the delineation of some defensible visions of moral maturity, and while clearly useful in the explication of empirically given variations and idiosyncrasies, requires strict warnings and qualifications if it is to be allied with the idea of shame. Because of the implication of the other in the very structure of self-consciousness, we cannot understand the reflexive attitudes in general, and shame in particular, apart from a reference to the social embeddedness of every individual.

THE SOCIAL PECULIARITIES OF SHAME

The claim that shame discloses our social ties is not in tension with the fact that shame fractures social harmony. Chekhov (1994) remarks that "when people are ashamed they hold aloof, above all from those nearest to them" (p. 157). When shame comes to Adam and Eve, they cover themselves, they hide. Emerson (1972) describes fleeing, hiding from himself, from the great light within. Shame may be a desperately private emotion, "the most isolating of feelings," according to Stanley Cavell, but it is also, Cavell (1969) notes,

> the most primitive of *social* responses. With the discovery of the
> individual, whether in Paradise or in the Renaissance, there is the

simultaneous discovery of the isolation of the individual; his presence to himself, but simultaneously to *others* [p.286].

Our presence to others is what both allows and reveals their gaze, Sartre's "look." The genesis of shame for Adam and Eve is described as the opening of their eyes, and Aristotle (1984) quotes as a proverb already old, "Shame dwells in the eyes" (p. 2205). The Cartesian individual, the self-assertion of "*I am, I exist*," is produced when the world and others—my perception of them and theirs of me—have been swept away by radical doubt, a procedure the exercise of which leaves Descartes (1984) feeling, he says, "as if I have fallen unexpectedly into a deep whirlpool which tumbles me around so that I can neither stand on the bottom nor swim to the top" (p. 16). The individual isolation of the *cogito*[5] is then given its exact mirror image in Nietzsche's (1982) *Daybreak*: "*Centre*—The feeling 'I am the mid-point of the world!' arises strongly if one is suddenly overcome with shame; one then stands there as though confused in the midst of a surging sea and feels dazzled as though by a great eye which gazes upon us and through us from all sides" (p. 352).

Cavell (1969) discerns the origins of shame in

> the specific discomfort produced by the sense of being looked at[;] the avoidance of the sight of others is the reflex it produces. Guilt is different; there the reflex is to avoid discovery. As long as no one *knows* what you have done, you are safe; or your conscience will press you to confess it and accept punishment. Under shame, what must be covered up in not your deed, but yourself. It is a more primitive emotion than guilt, as inescapable as the possession of a body, the first object of shame [p. 278].

And pondering the depths of our recurrent shame in the body can help us to delineate, and perhaps reform, our social relations. Bernard Williams (1993) cites an example of shame originally suggested by Max Scheler, an example that both rings instantly true

---

[5]*Cogito ergo sum*—"*I am thinking, therefore I exist*"—is the way the *Discourse on Method* presents Descartes's (1985) "first truth." It is observed as Descartes entertains what he calls "extravagant suppositions"—the idea that sense perception is always deceptive, the rejection, as fallacious, of all logical and geometrical proofs, and the pretense "that all the things that had ever entered my mind were no more true than the illusions of my dreams" (p. 127).

and yet reverberates with lasting perplexities: A woman who has for an untroubled time posed nude for an artist comes to feel shame when she realizes that the artist is now not looking at her as a model but as a sexual object. Williams explains her sense of shame—and shame generally—as rooted in a loss of power, in being at a disadvantage:

> [T]he change in the situation introduces the relevant kind of unprotectedness or loss of power: this is itself constituted by an actual gaze, which is of a special, sexually interested kind. She has previously been clothed in her role as a model; that has been taken from her, and she is left truly exposed, to a desiring eye [p. 221].

There is something obviously sound in Williams' contention that shame involves being at a disadvantage, that suffering shame is suffering a loss of power. But the example, also obviously sound, is not immediately explained by this account. What power did she have as a model that she has now lost? It will not do to say she had the power of her role, because the question is exactly what power that is. Why is it that her having aroused sexual interest is not taken as a sign of augmented power? The change in the situation also amounts, after all, to this: she is no longer merely employed by the artist; she now commands his desire. Why is this not a gain in her power? If it seems it is not, if the sexually interested gaze is understood as inherently damaging or diminishing this woman, understood as putting her at risk, rendering or exposing her as "unprotected," what does this tell us about our understanding of the everyday economy of sexual interchange and expression? What does it tell us about the function and the nature of the standing balance of power?

The crookedness of another range of familiar cases can raise similar questions. Many rape victims suffer, in addition to the crime, a sense of shame. How can this be understood? Williams's language is too mild for the outrage, but his description is weakly accurate: the rape victim is conscious of a loss or inadequacy of power, of being at a disadvantage. The Hegelian and Sartrean descriptions of the contestations of self-consciousness may also be recalled, and they here seem no longer hyperbolic: the master/slave relationship is effected; the rapist objectifies, destroys the subjectivity and freedom of the victim.

Even Kant (1959), though he resolutely separates his moral philosophy from a concern with shame, supplies notions that are remarkably salient: the centrality for Kantian morality of the idea of autonomy, his linking of autonomy and freedom of the will, and the version of the categorical imperative that forbids the treatment of any human as a mere means. Kant himself would not countenance the following train of thought, but there is certainly an emotional logic from which one might draw the conclusion that, if one's autonomy, one's freedom of will is denied, if one is treated as a mere means, one's *humanity* is denied, degraded, diminished. One is *humiliated*, turned, as the etymological roots of this synonym of "shamed" suggest, into dirt.

The insistence on autonomy is, though, part of what protects Kant's moral philosophy from the vagaries of shame. Practical social protection was also the aim of the Enlightenment's political development of the ideal of autonomy. Legitimate government, it came to be claimed, depends on the consent of the governed. Respect for the individual citizen involves recognition of, and respect for, the individual's capacity for choice, and political freedom involves mechanisms for the efficacy of choice. The removal, in rape, of the efficacy of the victim's choice, the tyranny of overriding her refusal to consent, are personal horrors; but they might also be expected to reverberate politically, as they confute what are often taken to be our founding ideals of social association.

But the rape victim may find that the social reverberations are not those for which she might have hoped. An additional cruelty often associated with rape is that the victim may discover the fragility of her standing with others, the precariousness of social respect. Sometimes she suffers, in addition to the crime, a sense of shame that is exactly captured by Spinoza's (1955) definition: she suffers pain, together with the thought that others blame her.[6] Why *is* this victim blamed? It is true that some of the motivations to this social reaction may work, as well, in the context of other crimes and misfortunes. Blame helps us to put distance between ourselves and those we blame; and if we can see someone's difficulty or suffering as somehow his or her own fault, we can imagine ourselves less

---

[6]It should be clear from what has already been said that I do not take the rape victim's sense of being blamed, when that is present, to be the only, or even the most important, element in the horrors she suffers, not even in the sense of shame, when that is elicited. It is important to note the peculiarity of this blame, however, no matter how peripheral it may be to the experience of some victims of rape, in order to highlight not just the psychological and the sociological but also the *political* import of shame, as well as a particularly vexed intersection of our moral and metaphysical uncertainties.

susceptible to the same fate, conceive of ourselves as without that fault and so with more security headed to a better destiny.[7]

Our evasions and self-deceptions seem particularly severe, however, in the case of rape. If the crime is tried in a court of law, consent is at issue, and what is to be adjudicated is the victim's will and whether she has made it plain. Rape victims often complain of feeling violated again by our system of criminal justice, and that is not surprising. What is tested there, probed, what is at stake—once again—is her integrity, her self-assertion, its power and its relation to sexual intercourse. The cruel social reaction to the cruelty of rape may be yet another manifestation of the uneasiness of our individuality, our unsureness about the limits of our own autonomy, our anxiety about the extent to which we are subject to contingencies not freely chosen.

If the uneasiness of our condition is unavoidable, however, it certainly does not follow that we must express our vulnerability in just that vicious way. We can imagine and act upon strategies to spare people—ourselves and others—some of these shames. Politics may effect some of these liberations, but how is politics here to be conceived? Morality must guide it, but what are the dictates of morality? Kant may have expected, and others may have continued to hope, that grounding morality in reason alone would sweep aside some of the problems about shame that we have here explored. But the Kantian emphasis on autonomy proves double edged, and the willful setting aside of cultural and personal experience proves unhelpful. An alternative approach, represented by such figures as Hegel and Sartre, sketches the moral and metaphysical acknowledgment of our mutual dependencies, our social embeddedness; but it offers no standards for the evaluation and amelioration of the *quality* of our mutual self-definition, no particular prospects for social or individual improvement.

Our best hopes may reside in continued thought, thought that comprehends not just the motivation but the rationale for the Kantian drive toward autonomy, thought that discerns not just the standing structures but the implications and possibilities for improve-

---

[7]Contributing as well to our conceptual difficulties here is the idea, once again broadly Kantian, that victims will be deprived of their humanity if they are not understood as retaining a capacity for choice. A series of small steps then takes one from this notion of moral *respect* to the idea that victims must have ascribed to them some *responsibility* and, finally, to the idea that victims may somehow be *blamed*. It is not just the logic of these moves but also the conceptual framework that needs reexamination.

ment of our social reciprocities. This is a call, then, for further philosophy. As we have seen, reason will not always be the final arbiter, the judge of all our values and the dispeller of our untoward emotions. Still, any strategy to release us from inappropriate shame will require passion and reward thought, will entail, that is, philosophy.

REFERENCES

Augustine (1961), *Confessions*, trans. R.S. Pine-Coffin. London: Penguin Books.
Aristotle (1984), *The Complete Works of Aristotle*, Vol. 2, ed. Jonathan Barnes. Princeton, NJ: Princeton University Press.
Beck, L. W. (1965), *Studies in the Philosophy of Kant*. New York: Bobbs-Merrill.
Cavell, S. (1969), *Must We Mean What We Say?* New York: Charles Scribner's Sons.
Chekhov, A. (1994), *Stories of Women*, trans. P. P. Ross. Amherst, NY: Prometheus Books.
Descartes, R. (1984), *The Philosophical Writings of Descartes*, Vol. 2, trans. J. Cottingham, R. Stoothoff & D. Murdoch. Cambridge: Cambridge University Press.
_____ (1985), *The Philosophical Writings of Descartes*, Vol. 1, trans. J. Cottingham, R. Stoothoff & D. Murdoch. Cambridge: Cambridge University Press.
Emerson, R. W. (1972), *The Early Lectures of Ralph Waldo Emerson*, Vol. 3, ed. R. Spiller & W. Williams. Cambridge, MA: Harvard University Press.
Hegel, G. W. F. (1977), *Phenomenology of Spirit*, trans. A.V. Miller. Oxford: Oxford University Press.
Hume, D. (1888), *A Treatise of Human Nature*. Oxford: Clarendon Press.
Isenberg, A. (1973), Natural pride and natural shame. In *Explaining Emotions*, ed. A. Rorty. Berkeley, CA: University of California Press, pp. 355–383.
Johnson, S. (1953), *The Rambler*. New York: Dutton.
Kant, I. (1959), *Foundations of the Metaphysics of Morals*, trans. L. W. Beck. New York: Bobbs-Merrill.
Nietzsche, F. (1972),*Beyond Good and Evil*, trans. R. J. Hollingdale. London: Penguin Books.
_____ (1982), *Daybreak*, trans. R. Hollingdale. Cambridge: Cambridge University Press.

_____ (1974), *The Gay Science*, trans. W. Kaufmann. New York: Vintage Books.

Pascal, B. (1966), *Pensees*, trans. A. J. Krailsheimer. New York: Penguin Books.

Plato (n.d.), *The Collected Dialogues*, ed. E. Hamilton & H. Cairns. New York: Pantheon Books, 1961.

Rawls, J. (1971), *A Theory of Justice*. Cambridge, MA: Harvard University Press.

Sartre, J.-P. (1956), *Being and Nothingness*, trans. H. Barnes. New York: Philosophical Library.

Spinoza, B. (1955), *Works of Spinoza*, Vol. 2, trans. R. H. M. Elwes. New York: Dover Books.

Williams, B. (1993), *Shame and Necessity*. Berkeley: University of California Press.

7

LÉON WURMSER

Nietzsche's War Against Shame and Resentment*

Throughout the work of Nietzsche it is a *philosophy of inner conflict* that makes the manifest aphorisms and essays understandable and coherent—not just a psychology of inner conflict, but, in the full sense, *a philosophy* that attempts to understand *the essence of man, his history and culture, and, most of all, his comprehension of the world and of himself, including all science, all valuation, all art, on the basis of inner conflict.* This is a philosophical revolution of the first rank, adumbrated by only a few: Plato and Augustinus, Shakespeare and Goethe, and of course, Schopenhauer.

It is an epistemological and metaphysical revolution that re-examines basic philosophical questions from a vantage point in psychology, specifically from that of a psychology of multiple, contradictory, fighting parts within man. Nietzsche's emphasis is on the multiplicity of the person and one's inner conflicts. Psychology, and a radically new psychology at that, is being used as cornerstone for a new philosophy. It is being counted on to reveal to us what is deepest and most relevant for understanding the human self, for our insight into the universe, for our history and culture, art, and, of course, our religion and morality. In this revolution Nietzsche is, even today, the pioneer of an entirely new, highly relevant, profoundly inspirational philosophy.

---

*The thoughts summarized here have been published in a detailled study as chapter 13 of Wurmser, 1993

Nietzsche speaks of the "war history of the individual" in which various cultures, ages, and generations are in the most ferocious battle within the individual. He speaks of the thinker whose thoughts are like persons with whom he has to fight; whom he has to protect, nourish, join; whose tyranny he wants to defy; whose faltering he meets with pity; whose power he fears; and to whom he gives the authority to honor his self, to praise or to chide it and treat it with contempt—"that we deal with them as with free intelligible [mental, spiritual] persons, with independent powers, equal to equal—this is the root of the curious phenomenon that I have called 'intellectual conscience'" (1878-1880, II, I, 26)[1].

Nietzsche writes:

Is it not evident that . . . man prefers *one part of himself*, a thought, a desire, a product, over *another part of himself;* that he therefore *splits up* his nature [being] and sacrifices one part to the other? . . . In morality man does not treat himself as individuum [indivisible], but as dividuum [divisible] [p. 68].

THREE STATIONS AND FRACTURED SYNTHESIS

Löwith (1956) dramatically describes Nietzsche's system as a movement of thought marked by three stations: the death of the Christian God, man as being confronted by nothingness, and the will for eternal return [of the same] ["die Lehre von der ewigen Wiederkehr des Gleichen"]. His thinking goes from "you ought to [Thou shalt]" to the birth of the "I want to [I will]" and then to the rebirth of the "I am" as the "first movement" of an eternally returning existence within the natural world of all living things.

The old conscience, the old morality is at the core of Nietzsche's rejection. *"Dead are all Gods: Now we want, that the superman live*—this should be, at the time of the great noon, our ultimate Will!" The precondition for Superman's advent is the radical destruction of traditional morality, the rule of the "you ought." To Nietzsche (1888a), morality is "the true poisoner and slanderer of life" ["Die vier großen Irrtümer"] (The 4 Great Errors), 6, p. 113). He wants to remove "the instinct of *wanting to punish and judge"* and engages

---

[1]All translations are mine. I have tried to remain as close to the original as possible, occasionally at the cost of stylistic considerations in English, in order to increase the validity of the psychoanalytic conclusions. Accordingly, all the references are to the German edition.

in the resolute reversal "where we immoralists together again with all our might take away from the world the concept of guilt and punishment" (p. 115). The image evoked is that of *castration*:

> The Church fights against passion by cutting it out in every sense: her practice, her "cure" is *castratism*. She never asks: "how may one change desire into something spiritual, beautiful, godlike?"—at all times she has put her emphasis of discipline on [the] extirpation (of sensuality, of the pride and will to rule and to possess, of revenge). ["Moral als Widernatur" [Morality as Counter-Nature], 1, pp. 101–102]

The anthropological postulate of Nietzsche's nihilism points to the elementary "will" for power. In Löwith's (1956) words: "Life itself is understood as a universal 'will' to power, and thus Nietzsche's basic distinction is that the phenomena of life are ranked according to strength and weakness and these are related to the strength and weakness of the will founded in life" (p. 57). In that philosophical revolution he sees as most central the antithesis between life as growing and life as declining—rich life and impoverished life, well-formed life and degenerate life. Nietzsche (1888b) puts this antithesis most poignantly, most crisply:

> What is good?—Everything that heightens in man the feeling of power, the will to power, power itself. What is bad?—Everything that stems from weakness. What is happiness?—The feeling that power *is growing,*—that a resistance is being overcome. *No* contentment, but more *power*; *no* peace at all, but war; *not* virtue, but competence (virtue in the Renaissance style, virtú, virtue free of moralin[2]). The poor and degenerate ones should perish: that is the first axiom [lit: sentence] of *our* love for man. And one should even help them to it [to perish]. What is more harmful than any vice?—Pity in action with all those degenerate and weak— Christianity . . . [2, p. 192].

The turnabout from the Will-to-Nothing into the Will-to-Eternal-Return is based on this main distinction.

Persuasively, Löwith (1956) points to the inner fracture in Nietzsche's "ideal sequence" (the movement of thought just described):

---

[2]"moralinfreie Tugend"

His doctrine breaks apart because the will for the *eternalization of the modern ego* whose existence has been thrown into Being, is incompatible with the contemplation of an *eternal circle of the natural world*[3] [p. 126] . . . The *problem* with the doctrine of return is how to [create] *unity* of this *split* between the human will directed at an aim and the aimless circling of the world [pp. 66–67] . . . the real difficulty consists in bringing the vision of the eternally circling Universe into accord with man's purposeful will toward the future [p. 74] . . . This duality of interpretation [zweifache Deutbarkeit] as an *atheistic religion* and as a *physicalistic metaphysics* shows that the doctrine as a whole is the *unity of a split [Einheit eines Zwiespalts]*, between the *nihilistic* existence of man who has gotten rid of God and the *positivistic* presence of physical energy [p. 87, italics added].

Thus Nietzsche puts his core vision of Being both as an *ethical imperative* and as a *theory of natural science*. This attempt to reconquer a lost world and its unity fails signally; it breaks critically apart "in the irreconcilable double meaning of a practical-moral postulate and of a theoretical claim [in Löwith, 1956, p.92]. . . . *The cosmic meaning stands in conflict with the anthropological [meaning]* so that the one turns into the nonsense of the other" (p. 64).

What can we add as psychoanalysts to this philosophical finding? Specifically: Is not this thinking in extremes, and are not its results as a fracture in the philosophy something we are acquainted with and about which we may have some comments?

"A LAUGHTER OR A PAINFUL SHAME"

Nietzsche (1888c) calls himself "a hybrid of illness and will for power." The depth of this split is revealed when he writes:

I know my lot. Some day there will be tied to my name the recollection of something immense, of a crisis the likes of which there never has been on earth, of the *deepest collision of conscience*, of a decision conjured up *against* everything that had hitherto been believed, demanded, sanctified. I am no human being,

---

[3]"Seine Lehre bricht entzwei, weil der Wille zur Verewigung der ins Dasein geworfenen Existenz des modernen Ego mit der Schau eines ewigen Kreislaufs der natürlichen Welt nicht zusammenpaßt" (p. 126).

I am dynamite ["Warum ich ein Schicksal bin" [Why I am destiny],
I, p. 399; italics added].

It is this "deepest collision of conscience," or, as we would say,
the conflict within the superego, that is for us the psychoanalytically
relevant center of the problem faced by Nietzsche and all those
deeply influenced by his revolutionary thinking.

Duties, reverence, and guilt have to be abolished in this "transvaluation of all values" that liberates from the "you ought": "Being
ashamed of one's immorality: that is a step on the ladder at the end
of which one also becomes ashamed of one's morality" (Nietzsche,
1885, 95, p. 81)

What, then, lies at the core of this transvaluation? The killing of
God—of authority, of the father? The removal of guilt? Can it simply
be coerced into the oedipal schema? Surely, it is all that in some way.
Yet, it seems to me, it is *Nietzsche's relentless battle against
weakness (weakness of will, of control, of being oneself), a
desperate fight against feeling ashamed*. All obligation, all guilt is,
lastly, a burden that makes one weak and invites the abysmal
humiliation that his entire fight against Western morality tries to
eradicate.

> *I teach you the overman [superman].* Man is something that shall
> be overcome. What have you done to overcome him? . . . What is
> the ape to man? A laughingstock or a painful embarrassment [lit.: a
> shame]. And man shall be just that for the overman: a laughingstock
> or a painful embarrassment. You have made your way from worm
> to man, and much in you is still worm. Once you were apes, and
> even now, too, man is more ape than any ape [Nietzsche, 1883–
> 1885, "Vorrede" [Preface], 3, p. 8].

The sharpest formulation of this value philosophical revirement
appears at the end of the third book of "Joyful Science"

> *What makes you heroic?*—Meet at the same time your highest
> suffering and your highest hope.
> *What do you believe in?*—That the weights of everything need
> to be calibrated anew.
> *What says your conscience?*—"You shall become who you are."
> *Where lie your greatest threats?*—In compassion.
> *What do you love in others?*—My hopes.
> *Whom do you call evil?*—Him who always wants to shame.
> *What is for you the most humane thing?*—Sparing somebody
> shame.

What is the seal of freedom attained?–Not being ashamed anymore in front of oneself [Nietzsche, 1882, p. 177].

The antitheses of pride and shame; of respect (or honor) and contempt (or derision, jeering, scorn); of courage and cowardice; of sincerity and guileful, insidious deception; of open revenge and resentment (understood as vindictiveness without strength and courage); of purity (cleanliness) and impurity (uncleanliness); of power (self-control) and décadence; of nobility and being part of the herd (the much too many, the superfluous)–all these form, as it were, a kind of "counterpoint" to most of his work. They all belong to the *spectrum of shame conflicts*. They all express his own struggle against fearing to be exposed, fearing to be "ashamed"–as the physically and emotionally suffering and lonely man he really was and as the weak human being he dreaded being: "One kills not by wrath, but by laughter," ("Nicht durch Zorn, sondern durch Lachen tötet man" [Nietzsche, 1883-1885, "Vom Lesen" [About Reading], p. 47]) and he speaks of "the horrible torture of offended honor," ("jener furchtbaren Marter der verletzten Ehre" [Nietzsche, 1878-1880, I, II, 61, p. 71]) which may repesent more suffering than life is worth. Hence the refrain: "Man is something that must be overcome"–man as a weak, shameful, suffering being, burdened by conscience and an animal of the flock, contemptible and resentful.

What is meant by "shame"? The word shame really covers three concepts: shame is, first, the *fear* of disgrace. It is the *anxiety* one has in fearing to be looked at with contempt for having dishonored oneself–a danger looming. Second, it is the feeling one has when one is looked at with scorn, the feared event having happened. In this second form, it is the *affect of contempt* directed against the self, by others or by one's own conscience. Contempt says: "You should disappear for being the person you have shown yourself to be– failing, weak, flawed, and dirty. Get out of my sight! Disappear!" One feels ashamed for *being exposed*. Third, shame is almost the antithesis of the second concept, as in, "Don't you know any shame?" It is an overall *character trait* preventing disgraceful exposure. It is an attitude of respect toward others and toward oneself, a stance of reverence–the highest form of such reverence being called by Goethe "die Ehrfurcht vor sich selbst," reverence for oneself. This third form of shame is discretion, tact, sexual modesty. It is respect and a sense of awe–a refusal "to touch, lick and finger everything, a nobility of taste and tact of reverence" (Nietzsche, 1885, 263, p. 221). Thus, we can discern three forms of shame: shame anxiety, shame affect as a complex reaction pattern, and shame as a preventive attitude against dangerous self-exposure (exhibition) and curiosity (voyeurism), a character attitude built on the defense by reaction formation (Wurmser, 1981, 1987b).

Nietzsche's most intimate concern is to fight off the exposure of weakness, the categorical avoidance of shame in its second meaning, the complex shame affect: of feeling ashamed, of being shamed, humiliated, disgraced, and of accepting such a verdict. When I say Nietzsche is waging war against shame, I mean it strictly in the first two ways of understanding it; his main defensive attitude is shame in the third sense, and that is actually also how he usually employs the word *Scham*.

All his outrageous, proto-Nazi demands, all those defiantly sadistic outbursts appear like weapons in a last-ditch fight of spite, of defiance and scorn against this pervasive sense of inner shame, or, rather, the pervasive fear of being shamed, of being discovered as weak—a defense by reaction formation.

> The darkening of the sky above man has always prevailed in proportion to how much man's shame *in front of man* has grown [Nietzsche, 1887, II, 7, p. 297].[4]

The ideal is the "noble man"—*der vornehme Mensch*, living in the *"pathos of distance,"* (*das Pathos der Distanz*, Nietzsche. 1885, IX, 257, p. 197)—who exploits and conquers the others and is full of contempt for the coward, the weakling, the liar, the herd animal. His moral is "self-glorification," *Selbstverherrlichung*: "The noble human being honors the powerful within himself." ("Der vornehme Mensch ehrt in sich den Mächtigen" [Nietzsche, 1885, IX, 260, p. 202]).

The new morality and metaphysics of Nietzsche stands in the service of this fight against the sense of shame—the freedom of a "man to whom nothing is prohibited anymore, except *weakness*, be it now called vice or virtue" (Nietzsche, 1888a, "Streifzüge eines Unzeitgemäßen" [Wanderings of an Untimely Man], 49, p. 173). It is the advocacy of a value system built on ruthless strength, self-control, will power, and an absolute avoidance of any vulnerability, of any exposure, of any weakness—all in a crescendo of power. It is the precedence of this fight against feeling ashamed and against shaming others, a fight at times approaching "shamelessness," that gives us

---

[4]"Die Verdüsterung des Himmels über dem Menschen hat immer im Verhältnis dazu überhand genommen, als die Scham des Menschen *vor dem Menschen* gewachsen ist."

the key to so much that appears enigmatic and paradoxical, often shocking, in Nietzsche's morality.

His value system, built on the battle against shame, culminates in the adoration of beauty, beauty being understood as the expression of strength of will, as freedom from any restraints that could weaken the will, the "audacity [supercourage] of the superman" (*[den] Übermut des Übermenschen*), as Löwith (1956, p. 63) calls it. Beauty is based on "appearance," even on "seeming"–to being seen with admiration; the value of beauty is thus intimately related to the spectrum of the affects of shame and the battle against shame. Is beauty not the ultimate, though transient victory over shame? "Art where the *lie* sanctifies itself, where the *will to deceive* has good conscience on its side is much more fundamentally opposed to the ascetic ideal than is science" (Nietzsche, 1887, III, 25, p. 402).

In this ideal opposed to shame, purity is important: "What most deeply separates two persons is a different sense and degree of cleanliness" (Nietzsche, 1885, 271, p. 219); the highest instinct of cleanliness leads to holiness–and utterly isolates. And this description again turns into prescription when he adds later on, again in the context of the analysis of nobility: "loneliness is for us a virtue, in form of a sublime tendency and urge for cleanliness, that guesses how the contact between man and man–'in society'–is inevitably impure. Every community somehow, somewhere, sometime makes– 'vile'" (Nietzsche, 1885, 284, p. 225).

Thus one can say that this "new" superego is deeply rooted in categories of "anality"–purity, control, willfulness, defiance, horror of all shame and submission; and with that is characteristically "split" into absolute extremes of judgment, always, in fact, judging, and with a bitter resentment underneath.

We may call this "new" ideal "narcissistic" or "anal" or "a war against shame" or "preoedipal"–all these are correct. Yet are these characterizations sufficient?

THE "RESSENTIMENT"[5]–"THE SLAVE-REVOLT IN MORALITY–A DISGRACE OF MAN"

With this heading I refer to a passage in the *Genealogy of Morals* (Nietzsche, 1887, I, 11, pp. 269–270): "All those instincts of reaction

---

[5]Nietzsche uses also in German this specific and very strong French term. The English word "resentment" is far weaker.

and resentment . . . these 'tools of culture' are a disgrace to man."[6] I have already mentioned the poison stream of resentment flowing out of the core weakness. It is exactly about resentment, "das Ressentiment," that Nietzsche has to say much that is of the greatest relevance and expresses even more without directly putting it into words.

He ascribes its origin to the "priestly people of the Jews":[7]

> Out of powerlessness their hatred grows into something immense and uncanny, into what is most spiritual and most poisonous . . . the Jews, that priestly people that gained satisfaction against its enemies and conquerors ultimately only by a radical transformation of their [the enemies'] values: by an act of the *most spiritual revenge* (der *geistigsten Rache*) [Nietzsche, 1887, I, 7, p. 259].

They replaced the aristocratic value equation of good = noble = powerful = beautiful = happy = loved by God by its opposite, "held by the teeth of the most abysmal hatred," namely, that "only those who are miserable are good; *the poor, powerless, lowly ones alone are good, the suffering, deprived, sick, ugly ones* are the only pious ones, the only Godly ones; only for them is there blessedness." With this value revolution the "uprising of the slaves in morality begins" (p. 260).

Soon thereafter comes a passage that seems to me particularly revealing of the *double message of resentment* expounded by this great, but dangerous thinker, a double message that, I believe, answers, to some extent, the question of why Nietzsche's philosophy came to carry such horrendous brisance:

> This Jesus of Nazareth, the embodiment of the Gospel of love, this "Savior," who brought blessedness and victory to the poor, to the sick, to the sinners—wasn't he precisely seduction in its uncanniest and most irresistible form, the seduction of, and the detour on the way to, just those *Jewish* values and reformations of the ideal? Hasn't Israel, by way of the very detour through this "Savior," through this seeming adversary and dissolver (Auflösers) of Israel,

---

[6]"alle jenen Reaktions—und Ressentiments—Instrinkte. . . Diese 'Werkzeuge der Kultur' sind eine Schande des Menschen"

[7]"Die Juden umgekehrt waren jenes priesterliche Volk des Ressentiment par excellence . . . " (Nietzsche, 1887, I, 16, p. 280). The reference is, of course, to Ex. 19.6: "You should be for me a kingdom of priests and a holy people" ("we'atem tiheyu-li mamlechet kohanim wegoy qadosh").

reached the last aim of its sublime vindictiveness? Is it not part of the black art of a truly *great* policy of revenge, of a farsighted, subterranean, slowly grabbing and precalculating revenge that Israel would, before the world, deny its real instrument of revenge as if it were some deadly enemy and crucify it, so that "all the world," that is, all the enemies of Israel, would, without hesitation, bite into this bait?

And, on the other side, could anyone, in all the refinement of his mind, devise an altogether more *dangerous* bait? Something that would equal in tempting, intoxicating, numbing, corruptive force that symbol of the "holy cross," that horrible paradox of a "God on the Cross"; that mystery of an unthinkable last and extreme cruelty and self-crucifixion of God *for the good of man?* . . . One thing is certain: sub hoc signo [under this sign] Israel has until now again and again triumphed with its revenge and transvaluation of all values over all other ideals, over all the *more noble* ideals [Nietzsche, 1887, I, 8, pp. 261–262].

That is, on one hand, a most trenchant analysis of the pernicious effect of resentment—an "analysis" not so much only of the "Jewish" resentment, but of the resentment hidden within Christian ethics and metaphysics; and, even beyond that, the entire old morality, the traditional conscience itself. Untruthfulness, inner and outer deception, and, most of all, a passive outward orientation, all born of pervasive weakness and impotence, carried by a vicious spirit of relentless but insidious revenge, and couched in terms of *poison*, dissolution, decay, and narcosis—these are the shameful attributes of the "Mensch des Ressentiment," the man of resentment, this antithesis of the man of nobility.

Yet, on the other hand, it is also a statement that itself shows all the influence of resentment. It is a bitter accusation of the insidious poisoning of the Western world by a Jewish conspiracy of more than 2000 years' duration, of a most cunning, skillful, and success-crowned emasculation of "noble man," the degradation of "tragic man," the sapping of the strength of the enemy. In short, it describes his humiliation and defeat by the most elegant means of revenge—self-castration with the help of a magic symbol. It is an indictment of the power of resentment, using the very magic of appealing to everybody's own, deeply buried sense of unfairness.

This is Nietzsche's philosophy of resentment at its purest, over and above his most intelligent descriptive analysis of resentment.

A CENTRAL DENIAL

Nietzsche's resentment is most centrally directed against Christianity and the human conscience built on guilt and self-punishment, but it also showers scorn and venom over mass culture, over everything bourgeois or socialist. Neither the concept of resentment nor the affect of resentment, however, can be understood without taking into account the underlying concept of justice and the deep sense of unfairness, the sense that one has not been treated justly. The concept and affect of resentment presuppose the sense of injustice and unfairness; this sense is an integral constituent part of resentment. Yet this reference to the polarity justice-injustice has been completely ignored by Nietzsche. Hence, psychologically resentment hangs in the air; it becomes the ultimate, supposedly basic reason to explain all the rest and is treated as if it were the main enemy. Yet, in fact, resentment is itself quite analyzable and in need of further explanation.

Analyzing resentment, we find that there may be such a sense of unfairness either because one feels that one has not been afforded due respect, recognition, honor, and dignity, and thus feels shamed; or because one feels shortchanged in regard to love, tenderness, sensuality, warmth, or possession as symbol of love; both lead to the affect of resentment. The common denominator is that the *sense of justice or fairness has been violated*.

Nietzsche's statement about the pervasiveness and perniciousness of the resentment turns itself out to be permeated by that gnawing feeling of injustice, powerlessness, and wish for revenge that mark resentment. Furthermore, Nietzsche's canvas showing in huge strokes resentment's history and psychology also turns into hypostatizing this idea into a general tool of explanation and condemnation without acknowledging its derivative character and its origins.

This discrepancy between the accuracy, even curious oversharpness, of his study of resentment and his partial blindness to it again represents a deep fracture in Nietzsche's argument.

Can this fracture in thought be broadened?

One line of his thinking leads from shame and suffering to resentment to revenge in the form of the destruction of all values and the creation of a new world of values, a world beyond weakness and shame. This line of reasoning, directed toward one pole of absoluteness, leads to the overthrow of the old superego and its replacement by *a totally opposite ideal and conscience*.

What is the other pole? It is self-discipline, even self-torment, on behalf of an absolute wish for truthfulness and selfless analysis, as unconditional a pursuit as the venomousness of that resentment and the war against shame have been. How can Nietzsche wage this war on two fronts at the same time and with equal radicalism, the war against lies and error and the war against shame and resentment?

To this quest for truth and its own inner rupture we turn now.

"THE ABSOLUTE WILL NOT TO DECEIVE ONESELF"[8]

Nobody who reads Nietzsche's works disinterestedly can fail to be deeply struck by the fervor of his search for truth and, in fact, by the profound truth of so much that search reveals. Truth is never treated by Nietzsche as absolute, but the search for truth is. Hence, he speaks of the *"unconditioned [i.e. absolute] inquiry into what is true"* ("die unbedingte Erforschung des Wahren" [Nietzsche, 1878–1880, II, I, 13, p. 17]). Similarly, he says about Zarathustra—not about the work, but his own alter ego (Nietzsche, 1888c, "Warum ich ein Schicksal bin" [Why I am destiny], 3, pp. 401–402):

> His teaching, and it alone, has truthfulness as highest virtue—that means the opposite of the *cowardice* of the "idealist" who flees from reality . . . The self-conquest of morality out of truthfulness, the self-conquest of the moralist [and the change] into his opposite— into *me*—this means in my mouth the name Zarathustra (das bedeutet in meinem Munde der Name Zarathustra).

Camus (1951) enthusiastically supports that side of Nietzsche that is uncompromisingly devoted to the pursuit of truth: "Yet one can derive from Nietzsche only a vile and mediocre cruelty that, in fact, he hated with all his might, unless one puts him first in his work as a clinician, far ahead of him as prophet" (p. 91).[9]

This may be, it is true, one of the creative tensions in Nietzsche's work—his creative "agon." Throughout we may note the sly oscillation between description and prescription, even proscription. This stylistic duality, this *conflict in rhetorical means*, is, however, nothing else than expression of a deeper conflict between the

---

[8]"Der unbedingte Willen, sich nichts vorzumachen" (Nietzsche, 1888a, "Was ich den Alten verdanke" [What I owe antiquity], 2, p. 177).

[9]"Mais on ne peut rien tirer de Nietzsche, sinon la cruauté basse et médiocre qu'il haïssait de toutes ses forces, tant qu'on ne met pas au premier plan dans son oeuvre, bien avant le prophète, le clinicien."

attitude of the clinician and therapist and that of the revolutionary prophet. The first wants the truth in order to demonstrate deception and to heal the suffering caused by it; the second wants revenge for his powerlessness and shame and needs power to redress the balance of unfairness, to heal his own resentment. These two attitudes are never reconciled for good; they only seem so. The fracture in the reasoning pointed out by Löwith (1956) is one outcome of this dichotomy. It seems to me that both lines of motivation were most powerfully at work in Nietzsche and that the immense duplicity and contradictoriness of his cultural and political effect is a result, writ in largest letters on the backdrop of the historical stage.

Thus there is that other side—the ethos of implacable truthfulness, with its inherent cruelty, especially against the self. In another formulation—one that gives deeper justice to the method of conflict analysis, specifically here in the sense of the inquiry into value polarities—there is a conflict between an absolute ethos of truthfulness and an equally absolutely set ethos of will and power, the avoidance of exposed weakness, hence of shame. Nietzsche appears to be torn between these two ethical postulates, both held absolutely. Although he is a master at working out conflict at its sharpest while setting the opposites as absolutes, he is torn by them; and every attempt at reconciliation fails, even the ultimate attempt in form of the synthesis of human life and cosmic being—"will for power" versus "the eternal return of the same." The fracture remains, the heroic effort fails, illness and destruction tear this most wonderful work asunder.

The conflict is sharpened even more. We find:

> In spite of all the value that might belong to what is true, to what is sincere [truthful, *wahrhaftig*], to what is selfless—it might be possible that a more basic value, one that is higher for all of life, would have to be ascribed to seeming [appearance], to the will for deception, to selfishness and to desire [Nietzsche, 1885, I, 2, p. 9].

Yet the crucial insight is this:

> The conception of the world forming the background to this book is peculiarly dark and unpleasant: among all the types of pessimism that have become known so far none appears to have reached that degree of maliciousness. The *opposition between a true and an apparent world is lacking*: there is only one world, and this one is false, cruel, contradictory, seductive, *without meaning* [italics added]. . . . A world like this is the true world . . . *We need [the] lie* in order to gain victory over this reality, this "truth," i.e., in order

to *live* . . . [The very fact] that the lie is necessary in order to live belongs to this frightening and questionable character of existence . . . [Nietzsche, 1980, p. 193].

Thus *"the philosophy of power becomes the philosophy of the lie,"* adds Giorgio Colli (in Nietzsche, 1980: italics added). The conflict between the will for truth and the will for power ends in an unsolvable paradox.

Camus (1951) speaks of the preeminence of the clinician over the prophet in Nietzsche. Is this really true? My own impression is that, especially in his later works, the prophet more and more subverts the clinician, cruelty and vindictiveness pervert curiosity and the impassioned search for truth, hatred infiltrates all interest, the sense of loss of love and of loneliness cries through the protests of strength and power.

From our distant vantage point, these contradictions and paradoxes, emerging from that double quest for truth and for strength, converge into an ever-deepening rift within.

THE TWO NIETZSCHES—"IT WAS AT NOON THAT ONE BECAME TWO."[10]

Let us review what we have found so far: There is the fierce denunciation of resentment and of its pernicious consequences—yet, at the same time, there is the unmistakable poison of that self-same feeling pouring out in his scorn.

There is the radical rejection of guilt and punishment, of remorse and pangs of conscience and their banishment from the new ethics. There is the ferocious rejection of any ethics built on the notion of "you ought"—yet it is hard to imagine a writer or thinker who is more condemnatory and critical, more judgmental and punishing, more corrosive in his contempt and ridicule.

I said that the prophet, no matter how much denied, always wins out over the skillful psychologist and clinically subtle diagnostician in the constant shift from description to prescription and from that to proscription.

---

[10]"Um Mittag war's, da wurde Eins zu Zwei".(Nietzsche, 1885, "Aus hohen Bergen" [From high mountains], p. 236).

Then there is the duality of thinker and poet, both being of the greatest brilliance and depth, both of enormous power, and yet forced together only to break apart.

And then something else: It has been said many times that Nietzsche was not an antisemite. Yet there are many passages in his work that are as vitriolic as the worst of any antisemitic tract. For example, when he extols "Aryan humanity" of "pure blood" and "nobility" against the "Anti-Aryan religion par excellence" (Christianity), a religion of hatred (Nietzsche, 1888a, "Die 'Verbesserer' der Menschheit" [Mankind's reformers], 4, pp. 120–121). I also find a passage like the following particularly hard to stomach: "Israel's history as the typical history of all the *denaturization* of natural values" with its "radical *falsification* of all nature, of all naturalness, of all reality, of the entire inner world" (Nietzsche, 1888b, 24–35, pp. 215–233).

But paradoxically there also are beautiful passages about the Jews. For instance, he writes:

> I would want to know how much one should, in the total account, forgive a people who, not without the guilt of us all, has had the most painful [suffering filled, leidvollste] history among all the peoples, and to whom we owe the most noble human being (Christ), the purest sage (Spinoza), the most powerful book, and the most effective moral law of the world. Furthermore, during the darkest periods of the middle ages, when the Asiatic pall was lying heavily over Europe, it was Jewish free thinkers, scholars, and physicians who, under the severest personal force [compulsion], held fast to the banner of enlightenment and intellectual independence and defended Europe against Asia. Not least it is owing to their endeavors that a more natural, more reasonable, and in any case nonmythical explanation of the world eventually could gain victory and that the ring of culture tying us together with the enlightenment of Greco-Roman antiquity has remained unbroken. If Christianity has done everything to orientalize the occident, so Judaism has essentially helped to occidentalize it again: which means as much as to make Europe's task and history into a *continuation of that of Greece* [Nietzsche, 1878–1880, I, VIII, 475, p. 305].

Isn't this perhaps just the point: that he is both a virulent antisemite and a reverent friend and lover of the Jews; categorical about everything, yet despising the categories others use and abuse; full of contempt and of respect, of hatred and of love? Here again is that extreme polarity and duality in him which he tries to, but cannot, reconcile.

Another overarching contradiction: *Justice* keeps coming up as one of the most important virtues. Albeit in historizing onesidedness (as opposed to a primarily psychological understanding), he very correctly develops it as emerging from the need for equilibrium, specifically in the archaic community: "*Equilibrium* is therefore a very important concept for the oldest teaching of law and morality; *equilibrium is the basis of justice*" ("Gleichgewicht ist die Basis der Gerechtigkeit," Nietzsche, 1878–1880, II, II, 22, p. 184). The decisive issue is his recognition of justice as based on an original concept of equality—an equality of rights, of opportunities, not necessarily of results. While it may be traced back to allegedly deeper reasons of advantage and utility or of pleasure, the fundamental quality of that equation for all kinds of social life is maintained. Thus, by grounding justice in equality (equilibrium), his appeal to justice on so many levels throughout his writings is effectively and convincingly supported. He uses the notion of "justice" not infrequently and says that "it will give everything its due" (I, IX, 636, p. 354). He even adds: "[we] want to kneel down in front of Justice as the only Goddess we recognize above ourselves" (637, p. 355).

Yet, much to the contrary, we also keep hearing the opposite message sounded with great vehemence: "you who make souls whirl, you preachers of *equality*. To me you are tarantulas, and secretely vengeful . . . to *me* justice speaks thus: 'Men are not equal.'" (Nietzsche, 1883–1885, "Tarantulas," p. 106). His hatred and scorn for the socialist gospel of justice based on the equality of man and for the democratic pronouncements of equal rights keep breaking through. He states the contradiction himself that human beings need equality for safety's sake, but that is, at the same time, something that runs profoundly counter to our individual natures, something forced upon us. He concludes that there is neither natural law [justice] nor natural injustice ("Es gibt weder ein Naturrecht, noch ein Naturunrecht") (Nietzsche, 1878–1880, II, II, 31, p. 191).

Recognizing in the contradiction a fundamental conflict between two basic needs—that of the will to overpower the other and that of living together for safety's sake (or other deep motives)—would state a basic human quandary intrinsic to human nature. To choose, however, one, the will for power, as primary nature and to derogate the linkage of safety = community = justice as against nature appears to me to beg the question. Why would one be for nature, the other suddenly against nature?

It would be facile to dismiss much of this duality and contradiction as part of pathology. On the contrary, I think that some of the duality precisely expresses Nietzsche's deepest insights and prophetic anticipations. Later on it became, in fact, relevant for the philosophy underlying the Complementarity Principle as a basic epistemological tool but has by no means been fully integrated into our own psychoanalytic thinking.

Nietzsche (1878–1880) himself describes and justifies this duality of acknowledgment and denial (which we know, of course, from Freud's writings about the "ego split") in an aphorism under the heading "Zweimal ungerecht" (Twice unfair):

> Sometimes we enhance the truth by a double injustice, namely when we see and present, one after the other, both sides of a matter, which we cannot see together [at the same time]; yet, in a way, each time we mistake [misunderstand] or deny the other side, deluding ourselves that what we see is the entire truth [II, I, 79, p. 41].

It is also in Nietzsche's spirit of relentless questioning and probing, however, that we go an extra step and ask ourselves, Is this duality not also, and decisively, part and expression of the underlying conflict? Has it not been used, as a tool of thought, for the self-destruction, the self-abolition of his philosophical intent? And how? Is it not used, in addition to its epistemological credentials, for a purpose that stems from what Nietzsche himself called his "suffering and deprivation"?

AN INTERPRETATION OF THE IDENTITY SPLIT

From all the unreconciled "splits," I have selected one that I consider fundamental and decisive for a further understanding of Nietzsche. He speaks so much and so well about the cruelty of conscience, but his own conscience is pitiless, especially when it is turned against others; thus it endows those who identify with his value priorities with the right to commit violence without mercy. It was Nietzsche's conscience turned outward—his brand of archaic superego, his ferocious judgmentalness, his peculiar eloquence of contempt and ridiculing, and, most of all, his power to shame others by the very vehemence of his own resentment—that lent its immense impetus, its force of mythopoesis, to a historical movement he would have abhorred had he met it.

Does not his appeal lie precisely in this doubleness of judgment and overthrow of conscience, in the doubleness of a superego based on the systematic prevention of being shamed and the elimination of those superego features having to do with guilt and punishment? His is an appeal rooted in just such a juxtaposition, where the yoke of conscience is thrown off, yet the severity of judgment, the most pervasive judgmentalness, is maintained.

So much of life appears in Nietzsche to be "cut out"–ignored or omitted: the depth of love, the intricacy of human relations, the questions of tenderness and attachment, and especially the issue of justice, without which no social system can endure and which forms such a deep part of human nature. I have noted his increasingly shrill denunciation of the basis of justice in any concept of equality and the related dismissal of the ethics of guilt.

As much as one has to agree with him that man's judgmentalness is one of the greatest banes of human relations and one of the most powerful poisons in the inner life, and as much as one may wonder with him about the ultimate source of the concept of justice, the concept of justice cannot simply be eliminated by pointing to its abuse by vindictiveness or by demolishing the quest for equality.

What "cutting out" ("Ausschneidung," his own frequently used metaphor) eventually all comes down to is a resolute "revolution against conscience," and, at that, a revolution against a specific form of conscience: at first simply the "feeling of 'sin' as a transgression against divine order" (Nietzsche, 1878–1880, I, III, 133, p. 121), yet also against guilt and remorse altogether: "the displeasure of remorse, the sharpest sting in the feeling of sin, is broken off." Eventually guilt and conscience become crimes against mankind. Thus, by imposing "the concept of guilt and punishment, the entire 'moral world order' . . . one has committed the greatest crime against mankind. Sin, . . . man's way of self-dishonoring par excellence, has been invented to block science, culture, any elevation and nobility of man; the priest *rules* with the help of the invention of sin" (Nietzsche, 1888b, 49, pp. 255–256).

This argument uses one giant myth: that such deep aspects of human nature as guilt, sense of sin, or morality are solely created from the outside, in this instance through the malignant cunning of some power-greedy priests, led by that mythical Israel. It is, for such a skillful psychologist as Nietzsche, a remarkably naive view of human nature: that it is shaped into these depths and to such considerable uniformity by external forces of a mythical character. This sort of blaming is the real ideological precursor of the totalitarian state–of what I have called "the three paranoid catastrophes" of this century–the totalitarian systems of Hitler, Stalin, and Mao Ze Dong (Wurmser, 1989, p. 506).

What else can we call this attitude of blaming human nature on sinister outside forces other than a basically paranoid attitude of externalization, projection, and denial, that claims the cause of weakening as lying on the outside, or in a basic degeneracy ("weakness") of nature that must be extirpated?

THE DEFENSE AGAINST SHAME

I have spoken of shame's third form as a reaction formation against being shamed for (wishes for) exposure and curiosity and against the traumatic sense of shame anxiety. There are in Nietzsche's writings countless examples of this *attitude of shame* and the necessity of hiding, of disguise, of silence, of veiling oneself, as a protection. Take, for example, the following: By killing God the eye that saw everything had to be eliminated; the "ugliest man" commits the deed of murdering God because "the man who obeys God's 'you ought' does not want to command himself" (Löwith, 1956, p. 50):

> He—*had* to die. He looked with eyes that saw *everything*—he saw man's depths and reasons, all his concealed disgrace and ugliness. His pitying knew no shame: he crawled into my dirtiest corners. This most curious, overintrusive, overpitiful one had to die. He always was seeing *me*: I wanted to take revenge on such a witness— or to cease living. God, who saw everything, saw *also Man*: this God had to die! Man does not *tolerate* that such a witness lives [Nietzsche, 1883–1885, IV, "Der häßlichste Mensch" [The ugliest man], pp. 294–295].

This deed spares man the shame from now on: "'How poor man is after all!' he [Zarathustra] thought in his heart; 'how ugly, how wheezing, how full of hidden shame!'" (p. 295).

The "second Nietzsche," his entire transvaluation of values, seems to me based on the magic of the *reaction formation* against shame, especially in the sense of a character and superego defense against the content of shame. There are also certain affects that serve as *affect defenses* against shame and may be used as precursors to the reaction formation: pride and vanity, spite and defiance, scorn and contempt.

Subsidiary to these two closely intertwined defenses against shame (reaction formation and affect defenses) is his magical undoing of suffering by creativity and beauty, a particularly lasting form of power proving that unworthiness has been transformed into the highest and most enduring worth, that "man has indeed been overcome" (Nietzsche, 1883–1885, passim), that his shame has been wiped out, once and for all.

Another defense against shame is *denial*: Would we not have to say that the massive "cutting out" of important areas of life might be dictated by that peculiar superego stance, that of the war against being shamed and hence against the need to be resentful? Yet would not that denial have to be sustained by a constant battle against the old conscience, an opposite superego figure? The player's jugglings and the shamer's dazzlings and the high-wire act are clearly only half the truth. This forced weightlessness, which yearns at the same time to fly and to be grounded, to dance and to find the point of gravity, has to disguise some crushing heaviness and hide the deep suffering behind courageous laughter and play.

Who is the relentless enemy? What is the other half?

Nietzsche himself is a man who is himself burdened by a monstrously crushing conscience, but all his thinking is an incessant attempt to prove that this is not so anymore; that he has killed, "overcome," that inner enemy; that he has wagered his life and sanity, his reputation and companionship on its overthrow—yet has never succeeded for more than "intoxicating" moments of inspiration. He is burdened by a conscience that is as much fraught with guilt as with shame (in the sense of being ashamed) and is accompanied by pain, helplessness, and anxiety.

His entire creative life appears to be a compulsive repetition of the shaking off of an overbearing conscience, the message being: "That bane of the Protestant ethic, that Christian superego of duty and categorical imperative, does not exist anymore; I have really killed it, haven't I? killed it for good, made it ridiculous forever as the malicious inner dwarf that it really always has been. Just look at me, how light I am, how unburdened of that dwarf! Look!" Parallel with such denial is the resurgence, in the form of projection and externalization, of what has been denied.

Thus we see, side by side, the widest opposition: deepest insight into inner conflict, guided by the absolute ideal of truthfulness, and paranoid externalization accompanying the denial of vast areas of inner conflict, namely, all those having to do with the "old conscience"—guilt, remorse, responsibility toward others, and, most of all, being ashamed, failing an equally absolute ideal, that of strength and power. The tension between these two absolute ideals or superego figures—truthfulness versus power—is never resolved. It is the basic split that fractures all of Nietzsche's philosophy and underlies the doubleness: the division into a clinical-diagnostic *philosophy of psychological truth and analysis* and a prophetic-apocalyptic *anti-shame-resentment philosophy*. These two, I claim, stand in an irreconcilable combat. The latter demands a paranoid solution; the former accepts the basic conflict-nature of man. The second is historically and culturally devastating; the first often evokes our enthusiastic admiration and assent and is capable of teaching us a great deal even today, after 100 years of psychoanalysis. Nietzsche (1883–1885) may have come closest to a convergence of the two, a partially successful synthesis, in a work more poetic than philosophical, the *Zarathustra*. Otherwise the Nietzsche of truthfulness stands in "sheer oppugnancy" to the Nietzsche obsessed with the fight against weakness, his unsuccessful war against shame and resentment. This fracture between truthfulness and strength, betweeen honesty and power underlies the fracture in his doctrine between the anthropological "will to power" and the cosmological "myth of the eternal return (recurrence) of the same," observed by Löwith (1956).

THE APOCALYPTIC RESULT

Historically it is decisive that in none of these works is there an elimination of the superego. Quite the contrary, we witness its massive reinforcement, although in profoundly altered form—from our clinical view, we would say in deeply regressive form. The "second Nietzsche," the ideal of *Zarathustra* and his conscience, became a leading superego figure for Germany, in fact for much of Europe, but with the most devastating consequences. The graver Germany's and Austria's humiliations were, especially after the World War I, the more the new superego, fighting with all its weapons against the inner and the outer shame, assumed mythical proportions and real power as a historical, political, military, and finally genocidal force. And Nietzsche anticipated it, hoping to "overcome" it in general terms, yet deceiving himself and even decisively bringing it about in its most horrible form: by his own pervasive judgmentalness in sarcasm and reproach and by his own drenching, yet denied, resentment. By reducing the guilt-oriented conscience to a matter of shame and, to a supposed external imposition of sanctions that left the individual helpless and passive, he accomplished the entire "transvaluation of values." Might it not be his very doubleness—the claim that all great insight requires the *Doppelblick*, "the double view"—combined with his depth of insight, the brilliance of his language, and his artful use of metaphor that has endowed his message with such an enormous echo and appeal for such a broad following? And is it not this doubleness of rebellion and loyalty in his "double sight" which has such a disastrous mass appeal because of the severity of superego conflicts at a time when old securities are shaken and the allegiances of the past have been overthrown?

Nietzsche's importance consists in his having drawn our attention to an ethic built on categories of shame, that is, a morality of inner consistency and its own truth and value, its own autonomy, and that he has laid out its huge significance as part of our own inner nature, its validity for us. He made the fundamental mistake, however, of putting this ethic in absolute, categorical terms: he reduced guilt to shame, attributed the facets of human nature to externally, historically, and culturally imposed ones, and left out the centrality of the need for *justice* in human nature and as *the causal issue behind the corrosive power of resentment.*

Yet Nietzsche could not have made those mistakes if he had not been, prior to Freud, the foremost explorer of inner conflict of the "laws" of human nature. His errors honor his genius as much as his discoveries do.

REFERENCES

Camus, A. (1951), *L'homme révolté* (Man in Revolt). Paris: Gallimard.
Löwith, K. (1956), *Nietzsches Philosophie der ewigen Wiederkehr des Gleichen* (Nietzsche's Philosophy of the Eternal Return of the Same). Stuttgart: Kohlhammer.
Nietzsche, F. (1878–1880), *Menschliches, Allzumenschliches* (Human, All Too Human). Stuttgart: Kröner, 1978.
――― (1882), *Die fröhliche Wissenschaft* (Joyful Science). Stuttgart: Kröner, 1976.
――― (1883–1885), *Also sprach Zarathustra* (Thus Spoke Zarathustra). Stuttgart: Kröner, 1988.
――― (1885), *Jenseits von Gut und Böse* (Beyond Good and Evil). Stuttgart: Kröner, 1976.
――― (1887), *Zur Genealogie der Moral* (The Genealogy of Morals). Stuttgart: Kröner, 1976.
――― (1888a), *Götzendämmerung* (Twilight of the Gods). Stuttgart: Kröner, 1964.
――― (1888b), *Der Antichrist* (Antichrist). Stuttgart: Kröner, 1964.
――― (1888c), *Ecce Homo.* Stuttgart: Kröner, 1964.
――― (1980), *Nachgelassene Fragmente* (Posthumously Published Fragments). Bd. 13 der Sämtlichen Werke (Complete Works). Hgb. Colli & Montinari. Berlin: de Gruyter.

Wurmser, L. (1981), *The Mask of Shame.* Baltimore, MD: Johns Hopkins University Press.

———— (1987b), Shame: The veiled companion of narcissism. In: *The Many Faces of Shame*, ed. D. L. Nathanson. New York: Guilford.

———— (1989), *Die zerbrochene Wirklichkeit.* (Broken Reality.) Heidelberg: Springer.

———— (1993), *Das Rätsel des Masochismus.* (The Riddle of Masochism). Heidelberg: Springer.

8

THOMAS J. SCHEFF

Shame in Social Theory

Over the last 200 years in the history of modern societies, shame virtually disappeared. The denial of shame has been institutionalized in Western societies. Two of the leading theories of human nature, behaviorism and Marxism, give it short shrift. The other leading theory, psychoanalysis, has both promoted and denied shame. Although much of the creative work on shame was developed by psychoanalysts, in orthodox psychanalysis shame is ignored in favor of guilt and anxiety.

Shame is almost recognized as a real entity in only one institutional sphere, the self-help recovery movement, now quite large, that grew out of Alcoholics Anonymous. Within this movement, shame is often seen as a vital aspect of recovery. Participants may speak of shame openly and frequently. Most of the popular writing on shame has come from those involved in AA. In all other institutions, however, shame leads a shadow life. The dynamics of shame in our society are as connected to social structure as they are to individual personality. The emotions of pride and shame are intimately connected to their social correlates, acceptance and disgrace. Like the emotions themselves, their social correlates are also under a ban.

This chapter is based in part on sections of chapter 1 of Scheff and Retzinger, 1991, and chapter 5, Scheff, 1991.

My colleague and I (Scheff and Retzinger, 1991) have outlined an approach that allows free movement back and forth between individual emotions and social relationships. We propose that pride is the emotional correlate of a secure social bond; and shame, the emotional correlate of a threatened bond. If this is the case, then the state of the bond can be determined immediately and directly from discourse: a preponderance of cues to pride suggest a secure bond, just as a preponderance of cues to shame suggest a threatened one. In this chapter I use this idea in order to locate the emotion of shame within psychological and social theory.

A BRIEF HISTORY OF SHAME

A brief review of the history of shame in Western societies may help us to understand how we got to this point. This chapter introduces these topics, beginning with the Bible and classic Greek thought and progressing through early modern discussions and recent formulations. Although emotions have been a topic of serious discussion for thousands of years, they form one of the cloudiest regions of human thought. Any investigation of emotions is at hazard from its beginning, since the concept itself is undefined. Even the most scholarly and scientific analyses depend on the use of vernacular terms such as anger, fear, grief, shame, joy, and love and the underlying presuppositions about emotion in our society. The field of emotions is less a body of knowledge than a jungle of unexamined assumptions, observations, and theories. Some of the roots of our contemporary attitudes toward emotion, and some of the puzzles we still share, can be seen by reviewing usage in the Bible and other sources.

The issue of shame arises very early in the Old Testament. Although the word is not used, it is implied in the story of Adam and Eve. When Adam tells God that he hid from him because he was naked, God asks, "Who told thee that thou wast naked?" God inferred that, since Adam was ashamed of being naked, he had become self-conscious, that he had eaten of the forbidden fruit. In the biblical story, shame arises simultaneously with human self-consciousness. This event is portentous; it hints that shame may play a central role in the human drama.

The shame context of the story is shown in most portrayals of the expulsion from the Garden, with both Adam and Eve showing embarrassment or shame. In the painting by Massaccio, Eve shows her embarrassment by covering her breasts and loins, but Adam covers his eyes with both hands. Perhaps Adam is more profoundly ashamed than Eve, who covers only parts of her self. Adam, by covering his eyes so that he won't see or be seen, like a child, may be trying to escape entirely from regarding God and from being regarded by him.

Adam and Eve are completely submissive to God's punishment: they are silent in the face of his harsh judgment. The very possibility of standing up to authority has not yet arisen. Their silence implies not only that God has condemned them but that they have condemned themselves; their shame is complete.

The book of Genesis implies two crucial episodes in human development: the physical creation of humans by God and the shift from the paradisiacal life of human animals to that of self-conscious human beings. A third significant episode occurs in the book of Job. The protagonist does not suffer in silence under God's wrath, as Adam and Eve did. Rather he confronts God with his misery, questioning the justice of his fate. The story of Job provides the first suggestion that hierarchy in the human social order is not inexorable, as it is in animal societies, but can be challenged. Job's confrontation with God is a stirring toward freedom from rigid compliance to the status quo, just as the birth of self-consciousness created the potential for partial liberation from animal existence.

A historical equivalent can be found in Vico's (1744) pronouncement "the social world is the work of men" (rather than God or nature). Unlike all other living creatures, humans have the potential for creating their own society. Vico's statement was courageous; he was in danger of his life for challenging the absolute authority of the Church and State.

Even today, escape from inexorable authority is still only partial. Most of us, most of the time, are enmeshed in a status quo, the taken-for-granted social arrangements of our society, which seem to us absolute and unchangeable. Even though the status quo is only one particular version of many possible social orders, to those enmeshed in it, it seems eternal. To a large degree, human beings, like other animals, are cogs in a social machine.

The three biblical episodes can be taken as emblematic of the physical, psychological, and cultural evolution of human nature. As will be seen, shame may be intimately connected with all three of these steps. First, shame has a basis in biology, as one of what William James (1890) called the "coarse" emotions, in that it has a genetically inherited component. According to child development studies, precursors of shame occur very early in infancy, too early to have been learned (see, e.g., Tronick, 1980; Tronick, Ricks, and Cohn, 1981). Second, the universality of facial expressions of shame in all cultures that have been studied, and in linguistic studies, also suggest a biological component (Scheff, 1987b). Third, there is a psychological component: shame arises in situations of self-consciousness, seeing oneself from the viewpoint of others. Finally, there is a cultural component. The situations that produce shame, the labeling of shame, and the response to it show immense variation from one society to another. Shame may be the most social of all emotions, since it functions as a signal of threat to the social bond, an issue to which I return later.

In the Old Testament there are many references to pride and shame, but few to guilt. In the New Testament, this ratio is reversed: there are many more references to guilt than to shame. One possible interpretation would be in terms of a difference between a "shame culture" and a "guilt culture." From this perspective (Benedict, 1946; Dodds, 1951), the writers of the Old Testament would have been members of traditional society in which shame was the major method of social control; and the writers of the New Testament, members of a society in transition to modernity, in which guilt was the major method of social control.

I propose, however, that the difference between shame and guilt cultures is misleading, in that it assumes that shame states are infrequent in modern societies. It is possible that the role of shame in social control has not decreased but gone underground. In traditional societies, shame is openly acknowledged; the word itself appears frequently in everyday discourse. In modern societies, references to shame appear infrequently or in disguised form.

The disguises of shame include hundreds of words and phrases that seem to be substitutes or euphemisms for the word shame or embarrassment; lose face, feel insecure. Our very language in modern societies conspires to hide shame from display and from consciousness.

A second issue concerns the meaning assigned to pride in the Old Testament. Virtually every reference places pride in a disparaging light. Perhaps the most familiar example occurs in Proverbs 16–18: "Pride goeth before destruction, and an haughty spirit before a fall." (In everyday usage, this quotation is often shortened to "Pride goeth before a fall.") A similar use occurs in 16–19: "Better it is to be of a humble spirit with the lowly, than to divide the spoil with the proud." Many more similar examples could be cited.

As in these biblical passages, contemporary usage implies that the word pride alone carries a negative connotation. To escape that connotation, it is necessary to add a qualifier, for example, *justified* pride. There might be less confusion if it were the other way around, that pride alone signified normal or justified pride. In this usage, it would be necessary to add a qualifier, for example, *false* pride, to refer to the kind of pride so prominent in the Old Testament. There is a hint of this usage in the passage from Proverbs just cited, when it is quoted in full: the kind of pride that leads to a fall is the kind that is marked by haughtiness. Perhaps false pride is unrelated to normal pride, but to its antithesis, shame. Insolence and haughtiness may mask deep-seated feelings of inferiority, i.e. shame.

False pride corresponds exactly to the meaning of the Greek word *hubris*, the kind of pride that leads certainly to Nemesis (punishment by the Gods). It appears that pride and shame played key roles in Greek thought, there being many shadings of each in classical Greek. In contrast to hubris, Aristotle depicted another kind of pride, which he saw as the supreme virtue, the interest in honor above all else, a pride that means "greatness of soul." (For a fuller discussion of Aristotle's conception of pride as a virtue, and many other classical and medieval treatments of pride as well, see Payne, 1951.)

Among the various kinds of shame in the Greek language, the distinction between shame as disgrace (*aischyne*) and shame as modesty or shyness (*aidos*) has survived in all European languages except English:

	Disgrace	*Modesty*
Greek	aischyne	aidos
Latin	foedus	pudor
French	honte	pudeur
German	schande	scham
Italian	vergogna	pudore

Schneider (1977) has urged the importance of shame in its second meaning, "a sense of shame." The connotation of this type of shame, especially in its root in the Greek word *aidos*, connotes not only modesty or shyness but also awe and reverence. Perhaps the closest equivalent in English is *humility*. It should be noted that Hume (1739), in his 18th-century treatise on the passions, devoted considerable space to pride and shame. He noted the relationship of shame to humility just mentioned and also made a distinction between normal pride and false pride. (He called the latter "vanity.") A very precise analysis of Hume's approach to the emotions can be found in Taylor (1985).

Ovid (7 a.d.) depicted a relationship between shame and stages of society in his Four Stages of the World. His first stage, the Golden Age, corresponds to the Garden of Eden, a world without fear and punishment. But this paradise was disturbed in the succeeding stages, until the last stage became an age of wickedness: "every species of crime burst forth" and "shame (*pudor*), truth and honor took flight." This last passage suggests that wickedness involves, among other things, shamelessness, a loss of the sense of shame.

The connection between shamelessness, evil, and self-destruction is made quite explicit in the Greek myth of the Goddess Aidos, as told by Hesiod and others (Heller, 1984). This myth makes clear that Nemesis is the avenger of Aidos. That is, a shameless attack on decency, personified as the Goddess of shame, is tantamount to self-destruction.

In modern societies it is assumed that shame is a rare emotion among adults and is bandied about only among small children (e.g., "shamey, shamey," and the odd gesture of pointing the index finger of one hand at the victim while stroking it with the other index finger). This assumption is reflected in the division made in anthropology between shame cultures and guilt cultures, with traditional societies relying on shame for social control, and modern societies, guilt. A similar premise is found in orthodox psychoanalytic theory, which places almost total emphasis on guilt as the adult emotion of self-control, and shame is thought of as "regressive," that is, as childish. (An early attempt to break away from both premises can be found in Piers and Singer, 1953.)

For many years, however, the literature has suggested that shame is the primary social emotion, in that it is generated by the virtually constant monitoring of the self in relation to others. Such monitoring, as already suggested, is not rare but almost continuous in social interaction and, more covertly, in solitary thought. *If this line of thought is correct, shame is the most frequent, and possibly the most important of emotions, even though it is usually invisible.* This thread can be found in Darwin (1872), Cooley (1922), and McDougall (1908), and more recently, in Lynd (1958), Lewis (1971), Goffman (1967), and Braithwaite (1989).

Much of Goffman's early work on the basic contours of social interaction implies that avoidance of shame is an important, indeed a crucial, motive in virtually all social behavior. Shame is not named explicitly in his first studies, but his basic categories strongly suggest it. For example, in his study of self-presentation (Goffman, 1959), he continually suggests that most public behavior is concerned with "impression management," much more than with supposedly rational or instrumental goals. One tries to control the impression one makes on others, even others who are not signficant to one's life. The implication that one is continually seeing oneself from the viewpoint of others implies frequent shame states, as Cooley, Lewis, and others have proposed.

In a later study, Goffman (1967) makes explicit the relationship between the motives involved in self-presentation and shame. (The term that Goffman used is not shame but embarrassment, which I will treat as a member of the shame family, as most commentators have also done.) In this study, Goffman states clearly and forcefully that "saving face" is a central motive in human activity and that this metaphor means the avoidance of embarrassment. Goffman envisioned embarrassment and the anticipation of embarrassment as crucial in *all* social interaction. He clearly states that embarrassment (and its anticipation) is not a deviation from normal social intercourse, but a principal feature of it.

Lewis (1977) has linked shame to social solidarity and the social bond. Drawing on studies of infant–caretaker interaction, the first step in her argument is that humans are genetically programmed to be social and cooperative. The infant–caretaker studies show, with a wealth of detail, that very young infants do not need to learn to be socially responsive. One example is the ability to take turns, a basic building-block for cooperative activity. Very young infants quickly show the rhythm of looking into the caretaker's eyes, then away. The precise rhythm of periods of mutual gaze, alternating with first one, then the other party looking away, appears to be crucial in the development of a strong bond. The studies point to the management of turn-taking as necessary to the development of mutual delight and love. As Yeats suggested, love comes in at the eyes. When a secure bond has been formed, both parties would be expected to feel pride. Social solidarity begins in the nursery.

In the second step of her argument, Lewis proposes that shame is the most important of the social emotions because it arises when there is a threat to the social bond. In her scheme, shame has a signal function, alerting one to threats to the bond. Just as feelings of pride signal a secure bond, feelings of shame signal a threatened bond. These two conjectures can serve as a foundation for a structure/process theory of social solidarity. Before proceeding further with such a theory, all me first to review earlier discussions of pride and shame.

EARLY STUDIES OF SHAME

Darwin (1872) devoted a whole chapter, the last substantive one, to "Self-attention–Shame–Shyness–Modesty: Blushing." As his punctuation suggests, his primary interest was the phenomenon of blushing: what evolutionary function could it serve? He proposed that blushing may be universal in the human species, even among the darkest skinned people. He suggested, in passing, by way of comments on the blushing of Australian aborigines, that blushing is caused by shame.

Under the section heading "The Nature of the Mental States which Induce Blushing," he stated his thesis: "These consist of shyness, shame, and modesty, the essential element in all being self-attention." For my purposes, the most essential proposition comes next, where he explains what he means by "self-attention": "It is not the simple act of reflecting on our own appearance, but the *thinking what others think of us, which excites a blush"* (p. 325). His preliminary discussion suggests that blushing may be caused by perceptions of evaluation of the self whether positive or negative. The bulk of the complete discussion suggests, however, that more frequently than not, the social perceptions of self which cause blushing are negative. Take his summary statement: "Blushing, whether due to shyness, to shame for a real crime . . . or a breach of the laws of etiquette . . . or humility . . . depends in all cases on . . . a sensitive regard for the opinion, more particularly the *depreciation* of others . . . " (p. 335).

Darwin's argument about the relationship between blushing, emotions, and "self-attention" can be restated as two propositions connecting blushing with emotions, on one hand, and social perception, on the other. First: *blushing is caused by shame.* "Shyness" and "modesty," Darwin's two other "mental states" that induce blushing, can be considered to be shame variants.[1] Second, and more important for my purposes here, *shame is caused by the perception of negative evaluations of the self.* Blushing is only one of several visible markers of overt shame and therefore is not a primary concept for a theory of social influence. The second statement, however, contains the basic proposition for the whole theory: shame is *the* social emotion, arising as it does out the monitoring of one's own actions by viewing oneself from the standpoint of others.

---

[1]Lewis (1971) uses the term variants; Wurmser (1983), cognates. Variants seems to be the more appropriate word; the various terms refer to states that are similar, in that they all involve shame, but vary in other ways. Embarrassment, for example, refers to a shame state of mush less duration and intensity that humiliation or mortification.

Shame as a crucial emotion for adults is prominent in the thought of William McDougall (1908). He considered shame as one of what he called the "self-regarding sentiments," the most important one: "Shame is the emotion second to none in the extent of its influence upon social behavior" (p. 124). Like Darwin, he seems to have understood that shame arises as a result of self-monitoring, although he was not as precise on this point as Darwin or Cooley: "The conduct which excites our shame is that which lowers us in the *eyes of our fellows*, so that we feel it to be impossible for our positive self-feeling to attain satisfaction" (p. 127, italics added). He seems clear on one important point, that, although shame undoubtedly has a biological basis that we share with the higher mammals, the human emotion of shame in adults is considerably more elaborate and complex (p. 56).

We next turn to Cooley (1922), a prophet of the role of shame in human behavior. He considered pride and shame as examples of what he called "social self-feelings," a conception very close to McDougall's "self-regarding sentiments." At some points in his discussion he seems to regard as a self-feeling any feeling that the self directs toward itself and implies that pride and shame have no particular prominence in this large group. This passage about the extraordinary importance of the self-feelings in human behavior, at first glance, seems to be in this key: "with all normal . . . people, [social self-feeling] remains, in one form or another, the *mainspring of endeavor and a chief interest of the imagination throughout life*" (p. 208, italics added).

Cooley continues:

As is the case with other feelings, we do not think much of it (that is, of social self-feeling) so long as it is moderately and regularly gratified. Many people of balanced mind and congenial activity scarcely know that they care what others think of them, and will deny, perhaps with indignation, that such care is an important factor in what they are and do. But this is illusion. If failure or disgrace arrives, if one suddenly finds that the faces of men show coldness or contempt instead of the kindliness and deference that he is used to, he will perceive from the shock, the fear, the sense of being outcast and helpless, that he was living in the minds of others without knowing it, just as we daily walk the solid ground without thinking how it bears us up [p. 208].

Although neither pride nor shame is mentioned by name in this passage, they are implied, especially the almost continuous presence of low-visibility pride in ordinary discourse. Moreover, the two examples he gives to illustrate his point are rich in implication:

> This fact is so familiar in literature, especially in modern novels, that it ought to be obvious enough. The works of George Eliot are particularly strong in the exposition of it. In most of her novels there is some character like Mr. Bulstrode in *Middlemarch* or Mr. Jermyn in *Felix Holt*, whose respectable and long-established social image of himself is shattered by the coming to light of hidden truth [p. 208].

Both examples, Bulstrode and Jermyn, involve the coming to light of shameful truths, truths which resulted in immediate public disgrace. In stressing the central importance of social self-feelings in this passage, Cooley may have been thinking primarily of pride and shame.

This possibility is confirmed when we examine his concept of what he called "the looking-glass self," his description of the social nature of the self. Cooley saw self-monitoring in terms of three steps: "the imagination of our appearance to the other person: the imagination of his judgment of that appearance, and some sort of self-feeling, such as pride or mortification" (p. 184).

In that passage, he restricts self-feelings to the two that he seems to think are the most significant, pride and shame (considering "mortification" to be a shame variant). To make sure that we understand this point, he mentions shame three more times in the passage that follows.

> The comparison with a looking-glass hardly suggests the second element, the imagined judgment, which is quite essential. The thing that moves us to *pride or shame* is not the mere mechanical reflection of ourselves, but an imputed sentiment, the imagined effect of this reflection upon another's mind. This is evident from the fact that the character and weight of that other, in whose mind we see ourselves, makes all the difference with our feeling. We are *ashamed* to seem evasive in the presence of a straightforward man, cowardly in the presence of a brave one, gross in the eyes of a refined one, and so on. We always imagine, and in imagining share, the judgments of the other mind. A man will boast to one person of an action—say some sharp transaction in trade—which he would be *ashamed* to own to another [pp. 184–185, italics added].

Cooley's analysis of the social nature of the self can be summarized in three propositions:

1.   In adults, social monitoring of self is virtually continuous, even in solitude. (We are, as he put it, "living in the minds of others without knowing it." p. 208); and

2.   Social monitoring always has an evaluative component and gives rise, therefore, to either pride or shame. These two propositions, taken together, suggest a puzzle. If social monitoring of self is almost continuous and if it gives rise to pride or shame, why is it that we see so few manifestations of either emotion in adults? Among the possible answers to this question, one would be that pride/shame is ubiquitous, but of a kind that has such low visibility that we do not notice it, giving rise to a third proposition:

3.   Adults are virtually always in a state of either pride or shame, usually of a quite unostentatious kind.

In his discussion of grief (he calls it distress-anguish), Tomkins (1963) observes a parallel puzzle: "The reader must be puzzled at our earlier affirmation that distress is suffered daily by all human beings. Nothing seems less common than to see an adult cry. And yet we are persuaded that the cry, and the awareness of the cry, as distress and suffering, is ubiquitous" (p. 56). His answer also parallels the one I have suggested for pride and shame: "The adult has learned to cry as an adult. It is a brief cry, or a muted cry, or a part of a cry or a miniature cry, or a substitute cry, or an active defense against the cry, that we see in place of the infant's cry for help" (p. 56) He goes on to an extended discussion of various substitutes for, or defenses against, crying. For example, an adult suffering in the dental chair might, instead of crying, substitute muscular contractions: clamping the jaws, tightly contracting the muscles in the abdomen, and rigidly gripping the arms of the chair with the hands (p. 59). As an example of defending against the cry, Tomkins suggests masking the expression of sadness with one of anger, by becoming angry as well as sad (pp. 64–65). It can be observed that most men in our society use this transformation, but many woman do the opposite, masking anger with grief.

One way of summarizing the various gambits that adults use when they are suffering loss is to say that in adults most grief is of a type that would have low visibility, because its manifestations have been disguised or ignored.

Ekman and Friesen (1982), finding what they call "miserable" smiles by can be seen as partially supporting Tomkins's conjecture. They found that most smiles were not indicative of joy but were either "false" or "miserable." That is, most smiles are voluntarily enacted, rather than spontaneously expressing joy. Miserable smiles occur when a smile is used to disguise a negative emotion such as grief.

Proposition 3, the positing of almost continuous low-visibility pride or shame in adults, parallels Tomkins's conjecture about grief. Both Tomkins and Cooley imply the virtually continuous presence of low-visibility emotion.

The most dramatic of Cooley's (1922) views on shame, and the one that brings him closest to the position taken here, is his example of the power of what he calls "social fear," that is, the anticipation of shame:

> Social fear, of a sort perhaps somewhat morbid, is vividly depicted by Rousseau in the passage of his *Confessions* where he describes the feeling that led him falsely to accuse a maid-servant of a theft which he had himself committed. "When she appeared my heart was agonized, but the presence of so many people was more powerful than my compunction. I did not fear punishment, but I dreaded *shame*: I dreaded it more than death, more than the crime, more than all the world. I would have buried, hid myself in the center of the earth; invincible *shame* bore down every other sentiment: *shame* alone caused all my impudence, and in proportion as I became criminal the fear of discovery rendered me intrepid. I felt no dread but that of being detected, of being publicly and to my face declared a thief, liar, and calumniator [p. 29, italics added].

Rousseau's phrase, "invincible shame," will stand us in good stead in the discussion to come. Notice also that Cooley suggests this instance as an example of "morbid" (i.e., pathological), rather than normal, shame, a useful distinction.

MEAD AND DEWEY

Cooley's analysis of self-monitoring posits pride and shame to be the basic social emotions. At this point intellectual history takes a somewhat surprising turn. G. H. Mead (1934) and John Dewey (1894–95) based their entire social psychology on the process of role taking, the ability of humans to monitor themselves continuously from the point of view of others. Yet neither Mead nor Dewey ever mentioned what was so obvious to Darwin, McDougall and Cooley: that social monitoring usually gives rise to feelings of pride or shame. Mead and Dewey treated role taking, their basic building block of human behavior, as entirely a cognitive process. Neither had anything to say about pride and shame, as if Darwin, McDougall and Cooley never existed. Social psychology has yet to recover from this oversight.[2]

Mead was a social philosopher at the University of Chicago at the beginning of this century. Profoundly influenced by evolutionary theory, he considered himself a "social behaviorist." His behaviorism, however, had almost nothing to do with the Watsonian variety. Indeed, he was a profound critic of positivist behaviorism, because he gave what he called "internal behavior," that is, thoughts and feelings, absolute parity with external behavior. His principal theory concerned the origins and basic dimensions of mind and consciousness.

Mead attacked the problem of mind in a way exactly opposite from the way that Freud did. Mead was concerned with the sources of reflective intelligence. For this reason, he ignored virtually all forms of irrational behavior. Concerned exclusively with intelligence and problem solving as a mode of evolutionary adaptation, he ignored the terrain investigated by Freud, just as Freud slighted effective problem solving. The two theories share virtually no common ground.

One of Mead's most important contributions to social theory was to suggest the way in which mind and the self arise out of participation in social relationships. Mead (1934) proposed that humans develop selves by passing through three stages, which he called play, the game, and the generalized other. By the play stage he meant merely that children first imitate the external behavior of adults without understanding it from within. A child plays postman by simulating the appearance and actions of the mailman without understanding their significance.

In Mead's scheme, it is through participation in socially organized events that the beginnings of selfhood make their appearance. Even a simple game such as peekaboo requires coordinating one's own actions with those of another person. The infant must wait, for example, for the game to begin and understand when it has ended. More complex games, such as dancing or baseball, require understanding not only one's own role, but also the role of one's partner or teammates. For the shortstop to throw out the runner with the

---

[2]An early attempt to correct Mead's and Dewey's omission of emotions can be found in Shibutani (1961). Although he does not make explicit the central role of shame, his chapter "Self-Esteem and Social Control" partly anticipates the thesis here.

ball she has caught, she must have mastered at least the rudiments of the role of the first-base player, giving him time to get to the bag, for example, before throwing.

In this way, Mead pointed out, a person learns to take the role of the other, to see the world, at least in part, from a point of view other than her own. This movement is profoundly social. It sets up a chain of events inside of consciousness that opens to the social world. In the game stage, however, the person still captive to scripted activities, is tied mechanically to existing social games and rituals. Conformity, rather than creativity, is the hallmark of this stage.

In the course of participating in games and rituals, a person learns that improvised actions are not only possible but necessary for effective cooperation with others. In the game of baseball, for example, no double play is exactly like any other. Each is improvised, in part, so that it will be exactly appropriate for each new situation. Mead thought that improvisation was the crucial quality that human beings share with no other creatures. By the improvisation of actions that are exactly appropriate to never-before encountered situations, human intelligence, a general problem solver, is born.

In the stage that Mead termed the generalized other, the person breaks free both of instinct and of established social conventions. Rather than taking the role of some actual person or group, one can put oneself in the place of some imagined person or group. One can take the role, for example, of the ideal parent one has never had, or the point of view of posterity. In this way, one can create an imaginary world in which there is sufficient scope for intellectual maneuver.

This kind of role playing at the adult level gives birth to reflective intelligence, the dispassionate, world-ranging review of a complex problem that seeks resolution. By focusing so intently on rational problem solving, however, Mead neglected many aspects of human existence. In addition to neglecting irrational behavior, already mentioned, he also neglected virtually all the human emotions. Although there are passages in which emotionally charged situations are discussed, they are so few, so brief, and so narrow as to be useless for understanding emotions. Many of the passages concern only one emotion, anger. Of the few examples Mead offers, most are concerned with animals rather than humans. Although profound and useful for many purposes, Mead's work largely ignores human emotions.

Mead' s colleague and close friend, John Dewey (1894–95), went so far as to publish a theory of emotions, couched in "behavioral terms." Dewey argued that consciousness, in general, and emotional experiences, in particular, involve two movements: the arousal of internalized action sequences and blockage so that the sequences cannot be carried through to completion. In Dewey's model, an emotion is a particular kind of internal *act*, one that has been aroused preparatory to acting it out but not allowed to go to its completion. This is probably an important idea, because it suggests an elementary model of the genesis of emotional experience (Scheff, 1993). Dewey's proposal, however, is framed in extremely abstract and general terms of emotional arousal, rather than being applied to specific emotions. For this reason, it has not led to much further discussion and research.

If we apply Dewey's idea to specific emotions, some interesting issues emerge. Suppose, for example, we think of grief as an emotion whose source is loss and whose endpoint is crying. To the extent that grief is aroused and followed through to completion through crying, little grief will be experienced. It is only when grief is aroused but crying is impeded that one can feel grief. Both Mead and Dewey shied away from specific emotions, much to the detriment of their theories of human behavior. In advanced Western societies, emotions are seldom discussed, probably because of repression. Of all the emotions, shame is probably the most taboo.

In modern societies, adults seem to be uncomfortable about manifesting either pride or shame. This is to say that the emotions of shame and pride often seem themselves to arouse shame. (This proposition explains Darwin's [1872] observation that both positive and negative evaluations can give rise to blushing.) It seems likely, as both Darwin and McDougall suggest, that shame has a biological basis, that it is genetically programmed, not just in humans but in the higher mammals. It may also be true, as recent infant-caretaker studies suggest, that for infants and very young children, the arousal of shame is largely biological (Scheff, 1987b).

For adults, however, it seems equally true that shame is not only a biological process, but also, overwhelmingly, a social and cultural phenomenon. The discussion so far has suggested that adult shame is doubly social: shame arises in social monitoring of the self, and shame itself often becomes a further source of shame, depending on the particular situation and the normative structure of the culture.

In its early phases, psychoanalytic theory gave the impression that shame had been completely ignored. As both Lewis (1987) and Lansky (1995) have pointed out, Freud's early writings implied a key role for shame. But in his mature theory Freud's primary emphasis was on anxiety and guilt. His approach implies that shame is infantile and regressive. Furthermore, the psychoanalytic concept of shame as arising out of the disparity between the real and the ideal self individualizes shame by cutting out the social component.

Schneider (1977) makes a strong case that Freud was insufficiently sensitive to patients' desire to hide their secrets, their embarrassment, and their shame about their thoughts, feelings, and actions. He argues that Freud was shameless (in the sense of being disrespectful) in his relentless attack on what he thought of as the patient's "resistance" to knowing themselves. Schneider illustrates the problem in the case of Dora, where Freud's irreverence toward a patient's sense of shame led him to confrontational interpretations that "lost" the patient. Perhaps the downplaying of shame is one of the key flaws in orthodox psychoanalytic theory and practice.

Although largely ignored in orthodox theory, shame emerges as central in several of the variant psychoanalytic perspectives. The contribution of psychanalysis to shame theory has been a mixed heritage. Shunned by Freud and by his orthodox followers, many of the most brilliant and vital contributions to what we know about shame have been made, nonetheless, by psychoanalysts. Adler's approach (1907-37) centered on "feelings of inferiority," a phrase that surely refers to shame. The theory pivots about a crucial phase in a child's development when she needs a secure bond with her parents. Adler argued that children prefer love, and if it is unavailable to them, they will feel abandoned or rejected. When that is the case, their adult personality will develop in one of two ways. Either the adult will form an "inferiority complex," that is, chronic feelings of shame (low self-esteem); or the person will manifest a "drive for power." Both paths may be interpreted in terms of chronic shame: the inferiority complex as *overt* shame, the drive for power as *bypassed* shame. (These two types of shame will be discussed subsequently.)

In Horney's (1950) approach, pride and shame play a central role. She termed the neurotic part of the personality the "false self," proposing that it is organized around what she calls the "pride system." Her analysis implies that the pride in this system is false pride and that the system in driven by a sense of humiliation, that is, shame. She places considerable emphasis on a particular sequence of events: honor, insult, and vindictiveness or revenge. Her analysis of this sequence anticipates my proposition that unacknowledged shame causes destructive aggression.

Piers and Singer (1953), Lynd (1959) and Tomkins (1963) also developed important analyses of shame and humiliation, based in part on psychoanalytic ideas. For my purpose here, however, the most important approach developed from psychoanalysis was that of Helen Lewis. Since Retzinger and I discuss her work at length elsewhere (see chapter 5, this volume) my comments here will be brief.

HELEN LEWIS ON SHAME

Lewis's most important contribution was her discovery of *unacknowledged* shame, the kind of low-visibility emotion predicated in the work of Cooley and of Goffman, but only conceptually. By patiently analyzing the transcripts of hundreds of psychotherapy sessions, moment by moment, Lewis (1971) demonstrated that patients were often in a state of shame. This state was virtually always overlooked by both therapist and patient. Many of the patient's statements show concern for the therapist's view of her: "I'm wondering how you are thinking about me after telling you all this." Both the manner and the content of these statements suggest shame states, but these are virtually never articulated. As much as any explorer of the physical world, Lewis had hit upon an unknown continent of shame.

Lewis's (1971) work suggests that shame is a haunting presence in psychotherapy, a presence that is usually hidden, disguised, or ignored by both patient and therapist. Returning to Cooley's conjecture about low-visibility pride, and Goffman's on embarrassment, one might infer that unacknowledged pride and shame are ubiquitous in all human encounters, not just in psychotherapy. This conjecture would explain why most therapists are unaware of pride and shame in therapy, even though these emotions may turn out to be crucial elements in treatment: like the patient and most other adults, the therapist is accustomed to ignoring the manifestations of these emotions.

Lewis also noted that shame usually occurred as a part of *sequence* of emotions. Her analysis of the quotation of the patient's comment quoted earlier provides an example. The patient may have been imagining that he was seen in a negative way by the therapist: first, a brief moment of shame was evoked, followed quickly by anger at the therapist, then, just as quickly, by guilt about the anger. This whole sequence might occur rapidly, lasting only 15 or 20 seconds.

An important implication of Lewis's discovery of shame and shame-anger sequences concerns the emotions of guilt and resentment. Guilt is usually thought of as an elemental emotion like shame, and resentment as a form of anger. Lewis's analysis, however, suggests that both emotions are *shame-anger variants*: guilt is a shame-anger sequence with the anger directed back at the self, resentment, a shame-anger sequence with the anger directed toward another. In this conception, guilt and resentment are isotopic variations of the basic shame-anger molecule. The sequential nature of this model suggests how guilt and resentment can last indefinitely as chain reactions of emotional reactions to one's emotional reactions. That is to say, sequences of this kind can loop back on themselves, as when a patient feels ashamed for being so upset over "nothing," then angry because of the shame, and so on, ad infinitum. Lewis (1971) suggested that such sequences form "feeling traps," self-perpetuating chains of emotions. The idea of feeling traps may point to a solution of the puzzle of lifelong guilt, resentment, and hatred.

Finally, Lewis developed a method of detecting low-visibility shame in discourse. She noted that in a context that involved the patient's seeing himself from the therapist's point of view in a negative way, the patient's *words* and *manner* (tone of voice, loudness, speech static, self-interruptions, etc.) suggest a state of shame. These three contributions can be used as a foundation for investigating the role of shame in conduct (see chapter 5, this volume).

SHAME AND THE SOCIAL BOND

My earlier discussion of shame and guilt cultures raises a crucial question about the connection between shame and social structure. Why did references to shame virtually disappear in the New Testament, to be replaced by references to guilt? That is, what is the relationship between emotion and social structure? As noted earlier, I propose that pride is the emotion corresponding to secure bonds (social solidarity) and that shame corresponds to threatened bonds (alienation). Social structure and pride and shame are reciprocally related: normal shame is necessary for the regulation of all human interaction, but the repression of shame causes and is caused by alienation.

Sociology as a discipline arose out of the idea that modernization, the rise of urban, industrial societies, was destructive of *community*. With social and geographic mobility and free flow of information, modern societies have a potential for change unthinkable in a traditional society. Although limitless change has many advantages, it also gives rise to a substantial disadvantage: ***all social bonds are at risk***. Not just one bond or the other is threatened, but all bonds: for many members of modern societies, perhaps even the majority, their connections to others are never quite safe.

Suppose, as a basic premise, that everyone requires a sense of belonging, a web of secure social bonds, and that for the average person this minimum is never quite achieved. If that were the case, the human condition in modern societies would resemble a fish out of water. The sustaining web would have been lost. If one allowed oneself to be aware of the loss, every moment of daily existence would be exquisitely painful.

I am not claiming, as Cooley (1992) and others have, that social bonds in the earlier communities were necessarily more secure than in modern societies. My argument does not require the idealization of traditional societies. In his analysis of suicide, Durkheim (1897) made the very important suggestion that closely knit communities do not necessarily guarantee adequate bonds: what he called altruistic and fatalistic cultures may produces suicide rates as high or higher than anomic or egoistic ones.

Bowen (1978), who originated the family-systems approach in psychotherapy, makes a similar distinction. He characterizes a well-ordered family system as differentiated; that is, the needs of each member can be negotiated, as can those of the family as a group. In families characterized as *cut-off*, there is inadequate negotiation because family members are rigidly separated as individuals. The culture in this type of family is typified by what Durkheim (1897) called anomie or egoism. In families marked by what Bowen called *fusion*, there is also inadequate negotiation, but for the opposite reason: family members are insufficiently differentiated as individuals. Instead there is "fusion": members find it difficult to negotiate their individual needs because of the demand for conformity and loyalty. Such a system corresponds to the type of society that Durkheim thought produced altruistic or fatalistic suicide.

I am suggesting that modern societies are characterized by isolation more than by secure or engulfing bonds. From this point of view, it does not matter whether premodern societies were based on secure or engulfing bonds, or some mixture of the two. Bonds threatened because of isolation are continuously painful regardless of the antecedent conditions. How might a society defend its members against such pain?

One defense would be to deny the very existence of the social bond. A rigid individualism provides a defensive myth for organizing experience in an anomic society, implying that the isolated individual is the only conceivable unit of human existence. Given this presupposition, the need for social bonds would become an unmentionable secret, even an unthinkable one.

I propose that modern societies have institutionalized the myth of individualism, and the denial of pride and shame, as defenses against the pain of threatened bonds. The beginnings of rigid individualism can be seen in children who have undergone the loss of parental care at an early age. These children take steps to defend themselves against the pain of further separation. The case of Reggie (Burlingham and Freud, 1942) illustrates the point. Separated from his parents at five months, he formed a passionate attachment to his nurse in the orphanage. This attachment was suddenly broken when he was 2 years, 8 months old; his nurse, Mary-Ann, left to be married.

> He was completely lost and desperate after her departure, and refused to look at her when she visited him a fortnight later. He turned his head to the other side when she spoke to him, but stared at the door, which had closed behind her, after she had left the room. In the evening in bed he sat up and said: "My very own Mary-Ann! But I don't like her" [p. 247],

Reggie has defended himself against the pain of his second separation; he has rejected the rejector.

Burlingham and Freud (1942), Bowlby (1969, 1974, 1980), and others who have studied the effects of broken bonds repeatedly report the same syndrome. After a lengthy period of futile calling for the missing loved one, these children learn their lesson. In effect, they say, like Reggie, "Very well, if you are not coming, then I don't need you anyway. I am sufficient unto myself. I don't need anyone. *Ever*." This defense is what Bowen (1978) calls "cut-off." In effect, it is a self-inflicted wound in response to a wounding social environment. Since one has suffered from separation in the past, one protects oneself by giving up hope, producing a self-perpetuating system.

THE MICROWORLD OF SOCIAL INTERACTION

One important limitation of reports in developmental psychology requires attention. Bowlby and other researchers seem to assume that severed bonds create more disruption than do bonds that are threatened. In effect, those writers suggest that being a member of a physically intact household, no matter what its emotional dynamics, is less damaging than being an orphan. As Bowen's (1978) analysis of family systems suggests, however, this may not be the case. The threat to bonds in an engulfing or isolating family system are hidden and confusing. The disruption caused by such a family may be more enduring than the disruption suffered from severed bonds.

Extreme ideation of severed bonds can be found in the culture of peoples who have been enslaved. A spiritual of the Southern black slaves provides an example:

> Sometimes I feel like a motherless child.
> Sometimes I feel like a motherless child.
> Sometimes I feel like a motherless child.
> A long, long way from home.
> A long, long way from home.

The slaves were wrenched not only from their families but from their cultures; all bonds were severed. When the destruction of bonds is unmistakable, however, it may be possible to form new ones.

In the physically intact white middle-class family, anomie-egoism or altruism can occur even though hidden behind a façade of polite words. Conflict between members may be so disguised that its roots are virtually invisible to the members. These conditions give rise to underground conflict in the form of "interminable quarrels" or "silent impasses" (Scheff, 1987a). Retzinger's (1991) analysis of marital quarrels demonstrates such relationships; they are marked by politeness, but accompanied by emotional distance, boredom, lack of trust, and withdrawal of affection.

In a classic study (Labov and Fanshel, 1977) two sociolinguists made a detailed examination, moment to moment, of conversations with her family reported by an anorexic psychotherapy patient. They showed how the daughter and mother were locked in a hidden system of mutual threat: the daughter threatened self-starvation, the mother, abandonment. The threats, recriminations, and insults were exchanged through innuendo; they seemed outside of the awareness of the family members. To find the sources of conflict, it was necessary to examine the dialogue, utterance by utterance, for their implications—not just the words, but the nonverbal gestures that accompanied each word, and the combination of words and gestures. (For my commentary on this study, see Scheff, 1989)

In relationships marked by hidden conflict, the bond is continually threatened, but in a way that makes understanding and repair of the bond extremely difficult. Since their prototypic bonds are inadequate, the typical individual in such a family might find it just as difficult to form new bonds as to repair the old ones.

Is it possible for the relationships in a whole society to be physically intact but based on threatened or inadequate bonds? In such a society, we would expect to find individuals willing to accept relationships that do not meet their needs but are tolerated because they are felt to be better than isolation. In these circumstances, nationalism and other kinds of sectarian grouping may arise, providing what may be thought of as "pseudobonds." Rather than attunement, which balances the needs of the individual and the needs of the society, pseudobonds in nations, sects, cults, and other exclusive groups furnish only the semblance of community. In such sects, the members give up significant parts of themselves, their own needs, feelings, and points of view; they are engulfed. Engulfment damages both the individual and the group, because distinctive points of view are needed for group survival.

The ideology of individualism, and its subsidiaries such as the myth of the "self-made man," obscures the part/whole nature of social systems. *Such an ideology may be an adult parallel to a child's defenses against the intense pain that follows severed or threatened bonds*. Those approaches which insist on viewing human issues in terms of isolated individuals may be defenses against the anomic conditions in our society. In modern societies, manifestations of the social bond are suppressed, and the emotions that signal the state of the bond, pride and shame, are denied and disguised.

REPRESSION OF EMOTION: ANGER AND SHAME

A very good case has been made concerning the repression of anger in modern civilization. Stearns and Stearns's (1986) study illustrated the insidiousness of the repression of shame. They have shown a change in the "advice" literature concerning anger that has been occurring for the last 300 years. Using religious texts of the 18th century, educational and child-rearing texts of the 19th, and psychological and managerial advice of the 20th, they demonstrate that attempts to control anger have become increasingly forceful and insistent.

The Stearnses show that religious advice in the earliest era was not aimed at anger per se but only at *excessive* anger. The typical advice in sermons was not against getting angry, which was often encouraged (righteous anger), but against excessive anger and against aggression. The authors show that, beginning in the 18th century, there was a gradual shift toward a more restrictive stance, ending in what they call the modern ambivalence toward anger: it is not just excessive anger and aggression that are forbidden, but all anger.

It would be difficult to overstate the importance of the Stearnses's findings, because they can be interpreted as supporting and expanding a well-known psychoanalytic theory, connecting civilization with repression, the Freud-Reich-Marcuse thesis. This thesis has always been at the hypothetical level even with individual cases, much less with a whole society. Elias (1978), who makes the same point specifically about anger, compares examples from manuals of courtly etiquette with 19th-century advice manuals. The Stearnses's findings is the first comprehensive documentation of the civilization-repression thesis.

Although the Stearnses do not link shame and anger, their study can be used to show this link. Following Lewis (1971), I propose that anger is repressed because of shame; that is, all anger, not just excessive anger, is forbidden in modern societies because members have been socialized to be ashamed of it. The Stearnses come very close to this statement but never make it explicit. Instead they use what may be called code words for shame in describing members' feelings toward anger in modern societies: they say that increasingly over the last 300 years, people are "anxious" about anger, or "uncomfortable," "embarrassed," or "guilty" about it. (For examples of these terms in a single chapter, see Stearns and Stearns, 1986, pp. 232, 234, 235, 236, and 239).

Those are some of the very emotion words which, following Lewis (1971), I believe to be glosses for the more primitive emotion, shame. Inadvertently, in the very act of lifting the repression for one emotion, anger, they continue to maintain the repression of another, shame, by using code words that disguise references to shame. Repression depends on the use of language as part of an inadvertent conspiracy of silence

SUMMARY

The discussion of shame in this chapter is a brief review of an emotion that I propose to be much more complex and pervasive than contemporary usage would acknowledge. Several points deserve reiteration. Shame appears to be ignored and denied in modern civilization. It is considered openly in traditional societies, but hidden in modern ones. There is, however, a fugitive literature on shame. That literature contains powerful hints that shame is a crucial emotion in human conduct.

One of the implications of the scholarship of Cooley, Lewis, and other of the writers considered is that pride and shame are intimately connected with the structure and process of social bonds. Pride and shame seem to be crucial facets of social relationships. This conjecture provides a way of integrating psychological and sociological analysis, of connecting momentary personal events with social structure.

Since the denial of shame is institutionalized in our civilization, a vital new language is needed, an emotion language, which calls shame and other primitive emotions by their proper names. Contemporary language skirts emotions, particularly shame. In some ways, any theory is merely a verbal shorthand for a new language for naming the universe. If we are to understand the universe of internal experience, in its close connection with social contact, we will need to develop a new language that acknowledges rather than denies the existence of shame.

REFERENCES

Adler, A. (1907–37), *The Individual Psychology of Alfred Adler*. New York: Basic Books, 1956.
Benedict, R. (1946), *The Chrysanthemum and the Sword*. New York: Houghton Mifflin.
Braithwaite, J. (1989), *Crime, Shame, and Reintegration*. Cambridge: Cambridge University Press.
Bowen, M. (1978), *Family Therapy in Clinical Practice*. New York: Aronson.
Bowlby, J. (1969), *Attachment and Loss: Vol. 1*. New York: Basic Books.
———— (1973), *Attachment and Loss: Vol. 2*. New York: Basic Books.
———— (1980), *Attachment and Loss: Vol. 3*. New York: Basic Books.
Burlingham, D. & Freud, A. (1942), *Young Children in Wartime London*. London: Allen & Unwin.
Cooley, C. H. (1922), *Human Nature and the Social Order*. New York: Scribner's.
Darwin, C. (1872), *The Expression of Emotion in Men and Animals*. London: John Murray.
Dewey, J. (1894-95), The theory of emotion. *Psycholog. Rev.*, 1:553–569; 2:13–32.

Dodds, E. R. (1951), *The Greeks and the Irrational*. Berkeley: University of California Press.

Durkheim, E. (1897), *Suicide*. London: Routledge & Kegan Paul, 1952.

Ekman, P. & Friesen, W. (1982), Felt, false, and miserable smiles. *J. Nonverbal Behav.* 6:238–252.

Elias, N. (1978), *The Civilizing Process*. New York: Urizen.

Goffman, E. (1959), *The Presentation of Self in Everyday Life*. Garden City, NY: Anchor.

——— (1967), *Interaction Ritual*. New York: Anchor.

Heller, E. (1984), *In the Age of Prose*. Cambridge: Cambridge University Press.

Horney, K. (1950), *Neurosis and Human Growth*. New York: Norton.

Hume, D. (1739), *Treatise on Human Nature. Vol 2*. Oxford: Clarendon Press, 1968.

James, W. (1890), *The Principles of Psychology*. New York: Holtz.

Labov, W. & Fanshel, D. (1977), *Therapeutic Discourse*. New York: Academic Press.

Lansky, M. (1995), Shame and the scope of psychoanalytic understanding. *Amer. Behav. Sci.,* 38:1076–1090.

Lewis, H., ed. (1971), *Shame and Guilt in Neurosis*. New York: International Universities Press.

——— (1987), *The Role of Shame in Symptom Formation*. Hillsdale, NJ: Lawrence Erlbaum Associates.

Lynd, H. (1958), *Shame and the Search for Identity*. New York: Harcourt Brace.

McDougall, W. (1908), *An Introduction to Social Psychology*. New York: University Paperbacks.

Mead, G. H. (1934), *Mind, Self, and Society*. Chicago: University of Chicago Press.

Ovid (7 a.d.), *Metamorphoses*. Bloomington: University of Indiana Press, 1955.

Payne, R. (1951), *Hubris*. New York: Harper

Piers, G. & Singer, M. (1953), *Shame and Guilt*. New York: Norton.

Retzinger, S. (1991), *Violent Emotions*. Newbury Park, CA: Sage.

Scheff, T. (1987a), The shame-rage spiral: Case study of an interminable quarrel. In: *The Role of Shame in Symptom Formation*, ed. H. Lewis. Hillsdale, NJ: Lawrence Erlbaum Associates, pp. 109–150.

——— (1987b), Creativity and repetition: A theory of the coarse emotions. In: *Psychoanalytic Sociology*. ed. J. Rabow, G. Platt & M. Goldman. New York: Krieger, pp. 70–100.

————— (1989), Cognitive and emotional components in anorexia: Re-analysis of a classic case. *Psychiat.* 52:148–160.

————— (1990), *Microsociology*. Chicago: University of Chicago Press.

————— (1993), Toward a social psychological theory of mind and consciousness. *Soc. Res.*, 60:171–195.

————— & Retzinger, S. (1991), *Emotions and Violence*. Lexington, MA: Lexington Books.

Schneider, C. (1977), *Shame, Exposure, and Privacy*. Boston: Beacon Press.

Shibutani, C. (1961). *Society and Personality*. Englewood Cliffs, NJ: Prentice-Hall.

Stearns, C. & Stearns, P. (1986), *Anger: The Struggle for Control in America's History*. Chicago: University of Chicago Press.

Taylor, G. (1985), *Pride, Shame, and Guilt*. Oxford: Clarendon.

Tomkins, S. (1963), *Affect/Imagery/Consciousness, Vol 2*. New York: Springer.

Vico, G. (1744), *The New Science*. Ithaca, NY: Cornell University Press, 1968.

Wurmser, L. (1981), *The Masks of Shame*. Baltimore, MD: Johns Hopkins University Press.

9 | JACK KATZ
The Elements of Shame

If we review as wide a range of experiences of shame as we can collect and then search for the distinctive features that they share, we can develop an empirically grounded theory of the emotion. It may seem impossibly ironic, this project of seeking a definition of shame by collecting experiences of it, since the collection process seems to presuppose that one has in hand a definition that guides the decision of what to exclude and include. This is a troublesome issue, and the strongest defense of proceeding, even as it hovers continuously on the edges of the inquiry, is that it is inevitable, at least if we want to ground theory, not in what we would like to believe about experience and behavior on moral or other a priori grounds but in the facts of personal life. In practice, for this investigation, the problem is not terribly troublesome. The ultimate test of a procedure to develop a "grounded" understanding of a concept is whether the inquiry reaps a richly varied, internally coherent, and widely usable understanding. It turns out that there is a great deal of consistency, both in the types of experiences that are treated in a taken-for-granted manner as shameful in self-reports and in the examples of shame cited by analysts.

Like other everyday emotions (laughter, crying, anger, etc.), shame is commonly experienced when one is doing something with other people, and it takes a narrative form, beginning and ending, rising and declining, evolving in a process that has more or less emphatic phases. Within a given episode of shame, the way a person embodies the experience changes, often in relationship to the efforts he or she makes to overcome it. That shame has not often been addressed as a segment of lived experience is indicated by the relative absence of evidence on the exit process. The key data for the testing of any empirical theory are not only the facts that exist as the phenomenon in question emerges, but also the changes that occur as it declines.

The theory of shame presented here is a specification of the constituent elements of this type of emotional experience. The empirical claim is that all the specified elements are present in any shameful moment, although a given shameful experience may highlight one or another of the elements. The data come from the academic commentary on shame, a corpus that frequently draws on fictional literature; from autobiographies; from ethnographic observation; and from university students who, over several years, were asked to provide anonymous descriptions and to challenge a changing version of an explicit statement of this theory.

In effect, people generally know the causal contingencies of shame even if they cannot state what they are, because people get into and out of the experience routinely. This theory of shame contains 10 distinguishable elements. What everyone experiences in shame is a *fearful* and *chaotic* sense of an *irresistible* and *eerie revelation to self*, of a *vulnerability* in one's *nature* that, by indicating one's *moral incompetence*, *isolates* and *humbles* one in the face of what one regards as a *sacred community*. These various elements are intimately interrelated, and any given experience of shame could be used to illustrate any of the ten. As I comment on each element I will organize the discussion by grouping the elements in three categories. The first set of elements clarifies how shame is an interpretive process, or a way of seeing oneself from the standpoint of others. The second set shows shame to be a form of praxis, or a project of organizing a practical, problem-solving line of action. The third set describes shame as a distinctive sensuality that is lived as a particular form of corporeal metamorphosis.

SHAME'S INTERPRETIVE PERSPECTIVE

An Eerie Revelation to Self

Perhaps the most frequently noted element of shame is that of revelation. Powerful images of shame, from Adam and Eve's effort to mask a newly unbearable nakedness, to Hester Prynne's forced display of a sinful past, to John Updike's (1985) memories of periodic bouts with psoriasis, emphasize revelation in the form of exposure. Early in the life cycle, sphincter control becomes a challenge that provides a universal socialization into the phenomenology of shame, and later in the life cycle incontinence often provides a reminder that early concerns about involuntary exposure are not simply childish.

It is part of the unique complexity of shame that the exposure it implies is to an audience but that that audience is in the first instance oneself. Others' discoveries about oneself are not shameful unless one learns of their discovery. It is necessary to register the occurrence of a revelation about self from the perspective that others take on oneself. But concrete, face-to-face encounters with others need not be involved.

What Adam and Eve bought for us, *Genesis* tries to show, is a self-consciousness in which we can take a transcendent perspective on ourselves. After they ate from the forbidden fruit but before God saw them, Adam and Eve were ashamed. What was shameful was what was immediately revealed to them. It might be thought that their shame was only an anticipation of revelation to others. But as in the experience of shame, the emphasis in the biblical story is not on anticipated observation but on the godlike, immaterial, haunting threat of revelation that emerges in the capacity to turn on oneself (see Katz, 1996b).

University student reports are full of instances of shame at events like shoplifting in which the student successfully "got away with it" in a practical sense. Such accounts might suggest that revelation is not essential to shame, except that the construction of a scenario of exposure is part of the characteristic halo of these experiences. In a dreamlike manner, one imagines circumstances of revelation to others. As in a dream, it is not necessary to flesh out the faces or identities of those who are observing one; they are often present as phantoms. Even when they are identifiable in the imaginings of moments of exposure, the others whose observations create the revelation are phantomlike. One account, for example, was of shame experienced when the student was looking at photographs in the room of a friend who had authorized use of her room but had specifically forbidden inspection of the photos. When looking through the photos, this young man recalled the strange sense that "she would walk in the door and see me at any moment, even though I knew she was in San Francisco and that this was impossible."

It is important to emphasize the eerie quality of the revelation in shame because this feature of the experience points to the emergence of a problem in bounding one's identity from that of others.

When there is a moment of revelation to others, the ashamed person often cannot or will not lift his or her head to perceive the others' regard, and so he or she maintains a phantomlike sense of the "others" whose knowledge brings shame. In these cases, it is not actually seeing others seeing oneself that brings shame, since one may never quite catch their gaze. What brings shame is taking toward oneself what one presumes is the view that others would have were they to look.

This eerie quality is most fundamentally due to the dialectical character of shame, which is at once an experience of exposure and one of mystification. If there is a strong sense of revelation in shame, there is also a distinctive ambiguity about what is revealed. In many student accounts, the shameful experience was of being disloyal, "stepping out on" a romantic partner or, as one put it, "letting a fellow touch me where he shouldn't." This might be considered an experience of guilt, especially since the disloyalty is often never discovered or is revealed only through confession, but the students insist that something more disturbing is at stake. In the reports there is an element of wonder that proceeds from the self-observation that one may be "one of those people" who cannot stop looking over the shoulder of the person whom they are embracing to see if there is not a better prospect on the horizon. The haunting concern is not so much about a breach of moral reciprocity, or a failure to respect obligations to a particular other, as it is a new doubt about the self. What nags is not guilt but an anxiety that one may be a kind of soulless emotional capitalist, ever-ready to dislodge investments if a better deal turns up. It is glimpsing the power of one's own social and sexual narcissism that provokes shame.

What is eerie about the self-revelatory quality of shame is that the experience hovers between exposure and cover-up. What is revealed is something that one does not yet and perhaps cannot fully confront. Full revelation promises to overcome shame. When one truly cannot resist persistent exposure, for example after one is caught shoplifting and subject to public denigration, shame seems unbearably intense, but just for that reason typically it eventually fades.[1] Where criminality leads to shame, punishment may be

---

[1] John Braithwaite (1989) has constructed a theory of social control on such workings of shame and punishment, and indeed the American penitentiary system was constructed from the colonial version of a related philosophy. But such abstract moral schemes avoid being elaborate intellectual dodges only if one can empirically fill in the conditions, and in the U.S. the key problem is getting criminals to feel shame rather than pride in their "bad" images.

welcome for making public, and for defining, what is necessary for restoring the miscreant to the moral community. A student who was caught burglarizing neighbors' homes, recalled, "Being angry as my parents were, they punished me severely; I felt as if I deserved it. This punishment felt like the only outlet from such a wrong feeling." A star athlete who was caught "illegally" partying on a road trip expressed regret at a lost opportunity for catharsis. Drinking, drugs, and sex were involved; but what the coach actually knew about and objected to was never revealed owing to the discreet handling of the matter. The administrator in charge

> explained that this incident should never be spoken of because it would look bad for the program itself and to the whole UCLA athletic department. . . . I would of [*sic*] felt more at ease by suffering from a solid or noticeable punishment given by someone else. Instead, I suffered from my own shame, embarrassment and humiliation.

As long as it persists, shame carries the sense that an undeniable truth about the self is revealed. The matters that one is ashamed about are acknowledged as fundamental to one's character. But what that truth is remains mysterious. What is implied about a man's nature in the discovery that he regards his foot as shamefully ugly?[2] Shame is that paradoxical experience, the revelation of the existence of a personally powerful symbol. What is revealed in shame is not an answer, a solution, or the key to self-understanding. What is revealed is the existence of an abiding mystery, a personally resonant something-that-has-been-kept-hidden.

Thus there is an ambiguity in the self-revelation in shame. As Sartre (1956) wrote, "Shame is by nature recognition. I recognize that I am as the Other sees me" (pp. 221–222). But that it is the other that sees me means that the revelation is never complete, for I can never see myself quite from the same perspective as can another.

---

[2]In the humiliating police investigation that required that he take off all his clothes, Dmitri (Mitya) Fyodorovitch Karamazov, "feeling intolerably ashamed," was especially degraded by the command to take off his socks, as he "had thought both his big toes hideous. He particularly loathed the coarse, flat, crooked nail on the right one, and now they would all see it. . . . It's like a dream, I've sometimes dreamed of being in such degrading positions" (Dostoyevsky, 1950, p. 587).

The other can, paradoxically, know much about me that I cannot know myself. The other can see behind me, underneath me, the way I turn my torso and head to regulate my gaze; and the other can also see what I see by putting himself or herself in my position, at least in a spatial sense. What is revealed to oneself in shame, as Adam and Eve discovered, is an omniscience about oneself that only the other can possess. One of the terrible implications of shame is the discovery that "know thyself" is inevitably a compromised project if it is not done with the cooperation and through the knowledge that others have of oneself, in which case it must be done through faith in the beneficent spirit with which others provide indications of one's identity.

On one hand, it is surprising how warmly contemporary psychology has taken up the topic of shame, since shame is a recognition of the essentially social and spiritual foundations of personal identity. On the other hand, the phenomena of shame describe the classic data of depth psychology. Experienced as an attack on what is sensed as one's personally indispensable symbolic clothing, shame highlights rather than destroys a personally salient mystery.

Isolation from Community

Shame carries a sense of isolation from community. Any particular individual in relationship to whom one feels shame is regarded as representative (symbolic) of a diffuse group from which one feels isolated. "Soiling oneself" may provoke embarrassment by creating a problem in managing one's identity in a given social situation, but when it provokes shame it is through the implication that one lacks a fundamental capacity of self-control that would be required when interacting with any set of others.

Guilt is often specific to given relationships, but shame inherently generalizes. For example, guilt at not having cared sufficiently for one's mother during her final illness has a haunting power even as the sentiment emphasizes the uniqueness of that relationship. But in families where the father, through his work, is the primary bridge between domestic household and participation in the public institutions of society, the father's "discovery" of one's "weakness" often implies not only one's failure to meet family expectations but a devastating segregation from the community of responsible adults.

Isolation from community, if sufficiently extreme, will for many people provoke shame without any element of specifiable fault and independent of any relationship with a particular other. Imagine being given the assignment of walking across the football field during half time at the Rose Bowl, there to be observed by the tens of thousands of spectators who are present in the stadium as well as by the millions who are viewing through TV screens. Would-be actors and actresses delight in such a prospect, as they can anticipate roles they might adopt as vehicles for their performance, but most others would anticipate nakedness and horror. The problem is not one of a moral failing in any indictable sense, but one of being *before the community without being part of the community* in any recognizably competent way.[3]

The contingency of isolation helps explain the patterning of the experience of shame by elite suspects in the course of white-collar criminal prosecutions. During a study I conducted in the U.S. Attorney's office in Brooklyn, several prosecution and defense lawyers described the following pattern. While the common criminal defendant develops relationships with his defense lawyer and the prosecutor from the isolation of jail, white-collar defendants often manage to stay in a position of control in their business and political worlds right up until the moment they are sent to prison. Defense lawyers report dramatic swings, from refusals to provide necessary documents and personal information, to efforts by the client to participate in the case as a colleague (Mann, 1985). It appears that members of elites often appear shameless in the face of scandal because they have distinctive resources for putting off their isolation from their prior community. They become part of a spirited team during long periods of investigation and then trial. Even after conviction, isolation is avoided in a ritual process in which the defendant, often through his attorneys, family, and friends, appeals to personal and professional colleagues to write letters to the judge in praise of the defendant's character. Prosecutors report that they can easily dispose of character witnesses who assert that the crime is radically inconsistent with what they know about the defendant,

---

[3]An instructive set of contrasting examples from Los Angeles culture was the arrest in the 1980s of Olympic track star Edwin Moses for soliciting a policewoman/prostitute on Sunset Boulevard, and the arrest in the 1990s of actor Hugh Grant for sexual activity with a prostitute in the same neighborhood. Grant picked up the ball and ran with it, proving his acting talents in a novel way by elegantly mastering a series of self-effacing media appearances that further endeared him to his audiences. Moses' professional talents provided no ready path for renewing the embrace of the community that had adored him. (On the other hand, his lawyers got him acquitted).

simply by asking, "So if you had known of the crime, you would have had to revise your view of the defendant?" But defense lawyers understand that the ritual solicitation of support is in part therapeutic work that they do for their clients. The process elicits an emphatic, diverse community embrace of the defendant, one in which strangers often volunteer to participate. It is not until the defendant is sentenced to confinement that he must, for the first time, abandon control and anticipate the practical experience of isolation. Defense lawyers report that this stage in the process is rich in shame and, along with the initial need to break down the client's resistance to disclosing secrets, emotionally it is the most difficult transition for them and for the client to negotiate.

Isolation from a Sacred Community

Standing out "like a sore thumb" is a common reference to shame, but the interesting element here, the problematic characterization of the thumb as sore, is glossed by the familiar saying. The soreness depends on the person's nonreflective discomfort at being an outsider to the group. A student who moved from Boston to the San Fernando Valley when he was seven years old recalled vividly, some 15 years later, how the class laughed as he read out loud a story about "bahn yahd" animals. He quickly learned to lose the accent. It was irrelevant to his feelings that his classmates, delighted with his innocent idiosyncracy, might have shaped for him a unique place of affection in the group. The issue at seven years of age was not one of being seen positively but one of folding oneself into the cultural fabric of the group so as not to be subject to its devastating gaze.

In primordial understanding, the sacred is a power that, however beneficent, cannot be withstood when regarded directly by a person. Thus a mortal's encounter with the gaze of a Greek god who had become his or her lover would be devastating to the mortal, notwithstanding the lovers' desires. In shame one discovers the communities that one cannot but regard as sacred.

One may discover shame in self-reflections that find one's essential sensibilities existing outside of any group. This is a neglected dimension of the shame of masturbation, a shame that persists long after moralistic cultural prohibitions have weakened. Masturbation shame is not simply a result of "internalized" collective disapprobation. On the contrary, the shameful turn in masturbation can develop in the realization that one has in effect asserted, as a form of hubris, that one can be in touch with one's fundamental feelings independent of contact with others. Part of the justification for the moral condemnation of masturbation is an understanding that human identity is essentially social, an understanding that one cannot complete oneself except through actions with others. Shame's understanding is not that masturbation is damnable because of religious doctrine or because of conventional morality, but because it implies narcissistic self-satisfaction (see Scruton, 1986).

If shame can be created by acknowledging to oneself that one has pretended to have a kind of sacred core outside the group, simply being in conformity with others does not guarantee insulation from shame. The collectivity before which one feels isolated in shame is a community before which one feels a presumptive need for respect. Thus one may feel shame as a citizen of a society that has lost a war, but not because there is any other society that one views as more honorable. Sensing the disgrace of the "fatherland" as part of a defeated mass of people, one feels isolated not from others but from the group's rightful destiny and from the sacred version of community that collective mythology honors.

A wide range of shame experiences are triggered by the sense that one has primordial ties to another person whom one sees as shamefully exposed. It is common both for members of groups that are elite and for members of pariah groups to sense shame on the revelation of disgraceful doings by a group member. Such shame can be experienced when one is privately reading a scandalous news story about a stranger. Shame may emerge in these circumstances even though one does not feel personally exposed or at fault. What is critical is the realization that group membership does not provide a taken-for-granted basis of self-respect, and the realization, which may come for the first time only when public scandals unfold, that one has regarded a subgroup as a sacred community. Dual affiliations are revealed as the person recognizes that his or her self-respect depends on the respect that a larger community confers on a social circle to which he or she is inalienably tied. In a domestic variation on this pattern, one student reported shame about his father, who sported a ponytail and road a motorcycle, and shame about feeling this shame. Here the surprising revelation was not the young man's spiritual affiliation with the smaller group (his family), but the conventionality of his dependence on the larger community's whims of fashion.

Paradoxically, shame about the activities of a group in which one has been a member often emerges only when one no longer is in the group. The paradox is resolved if we appreciate the sacred or charismatic aura that a group may sustain. One student worked in a telephone sales job during graduate school, and until he left the job he failed to question the "borderline oil and gas company" whose stocks he was promoting. As he put it, "By believing your own performances, as well as that of others, you get caught up in the feeling of the group. You deceive yourself in order to avoid the shame of your actions." While he was in the salesgroup, he was part of a vigorously expressive, ritualized collective effort to enhance self-esteem, an effort like that which animates many charismatic Christian groups.

Shame is common when one has abandoned the group as well as when one feels that the group has abandoned oneself. It is a common subject for high drama but the fate of relatively few people to find that both dilemmas are present in one moment, a moment in which loyalty to the group is pitted against loyalty to the values that make the group an honorable collectivity. One such experience was provided by a student who attended the last show of the comedian Dick Shawn. Shawn had made a moderately successful career as an unusually eccentric or "mad" comedian. He characteristically played on the ambiguity of whether he was in or out of role; often he raised the unstated but provocative question for the audience, "Was he really that nutty or was he just doing 'being nutty'?" During his last performance, he collapsed on the stage without notice. Joking comments began to emerge from the audience: "Is there a doctor in the house?" "Take his wallet!" "I want my money back!" A bit later some ladies were heard to complain in disgust, "This isn't funny anymore!" The audience continued to laugh sporadically but in an increasingly nervous tone as the actor remained on the floor.

The student reported his mounting shame in three stages. First he debated the shameful possibility that he "didn't get it," that if he intervened he would stand out from the crowd as the only square who failed to understand the comedian's humor. But then, as the house lights were turned on, paramedics ran in from the wings to administer CPR, and the audience was asked to leave, the student became ashamed that he had been part of a mass of individuals who had been so reluctant to risk standing out from the group that each would let a man die before his or her eyes. What had been a group laughingly celebrating its shared, unconventional sensibility as an appreciative audience for this oddball comedian was suddenly revealed to be a collection of individuals who were clinging in mortal fear to a superficial appearance of conventional form. In retrospect the student was additionally ashamed that he had participated in a group that had, however unwittingly, made fun of a dying man. He was, thus, triply ashamed: first, that he might be too square to fit into this hip group; second, that he was a member of this audience, which for its insensitivity and timidity deserved no respect; and, third, that through a combination of collective self-deception and cowardice he had participated in a sacrilege.

Ivan Morris (1975), in his review of patterns of honorable suicide in Japanese history, points to further subtleties in the way that shame is related to isolation from a sacred community. When military and political leaders commit ritual suicide after losing a war, and when Wall Street leaders jump out of skyscrapers when stock markets crash and financial frauds are revealed, commentators often assume that unbearable shame motivated the suicide. Morris makes clear that, while these are shame-related suicides, they do not necessarily follow experiences of unbearable shame. Rather they may be ways of maintaining one's honor and thus of avoiding shame. Matters of fault are, again, not fundamentally relevant. Mistakes may have been made in military strategy, frauds may have been committed with the investors' money, but that is not necessarily the motivating concern. People who hold elite positions often know that mistakes and frauds are common in their fields and that their peers will not presume that a revealed mistake or a fraud was causally responsible for a disaster. There is no disgrace in failure itself; indeed, there is a "nobility of failure" if the disaster is taken as an opportunity to demonstrate, through the self-sacrifice of suicide, that one is committed to the group.[4]

What the commentators typically fail to appreciate is that members of elites know that they cannot escape the unbearable privileges of their status. When wars fail and markets crash, leaders know that they will not suffer as much as will the lesser participants whom they have long called on to sacrifice and maintain the faith. For those who were in elite positions, there may be no way to avoid living in the disgrace of relative comfort if they continue to live, and that comfort would now belie their long-professed commitments to the collective enterprise. In their suicides they honor their elite status as having always been based on a communal spirit. Through suicide the self is taken out of society in order that a noble spirit may remain in support of the community. In the eyes of the honorable suicides,

---

[4]Another instructive study of suicide is Jean Baechler's (1979) study of French cases. Several of the suicides, such as that of a mayor who, with 18 years of official tenure and an unofficial career as the soul of his town, was suspended after 13 people died in a tragic accident (case #37), were unrelated to personal fault and appear to have been ways of avoiding rather than exiting from shame. See also case #42.

their self-sacrifice is altruistic, helping those who remain sustain the faith that their sufferings are rooted in honorable commitments.

THE PRACTICAL DYNAMICS OF SHAME

Shame is not just a unique way of seeing oneself from the standpoint of others, it is also distinguished by one's sense of practical possibilities. The practical aspect of shame never unfolds coherently because the person in shame constantly confronts a sense of moral incompetence, personal vulnerability and the irresistibility of forces that doom efforts to organize a coherent self. Nevertheless, the tension of an existential protest against a determined fate is an ongoing, active part of the experience of shame.

Moral Incompetence

Whether or not shame is preceded by an act that one treats as one's fault, there is a sense in shame of an inability to do the right thing. This sense is prominent in the shame that frequently comes with unemployment due to plant closings or general economic downturns.[5] Student athletes commonly report shame when they fail to win a competition, without any feeling of guilt about a lack of effort or a breach in training routines. Women who have been raped often report a combination of anger at the rapist, anger at anyone who would suggest they were at fault for "inviting" the violation, and shame that they were unable to prevent the crime. Such instances of the victim's shame are not due to the women's "internalization" of oppressive versions of sexual morality; something similar often occurs in the wake of nonsexual crimes. Con men rely on their victims' sense of shame to help "cool out the mark" and facilitate

---

[5]In their methodologically pioneering study of a whole community of the employed in a southern Austrian village in the early 1930s, Jahoda, Lazarsfeld, and Zeisel (1933) found apathy rather than shame to be the dominant emotional problem. And apathy itself was by no means an inevitable response. The village had been dependent on a textile firm; when the industry failed, everyone suffered unemployment. The collective dimensions of the problem meant that unemployed persons were not isolated from the community. And, indeed, when they congregated, "whenever we had a chance to observe such gatherings" they "would strengthen optimism and cheerful sentiments" (p. 63).

their getaway (Goffman, 1952). The rape victim, like the person whose digestive system is suddenly and unexpectedly overwhelmed by an amoeba that he cannot resist, may feel shame that her body has betrayed her by being vulnerable to alien forces that transcend her will. The rape victim's suffering is dialectical and absurd in that it protests in vain against an event that was not the victim's fault yet leaves an ineradicable stain.

This existential sense of a shameful inability to shape one's identity along morally desirable lines despite one's will and best efforts appears in various forms of vicarious shame. A black student reported his sense of shame on seeing black employees working in a club at which he was refused entry on the grounds, he believed, of his race. In countless ways, this young man's identity in contemporary U.S. society will be shaped by others' perceptions of his race; he is linked, willy nilly, to the social identities shaped by others of his race. He is here triply impotent: unable to keep other blacks from working at such clubs, unable to resist sensing that he shares a responsibility for the decisions of others of his race to work in such places, and unable coolly to brush aside the suggestion that he would want to participate in a club that would not want him as a member.

Instances of vicarious shame include watching painfully awful performances in a theater. Having paid to attend a bad performance, one might more sensibly be outraged. But the performer's shameful incompetence may be experienced as one's own. Social situations are replete with undesired implications that one is the sort of person whose character complements the proceedings at hand. Thus an audience member may be uncomfortable with what he senses as his responsibility for calling out a performance that he likes too little, especially if he has brought friends to the event; and a therapist may sense shame in the implication that, through voyeuristic pleasure, he likes his work too much, perhaps especially if positions in the room facilitate eye contact (see Lewis, 1971, pp. 15-16).

Vulnerability

In guilt a person imagines how he might have acted to avoid a faulty act; in shame, the person feels that his fate is determined independent of his will. Poverty's shameful character is ancient because of the close connection between indigency and vulnerability. If poverty in its public display as homelessness seems surprisingly shameless today, still public welfare opportunities in the U.S. remain grossly underexploited, in part because of the persistence of the shameful implications of dependency.

Traditional rituals of begging are to be understood not only in the light of what must be done to put the would-be donor in a willing state of mind but also as a kind of occupational self-therapy. For centuries in Europe, beggars would offer bits of street performance or recite formulas of praise for the moral character of their would-be patrons (see, e.g., Isherwood, 1986). These rituals fight shame by overcoming implications of vulnerability in two ways. They clothe the beggar in a role of moral respectability, however thin, however cynically used; and their performance requires artfulness, however labored and conventionalized.

The element of vulnerability in shame is highlighted by experiences of false accusation. Many students reported that being caught shoplifting was an intensely shameful experience, but a few students noted that their most shameful experience was being falsely accused. Recalling incidents that remained vivid after a period of 10 years, they noted that in their culture, Asian-American in these cases, the very suspicion of such an act was sufficient to occasion shame. The aspect of frustration here—that one can unarguably win the battle of reason but still find that victory to be of no avail in resisting the emotion—is characteristic of the practical dimension of shame.

When sexual conduct is the shameful matter in student reports, what is shameful usually is not the violation of religious principles or conventional morality, but the loss of control, that is, the vulnerability of reason either to sexual urges or social pressures. The problem is that

> —"I could have been such a fool" as to have maintained an intimate relationship with a man, a coworker whom she'd been warned was a con man, and who, she progressively discovered, had a live-in girlfriend, owed her and many others a lot of money, and had given her a venereal disease;
>
> —He acceded to the other's urging and to his own desires when he slept in the same bed with another Mormon fellow from his mountain state home town, even though they promised they "wouldn't do it";
>
> —Her cover story disintegrated when she indiscreetly stayed out until 3 AM with a married man, after which she was upbraided both by her mother and his wife. For some time, she had cultivated a friendship with the couple by bringing them food and clothes, cleaning and cooking for them, and frequently conversing with him in the front room for hours after the wife, who was pregnant, had retired to sleep in the back room.

Each of these three reports has indications that the young adult in question was coyly playing with the ability to control his or her own conduct. In these cases, the potential for shame is so clearly signaled in advance that the circumstances seem exploited for titillation. How does titillation work? Consider the phenomenology of sex. It is distinguished by cyclical turns between subjectivity and objectivity, between an artful guidance of one's body and a letting go of control. What made these histories titillating was that their subjects wittingly structured a similar drama into unmanageably delicate relationships. The relationship between shame and sex was not simply that sexual activity provoked shame; sex became shameful only after shame had been exploited to make interaction sexy (see Broucek, 1991, p. 118).

Sex occasions shame not simply because of moral precepts but because shame and sex, as experiences of forces that transcend one's control, can evoke each other. That sex and shame share a powerful dimension of vulnerability is also indicated by shameful experiences of trying to reestablish family order after sexual conduct has shattered presumptions of stability. The family problem may arise because of one's own conduct:

—She attempted suicide when her parents decided to send her back to Korea for a while. A scandal had broken out after she woke up naked in the apartment of a fellow whose family was socially related to her own.

—At 22, within a three-year relationship, she finds she's pregnant. The problem wasn't the revelation of sexual activity; that had not been covered up. The problem was confronting a devout Catholic mother about abortion and that "I knew that if anyone were to talk to me about my situation, somehow they'd humiliate me and make me feel like an incompetent, inferior, unintelligent human being" because she was someone "who was not suppose [sic] to get pregnant, so anyone who found out or knew about it was compelled to ask why and how."

The sense of vulnerability implicated by sex is not always directly a matter of one's own frailties; it may emerge when a parent's secret sexual life is discovered. In one case, a young woman discovered her father's mistress through her boyfriend's socializing with her father.

While my mom was working her tail off from 9:00 a.m. to 2:00 a.m., he was parading around with his bimbo on a cruise ship in the company of my boyfriend. . . . To top it all off, it appeared that everyone, family members, friends, business clients even [her boyfriend] knew about my father's affair. [Twice she confronted her father's mistress.] I came face to face with the woman who had stolen everything I valued in life. But rather than "her" feeling beneath everything human, it was I who experienced shame. Here was this woman with no morality, snubbing her nose at us. Her friends stood there calling us names, one even called me a whore, end [*sic*] even though I am a virgin, I was ashamed, and I can't explain why.

In another case, a student reported her struggles with a long-term situation that still puts her identity unpredictably at risk. Her father lives with her mother and with another woman, simultaneously; he alternates sleeping at the two houses; she has "stepbrothers."

I have gotten used to the idea that all my relatives know about this, but I still feel ashamed. . . . when I would find out from another relative that my father had been there to visit them with his other family, I would turn red all over and that feeling of shame would come to me again. When I was in the public schools, I would dread one of my friends finding out about this, so I never discussed it with noone [*sic*]. When there was an event in school and my parents were able to attend, I would be very happy but at the same time I would be tense to have anyone recognized [*sic*] my father as to be living with another family and now they find out he has another family and another wife. I feel shame for something I can not control but that at the same time it is painful to me.

Again, note that it is not just the sense that the young woman's identity is out of her control that sustains her shame, but the absurdity in the situation. Despite the awareness that their fate is beyond their control, the young women in the last two examples cannot resist trying to escape their fate. As symbolized by Adam and Eve's hopeless, frantic effort to hide from God, shame is an experience of frustrated efforts to escape.

Irresistibility

Closely related to the sense of vulnerability in shame is the sense that the feeling is irresistible. Both features are highlighted in the experience of unrequited love and that of being abandoned by a lover. One can in these circumstances struggle for expressions of affection, but the effort risks humiliation since what is desired is an unconditional acceptance. Here is the classic setting, both fictional and factual, where attempts to resist shame fail and turn into irresistible rage.

It is frequently the defeat of an effort to treat loss as emotionally resistible that leads to the powerful devastation of shame. In everyday amateur athletic competitions, for example, it is common for participants to sense shame on losing a contest that they have taken pains to treat lightheartedly as not bearing any characterological implications. Shame in these circumstances reveals the difficulty of limiting the investment of self to a situational identity.

This line, it is useful to note here, is the very one that separates shame from embarrassment. Embarrassment is a situational problem in managing face;[6] shame is a disturbance that transcends the machinations of situational self-definition. Thus one may privately sense shame when losing a game even though, or just because, one's opponent graciously attempts to save one's face by brushing off the outcome as "only a game." It is also common that games end in a mixture of embarrassment and shame. One middle-aged student reported shame on losing a game of monopoly, after having humorously taunted his opponent with remarks like, "You don't have a chance. You can't beat me. What gives you the idea you could beat me?" When the game ended, he had an embarrassing problem of negotiating a transition from his arrogant posture as well as a sense of shame that he could not resist the moral implications of the loss.

A common feature of the experience of shame that is directly related to the sense of irresistibility is a desire to turn the clock back and take another course of action. Fantasies of escape are common; one may think, for example, that "maybe it's not too late to change my name and move to Costa Rica." The anguish in this dynamic of hoping against reason is crystalized in those experiences when one realizes, on acquiring some new bit of knowledge, that long ago everyone present in a given scene had privately understood that one was pretentiously using language, invoking a reference, or claiming a friendship. Even if the original misuse was innocent, and even if no one else actually took notice of the fault, the immediate experience is an excruciating awareness that one cannot go back to the situation and correct oneself and that it is improbable that one will ever have an opportunity to put a new, face-saving gloss on the revelation.

---

[6]Whatever else, embarrassment has to do with the figure the individual cuts before others felt to be there at the time. The crucial concern is the impression one makes on others in the present—whatever the long-range or unconscious basis of this concern may be (Goffman, 1967, p. 98).

THE METAMORPHOSIS OF SHAME

In addition to its features as a way of seeing oneself from the standpoint of another (as isolated from some community that one regards as sacred), and its features as a form of practice (an absurd struggle against an irresistible sense of vulnerability due to moral incompetence), shame, like other common emotions in everyday social life, is a corporeal experience of a transforming sensuality. That is, shame is not only a way of looking at oneself or trying to do something, it is also a dynamic feeling.

A Fearful State

Shame is a fearful state. In an illuminating study that asked people to describe what they were feeling in a recent shame experience, Lindsay-Hartz (1984) turned up descriptions of cringing, of wanting to run away but being unable to do so, and of related fantasies of becoming invisible. Like Adam and Eve, people in shame not only try to cover up, they also want to run away but know that the others from whom they would escape are omniscient. People look down in shame, Georg Simmel (1924) noted, so that others cannot easily see how they are responding to the moment.[7]

The fear that animates shame finds its most perfect expression in a desire to return to the womb.[8] Several of Lindsay-Hartz's respondents describe their wish that the earth would open up and swallow them:

---

[7]"Shame causes a person to look at the ground to avoid the glance of the other. The reason for this is certainly not only because he is thus spared the visible evidence of the way in which the other regards his painful situation, but the deeper reason is that the lowering of his glance to a certain degree prevents the other from comprehending the extent of his confusion. The glance in the eye of the other serves not only for me to know the other but also enables him to know me" (Simmel, 1924, p. 358).

[8]Salman Rushdie's (1983) *Shame* revolves around the relationships between a man born of three mothers but who is immune to shame and a woman whose father imagines her to be male, and who lives constantly in shame. He has an overabundance of wombs; she must deny her own womb.

> Let me just cover myself up and nobody can see me. Shame is just total—and you want to disappear. . . . I can't put it a better way than to say, like there could only be a hole in the ground, I could sink into and nobody would see me. . . . You want to hide yourself. You want to be where you cannot be seen. There is no way out. Just by your mere existence is causing you shame. . . . I kind of even sank into my chair. . . . You hope for yourself not to be there. . . . You feel like burying yourself. . . . It's like if you hide someplace, that's what I think of as sinking into the ground [p. 692].

The desire is not for death, not for the punishment of being buried alive. It is, instead, a desire to be alive but without so much as breathing, so as not to draw attention to oneself. The wish should be read as: "I wish I could get rid of the visible evidence that this damned body makes of my spirit"; that is, for a secure refuge for the spirit, not for its destruction. The fantasy of being taken up by "Mother" earth and to exist but in a nonbreathing and invisible state, protected by a power that one cannot see, imagines a form of prenatal life. Lewis (1971) writes: "One could 'crawl through a hole,' or 'sink through the floor' or 'die' with shame. The self feels small, helpless and childish" (p. 41)

Chaos

The phenomenology of shame begins in fear and moves immediately to a sense of chaos. Adam and Eve are frequently depicted as running helter-skelter in search of a hiding place.[9] Again, something similar is part of everyday experiences of shame. We have seen some of the indications of chaos already, in the dead-end maneuvers of imagining the clock turned back, in the realization that one's identity is linked to a dishonored group or historical event and so will be irremediably stained, in the effort to exist without breathing. Lewis (1971) observed that "shame is a relatively wordless state" (p. 37). Helen

---

[9]In this respect, too, shame may be distinguished from guilt. People not uncommonly nourish and take pride in cultivating their guilt. Shame—but not the posture of modesty that would avoid shame—is terrifying in the chaos it embodies. Pagels (1988) offers the provocative observation that "were it not that people often *would rather feel guilty than helpless*—I suspect that the idea of original sin would not have survived the fifth century" (p. 146).

Merrill Lynd (1958) earlier had observed that chaos is one of the ancient meanings associated with shame. In Greek tragedy, it is unspeakably shameful events that throw Thebes into chaos.

Decades after Freud noted the phenomenon, it is still a common nightmare for college graduates, years after receiving their degree, to dream that they are shamefully unprepared for an exam the next day. Typically such dreams are unrelated to any real experience. It is specifically the sort of problem that one can do nothing about that is represented by this kind of dream, which transforms a mysterious self-doubt into a practical problem that, were it real, one could solve. When seriously disturbed patients have nightmares about long-past traumas, they often use their troubling dreams to construct a false biography that only indirectly represents haunting matters of shame (Lansky, 1995).

Dreams of having forgotten an obligation to attend an exam provoke a sense that parallels the everyday anxiety of being late for social obligations. Being late carries for many people a fear that it will convey to others the characterological implication that, if one cannot shape one's private affairs to the social calendar, one must be incompetent for virtually any social responsibility. In the frantic frustration that a person may experience in anticipation of being late, some form of emotional chaos is in motion.

Essential, Holistic

The fear in shame and in its nightmares is that the chaos cannot be limited to any specific act or fact. The experience of shame may start with the revelation of some minor stigma, like an ugly foot or a malapropism, but it quickly sweeps through the self. Lewis (1971) again:

> Shame is about the whole self. It is possible in moments when one is not ashamed to regret or grieve over a specific disfigurement or personal failing. At the moment when one is ashamed of specific shortcomings, shame affect involves the whole self. This global target of hostility makes it difficult to find a solution short of a sweeping replacement of self by another, better one [p. 40].

Shame may be about intimate matters, such as private parts or secret corruptions, or it may be about matters that are superficial in the general regard but that are intimately meaningful to the person ashamed.[10]

Humbling

Shameful feelings move from fear to chaos to humility. When "put to shame," one is cut down, forced to abandon a prior, arrogant posture. When one stumbles into shame, one shrinks down, trying to become small so as to escape notice.

Occupants of honored, elite positions confront a distinctive dilemma of shame precisely because of their difficulty in negotiating a posture of humility. It is a peculiar feature of recent U.S. politics that powerful forces in the public stubbornly insist on uncovering matters of personal biography that are inconsistent with the honor that large parts of the public insist on conferring on their leaders. The days have passed when such matters as presidential mistresses and habits of smoking would be kept off the record by opposition leaders and the press. Whether the matter is lascivious desire or a playful act, leaders are ridiculed when they acknowledge their "human frailties," as occurred with Jimmy Carter's report of "lust in the heart" and Bill Clinton's description of smoking but not inhaling marijuana. Leaders cannot as a practical matter avoid setting themselves up for shameful revelations because they cannot themselves control the forces of adoration that motivate their followers. Similarly, people who receive routine demonstrations of

---

[10]Simmel shrewdly focuses on the imputation of essential character in shame in order to suggest the structure of relationships in which shame is more and less likely. Others' perceptions of given acts are relatively unlikely to elicit shame where the others are either intimate associates or bare strangers. In the former case, the other has far richer sources for constructing one's character than an isolated act; in the case of the stranger, the other has little basis to presume how characteristic the act is. In Simmel's time, this helped explain the surprising openness of people who would meet for the first and presumably last time when they shared a train compartment: "travelling companions, who were unknown to one another until an hour ago, and who will not see one another again an hour later, are often prepared to entrust one another with intimacies." He expected that shame would be most likely in relationships that were, in these terms, of the middle range (cited in Gerhards, 1986).

respect, such as the maitre d's fawning, "Doctor, your table is ready," live within walls of dignity that would be undermined if a professional license were stripped away.

On the domestic front, fathers often must walk a tricky line between leading their children to unfounded adulation and attacking their children's need for faith in parental perfection. A son catching his father stealing something cheap, like coins from a phone booth, can put both to shame, even though the father never assumed a character that would make such a discovery the revelation of hypocrisy (see Morano, 1976, p. 79). Conversely, and perhaps empirically related to children's adulation, a form of shame frequently reported by my UCLA students is shame over disappointing parental expectations about grades, sexual behavior, drinking and driving. Whatever the reality may be on the parental side, these students indicated a sense that they lacked any means of downscaling parental expectations to a level that they would regard as realistic. On one hand, glorifying the other is, for many at least, an inextricable part of loving the other; on the other hand, the child and the parent, each unable to have his own limitations accepted by the other, collaborate to institutionalize a vulnerability to shame on both sides of the generational divide.

Common folk practices for extricating the self from shame contain a socio-logic about humility that is well worth noting. After a shameful experience that appears to be ineradicable, people often report that they returned home and began to busy themselves with tasks of restoring their domestic environment.

Tolstoy made clear both the shame of discrepancy arising from "the sudden loss of all known landmarks in oneself and in the world, and the way in which one seizes upon familiar details of daily life in an effort to regain a sense of one's own identity and rootedness in the social situation" (cited in Lynd, 1958, p. 39). Thus Anna Karenina, recognizing her feelings for Vronsky, busies herself with details of everyday life at home to dispel shame, although no one else knows of her feelings and no shameful act has occurred.

Compulsive housekeeping may be understood as an effort to build up a private sense of self that is independent of and immune to the threats of participating in society; but that formulation is only partially accurate. The busy-ness of perfecting the domestic order, by cleaning and putting things in their place, by taking up neglected responsibilities, or just by polishing an order that is already well established, has no substantive relationship to the matters that provoked shame. These must be understood as ritual practices that honor the congruence of one's nature and an order—any order— that is clearly moral. In cleaning, putting things in their place, paying one's bills, and so on, one humbles the self, becoming a servant of a predefined, typically conventional notion of propriety. Symbolically, the logic of self-salvation here is to do a kind of penance to some version of collective morality, trusting that in the process the environment will once again take up and silently embrace the self. But symbolic logic is not enough. A metamorphosis, or change in the lived corporeal vehicle of action, is necessary; and, as a practical matter, in taking on such tasks one changes the employment of one's body in thorough and precise detail.

NEGOTIATING A PASSAGE BETWEEN THE DUAL RISKS OF SHAME

Max Scheler (1987) developed a dualistic perspective that appreciated a distinction between "body shame" and "spiritual shame." Body shame is a matter of not staying covered by social clothing. It is occasioned by the faux pas that indicates a general lack of education; by "animal" releases or other indiscretions that occur when social actions are not properly embodied; by incompetencies due to poverty, poor health, membership in stigmatized groups, new immigrant status, and so forth that put one below the minimal level for leading a "normal" social life. If body shame is a matter of sensing that one is not capable of being competently human according to the definitions prevailing in a given society, spiritual shame is occasioned by claims to transcend conventional restraints because of extraordinary qualities. The fall of "body shame" is to a childish or animal nakedness; the fall of "spiritual shame" is that of Icarus, a fall from arrogant pretension. Body shame often emerges independent of imputations of personal fault; spiritual shame emerges where there is a lack of appropriate humility.

Dick Gregory (Gregory and Lipsyte, 1964, pp. 43-46) neatly reviews both forms of shame in his autobiography. As a poor child, he was ashamed to wear the Mackinaws that were known by everyone in the community to be distributed by the local charity. Ashamed of his poverty, the signs of which he literally wore as a constant provocation of body shame, he risked spiritual shame when, during a campaign in school to raise money for the Community Chest, and in order to impress a female classmate, he offered to bring several times the average class contribution from his father. This is how he recalled the teacher's response:

"We are collecting this money for you and your kind, Richard Gregory. If your Daddy can give fifteen dollars [it was during the Depression] you have no business being on relief. And furthermore," she said, looking right at me, her nostrils getting big and her lips getting thin and her eyes opening wide, "we know you don't have a Daddy" [p. 45].

Frequently the two forms of shame are merged in a given event, but they are still distinguishable, as in the double-whammy of a sucker's realization of his fallen status. Con schemes typically proceed from the sucker's willingness to believe that he is "wise," that is, a partner in a scheme to con others (Leff, 1976). In a "pigeon drop," for example (the following is from an experience in Mexico City's Chapultepec Park that was related to me some 25 years after it occurred), you stumble across a bag of money at the same time as does a stranger. The stranger offers to leave the bag with you while he searches around to find someone who would claim title to it. In the meantime, he must trust that you would split it honestly with him when he returns. To show your reciprocal good faith, he suggests that you entrust him with your watch. Before the stranger returns, you run off with the bag. When you have time to look more closely into it, you find that only the top bills are real. Now you must confront 1) the hubris in your assumption that you naturally would have the luck to fall upon an abandoned treasure, 2) the pretentious-ness in your effort to trick both the fictitious stranger you never met and the real one that you did meet, and 3) your fundamental incompetence to recognize an ancient con trick. The shame of the experience rings in two keys: it was just by pretending that you were especially smart that you came out a fool.

One may err painfully in being overdressed for an occasion or in being underdressed; when arriving at an appointment much too early or much too late; by failing to bring a gift of value sufficient to honor the recipient, by bringing a gift that is so valuable that it becomes an insulting attempt to lord one's status over the recipient, or by bringing a gift either too soon or too late, since errors of timing in either direction can indicate the lack of an appropriate sense of the social relationship (Bourdieu, 1990, p. 105).

Each of the 10 features of shame that we have reviewed char-acterizes spiritual as well as body shame. In the presence of what one regards as genius, stunning beauty, or unsullied innocence, one may cringe or *humble oneself*. There is evidence here of *chaos* and *vul-nerability*: "For many there is a reticence, awkwardness, speechless-ness, diffidence and fumbling before great people" (Morano, 1976,

p. 79). There is *fear* in meeting the great scholar at the cocktail party, fear that one may defile the scene by undermining the other's comfortable display of his or her marvelous sensibilities and talents. One cringes at the risk that something *sacred* may be defiled because he or she is too conventional.

At children's first music recitals, it is not uncommon for parents to find an *irresistible* catch in their throats as they watch precious performances in awe-struck silence. Such experiences are often surprising *revelations to self* of the profound dependence of one's *nature* on others' lives. When receiving awards or praise, one may realize that such ceremonies have value in sustaining others' motivations to an institution, but that the very conventionality of acceptance speeches, with their rituals for acknowledging equally worthy candidates and the less visible contributors to one's own success, distance oneself from the event. Even as one is being embraced by a community regarded as sacred, *one feels isolated* before it.

For some, a creative sensibility depends not on overcoming fear but on sustaining *a fear* not of shame but *of shamelessness*. Henri Matisse was instantly horrified when reviewing a slow-motion film that revealed the motions he made before his pencil touched the paper. "I never realized before that I did this. I suddenly felt as if I were shown naked—that everyone could see this—it made me deeply ashamed" (in Johnson, 1993, p. 21).[11] As a blush is a form of shame about shame, so modesty, when it is not merely a pose but a sensually lived experience of humility, is a kind of self-inoculating experience of spiritual shame that guards against the naked feelings of body shame.

The transcendence of body shame is not necessarily to shamelessness but commonly to a new embrace of the spiritual power of shame. John Updike (1985) recalls that after the sun would cure his periodic bouts of psoriasis, he could walk with his family on the beach in a bathing suit, with a pride that was at once a form of humility: "It was, for me, a matter of pride, a willed achievement, to be among these nearly naked strollers, to be an inconspicuous part of this herd, to be in this humble sense human" (p. 50).

---

[11]Contrast the more familiar perspective that creative achievement is a strategy against personal shame. An entertaining example is John Cuddihy's (1974) somewhat facile argument that Marx, Freud, and (by extension) Goffman worked to undermine different anti-semitic stereotypes of Jewish motivations (money, sex, interpersonal manipulation) by generalizing them to everyone.

In some discussions, what I am here calling spiritual shame is distinguished as modesty or the practice of protecting oneself against shame by living it constantly in a mild form. What is crucial for theory is not a specific vocabulary but an appreciation of the existential dilemma that animated Scheler's (1987) discussion, as it points to the challenge of personal identity in society as one of constantly negotiating a path between the Scylla of body shame and the Charybdis of spiritual shame. A dualistic perspective on shame is inconsistent with the prevailing thrust in American culture and in much psychological commentary that sees shame as inherently negative and to-be-transcended.[12]

The empirical reality of spiritual shame is distinctively tricky to see in data, just because it is a matter of the style, spirit or manner of conduct. As Goffman (1959) wrote, the obligation to present a self in society is not simply one of giving an impression that one is a particular kind of person (father, professor, market shopper, car driver), but also of "giving off" that same impression, that is, of acting one's roles and features of identity "naturally" or with a grace that makes them appear to be effortless emanations of one's character. "The expressiveness of the individual . . . appears to involve two radically different kinds of sign activity: the expression that he gives, and the expression that he gives off" (p. 2).

If we know, through cross-cultural research, that much about styles of masculinity and femininity, character features that change with age, and personality dispositions associated with high and low statuses in work institutions, vary enormously among societies, we also know that, in any given society, gender, age and status characteristics are always enacted as already there. Personal identity everywhere is an achieved performance of ascriptive characteristics. One learns how to enact fundamental features of personal identity in ways that suggest that the features are inherent, natural, matters of grace, and not products of years of culturally guided practice. It is difficult to see how members of society "give off" their personal characteristics just because members work so hard to obscure the machinations of producing their identities.

The posture that risks spiritual shame by implying a natural guarantee for the accomplishment of social life has its rationale in the faith that it produces, a faith that is a necessary precondition to

---

[12]A prominent recent example is Mecca, Smelser, and Vasconcellos (1989). For a critique of the monolithic culture against shame, see Schneider (1992) on Nietzsche's perspective, and Broucek (1991).

ordinary social interaction. Were Matisse to have watched his hands as he attempted to draw he would have lost his genius.[13] Any line of social action, from a casual conversation to an artistic performance to sexual interaction, is vulnerable to breakdown from too close attention to its necessary machinations (on sex, see Broucek, 1991). Awkwardness, not just practical ignorance and incompetence, threatens to provoke a destructive shame. But the alternative is not the transcendence of shame. A certain disattention, an implicit reliance on understanding even as it is emerging in explicit form, indeed a constant running on the surface of shame, is a necessary foundation of social action.

The implications of a dualistic conception of shame are decisive for the study of emotions in general. Just as there are two forms of shame, so are there two forms of humor (slapstick comedy and inspired wit; see Katz, 1996a), of anger (hot and cold, see Katz, 1988, chapters 2 and 3), and of crying (crying that proceeds from loss and crying that recognizes what is awe inspiring) in everyday social life (Katz, 1997). Just as it has been especially difficult for scholarship to grasp spiritual shame, so is there a parallel failure to appreciate inspired as well as tendentious forms of humor, the pleasures of meanness and cruelty as well as the dynamics of rage, the tears that issue in joyful celebration of innocence and creativity as well as the tears that wash over destructions of the self.

It is instructive that a "fall" can lead alternatively to shame, to a humorous appreciation of slapstick comedy, to a tearful recognition of a painful loss of a situational self, or, if one sees the fall as the result of another's intentions, to an angry sense of humiliation. Shame hovers in the near background of various everyday emotions. Research has yet to pin down just how systematic the relationships are, but there is strong evidence that the causal path into hot anger can be traced to humiliation and that the typical joking situation poses the challenge that one either "get it" or be "out of it" in the sense of being left awkwardly isolated from the sensibilities of others. Initial inquiries into "loss" cryings reveal a similarly close empirical relationship to shame. For toddlers, bouts of crying often flow only indirectly from falls; one can often see a pause before crying begins, a pause in which the child searches for his or her guardian so that, when the crying comes, crying will not isolate the child from others

---

[13]For an application of this line of argument to piano playing, see Sudnow (1978).

but will, on the contrary, literally throw the child into an embrace that overcomes a dramatized moment of isolation from communion.

The causal routes into the "spiritual" and the "body" forms of emotions appear to follow inversely related paths, whether the emotion is that of anger, laughter, or crying. The "badass" criminal who delights in a spirit of cold meanness does not respond to an immediate threat of humiliation, as does the everyday passion murderer. On the contrary, the badass inventively constructs a godlike power to humiliate others at will and without apparent reason. Laughter often begins around slapstick images of people falling out of conventional roles and into what otherwise might be taken to be shameful postures. But laughter sometimes then moves into a distinct second stage in which participants celebrate their collective manifestation of a common positive spirit and also face a new order of interactional challenge for maintaining their unity. When laughter becomes inspired, participants sometimes find that they must rush out of the scene in order not to betray it. What they then sense is that their laughter is about to change from a graceful contribution to the group into an attack on the group's shared focus. And joyful crying often develops as one becomes flooded with a shamelike sense of silent awe. Tears of joy emerge as a veil of modesty that recognizes the sacred character of the inspiring object by creating a discreet distance from it.

In short, a specification of the elements of shame, and an appreciation of the dual forms of shame as posing an existential challenge for social action, appears to be a promising standpoint for closely examining the empirical dynamics of everyday emotions. More generally, the study of shame argues for a social-psychological form of analysis. So long as the emphasis in the study of shame remains psychological, analysis is likely to highlight the destructive, inhibiting, and negative aspects of the emotion. The valuable features of shame are more visible when we ask, what is necessary *so that people may act together*? Then we can appreciate that manner, style, grace, and other ways of acting so that one's role appears to emanate naturally, as if through some kind of transcendent guidance, are always difficult, always contingent, but always necessary elements in the process of sustaining the identities of the others with whom we interact. Psychologists may find this perspective useful on the understanding that it is, after all, through the process of sustaining others' identities that each person elicits the responses that sustain his or her own.

The dimension of grace that is necessary for competent personal action need not be morally admirable or aesthetically appealing. Its typical vehicle may be a combination of national or regional cultural style, an ethnic or racial or gendered way of doing things, a professional demeanor, a personally distinctive, even eccentric manner— some mixture of collective forms that are invoked as inherent, insured, already there, confidently guiding the production of particular acts. Through the matter of manner, one provides a basis for others to take for granted that there exists a collective ground, independent of the participants' machinations, for the conduct on which they collaborate. The social order appears to demand not only that naked self-interests be covered by the substance of conventionally recognizable social roles, but also that each put the self aesthetically at risk of spiritual pretentiousness in order to sustain the identity of others.

REFERENCES

Baechler, J. (1979), *Suicides*. New York: Basic Books.
Bourdieu, P. (1990), *The Logic of Practice*. Stanford, CA: Stanford University Press.
Braithwaite, J. (1989), *Crime, Shame and Reintegration*. New York: Cambridge University Press.
Broucek, F. J. (1991), *Shame and the Self*. New York: Guilford Press.
Cuddihy, J. M. (1974), *The Ordeal of Civility*. New York: Basic Books.
Dostoyevsky, F. (1950), *The Brothers Karamazov*. New York: Random House.
Gerhards, J. (1986), Georg Simmel's contribution to a theory of emotions. *Social Sci. Inf.*, 25:901–924.
Goffman, E. (1952), On cooling the mark out: Some aspects of adaptation to failure. *Psychiat.*, 15:451–463.
———— (1959), *The Presentation of Self in Everyday Life*. Garden City, NY: Doubleday.
———— (1967), *Interaction Ritual*. Garden City, NY: Anchor Books.
Gregory, D. & Lipsyte, W. R. (1964), *Nigger*. New York: Dutton.
Isherwood, R. M. (1986), *Farce and Fantasy*. New York: Oxford University Press.
Jahoda, M., Lazarsfeld, P. F. & Zeisel, H. (1933). *Marienthal*. Chicago: Aldine Atherton, 1971.
Johnson, G. (1993), *The Merleau-Ponty Aesthetics Reader*. Evanston, IL: Northwestern University Press.
Katz, J. (1988), *Seductions of Crime*. New York: Basic Books.

———— (1996a), Families and funny mirrors: A study of the social construction and personal embodiment of humor. *Amer. J. Sociol.,* 101:1194–1237.

———— (1996b), The social psychology of Adam and Eve. *Theory & Soc.,* 25:545–582.

———— (1997), What is crying? Department of Sociology, University of California, Los Angeles. Unpublished manuscript.

Lansky, M. (1995), *Posttraumatic Nightmares.* Hillsdale, NJ: The Analytic Press.

Leff, A. (1976), *Swindling and Selling.* New York: Free Press.

Lewis, H. B. (1971), *Shame and Guilt in Neurosis.* New York: International Universities Press.

Lindsay-Hartz, J. (1984), Contrasting feelings of shame and guilt. *Amer. Behav. Sci.,* 27:689–704.

Lynd, H. M. (1958), *On Shame and the Search for Identity.* New York: Harcourt, Brace.

Mann, K. (1985), *Defending White-Collar Crime.* New Haven, CT: Yale University Press.

Mecca, A. M., Smelser, N. J. & Vasconcellos, J. (1989), *The Social Importance of Self-Esteem.* Berkeley: University of California Press.

Morano, D. V. (1976), *Existential Guilt.* Atlantic Highlands, NJ: Humanities Press.

Morris, I. I. (1975), *The Nobility of Failure.* New York: Holt, Rinehart & Winston.

Pagels, E. (1988), *Adam, Eve, and the Serpent.* New York: Random House.

Rushdie, S. (1983), *Shame.* New York: Knopf.

Sartre, J.-P. (1956), *Being and Nothingness.* New York: Washington Square Press.

Scheler, M. (1987), On shame and feelings of modesty. *Person and Self-Value,* ed. M. S. Frings. Hingham, MA: Martinus Nijhoff, pp. 1–85.

Schneider, C. D. (1992), *Shame, Exposure, and Privacy.* New York: Norton.

Scruton, R. (1986), *Sexual Desire.* New York: Free Press.

Simmel, G. (1924), Sociology of the senses: Visual interaction. In: *Introduction to the Science of Sociology,* ed, R. E. Park & E. W. Burgess. Chicago: University of Chicago Press, pp. 356–361.

Sudnow, D. (1978), *Ways of the Hand.* Cambridge, MA: Harvard University Press.

Updike, J. (1985), At war with my skin. *The New Yorker* 61:39–40, 43–44, 46–57.

BENJAMIN KILBORNE

The Hunting of the Red-Faced Snark: Commentary on Chapters 4, 5, 6, 7, 8, 9

In the chapters we are considering here, shame is what we are hunting. All approach the hunt well equipped, and there is a great deal to be learned in these pages. Donald Nathanson writes on the affect theory of Silvan Tomkins (chapter 4); Karen Hanson writes on philosophy and shame (chapter 6). Leon Wurmser, contributing a paper on Neitzsche (chapter 7), has brought his extensive erudition to the subject of shame in psychoanalysis. Scheff and Retzinger, the most prominent contemporary "shameniks" from the sociological tradition, review the contributions of Helen Block Lewis (chapter 5), and Scheff also writes on shame in social theory (chapter 8). Jack Katz (chapter 9) contributes an empirically based sociological study of shame.

The snark should be flattered to be the object of so much interest. Yet, since this is a book about shame, we can imagine the snark blushing at being so invisible that he has occasioned such a hunt. Picture a glorious hunt the object of which is imagined through the equivalent of the sounds of bugles, the sweat of horses and riders, the excitement and fever of the chase, and the lunge toward anyone who believes he has caught a glimpse of places where the quarry has recently passed.

Nathanson (chapter 4), with all the fervor of a collector of antique medical instruments, follows Tompkins in linking the behaviors of shame to biological concepts and in subscribing to his logic and yearning for precision. "If shame is an innate affect, it must have an activator capable of triggering a highly specific mechanism." And he proceeds to demonstrate how Tomkins searches for such a "highly specific mechanism." The search leads to the discovery of an "algebra of affect theory," the basic theorem of which is an "analogic amplifier." For Nathanson and Tomkins, such "analogic amplifiers" intensify the same affect: "Each affect is therefore a compelling stimulus for the production of more of that affect."

For Nathanson and Tomkins, science and language meet in a new scientific language of the emotions. Their "affect mechanism" is, they believe, "similar to the set of complex relationships between an alphabet, words, grammar and semantic rules." Both Nathanson and Tomkins reflect the longing for a precise, common language (the "algebra") of the emotions the modern roots of which strike back to the 18th-century Ideologues and the Champollions of this world, a Romantic desire to find a universal Ur-language, a passion for decoding previously unknown languages like Egyptian hieroglyphics.

Yet any universal language, any algebra-like formulation, necessarily departs from everyday experience. As Tomkins notes, shame is not always what it appears to be, so a logic and a set of hierarchies that depart from common experience seems essential for an "algebra of the emotions." "Discouragement, shyness, shame, and guilt are identical as affects, although not so experienced because of differential coassembly of perceived causes and consequences. Shyness is about strangeness of the other; guilt is about moral transgression; shame is about inferiority; discouragement is about temporary defeat; but the core affect in all four is identical, although the coassembled perceptions, cognitions and intentions may be vastly different."

Tompkins and Nathanson redefine shame in the context of a revised language of the emotions in which the ordinary links between our feelings, our notions of causality, and our ability to classify what we feel and what others feel can be called into question. There are great advantages to such an approach, for it allows us to look at feeling clusters in new ways. But there are also risks in proposing a model of algebraic clarity, in describing a (by definition new and unfamiliar) language of the emotions which has to be learned. And it raises an important question: how discrepant from everyday experience can a theory and language of emotions be and still be useful? And, correspondingly, to what extent does a preoccupation with a universal language of the emotions preclude attention to the range of meanings commonly associated with shame?

Scheff and Retzinger share with Tomkins and Nathanson this vision of themselves as decoders of a universal language of the emotions and, in the search for universals, as a hallmark of the scientists they see themselves to be. In their discussion of the world of Helen Block Lewis (chapter 5), Scheff and Retzinger remind us that she too seeks to redefine shame by including sequences of shame-related feelings ("shame loops") and by wondering about the extent to which shame (and its related feelings) are unconscious. And Scheff and Retzinger usefully provide five themes in terms of which Lewis's writings can be organized: 1) the prevalence of shame and its preeminence as an emotion; 2) "unacknowledged," "bypassed" shame, which Scheff and Retzinger point out might have been more effectively referred to as "unconscious" shame; 3) feeling traps, lengthy episodes involving "emotional reactions to one's emotional reactions"; 4) shame implies the experience of being disconnected from self and others; 5) the primary role of shame in treatment failures. As Scheff and Retzinger note, however, Lewis's notions of feeling traps do not include "shame-shame cycles" or "shame loops." Also, Scheff and Retzinger criticize Lewis for not clearly enough distinguishing between normal and pathological shame. This distinction raises an interesting question: can writers on shame themselves be organized into two groups—those who think that they cannot deal with shame without clearly distinguishing between the normal and pathological and those who would say there are no categorical differences between the two?

In chapter 8, Scheff, like Tomkins and Nathanson, looks for precise definitions and for a "new language" of the emotions. Yet in his enthusiasm to find universals, he makes telling assumptions. For instance, he writes: "false pride corresponds exactly to the meaning of the Greek word hubris." So far as I know, there is no word in another language that means exactly what some translation we would give it can mean. While this is a very small point, it has, I think, a wider implication: that the concern to establish a universal language runs counter to an understanding of context and meaning in specific situations, times and places. And although Scheff lists Greek, Latin, French, German and Italian "equivalents" for our terms "disgrace" and "modesty," he does not ground his ideas in a thorough examination of linguistic, etymological, cultural, and historical evidence. He does not provide us with the basis on which to judge the adequacy of the correspondence among these various terms or explore their meanings in the original language.

This seems to me useful to consider. Scheff underestimates the difficulty of translation in part as a consequence of his passion for finding a common language, a pan-human form of communication, universally the same. "Since the denial of shame is institutionalized in our civilization, a vital new language is needed, an emotion language, that calls shame and other primitive emotions by their proper names." Does the fact that our civilization "institutionalizes the denial of shame" necessarily mean that one has to view as useless whatever culturally specific meanings of the shame experience might be found? Can denial (or any other defense) be "institutionalized"? Is it necessary to reach for universals to say anything meaningful about shame at all? How do we know that the "names" that Scheff proposes are the "proper" ones if he does not demonstrate this? And in what does the "properness" of their names consist?

Writing as a philosopher, Karen Hansen (chapter 6) provides us with a shame-filled philosophical panorama of more than two millennia. Historical sequence and context are somewhat jumbled, as she careens vertiginously across the centuries, producing an impressive mass of ideas about shame. First she talks about Descartes, then Augustine, then Nietzsche, then Kant, and not too long thereafter Aristotle. By the end of her chapter, one's head is fairly spinning. Yet out of that emerges an extraordinary welter of ideas about shame and its complications which defies easy classification. Even a division between philosophers who see shame as negative (e.g., Isenberg) and those who see shame as positive (e.g., Descartes) cannot be made. The difficulty echoes the problems facing those who wish to distinguish between "good" and "bad" shame.

In *Beyond Good and Evil* (1885), Neitzsche wrote that, because there is no reliable opposition between a true and an apparent world, "there is only one world, and this one is false, cruel, contradictory, seductive, without meaning." Thus "the philosophy of power became the philosophy of the lie." Consequently, Nietzsche was caught having rendered inauthentic the primary basis for power, (and having given a sense of power to his inauthenticity) a position in which he could only emptily affirm antidotes to the shame at the core of his being. Wurmser (chapter 7) elucidates this fundamental and intractable problem.   As Wurmser so justly points out, "Nietzsche's importance consists in his having drawn out attention to an ethic built on categories of shame. . . . He made the fundamental mistake, however, of putting this ethic in absolute, categorical terms: he reduced guilt to shame." Wurmser writes, "By reducing the guilt-oriented conscience to a matter of shame and to a supposed external imposition of sanction that left the individual helpless and passive, he accomplished the entire 'transvaluations of values.'" And in the process provided shame with a disastrous mass appeal made still more disastrous by shared persecutory and megalomaniacal delusions severed from an essential sense of social justice.

Jack Katz (chapter 7) sets out to describe shame, not by redefining emotional categories or deciding which clusters of emotions shame might or might not fit into, but rather "empirically," by asking students how their understanding of shame relates to everyday life. Katz finds that there is a "great deal of consistency, both in the types of experiences that are treated in a taken-for-granted manner as shameful in self-reports and in the examples of shame cited by analysts." He states at the outset of his essay that, like other everyday emotions, shame takes a "narrative form, beginning and ending, rising and declining, evolving in a process that has more or less emphatic phases."

But then, having defined shame as a dynamic process existing in time (in contrast to the injection of time by other authors through sequences of emotions), Katz focuses on three categories with which to snare his Snark: an interpretive process ("how one sees oneself from the standpoint of others"); a "form of praxis or a way or organizing action"; and what he calls a "distinctive sensuality." These three approaches leave out individual fantasy and the unconscious. To see oneself from the standpoint of any particular other, let alone "others" (however they might collectively be imagined even by the most inventive sociologist), requires imagination and fantasy.

As Pirandello and others have eloquently observed, what we really have are idiosyncratic fantasies of how we appear in the eyes of specific others, and these are fundamentally and necessarily at odds with what might or might not actually be "there." Such a discrepancy is itself one of the driving forces of shame. After all, how did Adam and Eve imagine their nakedness? Did they necessarily know that God saw them naked? Or, feeling ashamed, did they imagine what God saw? And why does it matter?

Whether or not one accepts Katz's categories, one will be instructed by his examples. Linking shame to a sense of isolation from family and community, Katz suggests that a "wide range of shame experiences are triggered by the sense that one has primordial ties to another person who one sees as shamefully exposed." He illustrates this notion with the example of one student who felt ashamed of his father for wearing his hair in a ponytail and riding a motorcycle and felt ashamed of this shame. Or speaking about vulnerability in shame, linking it both to experiences of poverty and of false accusation (e.g., for many students it was more painful to be falsely accused of shoplifting than actually to be caught). Or his observation that "it is frequently the defeat of an effort to treat loss as emotionally resistible that leads to the powerful devastation of shame."

In all the chapters considered here, the subject of shame is sought out and imagined in various ways, as the object of a new and precise language of the emotions, as the model for a theory of affect regulation, as a means to describe the limitations of rational action, as the affect of the social bond. In closing, I wish to add a footnote on the extent to which shame is inherent in the human condition, an intractable part of being conscious, yet more than we can ever imagine it to be. Pirandello conveyed this point tellingly when he spoke of the difference between Orestes and Hamlet. "Suppose that, at the climax, when the marionette who is playing Orestes is about to avenge his father's death and kill his mother and Aegisthus, a little hole were torn in the paper sky above him? Orestes would still want his revenge, yet when he saw that hole, he would feel helpless. Orestes would become Hamlet! That's the difference between ancient tragedy and modern: a hole in a paper sky." Descriptions of shame will inevitably fall short of the mark not only because this is in the nature of the limitations of human description, but also because it is difficult to take into account the "hole in a paper sky." Shame can perhaps be said to be that hole in our paper sky, something that reminds us of our flaws, something that threatens our ability to communicate what we have in a way that can be taken seriously by others, something that punctures our image of ourselves and puts a rent in our experience of the social fabric, yet something without which human relationships and consciousness would be inconceivable.

Always and everywhere, ideals of precision and clarity run up against the untidiness and excesses of everyday meanings. Our "red-faced" Snark is difficult to hunt, in part because no fanfare and ceremony of the hunt can ever guarantee a quarry. And, because of the "hole in a paper sky," those who seek a "precise algebra," or a scientific language of the emotions will have trouble bringing home their Snark. Indeed, the Snark may have changed its name.

> *In the midst of the word he was trying to say,*
> *In the midst of his laughter and glee,*
> *He had softly and suddenly vanished away—*
> *For the Snark was a Boojun you see.*

> —Lewis Carroll, *The Hunting of the Snark*

REFERENCE

Nietzsche, F. (1885), *Jenseits von Gut und Böse* (Beyond Good and Evil). Stuttgart: Kröner, 1976.

III
THE FAMILY

10

SIDNEY LEVIN

A Common Type of
Marital Incompatibility

Marital problems are usually highly complex disturbances, and in most instances the etiological factors can be clearly delineated only after careful study of the personality structure of the partners and their interactions. Certain types of pathological interaction, however, may be shared by many couples and may have a similar etiology. Such a finding is the basis for this chapter. The pathological interactions considered here were usually not associated with pronounced individual psychopathology; it is well known that marital incompatibility may stem from not only severe neurotic problems but also from the inability of the partners to achieve a satisfactory synchronization of needs, regardless of the structure or severity of their neuroses.

In these marital problems, the difficulty seems to arise from the wife's tendency to reject repeatedly the husband's sexual advances and his masculine position, and to be barely aware not only of the rejection itself but also of the impact this rejection has on the husband's psychic economy. I am not referring to women for whom the rejection of the husband's advances is clearly a manifestation of pronounced frigidity and is therefore based on severe sexual inhibition; this situation represents a separate problem. Nor am I referring to instances in which the wife, when angry at her husband, avoids having sexual relations with him. After these two frequent types of response are eliminated, there remains yet another type of common response, the basis for which is deeply rooted in the woman's personality.

In this type of woman the tendency to minimize and deny her rejecting behavior is often quite dramatic. For example, she may state that she occasionally avoids her husband's sexual overtures when she is tired from a hard day's work or when she has a severe headache, but she may hasten to add that she does not believe she does this very often and, furthermore, that when she does, she is sure that it does not create any serious problem in her marriage. The significant aspect of this type of comment is that the woman making it appears totally unaware that she is stating matters incorrectly. Furthermore, it is often apparent that the excuses given for the admitted "occasional" rejections are flimsy and that the true motivation for them is being hidden.

The women to whom I am referring are not the type who manifest excessive penis envy and can be described as highly "castrating." On the contrary, the women I speak of are usually gentle and kindly, and are not strongly competitive with men. They are often attractive physically, and much of their narcissism may be invested in their bodies in a healthy way. When one of them enters psychotherapy or psychoanalysis, she typically evokes positive feelings in the analyst, with little or no negative countertransference, which thus cannot be used as a clue to the patient's rejecting behavior toward the husband.

The husband's reaction to his wife's rejections will vary considerably from case to case, depending on his own neurotic structure. Men who are more sensitive will have more intense reactions. Furthermore, those who are excessively demanding and feel that they are entitled to be satisfied on demand may actually provoke rejection. For purposes of exposition, however, I will bypass these individual differences and focus on what I have found to be some frequent common denominators in the marital interaction.

In many instances, as a result of the wife's rejections, the husband develops repeated depressive episodes of moderate degree which persist for several days or weeks at a time. I am using the term depression as it was used by Edward Bibring (1953) to refer not to severe depressive illness but to a depressive state of the ego, which may vary in intensity and may therefore be associated with any degree of depressive feeling. The husband may not be free to communicate to his wife the nature or severity of his reactions because her communications over the years have led him to expect that she will not understand the connection between her behavior and his responses to it. Furthermore, on those occasions when he has attempted to confront her with these connections, she has responded with an attitude of disbelief or with subtle indignation, leaving him feeling sorry that he brought up the issue and less likely to bring it up again.

In these marriages, the husband may experience a strong feeling of helplessness and frustration. He is repeatedly crushed by his wife's reactions but often cannot let anyone know how he feels, since he anticipates being told that he is too sensitive and that his wife is behaving in a perfectly normal manner. In many instances, he cannot tell anyone about his strong sense of disappointment because it is grounded in frustration not only of genital interests but also of pregenital ones, concerning which he may have intense shame.

The husband's depressive responses may manifest themselves in a variety of ways. He may develop insomnia, become irritable, or withdraw. The wife usually notices these responses and wonders what may have upset him. She may toy with the idea that it has something to do with herself, but she usually brushes this idea aside quickly and comes to the conclusion that he must be worried about his work or about other matters unrelated to their sexual life. Many times the husband will find substitute sexual satisfaction through masturbation, but since he feels ashamed of this outlet he usually cannot tell his wife about it.

Often, a day or two following a rejection, the wife may feel ready to have sexual relations; but since the husband is still depressed and filled with unconscious anger, he may show limited desire, sometimes accompanied by impotence. He may avoid making any overtures for a while, until his anger subsides and the depression lifts. The wife, in turn, may interpret his withdrawal as an indication that he is still worried about his work or about other matters unrelated to the marriage. He may even foster such an illusion because of a fear of exposing to his wife the basis for his sexual inhibitions, including the anger and disappointment he may feel over frustration not only of his genital desires but also of his pregenital interests.

Often an important feature of the interaction in this type of marriage is a clumsy attempt by the husband to make the wife realize the effects that her repeated rejections have upon him. He may decide, for example, to stop making sexual advances to her for a while, in the hope that this measure will frustrate her and give her a dose of her own medicine. But she usually does not get the message. She may even interpret his withdrawal as proof that he really does not need much sexual satisfaction. Furthermore, if she recognizes that he is angry at her, she often does not realize what he is angry about. She may consider him to be having a rather childish temper tantrum over a minor frustration and infer that he "will soon get over it." Or she may respond to him as though he were a demanding child who has to learn how to accept the inevitable frustrations of life in order to mature and live successfully in a grown-up world.

The tendency on the part of the wife to treat the husband as a child is often a major ingredient of this form of incompatibility. While frustrating his sexual needs, she may at the same time make great efforts to be attentive to his other needs. She may prepare good meals, keep the house in good order, be protective of him, and so on—all to prove to him and to others that she is really an excellent "mother." This behavior may not only evoke additional resentment in the husband; it may also put him in the predicament of having nothing to complain about except the frustration of his sexual needs, which he does not feel free to complain about because of his underlying shame concerning them and his anticipation of not meeting a receptive ear.

In one case that came to my attention, the wife found out that her husband had been masturbating. She became intensely angry and interpreted his masturbation as an indication that he really did not love her. Although there was some basis for this inference, since the husband was intensely angry at her at the time, her interpretation was incomplete, totally ignoring his intense love for her. When this issue was discussed in therapy, she responded with extreme naivete. She was completely oblivious to the fact that her husband's masturbation represented a substitute outlet that was used primarily because of her rejections. Furthermore, when she was first confronted with this possibility, she stated, "But if he really loved me, he would not masturbate but would wait until I'm ready for him." She usually behaved, however, as though she were not ready for him. Furthermore, when they had sexual relations, she had a tendency to adopt a mildly condescending attitude, as a mother might toward a fussy child.

Sometimes the husband may have the thought that if he threatened to leave his wife, or if he threatened to find another woman with whom he could have an affair, his wife might understand how he feels. It is common for the husband to censor the use of such threats, however, either because his superego is opposed to them or because he anticipates that, even if they are successful in altering some of his wife's overt patterns of behavior, they will not alter her underlying reluctance or help her to understand his plight.

Sometimes the husband uses another approach. He tells his wife how much he loves her and how much he needs her, in the hope that, when she feels the intensity of his love, she will respond with love in return. But this approach may not reach her either, because the wife's response is apt to be, "If he loves me so much, why can't he wait until I am ready for his sexual advances?" It is typical for the women who express such attitudes to consider their behavior as not truly "rejecting" but as merely "postponing." When one first hears these attitudes expressed in therapy, one gets the impression that the woman making them is extremely childish in her overall approach to human relationships. But when one realizes that she discusses other personal issues with a much more mature perspective, it becomes apparent that the childish attitudes are limited largely to sexual matters and are highly defensive in nature.

Sometimes the husband tries another strategy. He decides that his wife must be unhappy about what she considers to be her inferior role as a woman, and he therefore tries to elevate her self-esteem and to satisfy some of her narcissistic needs. He may praise her for her efforts, her accomplishments, her kindness, and so forth. But this approach may create a more complicated problem. Not only may it effect little change in the wife's rejecting responses; it may also put the husband in the predicament of appearing inconsistent if he now complains that his wife is inconsiderate in her sexual behavior when he has already committed himself to the proposition that she is such an unselfish and kind person.

When the husband reaches a point of desperation and decides that the only solution to his plight is to leave his wife, she often reacts to the news with amazement, which may be expressed as follows: "How could he do such a thing? I've been such a good wife: I've catered to him like a mother to a child." And it is characteristic for members of the community to support the wife in her indignant attitude and to consider the husband a "scoundrel" who has taken everything from the all-giving mother without showing any appreciation.

In these marriages, the husband's depressive reaction is usually based not only on the wife's sexual rejection but also on her lack of empathy toward him. If a man's sexual advances are rebuffed, this experience alone represents a narcissistic injury, contributing to depression. But if the woman also shows no awareness of or appreciation for the man's feelings—if she shows little empathy toward him—the narcissistic injury is thereby accentuated. The term empathy is being used as defined by Ferreira (1961). He defines empathy as "an ability correctly to perceive nonverbalized feelings and moods. It represents the backbone of nonverbal communication." A husband who has such experiences soon learns that, if he limits the frequency of his sexual advances, he can protect himself to some degree against narcissistic injuries. Often he goes through a complicated process of trying to figure out, on the basis of subtle cues, when the wife may be receptive and to limit his overtures to such occasions. In many instances, he becomes bewildered. He knows that his wife responds to his advances on certain occasions, but he cannot predict them accurately. In fact, the wife may be unable to make such predictions either, since she usually does not know in advance when she is going to be responsive.

As a result of the process of interaction I have described, it is characteristic for the husband to become increasingly cautious in his approach to his wife and to leave larger and larger intervals between the times when he makes his sexual overtures. The wife may then be left with the impression that her husband is fully satisfied with infrequent and limited sexual relations. If, on a later occasion, he should mention to her that he has been sexually frustrated for many years, she may adopt the attitude: "You've never shown any indication of it. Whenever you've made advances to me I've been receptive." This statement may be largely true in regard to the recent past. The husband may have cut down his demands in order to avoid being rejected, and the wife may remain oblivious of this fact.

In these marriages, it is not uncommon to find that both husband and wife are somewhat depressed and that they periodically resolve their depressions through sadomasochistic interactions, which involve a sequence of steps that can be summarized as follows: 1) The wife's repeated rejections are unconsciously aimed at provoking a hostile outburst in the husband. 2) Once this outburst has occurred, the wife dissolves into tears, thereby making the husband feel guilty and apologize for having hurt her feelings. 3) The wife, in turn, shows remorse for having frustrated her husband sexually, and a reconciliation results, often accompanied by satisfactory sexual relations. 4) The reconciliation is then followed by a temporary relief of depression in both of the partners, until the cycle is again repeated. (At times the husband anticipates his wife's rejections and initiates the cycle by provoking a fight over some minor issue.) In some instances a type of folie à deux develops in which the husband internalizes the wife's negative attitude toward sexuality and limits his advances to infrequent occasions. If he is asked why he has done so, he may answer that he does not believe it is fair for him to subject his wife to the discomforts of sexual relations, especially when she is tired or worried. Or he may consider himself "base" for wanting to have sexual relations so often or for wanting to have sexual relations in a manner that would cater to his pregenital interests. On the surface, the husband often appears to be quite content in his "considerate" attitude, but at a deeper level he may have intense resentment, often accompanied by some degree of impotence. Furthermore, once the impotence develops, he may make less frequent overtures in order to protect himself from the sense of humiliation that he feels when he cannot perform sexually.

In some of these cases, the husband's impotence may be relieved if he contracts for the services of a prostitute. He knows that in such arrangements it is highly unlikely that the woman will turn away from him at the last minute or postpone the encounter until some later date. A similar effect may occur if he enters into an affair with a mistress. Not only may his impotence disappear, but, surprisingly enough, he may be able to tolerate frustration much better in this relationship than in his marriage. His altered response may be partly attributable to the unconscious meaning of the specific sexual object; the wife may represent the incestuous object, whereas the mistress may represent the degraded sexual object. His altered response may also be attributable to the fact that the mistress may be a more truly feminine character who shows clearer evidence of appreciating his love. Another possible explanation should, however, also be considered, namely, the degree to which the sexual object is cathected with libido. If the husband is deeply in love with his wife, he may be more vulnerable to her rejections, whereas a less intense love toward the mistress may enable him to tolerate her periodic rejections without undergoing major narcissistic injuries resulting in depression.

The question I should like to raise is, Why is the wife so often oblivious of what is happening in the marital relationship?[1] Clinical experience indicates that once the wife is helped, through therapy, to become aware of her rejecting responses and of their effects on her husband's psychic economy, her behavior may change dramatically. In a case I treated recently, after the basis for the husband's depression was clarified, the wife found that she really had no strong need to refuse his sexual advances. She said, "I just didn't realize that he reacted with depression to my refusal. I enjoy having sexual relations with him on most occasions. And even when I'm tired and not terribly responsive sexually, it doesn't really bother me. If I had known what effect my rejection was having upon him and had realized how often I was rejecting him, I certainly wouldn't have

[1] I wish to express my appreciation to Drs. John M. Murray and Henry Wermer for their helpful suggestions in the preparation of this part of the paper.

done so." After this woman's receptiveness improved, the lifting of the husband's depression and his concomitant expressions of gratitude toward her acted to reinforce the change.

In the women under consideration, the underlying emotional basis for the avoidance of sexual relations may vary from case to case. This avoidance is often considered a form of "frigidity" and attributed to such factors as the castration complex (Freud, 1951), confusion between erotic and wounding penetration (Bonaparte, 1952), the "defilement complex" (Needles, 1966), and so on. When one studies these patients carefully, however, one often finds a variety of hidden emotional forces that do not indicate frigidity in the usual sense. For example, the wife may have an unconscious need to frustrate her husband because of an unconscious fear that if she does not do so, he may become bored and leave her. Or she may have an unconscious need to be loved in an aim-inhibited manner in order to quiet childhood fears of not being truly loved. In the latter instance, when yielding to the husband's sexual advances, the wife may feel that he really does not love her. If this feeling is intense, it may be expressed through the common cliche, "All he seems to want is my body." Many other childhood fears may contribute to the wife's pattern of rejection. One of the most significant of these is *the fear of experiencing shame*. This affect may be evoked by exposure of the body or by any type of normal sexual response—wetness of the genitals, erection of the nipples, increased perspiration, heavy breathing, and so on. In analysis one finds, however, that *the intensity of these fears of experiencing shame is usually not sufficient to make rejection imperative.* This likelihood is indicated by the fact that, once the wife becomes aware of the frequency of her rejections and their impact on her husband's psychic economy, she may show a dramatic change and become much more receptive to his sexual advances.

It appears, therefore, that in many instances one of the crucial issues centers on the wife's use of the *defense of denial* and the manner in which this defense has become consolidated and reinforced over the years as a means of avoiding minor degrees of tension. Such patterns of avoidance are often characterological ones. There are many individuals whose personality is characterized by the repeated ego-syntonic avoidance of mild degrees of tension. These patterns of avoidance tend to develop in early childhood, but, in order for them to remain ego syntonic, the person has to deny not only the severity of her avoidance but also that her avoidance has unfavorable consequences either to herself or to others.

Underlying the denial mechanism, at unconscious levels, one typically finds a basic defensive attitude of excessive "narcissistic entitlement" (Murray, 1964) to avoid the mastery of shame affect. This attitude of entitlement originates in childhood and, when it is later applied to the issue of adult sexual relations, can be represented by the following two propositions: 1) "I have a right to avoid sexual relations whenever I wish." 2) "My husband has no right to react unfavorably to my avoidance. He should love and admire me always." However, through various secondary defenses, including denial, these unconscious propositions have been modified into conscious ones that are more or less culturally acceptable. The first proposition has been camouflaged by "minimizing" the frequency of rejection and by "justifying" the basis for it. The derivative form of narcissistic entitlement is then expressed through the attitude, "I do not avoid sexual relations very often, and I never do so without some accept-able justification." The second proposition has been disguised by "minimizing" the husband's depressive reactions and by attributing them to extraneous events. The derivative form of narcissistic entitlement is then expressed through the attitude, "My husband does not react unfavorably to my rejections; whatever emotional disturbance he experiences is not my fault." The genetic basis for such underlying pathological forms of narcissistic entitlement in the wife, as well as the associated pathological inhibition of normal narcissistic entitlement that may occur simultaneously in the husband, is beyond the scope of the present paper. It is apparent, nonetheless, that pathological attitudes of narcissistic entitlement may undergo major defensive alterations as development proceeds. One might therefore think not only in terms of "manifest" conscious attitudes of entitlement but also in terms of "latent" unconscious ones.

As mentioned, the primary basis for the defensive process that has been outlined is the need to avoid shame. In the women under consideration there is usually a dominance of one aspect of the pleasure principle, in which the avoidance of displeasure has priority over the seeking of pleasure. Therefore, actions that bring satisfaction without any unpleasant shame tension are favored over actions that require the facing of mild degrees of such tension in order to reach satisfaction. As a consequence, there is often an arrest in the development of the ability to tolerate shame or to master it (Levin, 1964). A similar arrest in the development of the ability to tolerate other affects, such as disgust (Needles, 1964), may also be present.

It appears that the tendency toward ego-syntonic avoidance of minor degrees of tension, as described earlier, is a more or less feminine trait, to which early environmental influence contributes in a major way. It is more common for parents to permit a girl to avoid minor tensions or to cry her way out of a mildly unpleasant situation than to permit a boy to do so. Furthermore, in both boys and girls, the efforts to face tension and master it are often equated with a striving for masculinity.

It is a common observation that the type of woman under discussion rarely initiates sexual relations. On exploring the basis for this excessive "passivity," one often finds that during childhood these women were led to believe that to take the initiative sexually is highly "unfeminine" and shameful. Therefore, whatever tendency toward sexual passivity was initially present in early life has been reinforced and accentuated by the shaming attitudes of others (Levin, 1967), which are quite prevalent in our culture.

Even though these women may have strong needs to be loved and admired, genital sexuality is usually not very important to them. Many show a self-contentment, which Freud (1914) described in his paper "On Narcissism." In some instances, the narcissistic investment in their own bodies is such that they unconsciously equate their bodies with the penis and have no need to acquire one from a man. Freud (1933) stated: "we attribute a larger amount of narcissism to femininity, which also affects women's choice of object, so that to be loved is a stronger need for them than to love. The effect of penis-envy has a share, further, in the physical vanity of women, since they are bound to value their charms more highly as a late compensation for their original sexual inferiority" (p. 132). These women, therefore, do not become seriously involved with the husband's penis and accept it only weakly. This lack of involvement may spread to include a lack of interest in all of the husband's phallic strivings, including his work. Because of this attitude, the husband's masculine self-image may be gradually deflated (Murray, 1960), and he may eventually lose his sense of entitlement to a normally integrated masculinity.

In many instances, the husband is unaware of what is transpiring in the marriage and employs a complex set of defenses, which also includes a massive use of denial. Several years ago I undertook the analysis of a 35-year-old man who showed considerable depression, the basis for which he did not understand. He insisted that his marriage was a happy one, even though he occasionally sought extramarital affairs. These were temporarily satisfying, but left him feeling somewhat guilty. He was bewildered by his need for these affairs since, he insisted, his wife showed normal sexual responses. It took two years of analysis before he realized that, in having intercourse with his wife, he usually had ejaculated prematurely, which reflected his hostile responses to her repeated subtle rejections.

Needless to say, in these marriages psychotherapy for the husband is usually not adequate to resolve the incompatibility, although, when he understands himself and his wife better, he may be able to help her overcome some of her resistance to the mastery of shame affect. In most instances, however, it is necessary for the wife to enter treatment and for the long-standing and well-consolidated defense of denial to be carefully analyzed and eradicated. Such efforts can then be followed by careful analysis of the underlying immature attitudes of narcissistic entitlement and the longstanding resistance to the mastery of shame affect.

For treatment to be effective for the wife, her therapist must be free of the type of countertransference that might lead him to be oblivious of her use of denial or even to support it. Recently, in discussing with a colleague his treatment of such a woman, I was met with the response: "In my opinion, the main problem in this marriage lies with the husband. He should be able to accept the postponement of sexual relations when his wife is not receptive to his sexual advances. He has to learn to tolerate a little frustration." In focusing on the husband's difficulty in tolerating frustration, the therapist was supporting the wife's defense of denial, which left her unaware of the frequency and intensity of her rejections as well as of the severity of her husband's depressive reactions to them.

Not long ago I saw in consultation a 40-year-old woman whose husband had left her and sought a divorce, giving as his explanation that he had been grossly dissatisfied with their sexual relations for many years. She could not understand the basis for his complaints and remarked, "I never refused to have sexual relations with him during the entire duration of our marriage." Whether this statement was true or not was impossible to determine. During the interview, however, it was apparent that this woman could not concede that her own emotional difficulties had contributed to the marital problem. She was highly defensive on all issues and conveyed an attitude that she was invariably "right" and her husband "wrong." One could visualize this husband being subjected to constant narcissistic injuries and not being able to confront her with her contribution to them. Furthermore, it was obvious that she had falsified to herself and others the true state of affairs, since she showed an almost total lack of awareness of what her husband had been feeling throughout the course of their marriage. Whenever a husband or wife consults an analyst about marital problems without mentioning how unhappy the spouse must be feeling, one can usually infer that a massive use of denial is at work.

I had in treatment a middle-aged man who was intensely hostile toward his wife because of the control she had exerted in their marriage. He stated that, although she had never refused to have sexual relations with him, she insisted that the lights always be off, and she did not tolerate any foreplay. When he tried to discuss these issues with her, she minimized their importance. For example, she stated that, although she really did not mind having the lights on, she preferred having them off, and that since this issue was of minor significance, there was no reason for him to make a fuss over it. In actuality, he really did not make a fuss over it. On the contrary, he seldom brought up the issue, but when he did so she would often make a fuss over it. Here was a clear instance in which the wife's denial of the impact of her behavior on her husband was accompanied by an insistence that he accept her denial. It was only when she entered therapy that she became aware of the degree to which she had restricted their sexual relations.

I do not mean to imply that the defense of denial, as I have outlined it, can usually be easily resolved. When these patients undertake therapy, the resistances are often quite stubborn, and repeated clarification may therefore be necessary before they begin to yield. Furthermore, treatment requires a careful analysis not only of the long-standing defense of denial but also of the pathological attitudes of narcissistic entitlement. It is through such analysis that the patient can become aware of her tendency to avoid tolerable levels of shame and can eventually become free to achieve higher levels of shame mastery.

Although I have concentrated here on the rejecting behavior of the wife, in which the mechanism of denial is crucial, similar types of behavior may also occur in the husband. In such instances, the sequence of events that I have outlined may be seen in reverse, with the wife experiencing the repeated narcissistic injuries accompanied by depression. Furthermore, in the latter type of marriage, the interaction between husband and wife may take a more subtle turn, since the wife's sexual frustration may lead her to become much more assertive sexually and thereby to promote some reversal of sexual roles. This form of incompatibility is often based on a more primary impotence of the husband, for which he usually requires intensive treatment. In chapter 11, I discuss the husband's use of the defense of denial in marital incompatibility.

SUMMARY

A husband's depression often arises in response to his wife's egosyntonic patterns of rejecting his masculine position. These patterns of response in the wife, which are often denied by her, usually reflect her unconscious resistance to the mastery of shame affect. This resistance is typically supported by a pathological attitude of "narcissistic entitlement" which has been camouflaged through a variety of defenses, including the use of denial.

REFERENCES

Bibring, E. (1953), The mechanism of depression. In: *Affective Disorders*, ed. P. Greenacre. New York: International Universities Press, pp. 13-48.

Bonaparte, M. (1952), Some biopsychical aspects of sado-masochism. *Internat. J. Psycho-Anal.*, 33:373-384.

Ferreira, A. J. (1961), Empathy and the bridge function of the ego. *J. Amer. Psychoanal. Assn.*, 9:91-105.

Freud, S. (1914), On narcissism: An introduction. *Standard Edition*, 14:73-102. London: Hogarth Press, 1957.

———— (1931), Female sexuality. *Standard Edition*, 21:225-243. London: Hogarth Press, 1961.

———— (1933), New introductory lectures on psycho-analysis *Standard Edition*, 22:3-182. London: Hogarth Press, 1964.

Levin, S. (1964), Mastery of fear in psychoanalysis. *Psychoanal. Quart.*, 33:375-387.

———— (1967), Some metapsychological considerations on the differentiation between shame and guilt. *Internat. J. Psycho-Anal.*, 48:267-276.

Murray, J. M. (1960), The dynamics of reactive depressions. Presented at Conference on Depression and Antidepressant Drugs, conducted at the Metropolitan State Hospital, Waltham, MA. April 20.

———— (1964), Narcissism and the ego ideal. *J. Amer. Psychoanal. Assn.*, 12:477-511.

Needles, W. (1966), The defilement complex. *J. Amer. Psychoanal. Assn.*, 14:700-710.

11

SIDNEY LEVIN

Further Comments on a Common Type of Marital Incompatibility

In the previous chapter, I described a common form of marital incompatibility based largely on the tendency of certain women repeatedly to reject their husbands' sexual advances, with limited awareness not only of the frequency of the rejection but also of the disruptive effects that the rejection has on their husbands' psychic-economy. In the analysis of these women, it was found that, starting in childhood, the mastery of shame affect (Levin, 1967a) had been seriously arrested and that in adult life this developmental failure was manifested in part through excessive shame during sexual relations, with a consequent tendency to avoid such relations. In many instances this avoidance was unconsciously supported by attitudes of excessive entitlement, which also arose in childhood. The development of such attitudes has been discussed elsewhere (Levin, 1967b).

In considering the effects of the wife's rejections on the husband, I noted that the severity off his emotional reactions obviously depended not only on the degree and frequency of rejection but also on his own neurotic structure. Men who were more sensitive were likely to have more intense and prolonged reactions. In this chapter, I discuss some aspects of the excessive sensitivity evident in these husbands and point out how this sensitivity not only may contribute to the marital problems but also may lead to a vicious circle of interaction that not infrequently results in a severe breakdown of the marital relationship.

The group of men to whom I am referring are people who react strongly to frustration and whose responses in this regard involve two main components I) a partial emotional and physical withdrawal

from the disappointing object; 2) an attitude of grievance that usually
takes the form of feeling unfairly treated by this object. Since the
disappointing object is the wife, and since the frustration often
pertains to highly cathected sexual interests, the husband's attitude
of grievance usually focuses on his spouse. Although this attitude is
often suppressed or repressed, in some instances it is fully conscious
and may even be expressed openly. Even when it is totally unconscious, however, it may influence behavior in a variety of ways and
may be communicated in many subtle forms. Furthermore, when the
attitude of grievance prevails, whether it is conscious or not, it tends
to prevent a "reconciliation," for many days or weeks at a time,
regardless of how willing the wife might be or how much effort she
might make to achieve this goal.

The marital problems on which I am focusing, therefore, arise
not merely from the mobilization of the husband's angry feelings, but
from the fact that these feelings tend to be accompanied by
withdrawal from the wife and to become structured into attitude of
having been abused by her. For example, if the wife occasionally
comes late for an appointment with such a husband, even though the
lateness is not provocative and might occur with anyone, he not only
will become angry at her but will also withdraw from her; moreover,
he will also tend to develop the conviction that she is taking
advantage of him or neglecting him, and especially that she is doing
so intentionally.

It is apparent that the reactions of the husband may arise not
only with sexual frustration but also with any type of frustration. In
a 30-year-old scientist they occurred when he had difficulty finding
some papers after his ·wife cleaned up his office. He felt that she did
not care about his work and that she only wanted to have things
orderly. In discussing this issue during analysis, he accused his wife
of being excessively controlling, of treating their possessions as
though they were all hers, and of being generally selfish. These
accusations, in fact, represented projections of his own greedy and
monopolistic tendencies.

The mood that accompanies the husband's withdrawal is typically
one of mild to moderate depression and is often characterized by
sulkiness. At such times the husband may manifest lack of enthusiasm
for any interest that he and the wife ordinarily have in common. He
may also show limited cordiality toward her or become inattentive.
In some instances, his attitude is one of stubbornness, and he may
infuriate her with passive-aggressive techniques. For example, he
might find reasons to work overtime or to visit his club before
coming home at night, thus forcing his wife to serve him dinner at

a late hour. Some of his hostility may be expressed actively, through irritability, temper outbursts, sarcasm, or subtle forms of teasing, but much of it tends to be highly attenuated or to take the form of inactivity. It is common, therefore, for the husband to withhold his angry thoughts rather than to express them openly. Furthermore, when other people are around he may put on a false front in order not to let them know how he feels. His underlying bitterness, however, may at times be apparent to others.

The withdrawal seen in these patients usually represents a characteristic pattern of response, originating in early life. When children are hurt by their love objects, they tend either to strike out in some way or to withdraw. The men described here show the latter type of response, which is similar in some respects to the pattern of "depression-withdrawal" described by Engel and Reichsman (1956) in the well-known case of Monica.

The lack of communication by the husband, which usually accompanies his withdrawal, not infrequently fosters in him a paranoidlike attitude, since it prevents him from correcting some of his misperceptions of the wife's attitudes toward him and from counteracting his feelings of being maltreated.

It is characteristic in these marriages for the husband's anger about his sexual frustrations to be displaced onto other issues. He might criticize his wife for spending too much money or for a variety of minor inefficiencies when, in fact, he is angry that she has rejected his sexual advances.

When such a man enters psychoanalysis, he may at first not be aware of the intensity of his hostile feelings toward his wife. But when these feelings are eventually mobilized and the associated complaints brought to the surface, the attitude of having been treated unfairly also appears. In addition, the analyst may learn that there has been a temporary suspension of the husband's affectionate responses toward his wife accompanied by fantasies of being unfaithful to her, which may at times be acted out. Furthermore, the shame and guilt that may be thus mobilized can further complicate the husband's emotional responses.

In some instances, the husband describes the marriage in such a way as to almost convince his analyst that the wife is, in fact, a selfish, self-centered, and excessively narcissistic person. With careful exploration, however, it usually becomes apparent that he is not being fair to his wife, that he is exaggerating and distorting her difficulties and minimizing his own. In most instances, the husband's empathy toward his wife is seriously inhibited, and he talks about her in a manner indicating limited awareness of her unhappiness. It is this tendency to present a one-sided picture that often leads the analyst to recognize the severity of the husband's distortions. If the analyst does not recognize these distortions, however, the patient's tendency to blame his wife may become reinforced and he may even attempt to use the analysis for a defensive "pseudoanalysis" of the wife's emotional difficulties.

In analyzing this type of man, it often takes considerable time before one is in a position to clarify some of the basic interactions in the marriage. Many hours of preparatory analysis may be necessary, and a major part of this work often revolves around analysis of transference. The analyst, however, may at times become so involved in relating patterns of transference to childhood experience that he may not pay adequate attention to the way in which these patterns play themselves out in the marriage and to the defenses the patient may be using to avoid analyzing this. Furthermore, in some instances the patterns of response being played out in the marriage do not enter into the transference to any significant degree and may therefore continue to remain relatively obscure.

At some point, one has to clarify the defenses used by the patient to avoid analyzing the marital problems, and one must follow this up with a clarification of the patient's contributions to the marital incompatibility. For example, I might point out to the patient that he has not painted a clear picture of the wife and her difficulties; that the way in which he presents the facts about her leads me to believe that he has introduced some major distortions; that his general attitude is one of having withdrawn from his wife, with feelings of being abused by her; that he does not seem to show any empathy toward his wife; and that he appears to be caught up in his own hostility and in an attempt to structure it into an attitude of self-righteous indignation to a degree, which leaves no room for a satisfactory reconciliation. I may add that his indignant attitude could not help but make things worse. I thus try to build up a picture of a vicious circle of interaction, starting with the initial sexual frustration or disappointment, followed by withdrawal and a feeling of being abused on the part of the husband, which, in turn, evokes a depressive response in the wife. Furthermore, since the wife's depressive reaction may result in her being unable to function well, the husband can then feel more justified in complaining about her inefficiencies and inadequacies. I may also point out to him that he does not mention how hard his wife has been trying to make a go of the marriage and that he does not talk about the many efforts she makes on his behalf—that, in essence, he is ignoring many of the qualities in his wife that initially led him to fall in love with her. In clarifying these issues, I have found it helpful at times to indicate to the husband that he sometimes talks about his wife as though she ·were an enemy, when in fact she is his "closest friend." The use of this term may have a special impact, because it implies that he is suppressing the fact that his wife is the person closest to him and that she has been his ally through all types of trials and tribulations.

A further step in clarification has to do with helping the husband realize that, when he is in a phase of withdrawal, he sees his wife quite differently than he does during a phase of reconciliation, when his affectionate feelings are liberated. It is only during the latter phase that he talks about her in a manner that brings out her "good" qualities. This type of clarification may be especially helpful when the husband's bitterness is accompanied by a feeling that his love for his wife has finally disappeared. When he is reminded that on previous occasions his affection returned once he was able to reverse his withdrawal, he may realize that his love is still present but is being temporarily blanketed by his hostility

The most important effect of treatment, an effect that usually occurs only after a considerable period of time, arises when the husband finds that he can, on his own volition, reverse the process of sulky withdrawal and achieve a reconciliation, and that to take such a step is a sign of maturity. Once the husband understands the nature of his withdrawal and its consequences and has a clear understanding of the genetic basis for the withdrawal, he may begin to make attempts to counteract it and the phase of reconciliation will then start.

For one patient whom I treated, it took many months to clarify the patterns of withdrawal and to analyze their origins in childhood, but, once these aims were achieved, there was a fairly rapid resolution of his bitterness toward his wife. Shortly thereafter there was a dramatic change in their interactions, and he then informed me that he and his wife seemed to be "on a second honeymoon." He noticed that as soon as he started to communicate with her more freely she responded in kind and it was not long before they began to reexperience the love that had been present in the early phase of the marriage. At this point, the husband's empathic responses returned, and he now described his wife's relationships with the children in a manner that conveyed a growing understanding of her difficulties. Furthermore, he did not "drag his feet" at home, as he had been doing for many months On former occasions, whenever the wife would ask him to do something, he was apt to say, "I'll do it in a minute," but he would often procrastinate, so that she had a constant feeling of his reluctance to help her. As a consequence, she had gradually reduced her demands as time went on. Following the reconciliation, the husband's freedom to cooperate at home returned, and the wife's sense of intimidation in making demands disappeared.

In many instances, the husband's reaction of withdrawal is based on his sensitivity to specific types of responses on the part of his wife. A 32-year-old man reacted very strongly to his wife's tendency to remain silent when they were in the presence of his professional colleagues. She was a woman with considerable social anxiety, who became blocked easily in verbal interactions. When the husband's colleagues came to visit, he would feel embarrassed that his wife did not participate actively in the discussion. He would then become angry at her and would inwardly exaggerate her shortcomings. In analysis, this man's sensitive reaction was found to be based largely on childhood responses to his mother, who frequently became depressed and remained relatively silent for several days at a time. The patient had perceived his mother's silence as a total rejection, and this was how he now perceived his wife's difficulty in talking. Discussing this difficulty in analysis, he at first claimed that his wife intentionally "refused" to talk and that she did so merely as a means of expressing hostility toward him and his colleagues, since she was unusually quiet whenever they socialized with professional people. Needless to say, these inferences represented gross distortions, which the patient eventually recognized.

Another patient, about 30 years old, would become especially upset and withdraw whenever his wife lost her temper with the children. He would then conclude that she was emotionally unstable and that she really hated the children. This patient had been brought up in a home where tempers were never released and where he was indoctrinated into the attitude that to vent one's anger at children was a serious crime. In this instance, when the patient eventually became aware of his withdrawal, he made some efforts to reverse it. The reconciliation he was able to achieve was, however, highly unstable, since a new event would soon trigger off another phase of withdrawal. It was therefore necessary to analyze his sensitivity reactions over and over again. Gradually, his insight matured. He then remarked that, as he now saw matters, the stability of marriage depended on a fuller understanding of his sensitivity, so that he could more readily reverse what he called his "paranoid withdrawal."

Attitudes of excessive entitlement (Levin, 1967b) contribute in many ways to the type of incompatibility we are discussing here. Just as we find that many women have residual childhood attitudes of excessive entitlement to avoid sexual relations, we also find that many men have residual childhood attitudes of excessive entitlement to have their sexual needs satisfied by the wife, regardless of her emotional state. Such attitudes have a highly narcissistic quality and indicate some fixation or regression to pregenital modes of response, even though the sexual interests themselves may be largely genital in nature. When such a husband comes home at night, he may behave like a child coming home from school. He expects the wife to be like a "good mother," always ready to cater to his needs. These expectations may pertain to all types of needs, not only those which are clearly sexual. Such a husband may also feel entitled to have a wife who never gets upset. As a consequence, he may respond to her emotional states as an affront rather than as a manifestation of complex problems that he might help to resolve. Once he gains insight into his attitudes of excessive entitlement and realizes that he can help himself only by helping his wife, the marital relationship may improve. For example, he may find that, merely by listening to his wife talk about her daily problems, some of the tension may subside.

I recently clarified the attitudes of excessive entitlement of a man who often responded with indignation to his wife's emotional reactions. After gaining insight into his own indignant responses, for the first time in his married life he attempted to listen to what she had to say without jamming her conversation or offering her advice in a form that communicated his attitude that she should stop fussing over minor issues. In this instance, he was surprised to learn that she had considerable anxiety about an impending visit of her mother; and as she expressed her fears, he could empathize with her because he too had similar fears. As a result of this exchange, the wife felt that she had an ally, and her fears became less intense.

In many instances the husband finds it difficult to admit that he feels guilty about the manner in which he has been treating his wife. Once he expresses his guilt in therapy, however, he often finds that he can then expose it to his wife and thereby foster the process of reconciliation. Guilt is an affect closely related to object libido (Levin, 1967a), and when it is brought to the surface it can be a major vehicle through which affectionate feelings are liberated.

Many men may initially express some regret about how they have been treating the wife; but, on analyzing this regret, one may find that it is not true guilt but that it has a highly narcissistic quality. In other words, the husband may regret certain actions *of his own* because they have led to unpleasant consequences *for him*. In such instances true guilt may also be present, but it may require much analytic effort to bring this feeling to the surface.

True guilt goes beyond the self. Since its exposure, however, is often equated with "giving in," "weakness," "lack of masculinity," "dependency," and the like, the guilt may be enveloped in shame and may therefore be suppressed or even repressed. At the same time, the shame itself may also be suppressed or repressed. In treating these patients, therefore, considerable analysis of the shame and of the defenses to which it gives rise is often necessary before the underlying feelings of guilt can be brought to the surface. In these cases, it is often a major indication of therapeutic progress when the husband can eventually say "I'm sorry" to his wife. Such an apparently simple remark can represent an impressive "gift" to the wife, fostering the process of reconciliation.

In some instances, the husband's withdrawal from his wife is accompanied by regressive forms of behavior. These may take the form of compulsive masturbation, reactivation of previous homosexual interests and actions, various forms of heterosexual infidelity, and so forth. When the husband realizes that these activities have occurred largely as a result of the depressive state that accompanies his withdrawal from his wife and that they have brought him only limited relief from his tension, the motivation to exert control over them and to work toward achieving a reconciliation often increases.

In most cases, the intolerance for sexual frustration has to be carefully analyzed in terms of the unconscious forces at work. For one patient, this intolerance might be based on an unconscious fear of reverting to masturbation, an outlet that may still be enveloped in major conflict. For another patient, the intolerance for sexual frustration might be based on an unconscious fear of regressing to homosexual outlets. In many patients the intolerance for frustration depends on the fact that sexual behavior is being used to counteract depressive feelings. Sexual acts can represent a major proof of masculinity, a consolation for limited attainment of narcissistic aspirations, a reassurance that one is loved. Since the wife's refusal to participate in these sexual acts may deprive the husband of the antidepressive effects, some of the anger that is bound up in his depressive state may become liberated and then directed at her. It is therefore important for the husband to realize that his tendency to blame his wife for many of their difficulties may represent a means of trying to counteract his depressive feelings. Such blaming often includes powerful projections. It is not uncommon for the husband to complain about his wife's frigidity when, in fact, he is most concerned about his own impotence. He may also project onto the wife his own selfish motives, his own lack of considerateness. It is through such blaming that he tries to elevate his self-esteem and discharge some of his hostility. These techniques are essentially palliative in nature, however, since they do not help to resolve the underlying depressive state.

The patients described here are not men with paranoid character structures, but men who have a tendency to regress to a "paranoid-like" attitude toward a love object. They fall into a wide range of diagnoses; and, although some of them have strong narcissistic trends, they are not "borderline" or "psychotic" individuals. Furthermore, they do not show the same degree of regression in their responses to people in general that they do in their responses to their wives. In fact, they are often relatively mature individuals who are generally fairly reasonable in their attitude toward others. Furthermore, one often finds that friends leave little or no awareness of the degree of the man's withdrawal from his wife or of the degree to which he feels abused by her, because both aspects of the reaction may be carefully hidden from others.

Withdrawal may serve many purposes. It may enable the husband not only to protect his wife from the full brunt of his hostility but also to discharge hostility toward her in subtle forms, without feeling very guilty. The effect of the withdrawal, however, is usually destructive since it characteristically leads to a "cold war" atmosphere and prevents a reconciliation. The indignant attitude that accompanies it may inhibit the wife's expression of her anger, since she is likely to fear that if she expresses it the husband will feel doubly indignant. In this type of man, once the withdrawal sets in, the defense of denial is often prominent. He will deny not only that his wife is truly devoted to him, but also that he contributes in many ways to their difficulties. One of the most characteristic forms of denial is the denial of one's own sensitivity. In the treatment of such a husband it is absolutely necessary to clarify this denial, that is, to help him realize that he reacts excessively to frustration and that, when he does so, he magnifies the frustrating stimulus in order to minimize his own sensitivity, which produces an exaggerated response to the stimulus. A simple illustration can often help the patient understand this mechanism. For example, he can be told that a person ·who is sensitive to pain may have a strong fear of going to the dentist and when he does go he may become angry at the dentist whenever pain is felt. If such a person can admit his sensitivity to pain, he usually does not blame the dentist for it. But if he has to deny the sensitivity because he is ashamed of it, he may support this denial by postulating that the dentist is being cruel or sadistic, regardless of how gentle the dentist may be.

We are in the habit of considering the accusation that the dentist is cruel as a projection of the patient's repressed hostility. I believe, however, that this explanation does not do justice to the possible mechanisms involved. Although some people may repress their hostility toward the dentist and project it outward, in many instances the hostility is fully conscious and the forces of repression are directed mainly toward the excessive sensitivity which gives rise to the hostility. In the latter case, the person may admit that he is angry at the dentist, but he may consider his anger to be a normal reaction to the dentist's sadism, which he has postulated in order to maintain the denial of his own sensitivity. In some instances, he may actually provoke the dentist into a hostile response in order to point to this response as proof of the dentist's sadism.

Similar mechanisms may obviously occur in the husband who has a low frustration tolerance. He may become very angry when his wife frustrates some of his needs, but instead of admitting that he is overreacting he may insist that his wife is being sadistic and that therefore his anger is appropriate.

In such a person, the analysis often reveals that he equates sensitivity with lack of masculinity. The denial of sensitivity is therefore a means of protecting himself from the shame of feeling unmanly. The basis equation, sensitivity equals lack of masculinity, persists in the unconscious and is often projected outward in a form that leads the patient to anticipate that, if others consider him sensitive, they will also seriously question his masculinity. This unconscious conviction is often a basic one in these patients It is also worth noting that in such instances the patient's shaky sense of masculinity may be bolstered by his attitude of indignation toward his wife, since such an attitude is often felt to be a sign of strength. Regardless of whether the indignation is expressed openly or not, it may function as a support to the narcissistic equilibrium.

Once the analysis clears away some of the patient's defenses and enables him to accept his sensitivity, he may begin to master his shame about it and may then find that he can admit it to others, including his wife. This change may be followed by efforts on his part to find new ways of avoiding certain frustrations in the marital relationship and new ways of resolving his anger when inevitable frustrations occur. Meanwhile, through careful and continued analysis of the sensitivity, some of it may gradually drop away. Although this sequence of events is often referred to as a counteracting of the tendency to project, a basic component is a reversal of the tendency to withdraw into a paranoidlike state. Such a reversal may be difficult to achieve, since the pattern of aggrieved withdrawal yields considerable satisfaction and the patient is often reluctant to give it up. The satisfactions obtained through withdrawal are largely narcissistic ones, and the attitude accompanying it might be paraphrased as follows: "I don't need you any more. I will be independent and take care of myself. I will therefore give to myself the love you have withheld from me." Even though this attitude yields compensatory satisfaction, it does not relieve the underlying depressive state. Once the patient makes efforts to counteract his withdrawal and is successful in doing so, however, he may then find that his depressive feelings diminish, and he may therefore be more ready to repeat the efforts on subsequent occasions.

Many of the neurotic responses of these patients can be thought of in terms of a withdrawal of libido to a narcissistic position, accompanied by attempts to obtain excessive narcissistic satisfaction. The occurrence of such attempts, however, does not indicate that these patients are suffering from severe emotional disturbances, since the withdrawal of libido to a narcissistic position may occur to varying degrees in all types of disturbance.

The husband's tendency to point the finger at his wife as the source of his problems can often be compared to the typical responses of children and adolescents when things go wrong. It is characteristic of young people to blame others for their own difficulties, or at least to deflect attention from themselves by calling attention to the shortcomings of others. When this type of reaction occurs in adult life, it is usually less blatant than in childhood and tends to take more subtle forms, even though it may have a similarly narcissistic quality.

The question might be raised how the analyst knows when such a patient is distorting reality. Sometimes the distortions are evident because the patient's communications have a "paranoidlike" quality, and sometimes the distortions can be inferred from subtle inconsistencies. At other times, one has to press for additional information from the patient, especially when the details of events are conspicuous by their absence. Under these circumstances, the therapist often senses that the husband is hiding something in order to maintain the illusion that the wife is "to blame."

Many of the husbands to whom I am referring have serious difficulties in mobilizing their feelings of sadness, and especially in permitting themselves to cry. They feel that to cry is to be weak and unmanly; and they therefore struggle not only to avoid crying but also to avoid the sad feelings that usually precede crying. Such a patient may not be able to cry even at a very sad movie. He may sit with a lump in his throat, tears all bottled up, while others around him are "enjoying" a good cry. For such a person, to shed tears may he an extremely humiliating experience (Levin, 1967a). But it is not just the overt manifestations of weeping that are involved in conflict; the sad feelings associated with what one might call a "subclinical cry" are similarly involved. Most people, when they are sad, feel an inner cry, even though it may not appear on the surface. But others cannot permit themselves to feel this inner state, either because they fear that it might lead to a severe breakthrough of feelings with overt weeping or because they equate it with weakness. When these resistances are clarified in analysis, frequently through a gradual process of mastery, there is an improvement in the patient's ability to feel the inner cry. The patient may then find that he is able to obtain some relief from his depressive feelings by permitting the sadness to come to the surface in the form of a subclinical cry. The subclinical cry, therefore, is a highly abreactive type of experience. This may be true regardless of what one is crying about. I have also observed that the freeing of feelings of sadness is often a major step in the direction of reversing the withdrawal and relieving depression, since this freeing-up process may lead to an increased freedom to reach out to the wife with affectionate sadness, in an attempt to achieve a reconciliation. This type of response can be compared to that which is commonly seen when lovers return to one another after a separation. The husband who has been away in military service for a year and returns home usually finds that when he greets his wife he feels like crying. The man who cannot permit himself to tolerate at least a subclinical cry may have to remain somewhat aloof from his wife. It appears that the freedom to feel sad can release the libido so that it can be redirected outward rather than remaining pent up in a narcissistic position.

   At times one finds that the patient can feel sadness provided this affect is displaced onto events which are considerably removed from his own personal life. In such instances the therapeutic task includes an analysis of this displacement so that the sadness can be more directly felt in relation to those personal experiences which have given rise to it.

COMMENT

In this chapter, I have elaborated on my earlier attempts to delineate some common forms of marital incompatibility. I have chosen to accent the frequently observed sensitivity reactions of husbands and to point out that these reactions are often subjected to the defense of denial. I have also proposed that this defense is instituted largely because in the unconscious of these patients excessive sensitivity is often equated with deficient masculinity and therefore evokes feelings of shame. In other words, by denying his sensitivity to sexual frustration, the man can avoid shame affect. One might consider the husband's shame concerning his sensitivity to being rejected sexually as the counterpart to the wife's shame concerning her need to limit their sexual relations, which I described in chapter 10. One might also consider the husband's denial of the degree of his sensitivity as the counterpart to the wife's denial of the degree to which she limits their sexual relations. In both instances, the denial enables the person to blame the spouse for the marital difficulties. Furthermore, in either or both instances, attitudes of excessive entitlement may be present and add a narcissistic quality to the responses. On one hand, the husband may feel entitled to have a wife who never frustrates his sexual needs. On the other hand, the wife may feel entitled to avoid sexual relations whenever she wishes.

The patterns of response that I have described in each of these chapters are not confined to one sex and similar patterns may be seen in both. For example, responses of aggrieved withdrawal, as I have described, can be thought of as more or less universal and may create complications in all types of relationships. They appear to be quite common in men, however, and to have special significance in fostering marital incompatibility, since they so frequently contribute to vicious circles of pathological interaction between spouses. In concentrating on these interactions I have bypassed a discussion of many deeper problems. This decision was based on the contention that the patterns of response I have described are frequently not given adequate attention in analysis, since our interest in the depths of the unconscious may lead us to neglect what may appear to be superficial phenomena.

SUMMARY

In many instances a vicious circle of marital incompatibility results from a tendency on the part of the husband, when frustrated sexually by his wife, to react by withdrawing from her and by developing an attitude of bitter grievance, which prevents a reconciliation. Some aspects of the sensitivity which underlies these reactions have been discussed. Since such sensitivity is frequently equated in the unconscious with deficient masculinity, it tends to evoke unconscious shame, which in turn may lead to a denial of the sensitivity.

Successful treatment must therefore include a careful analysis of the unconscious shame and of the denial of sensitivity to which it gives rise, so that the underlying sensitivity can be exposed and the resulting withdrawal can eventually be reserved.

REFERENCES

Engel, G. L. & Reichsman, F. (1956), Spontaneous and experimentally induced depression in an infant with gastric fistula. *J. Amer. Psychoanal Assn.*, 4:428–52.
Levin, S. (1967a), Some metapsychological considerations on the differentiation between shame and guilt. *Internat. J. Psycho-Anal.*, 48:267–276.
———— (1967b), Some comments on pathological attitudes of entitlement. Presented at meeting of the American Psychoanalytic Association, Detroit.

12

SUZANNE M. RETZINGER

Shame-Rage in
Marital Quarrels

For years social theorists have pointed out the importance of the social bond, the innate propensity for sociability in human beings, and what happens when it is disrupted (Marx, 1844; McDougall, 1908; Cooley, 1902; James, 1910; Mead, 1934). The bond and emotions are social as well as psychological phenomena; they are means to and end results of bonds, whether intact or damaged. Emotions are a way to monitor relationships between self and other, separateness as well as togetherness. Both emeshment and isolation are states of alienation (for further discussion see Retzinger, 1991, and Scheff and Retzinger, 1991). The common thread is the primacy of connectedness with others and the feelings that result from alienation, the excruciating pain of being cut off or isolated from other people: impotence and indignation, rage and impotent despair. Feelings of genuine pride usually accompany secure bonds (see Scheff and Retzinger, 1991).

Studies of social isolation (e.g., Spitz, 1946; Harlow, 1962; Bowlby, 1973) suggest the importance of human sociability. A biosocial view of human behavior is supported by microscopic analyses of complex interaction between the neonate and caregiver (Ainsworth, Bell, and Stayton, 1974; Brazelton, Koslowski, and Main, 1974; Tronick, 1980; DeCasper and Fifer 1981; Stern 1981; Brazelton, 1982; Field, Woodson, and Cohen, 1982; Tronick, Ricks, and Cohn, 1982; Sorse et al. 1985). Emotions seem to be a social signal from the earliest interactions, as indicated by an infant's attempts at reinstating interaction when a caregiver is instructed to be still faced (Tronick et al., 1982) or an infant's stopping at the edge of a perceived cliff when the caregiver displays fear but continuing over the edge when presented with a smile (Sorse et al., 1985). There also seems to be an innate potential for turn-taking in early interaction that seems to regulate the inner states of the interactants.

Other work suggests the importance and power of the social bond, not only in infancy but over the lifespan. Shaver, Hazen, and Bradshaw (1987) have shown the similarities between adult romantic love relationships and attachment in infants, following Bowlby (1969). The concept of the social bond can help explain how high levels of conflict can emerge and continue to escalate. Emotions associated with threatened or broken bonds play a central role; they communicate both to self and other the state of the bond at any given time (Retzinger, 1991).

In a biosocial framework, the primary motive is to secure important bonds. Emotions are crucial—secure bonds are accompanied by feelings of pride, joy, and happiness; threatened, damaged or severed bonds, by feelings of insecurity, sadness, anger and shame. Survival itself is dependent on social bonds. Shame plays a prominent role in the maintenance of bonds; it is a signal of threatened or damaged bonds. The source of shame is a perceived injury to self: insult, rejection, rebuff, disapproval, unrequited love, betrayal, unresponsiveness, disrespect, criticism, imagined as well as real.

Large-scale studies of conflict (Coleman, 1957; Pruitt and Rubin, 1986) suggest in larger communities that bonds are weaker and thus people are more prone to conflict. These studies also suggest that escalation of conflict occurs when despite contact, no bonds have been established to protect from escalation. It appears that people with bonding difficulties, such as those with dependency needs that are unfulfilled and denied, are particularly prone to shame and high levels of conflict.

Vulnerability to violent escalation by dependent people was also suggested by Shupe, Stacey, and Hazelwood (1987) in their study of family violence: "The more violence in the relationship, the more dependence there was" (p. 36). Dependent men had poor skills for communicating emotional needs and frustrations, as well as a belief that dependency was a feminine trait. They attempted to drive off the very affection they sought, which made them vulnerable to the slightest threat. Lansky's (1987) study also indicates that violent men are dependent but cannot express this need.

Bowlby's (1988) work also gives support to the dependency hypothesis. He found the dependency needs in violent mothers to be especially strong; these mothers were unable to make close relationships; at the same time they had a great need for them. In another study, Hansburg (1972) showed that abusing mothers were extremely sensitive to any type of separation and responded with high levels of anger.

Separation and shame are interrelated. Shame can lead to further separation when not acknowledged, that is, when it is hidden from others. One is alone in one's pain. By itself, unacknowledged shame can create a form of self-perpetuating entrapment in one's own isolation; if one hides this sense from the other (because of shame), further shame is created, which results in a a heightened sense of isolation. This formulation should not be taken lightly. People kill for social reasons: lost affection, lost honor, and other highly moral reasons (Lewis, 1976; Katz, 1988).

When shame is ignored, one not only feels separated from the other person and hurt, but also identification with the other becomes difficult. The other person can then be experienced as the source of the hurt; each reciprocates with a more vehement assault against the perceived attack: withdrawal of affection, sarcasm, blame, demeaning criticism, threat, or worse. Each tactic separates people further from one another, generating ever more powerful emotions.

Separation can take the form of either isolation or engulfment; both are states of alienation, involving fragile bonds with others. For secure bonds, one must be able to be close but to also be separate. In engulfment, one's uniqueness is denied; one is unable to differenti-ate from the other (Bowen, 1978). In response to the inability to differentiate, one remains in a state of extreme dependency or is cut off emotionally; both render a person subject to shame states. The context for shame is important because it involves a message of separation (or threat of separation). The context reveals its intricate connection with *alienation* and threats of abandonment.

Several studies have explicitly shown the prominence of the role of shame in conflict and violence. Katz (1988) suggests that humilia-tion often underlies violent crime and homicide. Lansky's (1987) indicates that physically violent marriages are rampant with shame, the persons in violent relationships being particularly prone to shame. Scheff (1987, 1989, 1994) and Retzinger (1991) and Scheff and Retzinger (1991) have shown the prominence of unacknowl-edged shame in marital quarrels, psychotherapy sessions, prison riots, and warfare.

Self–other involvement in shame has several complications. Because of the invisibility of shame and its painfulness, it is often

difficult to communicate. When shame is evoked but not acknowledged, anger is aroused by indications that the other does not value
the self, usually experienced as an attack coming from the other
(which may or may not be the case). In either case the self feels like
the target of the other's hostility. "Hostility against the rejecting
'other' is almost always simultaneously evoked. But it is humiliated
fury, or shame-rage" (Lewis, 1976, p. 193). The special quality of
emotional communication in shame-rage is a "self-to-other message
or thought about how rageful the self feels at its inferior place 'in
the eyes' of the other" (Lewis, 1981, p. 190).

Unacknowledged shame acts both as an inhibitor and as a
generator of anger, rendering the person impotent to express anger
toward the other (withholding behavior), while simultaneously
generating further anger. Shame is the emotional signal of impaired
bonds; when it is not acknowledged, one ostensible result is
escalation. Shame-rage seems to be self-perpetuating. Each emotion
serves as a stimulus for the other.

Bowlby (1988) and others suggest that a lapse in the bond
generates emotions that serve a function: "This anger, the function
of which is to dissuade the attachment figure from carrying out the
threat, can easily become dysfunctional" (p. 30). Angry protest, in
Bowlby's sense, is an attempt to preserve social relationships by
signaling the need to repair lost bonds or lost face.

Escalation takes place when the bond is threatened and shame is
elicited: persons are alienated, shame is not acknowledged, manner
is perceived as disrespectful. The more emotionally reactive and
undifferentiated the parties, the more likely they are to engage in
dysfunctional conflict. Each needs the other in some way and feels
injured by the other; each person's behavior is perceived by the
other as unjust.

Lewis's (1971) working concept can be used to analyze the
following case. Her method carefully spells out the context for shame
and identifies the characteristics of a shame experience: stimulus
(context), experience of a shame state, relationship between self and
other, hostile reactions, and defenses. The self–other relationship is
crucial in shame experiences; the self is always perceived to be in an
inferior position to other.

To add credence to identifying shame through context, I have
developed a method of identifying shame through visual and
paralingustic cues, which occur in the context of shame events.
Some of the cues are listed in Table 1. (For an extensive description
of a method for identifying shame, see Retzinger, 1991.)

Table 1.

VERBAL MARKERS

SHAME:

alienated: rejected, dumped, deserted, rebuffed, abandoned, estranged, deserted, isolated, separate, alone, disconnected, disassociated, detached, withdrawn, inhibited, distant, remote, split, divorced, polarized.

confused: stunned, dazed, blank, empty, hollow, spaced, giddy, lost, vapid, hesitant, aloof.

ridiculous: foolish, silly, funny, absurd, idiotic, asinine, simple-minded, stupid, curious, weird, bizarre, odd, peculiar, strange, different, stupid.

inadequate: helpless, powerless, defenseless, weak, insecure, uncertain, shy, deficient, worse off, small, failure, ineffectual, inferior, unworthy, worthless, flawed, trivial, meaningless, insufficient, unsure, dependent, exposed, inadequate, incapable, vulnerable, unable, inept, unfit, impotent, oppressed.

uncomfortable: restless, fidgety, jittery, tense, anxious, nervous, uneasy, antsy, jumpy, hyperactive.

hurt: offended, upset, wounded, injured, tortured, ruined, sensitive, sore spot, buttons pushed, dejected, intimidated, defeated.

ANGER: cranky, cross, hot-tempered, ireful, quick-tempered, short fuse, enraged, fuming, agitated, furious, irritable, incensed, indignant, irate, annoyed, mad, pissed, pissed off, teed-off, upset, furious, aggravated, bothered, resentful, bitter, spiteful, grudge (the last four words imply shame-rage compounds).

Other verbal markers:

SHAME: Mitigation (to make appear less severe or painful); oblique, suppressed reference, e. g. "they," "it," "you"; vagueness; denial; defensiveness; verbal withdrawal (lack of response); indifference (Acting "cool" in an emotionally arousing context).

ANGER: interruption; challenge; sarcasm; blame

SHAME-RAGE: Temporal expansion/condensation or generalization ("You *always* . . . ," "you never . . . "). Triangulation (bringing up an irrelevant third party or object).

PARALINGUISTIC MARKERS

SHAME: (vocal withdrawal/hiding behaviors, disorganization of thought): over-soft; rhythm irregular; hesitation; self interruption (censorship); filled pauses (-uh-); long pauses (); silences; stammer; fragmented speech; rapid speech; condensed words; mumble; breathiness; incoherence (lax articulation); laughed words; monotone.

Table 1. (continued)

ANGER: staccato (distinct breaks between successive tones); loud; heavy stress on certain words; sing-song pattern (ridicule); straining; harsh voice qualifiers.

SHAME-RAGE: whine; glottalization (rasp or buzz); choking; tempo up/down; pitch up/down.

VISUAL MARKERS

SHAME: l) Hiding behavior: a) the hand covering all or parts of the face, b) gaze aversion, eyes lowed or averted. 2) Blushing. 3) Control: a) turning in, biting, or licking the lips, biting the tongue, b) forehead wrinkled vertically or transversely, c) false smiling (Ekman & Freisen, 1982); or other masking behaviors.

ANGER: l) Brows lowered and drawn together, vertical lines appear between them. 2) The eyelids are narrowed and tense in a hard fixed stare and may have a bulging appearance. 3) Lips pressed together, the corners straight or down, or open but tense and square. 4) Hard, direct glaring. 5) Leaning forward toward other in challenging stance. 6) Clenched fists, wave fists, hitting motions.

These markers are context-related; that is, their relevance depends on the relationship between self and other. You need to look for constellation of markers in context. The more markers from each category, the stronger the evidence.

CASE ILLUSTRATION

Karin and Randy are both in their 30s. He is a college student, an artist and sculptor; she is employed as a manager. They are both unhappy with their relationship and are destructive toward each other verbally and emotionally. Although there was no reported physical violence, Karin and Randy's quarrel is characterized by covert and overt demeaning criticism by both and "character assassination" by Randy toward Karin. Randy's hostility is overt, while Karin's is more subtle, emerging in disguised forms, such as innuendo.

The main focus of the quarrel is the weight that Karin has gained: "since the death of the last baby I've gained 80 pounds." She appears to be greatly overweight. Although Randy also appears to be quite overweight, little mention is made of his weight. During the 15-minute quarrel, at each point of escalation, they move from topic to topic: who gave whom support, their sex life, Randy's friends, and Karin's father. Each blames the problem on the other, neither takes responsibility for his or her own part. Randy and Karin's bond seems to be quite fragile; the humiliating way they treat each other and communicate grievances damages the bond further. This quarrel escalates eight times in 15 minutes; it ends with cursing and an extremely high level of anger.

In their initial dialogue, there is no evidence of anger, but Randy displays many cues for shame, seen in hiding behaviors: he averts his gaze, leans away, hesitates, triangles. He speaks with frequent pauses, uses filler words and mitigation, and generalizes. Shame is also indicated by his attempt at being casual and indifferent. Indifference can mark a state of bypassed shame: "It succeeds in warding off feelings of humiliation in the self and it can succeed in evoking them in others" (Lewis, 1981, p. 12).

The following excerpts illustrate various points of escalation. Shame is marked by italics, anger by boldface; when shame and rage occur together, underlined bold is used. The numbers indicate time in minutes and seconds.

06:11   K: . . . *who* **who needs it** *(1.3)* and if *you* happen to have gained weight because you've got problems in *your* life, then *you* gain weight because *you* got problems in *your* life. *That doesn't mean you're any less of a person ().*

R: *(4) Ya well () (long sigh) (8.26 pause)*

K: **Yeah, well what**? *(3.70 pause)*

06:34   R: *Yeah, but I hesitate to get into this at all I ()*

K: **Well**?

R: **(interrupts) AHH!** (guttural noise) *() cause I (3) you know* I don't want to () get into your () **character assassination** but I usually do *(3.20)*.

K: You don't have to say anything super personal but . . .

07:00   R: **(interrupts) But** you have to understand that *ah um (2.40) if uh you know that that I mean* you're living with one of the most anti-social men in the world (1.50) that anything that society would do I would automatically try to find a a completely different way to go about anything.

K: **But NOT when women are concerned**.

R: **(interrupts) But** you also—*we*—<u>**that's not true**</u>!

K: **Ya it is**!

07:21   R: **It's not true** *I mean* () I think *every* man has
           their dream woman () *every* man has their their
           dream uh silhouette () dream () shape *() you
           know uh* dream eyes *uh you know* <u>**whatever
           (2.35) and um (3.15) an I I hate to put it you
           this uh you know I hate to (2.62) to always
           harp on the same stuff but uh (2.75) I mean**</u>
           at your weight now *(2.35)* **you're just not
           doing it for me!**

In the beginning of the first excerpt, the context involves
ideation of deficiency of self: Karin explains that she is no less a
person because of her weight, and Randy values nonconformity.
Karin implies that he is a conformist. Randy is powerless to stay away
from Karin's "assassination" even though he does not want to get
into it. Here there is more shame present than anger. As we will see,
anger increases as the quarrel progresses, with anger taking the
forefront toward the end of the 15-minute quarrel.

Randy and Karin continue to argue, now about where the weight
problem originated. She complains that it stemmed from lack of
support; he claims that he gave her support. There are more
complaints and countercomplaints; each judges the problem as due
to the other. They are now in a blame-blame cycle, putting the
responsibility onto the other. The bond is damaged further as they
continue to argue.

10:13   K: **Ya but the support doesn't come in telling
           me not what to eat but realizing that I have
           some problems and I'm internalizing them
           is where the support and you should come
           in.**
        R: *Ya but I can't get into your mind.*
        K: *Well I I you know I ()* **fairly read you well**.
10:29   R: *Well* **I fairly read you well too** and *it it and I
           don't know I don't know what's going on it
           seems like () I mean* **we're both gonna be 65**
           someday () and **I'm not going** to *you know* I'm
           not gonna () **mind living with a 65-year-old
           broad when I'm 65** () **but we're in our 30s!**
        K: *I don't think I look like I'm 65.*
        R: (*clears throat*) **You have the same silhouette as
           a 65-year-old broad!**
10:53   K: *That doesn't matter.*

From the topic of the origination of the weight, they move into ideation of separation (*"Ya but I can't get into your mind"*) and then shame and then another episode of angry escalation. The foregoing excerpt is marked by gaze aversion, as well as repetition, fragmentation, and self-interruption (indicative of disorganized thought), all marking the presence of shame. The dense presence of shame is rapidly followed by escalated anger.

Intense escalation occurs in less than a minute as Randy responds to Karin's complaint about his lack of support: *("Ya but I can't get into your mind"*—ideation of separation). Karin responds with one-up-manship: *"Well I-I you know* **I () fairly read you well**." She starts out with repetition, hesitation, pausing, but finishes with a criticism of Randy. She says she is able to do something he is unable to do—she can understand and he can't.

Randy is affected intensely. His next response is defensive and dense with shame cues. Escalated anger rapidly follows as he demeans Karin by saying that she looks like "a 65-year-old broad." His verbal attack is preceded by shame cues, as it is in each instance of escalation. His words and manner humiliate Karin, in turn, who responds defensively, and so on as the quarrel continues to escalate. They move on to the topic of sex, trying to determine whose fault it is that sex is not good:

13:53   K: ...that sex isn't the greatest, **could any of it be
            your fault**?!
        R: **NO**!
13:56   K: **NONE of it**?!
        R: <u>Uhuh</u>!
        K: **None of it in BED was your fault it was all my
            fault that it wasn't the greatest (1.8) you see
            what you're saying**?
14:04   R: **Ya I do () and that's what I'm saying**!

Each new topic brings a higher level of escalation. Their quarrel becomes more nasty and personal. Each denies responsibility for their relationship; each claims the other to be deficient. The bond continues to be damaged.

14:21   K: *(laugh)* **You see you're not even facing the
            problem** and **maybe that's where the
            problem lies**!

R: **(interrupts) what do you mean—not no no**
see the problem is (1.63) just visualize () **you at
a 125!**

K: **Even if I weighed** a 125 we'd still have a
problem in bed!

14:32 R: **(interrupts) Wait a second I'm not finished
talking - that's not true () <u>what kind of a
problem would we have</u>**?!

K: The same problem we have now because of the
way you are!

R: **What do you mean that I don't kiss you**?!

14:43 K: **<u>You don't you're not really</u>**

R: **<u>(interrupts) That I don't that I don't get into</u>
foreplay, that I don't get into um being kind
and and <u>um being uh</u> () watchful for your
own** *um () you know* **climaxes** and your own
()

K: *(laughs)*

14:55 R: *Uh you know uh*

K: (interrupts) **All that type of stuff is still going
to be there when I'm a 125!**

R: **That's bull shit!**

15:00 K: **<u>What do you mean that's bull shit</u>**?!

R: **(interrupts) Cause all that stuff** would disappear.

K: **<u>You're gonna care more if I weighed a 125?</u>**

15:04 R: **(interrupts) HELL YA!**

Their quarrel is out of control. Randy has become extremely
personal about the details of the problems in their sex life. Cues for
overt anger are predominant where earlier unacknowledged shame
was at the forefront. Randy continues claiming that the problem is
Karin's weight. Karin now says the problem is that Randy doesn't
face the problem, which won't end if she loses weight because it's
Randy's denial that causes the problem. They interrupt and criticize
each other frequently and vehemently, both showing more disrespect
than previously. From sex the conversation has shifted to a discussion of their lips:

16:40 R: Simply because **I don't want to kiss you or
spend time kissing you** *doesn't mean* **I <u>don't</u>
<u>like you</u>** *() you see* **you got that backwards!**

K: **<u>(interrupts) Yes it does</u>**!

R: **No! you got that backwards**! *()* What that
  means *is () is* **that I don't like your FACE** *()*
  right now! () I mean **it used to be that had**
  some actual lips () **now your there's there**
  there's very little definition!

17:01 K: **(interrupts) You don't have any upper lip**
  don't talk about my lips!

They seemed to have lost track of what they were originally
quarreling about and to be looking for ways to attack and humiliate
each other. The final point of escalation moves them into arguing
about Randy's friend Kevin and Karin's father. The quarrel has
expanded to include others outside of their direct relationship. The
intensity of anger is at its greatest, but it is shame-rage:

19:11 R: . . . but **you have to begin to realize** that that
  that no matter how you were raised that peoples
  insides mattered **I can't understand why why**
  in the world your father would would say
  that about anybody **when that guy when**
  that guy (*inaud*) **when your father your**
  father.

  K: (interrupts) **Insides do matter** () **I was raised**
  that

19:20 R: (interrupts) **Never said a straight** () **ya but**
  your father never had a straight

  K: **(interrupts) Character and personality are**
  very important traits ya but look at Kevin
  and his relationship he's on his THIRD wife!

19:28 R: (interrupts) **Ya but** **Kevin Kevin has always**
  been able to say what he felt inside and to
  really give it!

  K: (interrupts) Ya but **he's also brusk**!

  R: **He's also brusk but he's real. See your father**
  was never able

  K: (interrupts) **He's losing**

  R: (interrupts) **Say anything real**!

19:36 K: (interrupts) **Randy stop a minute. He's losing**
  his third wife now and he's gonna be
  entering his fourth marriage. His ideal of
  women only looking through the magazines
  and not caring what their character's like!

> R: **(interrupts) That's not true! You don't know**
> **what what you don't - That's not true! ()**
> **that's not true! You don't even know that**!
> K: **(interrupts) A lot of this is based on external**
> **things**
> 19:53   R: **No it isn't! No it isn't!**

A third party has been drawn in, creating a wider gap between Randy and Karin. Nothing about the relationship is addressed, nor are the emotions between them. When outside parties become involved, polarization of positions can solidify into tribal warfare (Neuhauser, 1989).

Randy and Karin interrupt each other and show increased signs of anger; they use tactics that blatantly insult and humiliate the other. The quarrel escalates to include Randy's friend and Karin's father, denigrating the friend and father in demeaning and hostile ways.

> 19:57   R: **I don't know how the hell you were raised**
> **that way I mean your father is the most is**
> **the biggest liar () I mean you could ask your**
> **father what day it was . . .**

The quarrel continues to escalate at intervals. Each incident of escalation brings the quarrel to a higher level of anger; increase in cues for anger parallels increase in shame cues. The level of anger and hostility became very high as the 15-minute session came to a close. As a timer signalled the end of the session, Randy cannot stop "harping"; he finally ends with the line: "**GOD DAMN KARIN,** *I'm just gonna go the rest of my life with . . . .*" Continued cursing and hopelessness are an indication that shame-rage is present at a high level.

Each excerpt in sequence is more intense than the preceding one. Their changes in topics and utterances avoid the feelings between Randy and Karin and create further distance; as shame increases so does anger. Cues for anger multiply and alternate rapidly with shame cues. A characteristic feeling associated with shame-rage is that the situation is endless or hopeless. Four minutes, 18 seconds into the quarrel, Randy expresses this feeling: "this one seems like a never ending one" (09:17.51). By now the level of anger is high, but 1 minute, 5 seconds later the quarrel escalates further as they discuss whether they can get into each other's minds.

Shame remains unacknowledged; neither person comments on manner, emotions, or the bond. The tactics they use erode the bond between them, and generate further shame. Although shame cues are still present, anger is by far the predominant emotion at the end of the time period, when the researcher interrupts the quarrel.

CONCLUSION

Randy and Karin were not physically violent, but there was verbal and emotional violence. They dealt with *what* was said–the topic, and not the manner or *how* it was said (Watzlawick et al., 1967), which involves the bond between them; emotions were not acknowledged. The tactics they used showed disrespect, and feelings escalated. The bonds were further damaged in each case. Although preliminary, the results suggest that inadequate bonding and unacknowledged shame play a central role in escalating conflict.

Randy and Karin's quarrel began with a constellation of shame cues, rather than those of anger. Alternation between anger and shame steadily increased, reaching a high level of emotional violence; the quarrel ended with intense anger. Although the quarrel began with the topic of Karin's weight, it shifted from topic to topic; shame preceded each topic change, was never acknowledged, and was followed by increase in anger paralleling increasing shame. The rapid change of topics did not help; it was used to blame, to overwhelm the other, and to avoid the isolation that each felt in this relationship. Throughout the quarrel, the bond was being damaged; there were no moments of repair or building bridges. Each participant was alienated from the other.

Escalation involves several stages: 1) inadequate or threatened bonds, that is, emotional separation/alienation; 2) shame is evoked but is not acknowledged (the bond or feelings are not discussed); 3) anger follows shame, as if to defend against an attack (i.e., to save face), often expressed disrespectfully, leading to self-perpetuating sequences. This pattern was found in the escalation of conflict in three other cases (Retzinger, 1991).

Within a framework of human sociability, a new view of conflict emerges. If connection with others is a primary motive in human behavior, maintenance of bonds is crucial. Bonds are reciprocally related to and involve emotions: emotions are signals and means of both cohesion and disruption. In this framework, anger can be viewed as an attempt to ward off perceived attack and "save face," to deny the need for others, or to remain attached in the face of threats to basic emotional ties. Rage, a reaction against an injury to self, is a protective measure used as an insulation against shame.

Threatened or damaged bonds create an environment for escalation when the need for the other is denied.

Unacknowledged shame seems to be the critical factor in the inability to resolve conflict. When the self-monitoring system fails to serve its function (shame is denied), persons continue to feel alienated; the inability to communicate their feelings effectively further separates them from each other.

The exploration of shame is in the infancy state of development. Results reported here are tentative and exploratory, although other findings have shown shame to be prominent in many kinds of conflict, from internal conflict in nightmares (Lansky, 1995) to world wars (Scheff, 1994). Shame seems to have important implications in normal, everyday life, as well as in pathological human behavior. To the extent that parties in a relationship are alienated from each other and deny their feelings, they risk destructive behavior.

REFERENCES

Ainsworth, M. D. S., Bell, S. M. & Stayton, D. J. (1974), Infant–mother attachment and social development: "Socialization" as a product of reciprocal responsiveness. In: *The Integration of the Child into a Social World,* ed. M. Richards. New York: Cambridge University Press.

Bowen, M. (1978), *Family Therapy in Clinical Practice.* New York: Aronson.

Bowlby, J. (1969), *Attachment and Loss, Vol. 1.* New York: Basic Books.

——— (1973), *Attachment and Loss, Vol. 2.* New York: Basic Books.

——— (1988), *A Secure Base.* New York: Basic Books.

Brazelton, T. B. (1982), Joint regulation of neonate-parent interaction. In: *Social Exchange in Infancy,* ed. E. Tronick. Baltimore, MD: University Park Press, pp. 7–22.

——— Koslowski, B. V. & Main, M. (1974), The origins of reciprocity: Early mother–infant interaction. In: *The Effect of the Infant on Its Caregiver,* ed. M. Lewis & L. Rosenblum. New York: Wiley.

Coleman, J. (1957), *Community Conflict.* New York: Free Press.

Cooley, C. H. (1902), *Human Nature and the Social Order.* New York: Schocken Books, 1970.

DeCasper, A. & Fifer, W. (1981), Of human bonding: Newborns prefer their mothers' voices. *Science,* 208:1174–1176.

Field, T., Woodson, R. & Cohen, D. (1982), Discrimination and imitation of facial expression by neonates. *Science*, 218:179–181.

Hansburg, H. (1972), *Adolescent Separation Anxiety*. Springfield, IL: C.C. Thomas.

Harlow, H. (1962), The heterosexual affectional system in monkeys. *Amer. Psychol.*, 17:1–9.

James, W. (1910), *Psychology*. New York: Henry Holt.

Katz, J. (1988), *Seductions to Crime*. New York: Basic Books.

Lansky, M. (1987), Shame and domestic violence. In: *The Many Faces of Shame*, ed. D. Nathanson. New York: Guilford, pp. 335–362.

———— (1995), *Postraumatic Nightmares*. Hillsdale, NJ: The Analytic Press.

Lewis, H. B. (1971), *Shame and Guilt in Neurosis*. New York: International Universities Press.

———— (1976), *Psychic War in Men and Women*. New York: New York University Press.

———— (1981), *Freud and Modern Psychology, Vol 1*. New York: Plenum.

Marx, K. (1844/1964), *Economic and Philosophic Manuscripts of 1844*. New York: International Publishers.

McDougall, W. (1908), *An Introduction to Social Psychology*. New York: University Paperbacks.

Mead, G. H. (1934), *Mind, Self, & Society*. Chicago: University of Chicago Press.

Neuhauser, S. (1988), *Tribal Warfare in Organizations*. Cambridge, MA: Ballinger.

Pruitt, D. G. & Rubin, J. Z. (1986), *Social Conflict*. New York: Random House.

Retzinger, S. M. (1991), *Violent Emotions*. Newbury Park, CA: Sage.

Scheff, T. J. (1987), The shame-rage spiral: A case study of an interminable quarrel. In: *The Role of Shame in Symptom Formation*, ed. H. B. Lewis. Hillsdale, NJ: Lawrence Erlbaum Associates, pp. 109–149.

———— (1989), Cognitive and emotional conflict in anorexia: Re-analysis of a case. *Psychiat.*, 52:148–161.

———— (1994), *Bloody Revenge*. Boulder, CO: Westview.

———— & Retzinger, S. M. (1991), *Emotions and Violence*. New York: Lexington.

Shaver, P. (1988), Love as attachment. In: *The Anatomy of Love*, ed. R.J. Sternberg & M. Barnes. New Haven, CT: Yale University Press, pp. 68–99.

Shupe, A., Stacey, W. & Hazelwood, L. (1987), *Violent Men, Violent Couples*. New York: Lexington Books.

Sorse, J., Emde, R., Campos, J. & Klinnert, M. (1985), Maternal emotional signaling: Its effect on the visual cliff behavior of 1-year-olds. *Develop. Psychol.*, 21:195–200.

Spitz, R. A. (1946), Anaclitic depression: An inquiry into the genesis of psychiatric conditions in early childhood II. *The Psychoanalytic Study of the Child*, 2:313–332. New York: International Universities Press.

Stern, D. N. (1981), The development of biologically determined signals of readiness to communicate, which are language "resistant." In: *Language Behavior in Infancy and Early Childhood*, ed. R. Stark. New York: Elsevier North Holland, pp. 45–62.

Tronick, E. (1980), The primacy of social skills in infancy. In: *Exceptional Infant, Vol. 4*, ed. D. B. Sawin, R. C. Hawkins, L. O. Walker & J. H. Penticuff. New York: Brunner/Mazel, pp. 144–158.

———— Ricks, M. & Cohn, J. (1982), Maternal and infant affect exchange: Patterns of adaptation. In: *Emotion and Early Interaction*, ed. T. Field & A. Fogel. Hillsdale, NJ: Lawrence Erlbaum Associates, pp. 83–100.

Watzlawick, P., Beavin, J. & Jackson, D.D. (1967), *Pragmatics of Human Communication*. New York: Norton.

13

Shame: The Dark Shadow of Infertility[*]

Faces of despair pressed against the windows of the fertile world . . . this is the secret inner experience of the person enduring chronic infertility. While there has been much open discussion about the grief, anger, depression, and multiple losses associated with the predicament of infertility (Glazer and Cooper, 1988; Menning, 1988; Shapiro, 1988), probably the most excruciating emotion, and the one that is the least discussed, is the experience of shame. And, since this emotion is so frequently hidden, it is often not understood or empathized with by the environment.

For the infertility sufferer, as over and over, attempts to get pregnant come to naught, a recognition approaches that an intensely strived-for goal has not been, and may never be, attained. As this failure becomes more and more evident, one's self-image is assaulted. It is easy to move from treatment cycles or in vitro fertilizations that have failed to feelings that "*I* am a failure." There is a rupture in the sense of adequacy and effectiveness, the "sudden experience of a violation of expectation, of incongruity between expectation and outcome result(ing) in a shattering of trust in one's self, even in one's own body and skill and identity . . . " (Lynd, 1958, p. 46).

As the blow of infertility exerts its impact on the self and its surround, there is an interplay of intrapsychic forces, interpersonal expectations, and social consequences. Anguish, self-doubt, and

---

*An earlier version of this paper was published in the *Resolve National Newsletter*, Volume 18, No. 2, April 1993.

313

chronic sadness converge as the person comes to experience the *self* as failing, not only in the realization of its own dreams to reproduce and nurture, but also failing the hopes and expectations of significant objects—spouse, parents, and siblings as well. For the infertile patient, then, there is a double insult: the private failure to live up to one's personal goals and ideals, and the more public humiliation, since the defeat of the wish to have a child is so visible to others and also so potentially depriving to loved ones. Not only does one see oneself as defective and failing, but also one is exposed to an audience who can bear witness to the flawed self. The tragic story of chronic infertility is that, over time, the sense of failure gradually and imperceptibly spreads like a dark shadow over a person's experience, while simultaneously the sense of a person's other competencies or abilities gradually becomes more and more eclipsed and obscured.

Both Morrison (1989) and Broucek (1991) emphasize how shame can arise from a sense of failure of the self or from failure of the responsiveness of the other. Both failures are dramatically visible in the life of the infertility patient. It is safe to say that most people who have not either suffered infertility themselves or been close to someone who has are innocently unaware of the devastation that can be wreaked on a person's sense of worth and psychological comfort merely by having to live in the fertile world. The first therapeutic goal, then, is to help sufferers acknowledge and tolerate their own sense of failure. Next, they need to be assisted in finding words for their confusing reactions to the failed attunement of those who, although perhaps well intentioned, are naively unaware of the powerful impact of the state of infertility. Ultimately, if sufferers become able to share their subjective experience with important others, they will have a better chance of "creating" or "shaping" (Morrison, 1994) the attunement that is so essential if feelings of shame are eventually to be ameliorated.

One can consider two basic areas of shame related to infertility: bodily shame and shame related to other vital aspects of the sense of self. Although soma and psyche are interwoven, it is helpful to separate them in order to elucidate more precisely the feeling of helplessness and failure embedded in each.

BODILY SHAME

The familiar term "inferiority complex" at first referred to a feeling of shame based on the feeling of inadequacy of body parts (Adler, 1927). Although the dynamics are different for each gender, one cannot dispute that, for both men and women, potency, fertility, sexuality, and reproductive competency are intimately intertwined with the sense of self-worth. It is common, for example, for men's feelings of pride or humiliation to fluctuate with the numbers that appear on their sperm counts. And, not only are there private feelings, but also the anguish of exposure of one's infertility to the public eye further increases the sense of shame.

> If the Hebrew Scriptures have it right, long before Yahweh intervened to liberate a whole people from slavery, His overriding concern was domestic politics: the act of relieving women like Sarah, Abraham's wife, of the shame of barrenness. Hagar's fruitfulness only deepened Sarah's bitterness and set the two women fighting . . . or take Rachel. Is there any more heart-rending cry in the Old Testament than hers? "Give me children, or I die!" To which Jacob retorts: "Can I take the place of God, who has denied you the fruit of the womb?" [Gen. 30:1–2, in Editorial, 1993].

And also from the Bible, the aging wife of Zechariah, Elizabeth, said, "This is what the Lord has done for me when he looked favorably on me and took away the disgrace I have endured among my people" (Luke 1:25–27). The gruesome fate of Ann Bolyn dramatically and drastically attests to the extremes of devaluation to which a person can be subjected because of his or her perceived reproductive inadequacy.

Infertile people do not literally get executed these days, but it is true that, with chronic infertility, there is a gradual erosion in confidence in one's body-self and one's sexual self that can be likened to a slow and painful psychic demise. The cumulative effect of messages of failure deflate both the sense of self and the pride and arousal of sexuality. Failed fertilizations, failed implantations, and underlying messages of "maybe *this* is what is wrong with you" bring a dark cloud over one's feeling of being intact, sexual, alive, and alluring. A highly invested function is not working correctly and the person comes to feel progressively more and more defeated, deflated, and humiliated.

Although perhaps too simplistically, shame has traditionally been viewed as "the enemy of healthy sexuality" (Broucek, 1991, p. 107). It is clear that healthy and vigorous eroticism must involve a sense of vitality and enhancement—the desire to appreciate and be appreciated in all one's sexual splendor and vigor. But how much revelling in a feeling of splendor can occur with semen specimen cups, vaginal ultrasound probes, daily injections and blood tests, mucus and urine measurements? There is a cumulative effect of multiple tests and treatments that remove the mystery, fantasy, and intrigue from the sexual. For, in order to feel aroused, one has to imagine intrigue about one's body and to be able to picture the glimmer of fascination in the observer's eye. This healthy exhibitionism and need for mirroring is shattered by the mechanical, "unromantic," carefully scheduled procedures involved in infertility treatments and the ensuing feelings of inadequacy and defectiveness.

Broucek (1991) has said that "the erotic must remain veiled" (p. 119). The objectification of sexual parts, and the loss of any modesty, mystery, or privacy gradually evolves into an objectification of the self and neutralizes any subjective pride in the erotic. The "I-thou communicative mode" of sexuality (p. 118) disappears, and the person begins to feel like an "it" (Bacal, 1993, personal communication). The feeling of specialness about one's sexuality withers and dies. Given that treatments involve the intrusiveness and objectifying gaze of many clinicians, and the public exposure of the most intimate details of one's body, sexual parts, and functioning, the infertile person begins to feel like a clinical specimen. Self-loathing and disgust about one's body ensues.

Freud (1905) pointed to shame and disgust as the chief barriers to the instincts. In my opinion, shame is the chief reason for the frequent complaint of loss of interest in sex among chronically infertile people. Far more than depression, preoccupation, or exhaustion, it is shame that accounts for the common description of loss of libido. When sexuality must be summoned "regardless of our readiness, the situation becomes an analogue of the oral disgust situation and the same affect is apt to be aroused resulting in disgust towards the objectified other and oneself" (Broucek, 1991, p. 113). The patient "embraces objecthood" (p. 131) and loses the sense, sexually speaking, of being a "who" in an intersubjective mode. Instead, the person becomes a "what"—a "what" that there is something *wrong* with! The attitude toward the sexual self ceases to be erotic and becomes one of "critical detachment" (Sussman, 1993, p. 113).

How easily complicated and extended medical procedures can cause the sense of specialness about one's sexuality to shrivel is illustrated by the following brief vignette. An attractive woman patient told me she was waiting one day in the surgical suite all prepped for her IVF egg retrieval. As she lay there in the lithotomy position, her handsome doctor walked into the room, gazed at her spread legs, and exclaimed, "Wow! Beautiful!" At first she felt a bit flushed, flattered, and enhanced, until his further comments dashed that feeling when it became clear that he was commenting on her brand new bright red knee socks!

SHAME AND THE SENSE OF SELF

In infertility, needs for mirroring, twinship, and idealization (i.e., connection and affective resonance) are all traumatically disappointed, leading to intense feelings of shame, inferiority, and failure. An infertile person is painfully aware of the absence of affirming and confirming responses that fertile people take for granted. When couples first meet, it is typical to inquire about who has what offspring. It is not uncommon for people to brag about their children in a totally expansive and unabashed way, with little awareness of the sting of feeling diminished they may be inflicting on their infertile friends. Exchanging "oohs" and "ahhs," confirming and approving thrilled reactions, gives the stamp of approval to the proud parents' or grandparents' own success; while, for the infertile person, it magnifies and illuminates the sense of being flawed or defective. And these injuries happen frequently, since exhibitionism and pride of procreation is socially sanctioned in a way that displaying one's other assets (one's investment portfolio, jewelry collection, or bank account) would be frowned upon. Bearing the feelings of shame and failure in an exhibitionistic environment can be overwhelming to the infertile person and can provoke intense rage and despair, reactions about which the infertile person, in turn, also becomes ashamed. For both men and women, there can be intense periods of disequilibrium, hurt, envy and rage as one contrasts oneself with others who are the "haves." Even the very yearning to share such affirmation and mirroring can become a source of shame. Bit by bit, the infertile person can come to feel more and more diminished, insignificant, and contracted (Morrison, 1994, p. 25). Feeling small, alone and separate, the sufferer may withdraw and eventually seek to avoid such social situations all together.

The impact of being excluded from the reproductive aspect of life may be greater for women, who typically have defined their femininity by their relationships and connectedness to others (Gilligan, 1982; Notman et al., 1986; Jordan et al., 1991; Barth, 1993). Socially and interpersonally, "a feminine sense of self is organized around giving to and caring for others, exemplified by the fantasy of a mother caring unambivalently for her child" (Barth, 1993, p. 175). An infertile woman is deprived of an avenue of approval and affirmation that she has come to expect throughout childhood as her due. The intensity of this wish can be understood as part of the need "to have the loving, giving aspects of the self recognized and confirmed through this special relationship" (p. 174). Many women report feeling "incomplete" or "missing a part of themselves," and they rely on the fantasy of having children as a means to correct or compensate for the sense of defect they see in themselves (Freud, 1925, p. 256). Men do not typically envision childbearing as a solution to these problems. Although attitudes are gradually changing culturally, a women's failure in the area of creating a family and children can, for all these complicated reasons, have a devastating impact on her core sense of worth and wholeness.

It is not just the absence of mirroring responses or positive affirmation that the infertile person must contend with, but the presence of negative input as well. People in the outside world can actually foist humiliation on the infertile person, totally oblivious to the fact that they are so doing. Often, there is the not-so-subtle implication that infertility is the result of a self-centered life or negative feelings towards children. Innocent comments like "So, you decided not to have children; I guess you're too busy with your career" can inflict deep wounds. And then there are comments that outright invalidate the infertile person's experience. Such comments range from, "Don't worry, there is nothing wrong; just take a vacation and relax like my niece did" to, "Shame on you for being so upset and not enjoying all the good things you do have in your life!", to: "What, are you crazy! You want this! You can have my kids!" Imagine hearing this one: "I saw your father—he is so wonderful with your sister's children, such a fantastic grandfather. You'd better hurry up—look what you're missing!" Such comments, so out of tune with the subjective reality of the infertile person, can lead to deflation, disequilibrium, loss of self-cohesion and multiple fragmentation experiences, such as hypochondriasis, intellectual disorganization, acting out, despair, and recoiling inward.

It is not only these external commentaries that cause shame and agony for an infertile person, but the internal feedback that the person may be generating as well. For example, some see their infertility as a shameful badge or confirmation that they have lived their life wrong—a visible sign that some deformity or mistake in their life style is responsible for their condition. Maybe they delayed childbearing too long in their quest for a career, or because of difficulty in consolidating a marital relationship. Or maybe they harbor a private remorse or shame over drugs taken, abortions, or sexual activities that may have led to infections. When one attributes the heartbreak of infertility to some malformation in one's life, the private shame and anguish can be devastating.

In summary, when there is an absence of needed affirmation or the presence of invalidating or misattuned and unempathic responses, the shame provoked can lead to despair, anxiety, and rage. Many women have described episodes of throwing or smashing things, especially breaking china or glass, reflecting and expressing their own shattered self-image. And then, as the wish for a child seems to become ever more futile, the very yearning itself may become a source of humiliation. The discomfort deepens as friends and loved ones enjoy their growing families and it becomes painfully evident to everyone that all the time, money, and energy the patient has invested in this goal has been for naught. As a parallel, one would not want others to know that one has "stupidly" invested all one's resources in a stock that has failed. In a way, infertility results in a feeling of having been made a fool of—shamed—by nature, by the medical system, by God.

To sustain a feeling of self-cohesion, a person needs to experience a sense of twinship or "essential alikeness" (Wolf, 1988, p. 55) with others. A sense of comfort and support comes from being with people who seem to share a sense of sameness with us. This twinship feeling seems both to confirm the worth of the current sense of self and to offer hope about the possibility of new skills and competencies. Many women find that the experience of pregnancy and childbirth gives them a special bond with their mothers and with other women who exist now or who came before. Infertile persons must cope with feeling different and excluded from the peer group and the normal life cycle of children and grandchildren, not by choice, but because something is "wrong" with them. Being denied this "twinship" because of infertility can deprive one of the sense of normalcy. Eclipsed by feelings of shame and isolation, people in this state often defensively withdraw, contracting their social exposure even further. Feeling alien, they hide in the shadow.

Finally, one's sense of self can be strengthened and sustained when one feels close to and can emulate the attributes of someone who is, or has been, looked up to and admired; that person is seen as having qualities, or "action patterns" (Goldberg, 1988, p. 214), that one currently lacks but might hope to absorb in the future (idealization). For boys, these ideal images abound in the work world, but for girls (although this situation is slowly changing), the traditional female role models have generally had families and babies as part of the picture. "Contemporary analysts have suggested that positive identification with her mother plays a significant role in a woman's sense of herself as a woman and that her wish to have a baby is derivative of this identification" (Barth, 1993, p. 171). Picturing the images of admired women can fortify a young girl while she is growing up and can be a comfort in times of insecurity. And, even for the grown woman, as Barth (1993) has described, having a child can be seen as a way of enhancing feelings about oneself as a woman or compensating for negative feelings about the self, such as the fear of being inferior or selfish. If there is too big a gap between the ideal self and the actual self, and especially if the woman blames herself for this gap, despair and a sense of traumatic disappointment can ensue (Piers, 1953; Morrison, 1989). The defeated self, feeling powerless to attain dearly held ideals and aspirations, succumbs further to feelings of shame, powerlessness, and depletion. The shadow gains ground.

CONCLUSION

Because shame reflects not only an intrapsychic disturbance in the sense of self, but a disturbance as well in the social context (Morrison, 1989; Broucek, 1991), we must consider not only the patient's relation to himself or herself, but also relations with others. Within treatment, as the patient comes to feel that her pain is deeply understood, shame can begin to subside, thereby paving the way to understanding, and ultimately overcoming, the need for defensive withdrawal. As feelings of shame are labeled and are experienced as more tolerable, patients can be encouraged to share their feelings not just with the analyst but with selected others who will not just pass off the feelings of failure and deprivation as trivial, others who have suffered infertility themselves and with whom patients can experience a kinship.[1] The goal is to help people in the relational surround

---

[1]Certain organizations such as *Resolve* can provide medical information as well as psychological support. A patient can receive mirroring and twinship experiences by contact with others who also suffer from infertility or who even share the same medical condition. In addition to providing information and access to specialized medical treatments, *Resolve* provides access to the names of people who are willing to share their feelings and their actual medical situation. Bonding with other sufferers is important for the healing process because it legitimizes and validates the sufferer's experience, as well as providing a "twinship" reference group of others who are in the same minority. There is also information on "child-free" living and access to others who have survived the trauma of infertility and found a way

to be more attuned to the feelings of inferiority from which the patient suffers and to be more empathically responsive to her emotional state. Feeling fortified by such experiences, the patient might later be encouraged to share her feelings with the fertile world, such as family and friends. The fertile world often does not naturally link shame feelings with inferiority. But since shame is such a universal human emotion, and since everyone has some sort of failure to relate to (loss of job, being rejected from a college, getting a poor work review), patients can, ideally, have a role in educating significant others to sensitivity to shame and thereby feel strengthened by the more attuned responsiveness of important people in their lives. Being able to achieve such understanding in one's relations outside of the therapeutic relationship can by itself counteract the weakening feeling of shame by creating a sense of efficacy and empowerment.

From feeling weakened and withdrawn, the infertility sufferer may ultimately progress to being able to use her own personal reflections as an antidote to shame. Gradually she may be able actually to take pride in having been able to endure the stress. The thought that one has devoted time and energy to a treasured and worthwhile goal is, on its own, an accomplishment and represents something valuable about oneself, independent of outcome. The feeling of having poured oneself into something meaningful, even if the effort it has "failed," can, in itself, become a source of peace and self-esteem. Strengthened by the transference relationship, the person can also take pride in all the things she has done that have been painful, such as going to baby showers, ogling other people's children, sitting through child-centered Christmases—all the ways she has extended herself and been strong enough to overcome the pull toward humiliated retreat, all the ways in which she can feel pride in having been able to be altruistic even in the face of her own grief, feelings of inferiority, anger, intense suffering. Knowing that one has been able to face the world despite these intense private emotions can increase self-esteem and confirm a sense of strength and competency.

The process of coming to terms with and integrating the shame of infertility is a long and gradual one, but it is possible, with empathic attunement from the therapist and from others, for the

---

to move beyond it. Such "idealizable" objects are made accessible by the *Resolve* organization both through writings, in newsletters, or even through telephone contacts.

sense of failure to be transformed into an empathy with oneself, an affirmation of one's strength, an acceptance of one's limits, a pride in one's endurance, and, maybe most of all, an empathy with others, who as partners in the human condition, also face defeats. In time, the shadow cast upon one's life can fade and the light can shine through again.

REFERENCES

Adler, A. (1927), *Understanding Human Nature*, New York: Greenberg.
Barth, F. D. (1993), Conflicts over selfishness: one aspect of some women's wish for a baby. *Psychoanal. Psychol.*, 10:169–185.
Broucek, F. J. (1991), *Shame and the Self*. New York: Guilford Press.
Editorial (1993), Rachel's lament Jacob's Reply. *America*, 169 (16), November 20.
Freud, S. (1905), Three essays on the theory of sexuality. *Standard Edition* 7:125–243. London: Hogarth Press, 1953.
———— (1925), Some psychical consequences of the anatomical distinction between the sexes. *Standard Edition* 19:243–258. London: Hogarth Press, 1953.
Gilligan, C. (1982), *In a Different Voice*. Cambridge, MA: Harvard University Press.
Glazer, E. S. & Cooper S. L. (1988), *Without Child*. Lexington MA: Lexington Books.
Goldberg, A. (1988), *A Fresh Look at Psychoanalysis*. Hillsdale, NJ: The Analytic Press.
Jordan, J., Kaplan, A., Miller, J. B., Stiver, I. & Surrey, J. (1991), *Women's Growth in Connection*, New York: Guilford Press.
Lynd, H. (1958), *On Shame and the Search for Identity*. New York: Harcourt Brace Jovanovich.
Menning, B. E. (1988), *Infertility*. Englewood Cliffs, NJ: Prentice Hall.
Morrison, A. (1989), *Shame: the Underside of Narcissism*. Hillsdale, NJ: The Analytic Press.
———— (1994), The breadth and boundaries of a self-psychological immersion in shame: A one-and-a-half person perspective. *Psychoanal. Dial.*, 4:19–35.
Notman, M. T., Zilbach, J. J., Baker Miller, J. & Nadelson, C. (1986), Themes in psychoanalytic understanding of women: Some reconsiderations of autonomy and affiliation. *J, Amer. Acad. Psychoanal.*, 14:241–252.

Piers, G. (1953), Shame and guilt: A psychoanalytic study. In: *Shame and Guilt*, ed. G. Piers & M. Singer. New York: Norton, pp. 15–55.

Shapiro, C. H. (1988), *Infertility and Pregnancy Loss*. San Francisco: Jossey-Bass.

Sussman, H. (1993), *Psyche and Text*. Albany: State University of New York Press.

Wolf, E. (1988), *Treating the Self*. New York: Guilford Press

IV

CLINICAL AND RELIGIOUS

14

MELVIN R. LANSKY

Envy as Process

It was Melanie Klein (1946, 1957) who first recognized the profound psychoanalytic significance of envy. She clarified and extended Freud's ideas on penis envy to encompass a very wide clinical scope. Envy, in its essence, refers not to the vernacular sense of covetousness—that to envy something is to want to possess it—nor to simple admiration, and certainly not just to envy of or for the penis. In its more basic psychoanalytic sense, envy refers to destructive hatred of the other who, by self-conscious comparison with the self, seems to be better, more intact, more advantaged, more complete, more giving, more ideal, more important, more privileged, and more worthy of love. These Kleinian extensions of Freud's ideas provide the conceptual basis for a deep understanding of malignant, destructive wishes and actions that reside within the darkest part of human nature. Envy is especially malignant because the hate and destruction it engenders are directed at what is seen as good, not as bad. It is this feature of envy that is at risk of being neglected when envy is subsumed simply as an aspect of aggressive conflict.

Envy as a clinical problem is often unacknowledged by the envious person, partly because envy is more often than not disowned and partly because of the analyst's countertransferential difficulties in appreciating and acknowledging the full emotional impact of hatred for what is seen to be good rather than bad or merely frustrating.

Envy is still most appreciated today in Kleinian circles, where it is, in fact, privileged theoretically (Klein, 1946, 1957; Joseph, 1956; Bion, 1959, 1977; Boris, 1994).

While agreeing with the Kleinian emphasis on the clinical centrality of envy, I contend that envy is best viewed as a process, not simply as a manifestation of aggressive drive or destructive instinct. Recognition of the process in which envy is embedded is the key to understanding the clinical phenomenology of envy and its therapeutic handling. Further, such an understanding of envy—not as a thing or as a derivative or as a manifestation of a drive or as an instinct—requires a detailed knowledge of the different ways in which shame and envy are related in the clinical situations.

My contention that envy is a process and in complex ways is related to shame gives rise to epistemologic problems, however, since both shame and envy are often inferred from clinical evidence rather than experienced or acknowledged as such by the shamed or envious person. A full treatment of the topic would require discussion of the bases for such inferences, an issue too complex to be treated here.

Let me emphasize, however, the importance of adopting a perspicacious view of the clinical phenomenology of hostile and destructive behavior. To integrate theory with clinical understanding, one must bear in mind the entire natural history of envy and its embeddedness in narcissistic vulnerability and take into consideration fantasied attempts to establish a stable narcissistic equilibrium, however pathological. Failure to adopt such a broad viewpoint results in one-sided languages that capture only the pervasive, malignant, and destructive aspect of envy and consequent guilt (Kleinian) or the disturbances of narcissistic equilibrium and shame that form the context of envy and the result of exposure of envy (Kohutian). Neither language alone captures the impact of destructive envy either on the individual psyche of the envious person or on the interpersonal surround. The difficulties in attaining and keeping a balanced focus on the full clinical phenomenology place the clinician at risk for *pars pro toto* formulations that result in unbalanced treatment approaches. It is for that reason that I am attempting this sketch of the natural history of envy. I hope that these points will become clearer as my exposition unfolds.

SHAME AND ENVY

The terms shame and envy both require clarification.

Shame can be thought of in the narrow sense as the emotion manifestly painful, the result, developmentally, of interrupted joy (see

Nathanson's discussion of Tomkins, chapter 4, this volume), or, later in one's development, as the emotion resulting from an interrupted sense of the security of one's status or pride because of exposure to others or self as failing to meet certain standards or ideals.

But the family of shame-related phenomena includes much more than manifest, overt shame. The nuances of latent, bypassed, unconscious, or unacknowledged shame or shame-related emotions have come to be appreciated only in the last quarter century following the pioneering work of Helen Block Lewis (1971; see also chapter 5, this volume) and Heinz Kohut (1971; see chapter 3, this volume). Shame is not simply an emotion; it also is a defense against behavior that would lead to the experience of manifest shame. Shame in this sense refers to modesty, humility, and so forth. Shame is also a type of signal anxiety from the superego—the ego ideal in particular—that signals the loss of bonding, rejection, loss of status, denied status, relegation to inferior status or status outside the ken of what others are.

The situation is more complex if, as is usual in the shame prone or narcissistically vulnerable person, these dangers of loss of bond or status or pride are felt in conscious or unconscious fantasy to be connected to defects or basic unlovability in the self. In unconscious fantasy, such attributions concerning shameful status are often experienced as injustice, that is, of having been cheated or damaged. Let us recall the passage from *Richard III* quoted by Freud (1916). It captures this marvelously (see chapter 1, this volume).

> But I, that am not shaped for sportive tricks,
> Nor made to court an amorous looking-glass;
> I, that am rudely stamped, and want love's majesty
> To strut before a wanton, ambling nymph;
> I, that am curtailed of this fair proportion,
> cheated of feature by dissembling nature,
> Deformed, unfinished, sent before my time
> Into this breathing world, scarce half made up,
> And that so lamely and unfashionable
> That dogs bark at me as I halt by them;
>
> And therefore, since I cannot prove a lover,
> To entertain these fair well-spoken days,
> I am determined to prove a villain
> And hate the idle pleasures of these days.

> [*Richard III* (I,i 14–23 and 18–31; text selection, Freud's)]

This shame, through the nexus of unconscious fantasies connected with it, instigates Richard's envy.

Envy, not to be confused with its colloquial usage as simple covetousness, is less often reported clinically as the overt experience of an envious person than it is *inferred* by the analyst from acts or wishes that attack the status or envied attributes of the envied person or, to avoid the experience of envy, the bond with that person. In situations involving envy, we see or infer, as in the case of *Richard III*, a self-conscious experience resulting from a comparison with others, a sense of one's own inferiority or defectiveness that precedes, that is to say, instigates the envious attack. Though neither Shakespeare's verse nor Freud's essay refers specifically to shame or envy, the soliloquy clearly refers to both and to the relation between shame and envy. Except for rare insights into the soul, as given us in Richard's soliloquy, envy is mostly disowned both by others and by self. For reasons that I shall touch on later, disowning is a major clinical feature of envy.

I cannot in a communication of this length explore thoroughly the psychoanalytic literature on envy, much less the philosophic, sociologic, or recent developmental and clinical contributions to our understanding of envy (but see Klein 1946, 1957; Bion, 1959, 1977; Joseph, 1986; Etchegoyan, Lopez, and Rabin, 1987; Lansky, 1992; and Boris, 1994).

THE RELATIONSHIP BETWEEN SHAME AND ENVY

Any attempt to understand the natural history of envy requires an understanding of the complex interrelationships of shame and envy. Shame relates to envy in the following ways:

Envy results from the activation of a *predisposing sense of shame*, portrayed most tangibly in Richard's soliloquy as his sense of ugliness and physical inferiority, which make him unable to see himself as lovable.

> I that am rudely stamped, and want love's majesty
> To strut before a wanton, ambling nymph

> [*Richard III* I,i 16–17]

A surprisingly prevalent component of the preexisting sense of shame that gives rise to envy is a sense of *feeling as though one has become like the same-sex parent who has been held in contempt;*

that is to say, the apparent loss of a struggle against an identification (Greenson, 1954) with the same sex parent felt to be contemptible, especially by the opposite-sex parent.

Associative   connections   and   attributions   (unconscious fantasies) link this sense of defect to one's unlovability and deprivation. Richard sees himself as unlovable and deprived. This is sensed specifically as injustice—as his having been cheated.

> I, that am curtailed of fair proportion,
> Cheated of feature by dissembling nature,
> Deformed, unfinished, sent before my time
> Into this breathing world, scarce half made up

[lines 18–12].

The self-conscious comparison and sense of deficiency, deprivation, and unlovability are linked with the imminent and inescapable danger of loss of the possibility of lovability; of a fair chance to bond, to be loved, to be as others are; or to the likelihood of outright rejection. Associations connected with gender, race, class, and so forth may be involved, as may be unconscious identification, especially with the parent of the same sex. It is these shame fantasies that make the experience of shame (the emotion) unbearable. (See also Rizzuto, 1991.)

Envy is instigated by an experience of shame. The predisposing features, which always form the backdrop of the envious person's makeup, combine with shame fantasies and with circumstances that give rise to an experience of shame. In the case of Richard, peacetime, when the aggressive, entirely masculine activity of war is replaced by circumstances in which his physical unattractiveness and his unlovability make him see himself as unsuitable for amorous competition, is a circumstance that shames him by comparison with others. It is this combination of predisposing sense of defectiveness in the self, associated fantasies, and the immediate sense of shame from comparisons in precipitating circumstances that give rise to envy.

> And, therefore, since I cannot prove a lover, . . .
> I am determined to prove a villain . . .

[lines 28, 30]

This upsurge of shame usually arises when shame arising from self-conscious self-evaluative comparisons is unacknowledged as such; that is, it remains unconscious (Lewis, 1971; Scheff, 1990; chapter 5, this volume). Shame remains unacknowledged if its acknowledgment exposes something about the self that is felt to be unbearable. An upsurge of shame may occur especially at times of change or impending separation; in the therapeutic situation, around the times of vacations or termination. These predicaments instigate comparisons of the patient's feeling of lack of intactness with the (imagined) intactness and perfect emotional equilibrium of the therapist, who is free to enjoy life without needing the patient as the patient needs the therapist. The ensuing upset and turmoil are frequently (albeit misleadingly) covered over in dynamic formulations with the oversimplified label of separation anxiety.

Exposure of the self as envious gives rise to shame. An obvious corollary of this observation is that shame very often ensues from the interpretation of envy in the context of psychotherapy or psychoanalysis. This reaction to exposure as envious includes both obvious, narcissistic wounding and acute shame reactions and more subtle varieties of the spectrum of shame: not getting the point, not understanding, not appreciating the significance of the interpretation (Bion, 1959), leaving treatment, or attempting to relocate the shame onto others. The interpretation of envy (Etchegoyan et al., 1987) is a difficult matter especially until the time in treatment when the patient's awareness of his or her envy generates for the most part bearable rather than unbearable shame. Whether shame is bearable or unbearable is a neglected topic by and large for our theory of affect and of technique. The upsurge of shame when envy is exposed is, of course, one reason why envy so often remains disowned or hidden. Exposure of the self as attempting to tear down the envied other to even the score, even the field, surpass, or get even is humiliating. So is the exposure of the obverse, of grandiose daydreams, dreams of glory, to enhance or build oneself up following an experience of shameful comparison (Goldberger, 1995; see also James Thurber's (1947) *The Secret Life of Walter Mitty*). In both cases, exposure of the priority of adjusting one's narcissistic equilibrium, one's absolute uniqueness (see chapter 3, this volume), evidences unharnessed, infantile grandiosity and egotism that often give rise to fulminant shame reactions.

A NATURAL HISTORY

The foregoing preliminaries on the relationship between shame and envy put me in a position to sketch a natural history of envy, that is, to attempt a perspicuous view of envy as a process. This process includes predisposing factors (preexisting shame, conscious or unconscious); a precipitant (a self-conscious comparison); an instigatory experience (a shame experience); unconscious fantasies that make shame unbearable; the act or fantasy of envious attack; and the reactions, conscious or unconscious, to one's own envy. Although this sketch is, of necessity, overly schematic and somewhat mechanistic, I hope that it will help to locate the situation of envy as it is embedded in relationships of affects to each other, to unconscious fantasy, and to precipitating disturbance in narcissistic equilibrium.

1. *Predisposing (preexisting) shame* has been discussed in the preceding section.

2. *Precipitant*: Envy, like shame, is a self-conscious emotion. *Envy arises as a result of comparison*, conscious or unconscious, with either a source of love or a competitor for love or ideals or standards by the attainment of which one aspires in fantasy to attain love or the restoration of status as absolutely unique in the eyes of a love object or in one's own self appraisal (see Morrison, 1989; chapter 3, this volume). Comparisons—conscious or disowned—with one from whom one wants such esteem and status disturb narcissistic equilibrium when that other is seen to be full, abundant, giving, and intact in comparison with the envious person's neediness, felt deprivation, abjectness, and lack of status. With a competitor for love, envy arises when comparisons place that other in a light that makes the other seem more advantaged, more accomplished, more lovable, more successful in attaining goals and ideals than is the envying person. The impossibility of attaining a sense of lovability and absolute uniqueness in the face of goals, ambitions, and standards generates envy, even in the absence of a comparison with a particular person.

In the case of Richard III, the end of the war and the advent of peace that form the immediate context of the play's opening generate in Richard a sense of his own deficiency by comparison with those who are suited to the amorous pleasures of peacetime.

3. *Instigation*: These comparisons have in common that *they instigate envy because they give rise to an experience of shame*. That experience of shame need not be—in fact often is not—a conscious experience of the emotion, shame; more likely, in the case of bypassed shame, unacknowledged because it is unbearable, and transformed into rage (Lewis, 1971). In this sense, envy can be viewed as a variant of narcissistic rage (see also Morrison, 1989).

Shame that is unbearable dislodges the shamed person from the social and moral order. I believe, though I cannot develop the argument in detail here, that this is what Freud (1920) meant by the destructive instinct (Thanatos). Unacknowledged shame turns to narcissistic rage, one variant of which is envy. It is important to consider what it is, then, that makes shame unbearable as opposed to bearable.

4. *Unbearability: Shame becomes unbearable not so much because of the intensity of the emotion itself as because of its signal function.* That is to say, shame *is connected to preexisting unconscious fantasies that signify to the shamed person rejection from the social order, unlovability, loss of status, or relegation to inferior status.* Shame, or the imminence of shame experiences, serves as a signal of the danger of rejection, failure, and narcissistic mortification. Such a danger can occur only with (conscious or unconscious) preexisting fantasies about oneself as deficient, deprived, defective, unlovable, and unloved. This experience of oneself may be based on interpretations of prior experience, on actual deficits, or on a mood of deprivation that remains from early life. Such a sense of self accrues fantasies that are associations to this basic feeling. It is this mood, consequent fantasies, and the association of these with (what might be to others) even minor shame experiences in the here-and-now that must be analyzed in the treatment situation if malignant envy is to be successfully addressed. These fantasies include but are not limited to the following:

That one's being damaged or defective is such that it places the envying one outside the ken of lovability and meaningful bonding and dooms hope for the attainment of absolute uniqueness.

That the shameful comparison confirms that one deserved the humiliating role assignment made early in life or that one has become like an object of identification (often, in my clinical experience, the same-sex parent) held in contempt by the other parent.

The pain of comparison is accompanied by a distinct flavor of injustice. The comparison is seen as unfair, the envying person feels cheated or damaged, and the comparison situation seen as personified—cheated by someone.

That such unfairness carries with it an exemption from the moral order and an oblivion to the consequences. The envious attack is outside the order of justice. The rules are not felt to apply in the experience of the envious person.

This sense of righteous rage is sometimes accompanied by the psychological state of oblivion to consequences. (Those made anxious by anger are usually most anxious about this feature of narcissistic rage in particular; that is, that narcissistic rage, of which envy is one type, is accompanied by the short- or long-term risk of utter oblivion to the destructiveness of such rage.)

A presupposition of (i.e., fantasy underlying) envy is that the project of attaining absolute lovability and uniqueness is endangered by the comparison. The fantasy is that tearing down the envied person will somehow restore justice, even the field of play, or in some unspecified way enhance the envious person. The experience of envy carries with it the sense of removal of the last obstacle to union with the good (Katz, 1988).

The comparison, then, is seen as finalizing, confirming, or exposing the fact that the subject (in relation to an internal agent) is outside, rejected, inferior, deprived, unlovable, whereas the envied person is inside, bonded, secured, unique, and lovable.

The experience of the envious person is: because of the envied person, I am outside of the conditions set by an internal agent for status, pride, love, or connectedness. The comparison gives rise, then, not only to shame, but, because of status as inferior, failed, or rejected, shame that is unbearable. Envious tearing down of others emanates from the fantasy of undoing or reversing this situation. Such a fantasy, associated with the shame experience that makes it unbearable, is at the center of the psychotherapeutic or psychoanalytic handling of envy. Until it is analyzed and worked through, the experience of shame, so unbearable that it cannot be acknowledged, unites, by way of the unconscious shame fantasy, with destructive narcissistic rage, of which envy is one type. Envy, in fact, can be seen as one type of defense against unbearable shame.

5. *The envious act or intent* is more often than not inferred from the clinical phenomenology rather than experienced directly as envy. That is to say, envious intent rather than being manifest, is most often repressed or disowned and inferred from its impact on relationships. I cannot deal here with the details of the complex topic of the bases for the clinical inferences of envy.

6. *The reaction to envious wishes or acts* may be more prominent than envy or destructiveness itself. Such reactions include:

Conscious guilt (remorse) for the harm done to others. Frequently, remorse (concern for damage to others) covers over the intense shame that results from exposure of envious intent.

Unconscious guilt inferred from feelings of depletion, inhibition, unworthiness, fear of separation, or repetitive acts of otherwise mysterious self-sabotage: Since the effects of unconscious guilt are both weakening and disempowering, they ultimately synergize with and amplify the sense of shame.

Projection of destructive attack outside of self or of a relationship so that it is felt to be coming in from outside. Such projection is often deployed in dyadic relationships, where it is experienced by the dyad as free of conflict, and evil and destructive hate are projected outside of the relationship. Such projection is then buttressed by unacknowledged provocation. Regressive dyads felt manifestly to be entirely supportive and conflict free are fertile ground for such projections of envy. Many "selfobject" relationships and psychotherapeutic dyads seem manifestly free of conflict because the envy is projected outward. Such is the case with Richard III's striving for power (Nietzsche, 1885; Adler, 1927; chapter 7, this volume).

7.   Shame resulting from *exposure as envious* is either defended against by disowning envious intent; oblivion to the consequences—withdrawal, aloofness, distancing, not getting the point—attacks on linking (Bion, 1959)—or is experienced as mortifying shame (Lansky, 1996).

8.   The entire process, whether resulting from envious deed or wish, serves to amplify and confirm the shame fantasies discussed under 3.

CONCLUSIONS

This preliminary schema of envy as a process will, I hope, add to our understanding of why it is that, however pervasive envy may be in the therapeutic situation, it is difficult to focus on therapeutically. The difficulties in so doing all have to do with the veiled or disowned quality of envy as it appears clinically and with the intimate relationship of envy to shame. Envy hides shame and is, as well, hidden itself. It is for this reason that a feel for the natural history of envy, and not just an interpretive attitude, is required of the analyst.

The shameful sense of self that forms part of the predisposition to malignant envy, the shame or fear of it when one is exposed as envious, and the elaborated fantasies associated with shame that make the experience of the emotion shame unbearable—all these must receive a sustained and nuanced therapeutic focus for the problem of envy to be modified by therapeutic intervention. That they are hidden, screened, defended against by envy, which is itself usually disowned, compounds not only the tenacity of the envious patient's defensive organization, but also the analyst's sure-footedness in attaining a useful therapeutic focus on envy.

Specifics of the technique of analyzing envy carry us too far afield. It is my hope that I have helped provide a clear enough view of the phenomenology of envy so that clearer thinking on the specifics of technique can follow.

REFERENCES

Adler, A. (1927), *Understanding Human Nature*. New York: Greenberg.
Bion, W. R. (1959), Attacks on linking. *Internat. J. Psycho-Anal.*, 40:308-318.
——— (1977), *Seven Servants*. New York: Aronson.
Boris, H. (1994), *Envy*. Northvale, NJ: Aronson.
Etchegoyan, R. H., Lopez, B. M. & Rabin, M. (1987), On envy and how to interpret it. *Internat. J. Psycho-Anal.*, 68:49-61.
Freud, S. (1916), Some character types met with in analytic work. *Standard Edition*. 14:311-333. London: Hogarth Press, 1957.
Goldberger, M. (1995), The clinical use of daydreams in analysis. *J. Clin. Psycho-Anal.* 4:11-21.
Greenson, R. (1954), The struggle against identification. *J. Amer. Psychoanal. Assn.*, 2:200-217.
Joseph, B. (1986), Envy in everyday life. *Psychoanal. Psychother.*, 2:13-22.
Katz, J, (1988), *Seductions of Crime*. New York: Basic Books.
Klein, M. (1946), Notes on some schizoid mechanisms. *Internat. J. Psycho-Anal.*, 37:99-110.
——— (1957), *Envy and Gratitude*. London: Tavistock.
Kohut, H. (1971), *The Analysis of the Self*. New York: International Universities Press.
Lansky, M. R. (1992), *Fathers Who Fail*. Hillsdale, NJ: The Analytic Press.
——— (1996), Shame and suicide in Sophocles' *Ajax*. *Psychoanal. Quart.*, 65:761-786.
Lewis, H. B. (1971), *Shame and Guilt in Neurosis*. New York: International Universities Press.
Morrison, A. P. (1989), *Shame*. Hillsdale, NJ: The Analytic Press.
Nietzsche, F. (1885), *Thus Spoke Zarathustra*. In: *The Portable Nietzsche*, ed. W. Kaufmann. New York: Viking Press, 1954.

Rizzuto, A.-M. (1991), Shame in psychoanalysis: The function of unconscious fantasies. *Internat. J. Psycho-Anal.,* 72:297–312.

Scheff, T. (1990), *Microsociology.* Chicago: University of Chicago Press.

Thurber, J. (1942) The Secret Life of Walter Mitty. In: *My World and Welcome to It.* New York: Harcourt, Brace, Jovanovich.

15

DONALD L. NATHANSON

Affect Theory and the Compass of Shame

What differentiates affect theory from all previous systems for the explanation of human emotion is its insistence that the forms of emotion seen in adults are not the innate mechanisms themselves, but actually ideo-affective complexes made possible after years of individual experience with innate affect. As Silvan Tomkins said so often, the crisp edges of affect that we can identify with such ease in the neonate are blurred in the adult just as geologically young mountains are sharp and older ones are rounded. Although the newborn infant opens its mouth to scream in rage as instructed by the innate mechanism, just a few months later the same child will purse its lips and grimace rather than give forth the full-throated yell. We socialize children to make less noise, to mute the display of affect so they are less likely to take over our shared spaces. By the time we reach adulthood, we may be so limited in our expression of anger that some therapist may encourage us to shelve our embarrassment at being seen angry, to give up control and utter a scream that is primal because it comes from an era of our development when affect, the contribution of ancient subcortical structures, had not yet been placed under neocortical control. A science of emotion that mistook the affect production of an adult as equivalent to that of an infant, an archaeological theory that tried to explain the innate from the derived, might see the pursed lip as primal and the scream as primitive. Tomkins asked us to start with the world of the infant and build to the experience of the adult.

So it is for shame, an emotion described enough differently by its many scholars that it was not until Wurmser (1981) elucidated a shame family of emotions defined somewhat differently for and by each of us that we could move to a more general sense of our topic. Embarrassment, ridicule, contempt, the experience of being put down or shunned, humiliation, mortification—all these and more Wurmser explained as feeling different in ways that were more personal than scientific, more situational than innate. The work of Tomkins gives further credence to Wurmser's insight and allows us to extend the compass of shame much further toward another realm of clinical utility. I have defined four poles of this compass, four libraries of scripted behavior leading to four quite different realms of personal experience. In order to visit these libraries we need a brief tour of the building in which they are housed.

The work of Silvan Tomkins allows us to view all affect as a system of spotlights that takes one element of the possibly visible scenery and makes it the focus of our attention. As the mobile life forms evolved to assess so many possible sources of information, the ability to assign salience (and thus manage situations with the most appropriate part of our equipment) conferred greater ability to prosper. There are only nine innate affects, each a separate and different form of analogic amplifier of whatever has triggered it; nine spotlights, each a different color and capable of being assembled into a light show of tremendous variability. It is these nine mechanisms, built into the basic wiring of the human and responsible for all the action and power we used to attribute to the drive system, that govern how we will behave when we pay attention to anything. Nine separate forms of attention, nine completely different kinds of consciousness; combined with each other and all the possible sources or triggers of affect, a simple palette makes a seemingly infinite tapestry of human experience.

AFFECT THEORY

The affect we know best from our own lives, of course, is the one that covers the range of reaction to novelty from mild interest to wild excitement. Tomkins (1962) pointed out that interest-excitement, like all the affects, is displayed primarily on the face even though it involves characteristic vocalizations, accelerations of pulse and rate of breathing, and changes in posture. We know it immediately by the furrowed brow, the attitude of "track, look, listen," the slightly opened mouth, and the kind of rapt attention normally seen when any of us studies new material or is "entranced" by a novel stimulus. It would be difficult to imagine school, sport, study, entertainment, or most personal relatedness without the phenomenology of interest-excitement. Our understanding of shame is entirely dependent on the recognition of interest-excitement as an innate mechanism.

Steeped in a late 19th-century scientific culture that understood the brain as a tool for the management of energy rather than of information, and hoping to fulfil the early 20th century quest for grand unifying theories, Freud believed in a primarily sexual life force he called libido and misunderstood all excitement as a subset of sexual arousal, which is only one of its many possible triggers. The positive effects of this scientific assumption included the explosive interest in sexuality that transformed Western culture and our celebration of inner looking.

Since the culture of his time literally forbade free and open discussion of sexual wishes by shaming them into secrecy, Freud developed a psychoanalytic method that defined as "resistance" any embarrassment at sexual disclosure and overrode the shame that had stifled discussion. Once in the secret room, Freud tended to ignore its doorway. Furthermore, one of Freud's major contributions to the art of psychotherapy was his discovery that, if the analyst reacted minimally to the verbal and affective output of the patient, the resulting breach of normal conversational style increased the flow of information from the patient. Within this system it was necessary for the analyst to forbear from visible resonance with the patient's affect lest the analyst's affective contribution distort the process through which information was emerging from repression. The analyst might shape the flow of information by carefully phrased interpretations presented with exquisite neutrality, thus allowing the patient to process the cognitive part of the analyst's contribution and not be confused or misled by the analyst's affect. In my psychiatric residency (1966–69), lecturers and supervisors stressed that people could be interested in or excited by nonsexual ideation only when these affects had become separated from sexual arousal by repression and disavowal, and they suggested that it was more than a bit shameful for us to be excited in the therapeutic situation. It was a simple and unavoidable artifact of the technique invented by the founder of psychoanalysis that distracted scholarly attention away from the emotionality of both interest and shame, a point particularly poignant when the connection between them is made through affect theory.

So normal, so ubiquitous is interest-excitement that untrained observers forget to study it because they consider interest as the baseline or background of life. Within affect theory, we understand it as a patterned response not to the content of a message, but to some quality of the way that information has entered the central nervous system. We become interested only when information is acquired at an optimal gradient, at just the right increase in the amount of data per unit of time.

Only two affects animate the good feelings of life—interest-excitement, this evolved, programmed response to an optimal gradient of stimulus acquisition; and enjoyment-joy, the range of programmed responses to any decrease in the preexisting level of the flow of information into the system. We laugh when the decrease is rapid, smile when it is more gradual, and merely relax when our load is relieved even more gradually. An orgasm, the glass of water that slakes raging thirst, the Rolaid that really brings relief, and a good joke are all alike in that some stimulus source is reduced although at somewhat different rates of speed and in vastly different situations.

If it is through interest-excitement that the affect system registers and amplifies stimuli that cascade into our sensors from sources outside and inside the body at an optimal rate of acquisition, then how have we evolved to handle information that enters at a higher than optimal gradient? Through an almost macabre exaggeration of the attitude we saw as "track, look, listen" in the positive affect of interest, the face becomes frozen in a stare at or to the side of whatever has now evoked the range of affects from fear to terror, while the warm and rosy cheek of excitement is chilled and blanched. Pulse and respiration, amplified so pleasantly in excitement, are increased to thunderous and uncomfortable degree in fear-terror; this is the pounding heart of panic, the lump in the throat, the feeling that you're going to die that characterizes the upper end of this particular range. (It is lack of awareness or disavowal of minor grades of this negative affect that leads people with panic *disorder* to concentrate their attention solely on the meaning for the safety of their cardiovascular apparatus of this moiety of the affect. They miss the entire meaning of an affect—a mechanism that has evolved to call attention to its source—and instead get stuck in one of its subroutines.) The pure innate affect we see in the infant is but a small part of the picture of fear, for our growing experience with each of the possible sources of each affect forms the library to which we develop the associative links that make up our emotional life. Basch (1976) suggested that we use the term affect to denote the basic physiological mechanisms involved, *feeling* to represent the perceived or felt quality of the affect, and *emotion* to encompass the coassembly of an affect with our memory of previous situations in which that mechanism had been triggered. It is easy to understand that affect is biology, whereas emotion is biography.

What links the sound of a pistol shot, a hand or thunder clap, a scream in the otherwise quiet night, and a host of other sudden, brief stimuli is not our eventual cognitive assessment of the source that has triggered an affect over the range from surprise to startle, but its stimulus contour. Information that comes into the affect system with a rapid, sudden onset and an equally rapid offset, what in mathematics is called a "square wave," sets in motion the briefest of the affects. Surprise-startle provides a mechanism that, in the few hundredths of a seconds it lasts, turns off our attention to any other source of affect and prepares us to focus on what next will become the subject of our attention. Useful as this may be in normal life, when coassembled with terrifying scenes of battle that set in motion violent upheavals of the cardiovascular system, it may become part of the symptom complex of post traumatic stress disorder and require biological intervention.

Just as we have evolved to register and amplify differently three ranges of increasing stimulus gradient, and any decreasing gradient, we own two further innate affect mechanisms that amplify and call attention to stimuli that are held constant at higher than optimal levels. The sobbing affect of distress-anguish, which itself is of constant density and certainly a non-optimal experience, is another form of analogic amplifier. We see babies sob and cry (corners of the mouth down in the "omega of melancholy," eyebrows arched) when they are cold, hungry, lonely, tired, or in mild pain—all of which are constant density stimuli. It is axiomatic that no affect is linked to any particular source. (Rank, 1952, was wrong when he declared the birth cry a specific message about separation anxiety. It favored evolution for us to develop a system that could call attention to whatever needed attention acutely, no matter what its source.) Finally, when stimulus density is steady but even higher than that needed to trigger distress-anguish, a mechanism is set in motion that tenses muscles all over the body including clenched fist and flailing limbs, and produces the roar and reddened face of rage. Anger-rage calls attention not to the "reasons" one might be angry at something, but to nothing other than the contour of a triggering stimulus. We know your anger and my anger from the commonality of the situations that share this quality of steady-state overmuch, scenes that come to form complex emotions as they connect with the reference library of the angry mind. Affect, says Tomkins, makes good things better and bad things worse; the affects are a system of motivation because the good ones feel really good, and the unpleasant ones feel really bad.

If each affect is an amplifying analogue of its stimulus, then each affect itself is a competent trigger for more affect. Any time we experience an affect, that affect is likely to produce even more affect in us, simply because it bears the same stimulus contours as the original situation that triggered it and is an amplification of it. Affect tends to stop as soon as we pay attention to its source, and to get more intense as long as we ignore it. Similarly, since each affect is expressed on the display board of the face and by highly specific odors, cries, and postures, each affect that we express is also a competent trigger for that same affect in another person who happens to be watching or listening to us. Normally, we dig deeply into memory to locate previous episodes of any triggered affect in order to understand better the present episode. Basch (1983) pointed out that when we experience an affect because we have been in the presence of another person (infant or adult) who is broadcasting that affect (this is called "interaffectivity"), we perform the same procedure. Interaffectivity is innate because of the way the affect system has evolved, but mature empathy—the product of what we experience through interaffectivity and what we know from our own life history—depends on our ability to "make sense" of the affect we have experienced while interacting with someone else.

One of the peculiarities of human life is that we become so interested in other humans. Many scholars and philosophers maintain that we have evolved to become attached to each other, and they believe that such mechanisms cause us to have a built-in, primary attachment to the caregiver. Despite the importance of such a belief to Erich Fromm (1941) the emotional connection between mother and child is not present before birth, for there is no telephone-like structure or system linking the fetus with the mind of the mother. Others have suggested that we have evolved a biological system for attachment that is latent in the brain until developed or brought on line in the first two years of life. Elsewhere (Nathanson, 1992), I have commented at length on the distractingly colorful history of this theory: 1) the basic concepts that underlie attachment theory are based on Konrad Lorenz's work with aquatic fowls (described in Hess, 1958), life forms with neither an affect system nor facial affect display; and 2) Bowlby's (1982) work on infants shorn from their parents during war was undertaken in complete ignorance of the importance to attachment of the facial display of affect!

I believe that, rather than possessing any firmware specific for attachment, we humans are entirely separate entities launched at birth into a vast interpersonal void and become able to form attachments only because our ability to sense the inner world of others is made possible by the assessment of data derived from the analysis of interaffectivity. I have described as an *empathic wall* (Nathanson, 1986) the learned mechanisms that allow us to prevent such interaffectivity, and stressed their importance in the development of individual competence. We would be far less effective as adults were we forever at the mercy of the affects being broadcast into our environment by others, just as we would be terribly alone were we unable to drop the empathic wall and sense the inner world of others by sharing their affects. The simple fact that each human is a powerful broadcaster of the positive affects interest-excitement and enjoyment-joy makes us focus a tremendous amount of attention on others as a source of pleasant experience and to become extraordinarily sensitive to anything that can limit such pleasure. I believe that interpersonal closeness is entirely dependent on the history of our affective interaction and not on the operation of a built-in attachment system. If the mutualization of positive affect draws people together, then anything that interferes with positive affect must pull them apart.

There are, of course, other mechanisms built into our makeup, mechanisms important for the maintenance of life, capable of affecting our sense of well-being, and of importance in our interpersonal relationships. The basic difference between the system of drives and the system of affects, Tomkins (1962, 1992) points out, is that the affects call attention to whatever they have amplified, even though they contain no information about the content of that stimulus. Affect, then, is motivating but not localizing. It is through interaffectivity that the crying infant triggers distress-anguish in the mother, who then rushes to her child able only to guess which among many possible steady-state stimuli was responsible for this moment of motivation. She will have to examine the baby to find the specific cause of its tears. But the reason we do not have to learn how to be hungry, or that it is time to urinate, defecate, sleep, or seek sexual congress, is that we have evolved with a system of drives, an entirely separate group of mechanisms that have no motivational power whatever but inform us that a need now exists and tell us the specific location where that need must be satisfied. Like any other stimulus capable of triggering interest-excitement, the mechanism of sexual arousal starts gradually and increases at a gradient perfectly evolved for that affect. If it came on us more rapidly, it would trigger fear-terror; if suddenly, it would startle us. Your own personal experience, or that confided by patients in therapy, should confirm that steady-state sexual arousal is not only unpleasant but a competent source of distress or anger.

Hunger points us to the mouth with exquisite specificity, as does sexual arousal to the genital and a full bladder or rectum to our excretory function. We can ignore any of these sources of information when something else manages to trigger affect that gets our attention more effectively than drive-based data. Yet hunger is so vital to survival, and so powerful a trigger for distress-anguish or interest-excitement, that we would devour anything in sight were we not protected by two mechanisms Tomkins calls "drive auxiliaries." When something smells awful, no matter how enticing it looks, a mechanism is triggered in which the nose and upper lip are wrinkled and the head drawn back from the offending odor. This dissmell (a term coined by Tomkins) is capable of turning off hunger for that specific substance no matter how ravenous we were only a moment earlier. Additionally, when some substance has gotten past the sentry of the nose and entered the mouth, if foul-tasting, it will produce a programmed response in which the tongue is thrust out, the lower lip protruded, and the head moved forward to assist the expulsion of the distasteful substance. The mechanism we call disgust will also turn off hunger for a specific substance, no matter how hungry we had been just before it was triggered. These two protocols have evolved to the status of affects even though they arose as monitors of the drive hunger—dissmell monitoring interpersonal distance (who wants to be close to a "stinker"?) and disgust keeping us away from people we once loved but now cannot stomach. Although the affect, the physiological mechanism for shame, is quite different from these two drive auxiliaries, it is not possible to understand the mature experience of shame apart from its later assembly with them.

Just as dissmell and disgust have evolved to turn off hunger no matter how powerful, the affect underlying the complex and varied phenomenology of shame starts out as a simple mechanism that turns down the powerful positive affects of interest-excitement and enjoyment-joy when something has interfered with their operation. Think of it this way: if interest-excitement and enjoyment-joy are analogic amplifiers of rising or falling gradients, then these two affect mechanisms stand in relation to these gradients as in classical Newtonian algebra the equation for the first derivative of a curve might relate to the equation for the curve itself. By analogy, then, the mechanism for the "affect auxiliary" Tomkins calls shame-humiliation is set in motion only when something impedes the operation of the already triggered affects of interest-excitement or enjoyment-joy. The new affect is then an analogic amplifier of *impediment*, and stands in relation to the original situation (which only a moment ago triggered positive affect) as a second derivative of that rising or falling gradient. *Shame-humiliation has nothing at all to do with human relationships unless and until a relationship triggers positive affect!* If there has been nothing to trigger positive affect, there is no chance that shame can become involved. If I become interested in a situation or enjoy some source that has nothing at all to do with another person and something impedes (but does not terminate) the continuation of my positive affect, then the intrusion or impediment itself will trigger shame affect that turns down or further impedes my experience of positive affect.

No matter how much you may want to say that a particular moment of shame occurred *because* an exhibitionistic urge was revealed, or that someone "internalized" an episode of inadequacy or related an incident to some aspect of the self, it just isn't true. We can cry when we are not hungry, become enraged when overloaded by stimuli that have no dynamic significance whatever, and experience a moment of shame affect triggered in a situation that has nothing to do with the nature of self or other. The best analogy is to an automobile, which can be used to drive the family to the seashore, to assist at a burglary, or to ram into and kill a crowd of children. In each of these three scenes, the automobile is nothing more than a mechanism. So it is for each and every affect. Affects are always—and only—somatic mechanisms that amplify their triggering stimuli and thus bring them into consciousness. The reason there is so much shame associated with sexual arousal is simply and only that the stimulus gradient produced by arousal is a perfect trigger for interest-excitement, and to the extent that this excitement runs high, the possibility of impediment increases unless fulfillment is guaranteed. Adolescence is an era of shame for nearly every human because the sexual system has newly been turned on to its fullest during a period of development in which it is most likely to be impeded. Empirically, most of us learn to increase the level of our excitement whenever we encounter mild levels of shame during a sexual interchange; here the hope is that the new level of excitement will exceed the threshold at which this particular impediment can trigger shame. Much of the entertainments attended by adolescents and young adults involve opportunities for such sequences of excitement, shame, and highly magnified countervailing excitement.

THE SEQUENCE OF SHAME

We need only one more realm of terminology before we can enter the library where our scripts for the management of shame are stored. No matter how many times I tell you that shame involves amplification of an impediment to positive affect, you will respond that you know quite well what it feels like when you are embarrassed, and I have provided no links between that complex feeling-state and the neurobiology of affect theory. What happens between here and there to create the colorful palette of shame? What is the sequence of events leading to the experience of shame? First of all, shame can be triggered only when the organism has already been in the thrall of a positive affect. Next, there must be some event that interferes with the operation of that good scene.

Imagine that you are locked in mutual gaze—that most intimate of human activities—with your beloved and that both of you are laughing in shared pleasure at some fond memory. For no reason we can determine (an errant thought, a distracting association, some new idea that had been developing in background and now triggers enough affect to enter consciousness), the merest alteration in the expression of joy flickers over the display board of your partner's face. Love permits the mutualization of affect through affective resonance; it is one of the best reasons to drop the empathic wall to experience the world of another. Notwithstanding that this partner loves you not a whit less, you have experienced an impediment to your own experience of enjoyment-joy, an impediment that must now trigger shame affect.

All at once the physiological protocol for the affect is set in motion. Shame affect alters muscle tone in the head and neck, accounting for the bowed head so characteristic of the experience. The eyes are lowered, moved away from the previously enjoyable scene. Blood rushes to the cheeks, causing the blush, and for a moment we are unable to think clearly. This cognitive shock, to which Sartre (1948) referred as "an internal hemorrhage for which I am always unprepared" (p. 261), has occurred not because we have lost any of our neocortical prowess, but because all higher thought is focused where affect shines its spotlight. The positive affect that only a moment ago held sway has now been interrupted by the powerful negative affect of shame, the painful amplification of impediment; until we recover mental balance by shifting to where shame affect points its light, our thinking is as inchoate as Darwin (1872) described it a century ago.

Swiftly we recover from the abrupt shift in our ability to think about what was going on only a moment ago and enter the cognitive phase of the shame experience. It is the biographical part of the shame experience that happens next as we scroll through our memory of all previous moments in which physiological shame was released in order to make more sense of this particular episode. Elsewhere (Nathanson, 1992; chapter 4, this volume) I have outlined the list of all possible experiences within which this affect is normally triggered. Involved is the whole library of shame and pride— matters of size, shape, skill, success or failure at competition and sexuality, and the entire realm of how we are seen by others and the degree of our intimacy with them. No matter which category houses the triggering incident, thoughts referable to all eight categories appear any time the physiological affect mechanism is triggered.

Now that we have placed the current episode of shame affect within our history of previous similar episodes, it is time to make some decision. Shame, like all the affects, turns our attention to its trigger, here whatever has become an impediment to ongoing interest or contentment. Usually it calls to consciousness that we are less than we might have liked, that we do not measure up to our best hopes for ourselves. Now we must figure out how to use this new information, which conflicts with our sense of identity. Sometimes, rarely, we chuckle at the revelation that we are more paunchy or gray or stupid or ungainly or sexless than we had hoped; we chuckle and revise downward our self-esteem. More often, I fear, we defend against this knowledge by placing it in some other context.

Early in our schooling all of us were taught that one of the most important characteristics of living systems is that they respond to stimuli; the language of stimulus–response pairs dominated under- graduate education in psychology. Now we know that no event can be considered to be a stimulus unless it first triggers an affect, after which the nature of that stimulus is highlighted and our response engaged. Everywhere we must shift our language to that of stimulus- affect-response sequences and recognize that what we call an emotion is actually the gestalt formed by a scene in which these three events take place rather quickly. For shame, the possible responses form only four groups; I have characterized these as the Compass of Shame (see chapter 4, Figure 1). The four poles of the compass act as storage libraries for the many scripts that each may be quite different from the other but have in common the central directive that when shame affect is triggered, the individual will engage in *withdrawal*, *attack self*, *avoidance*, or *attack other* behavior.

When we allow full sway to the physiological part of the affect, shame makes us turn away from others in the mode we call *withdrawal*. At the more healthy or normal end of its spectrum, this set of scripts includes shyness and all the ways we hide when embarrassed; at the pathological end of its range lie the harrowing

illnesses sometimes called "depressions" when one is unable to greet
the eyes of another for long periods of time. Prolonged silence in a
therapy session is shame until proved otherwise; as Stoller (1987)
said, "I am uneasy when colleagues say 'resistance' or 'the
resistance' as if they believe in a special force with roots deep in
mystery. . . . Most resistance, to me, is simply a person's awareness—
conscious, preconscious, and unconscious—of fearing feeling
humiliated" (pp. 305–306).

Yet to give in to shame means that one really will be shorn from
the rest of humanity, an isolation all the more punishing for those
who have done poorly navigating the tricky shoals of independence
from others. The *attack self* pole of the compass is a devil's bargain
in which I realize that, since I seem to have no choice about
experiencing shame (it having been triggered for reasons I cannot
control and will be triggered again and again because I am helpless
in a loveless world with no one to solace my wounds), I would feel
safer shamed within a relationship rather than alone. Whereas most
of us, most of the time, try to avoid feeling inferior to others, in the
attack self mode we take pains to define ourselves as lesser then the
other person with whom we are interacting. At the normal end of
the spectrum, these are all the times we are deferential toward
authority ("Yes, officer, certainly, sir. Thank you for pointing out that
I was going five miles over the speed limit."), making certain that the
other person is well aware we know that he or she has all the power.
At the pathological end of its range lie *attack self* scripts for
masochism, in which we accept literally brutal treatment at the
hands of a powerful other in order not to feel the sting of abandonment. Masochism is often translated into complex sexual behavior
patterns because sexual arousal is so intimately connected with the
shame attending impediment to the interest-excitement it triggers,
and our methods of handling that shame link us to others through
the scripts housed in the compass of shame.

It is here especially that the experience of shame shifts from the
physiological mechanism, the innate affect of amplified impediment,
toward our mature definition. By the end of the toddler era, when
toilet training has taught us a great deal about dissmell and disgust,
the experience of shame affect has become immutably fused with
those two affects that also involve interpersonal distance. In order to
explain to others just why we should be treated as a lesser form of
life to be kicked, abused, or disdained, we take unto ourselves the
affects of dissmell and disgust as self-dissmell and self-disgust.
Whereas the intensity of the shame experience is directly proportional to the degree of positive affect that has been impeded, the toxicity

of that same shame experience is a function of the degree to which dissmell and disgust have been incorporated into the personal mixture of ideas, experiences, and innate affects that come to make up the mature *emotion* we call shame. If I am to attract someone who will be a cruel protector, I must define myself as a lowly worm, a sniveling misfit, a reject who is glad to be found of some use to the powerful one even if that use only defines more emphatically my dissmelling and disgusting nature. I will whimper, exhibiting the sort of distress-anguish found only in helpless creatures beneath dignity, and I will take your further reduction of me as a sign that I am worthy of your attention. Inwardly, I breathe a special sigh of relief, for I am no longer alone.

Pretty intense, this form of shame. So much do most of us eschew the ignominy of *withdrawal* and *attack self*, so much do many of us loathe and despise the very experience of shame affect in its combinatory forms just described, that we do whatever possible to prevent its expression. Using the scripts, the attitudes and behaviors housed at the *avoidance* pole of the compass, we learn several ways of warding off or detoxifying shame. When the spotlight of attention is turned on some aspect of our being that makes us feel lesser than we might like, it is a simple task to distract the viewing eye of the other to our newest source of pride—an automobile, summer cottage, jewelry, well-toned or surgically optimized body, or even entice that other into an escapade utilizing all of them. I define healthy pride as an efficacy experience undertaken in the spirit of positive affect. Nobody need know that a particular episode of sexual conquest served as a distraction from some awkward moment or attribute; if done well, the pleasure of the other will provide its own sort of reward as one who might have felt lesser is now thanked for being a lot more. Hedonism is often a defense against shame through which we substitute a source of pleasure for the source of pain that might well have pointed the spotlight of attention to a part of the self that needed repair.

Shame is pretty tricky, though, and no amount of skill will allow one to dance forever out of its reach. The quiver of arrows stored in the locker of *avoidance* still can protect us. As all of us learned early, the pain of shame is quite soluble in alcohol. We can drink away our failures and humiliations, belt down a stiff one as we walk into a party full of strangers, get drunk when that special person leaves us for a detested rival. Apply alcohol to an open wound and it will sting. Apply alcohol to shame and we start to sing. Such is the chemistry of the affect system—we should not be surprised that any member of this group of biological protocols might be sensitive to biological

treatment. Just as alcohol is shamolytic, cocaine and the amphetamines increase interest-excitement and thereby produce the same
sort of protection from shame as the excitement-shame-excitement
sequence discussed earlier. Heroin, so my patients tell me, produces
so much enjoyment-joy that it overrides any dysphoria. The drugs of
the street are always and only about affect, and most of them are
about shame.

And yet, no matter what we do, there will be times that the pain
of shame can neither be warded off nor its heat quenched. All of us
some of the time, and some of us all of the time, have moments
when the pain of shame is intolerable and the thoughts cascading
from the eight categories of memorialized experience produce
unbearable amounts of self-dissmell and self-disgust. Feeling lower
than we can accept, we seek a relationship within which we can
reduce the self-esteem of another person. Despite how much you, as
a psychotherapist or cleric or teacher or person of spirituality, might
disdain and avoid the brutality of the "action" genre of movies and
television shows, suspend for a moment your personal aesthetic and
watch a week's worth of this entertainment staple. Filmic interpersonal violence is always and only engaged within the compass of
shame, action undertaken from the *attack other* library of scripts.
Whenever we handle a moment of embarrassment by looking down
our nose at our tormenter, by issuing a put down, by turning another
person into a tool for our anger or a recipient of our dissmell or
disgust in order to produce shame in that other, we have worked
from this library. One of the reasons our society has become so
dangerous is that the preferred expression of shame has shifted from
withdrawal and *attack self* (neither of which is likely to hurt anyone
else), to *avoidance* mechanisms that magnify excitement and anger
and *attack other* systems that are meant to be dangerous. As in all
these script libraries, *attack other* scripts may range from the mildest
moment of irritability to the most pathological form of sadistic
violence.

If we are to understand shame, we must give up the simplistic
belief that shame *is* any one of these four patterns of response. There
is no unitary emotion to be called shame, only this quartet of script
libraries. Wherever we see fighting, we must look for shame.
Wherever we see narcissism, we must look for the defect that
appeared to need cover or distraction. The sadomasochistic interchange is always and only about shame, just as all forms of defensive
withdrawal are about shame. Those of us who are brought up in
homes or neighborhoods that give but little solace for the pain of
shame will move steadily toward the more pathological range of its

expression. If there is a biological glitch, an error in metabolism that makes some neurotransmitter (like serotonin) more or less available than normal, and this condition produces shame affect that can be reduced or ameliorated only by the use of medication, whatever shame is associated with this illness can be expressed only through one of these four poles of the compass. The logic is simple and inexorable. Although any behavior can be launched for a wide range of reasons, when we see a disturbed child or adult act in the ways described by the compass of shame, we must try to explain the resultant psychopathology in terms of what we know about affect itself and the specific pathways for shame.

The range of shame far exceeds anything ever dreamed in our earlier systems of psychology. As Wurmser (1981) said so clearly,

> I daresay there might hardly be one psychoanalytic or psychothera- peutic session without the more or less conscious presence of shame or its cognate feelings of embarrassment and put down, of slight and humiliation, or of shyness, bashfulness, and modesty. True, these feelings may themselves be used as defenses, but far more typically they serve as motive forces for defense, initiating repression, denial, projection, and so forth. This means that shame in its typical features is complex and variable, a range of closely related affects rather than one simple, clearly delimited one. It shades into moods on one side, into attitudes on the other [p. 17].

To this powerful message we have added the entire spectrum of narcissistic and borderline disorders (Nathanson, 1994), and the response to insult that now characterizes so much of modern interpersonal life. It is hoped that, with this expansion of the very concept of shame, embedded as it is within the affect theory of Silvan Tomkins, the cohort of psychotherapists willing to place the spotlight of attention on the entire compass of shame may enjoy a significant increase in both understanding and efficacy.

REFERENCES

Basch, M. F. (1976), The concept of affect: A re-examination. *J. Amer. Psychoanal. Assn.*, 24:759–777.
⎯⎯⎯⎯ (1983), Empathic understanding. *J. Amer. Psychoanal. Assn.*, 31:101–126.
Bowlby, J. (1982), *Attachment and Loss, Vol. 1*. New York: Basic Books.

Darwin, C. (1872), *The Expressions of the Emotions in Man and Animals.* New York: St. Martin's Press, 1979.

Fromm, E. 1941), *Escape from Freedom.* New York: Rinehart.

Hess, E. H. (1958), "Imprinting" in animals. *Sci. Amer.*, March; Reprinted in: *Readings from Scientific American*, ed. S. Coopersmith, pp. 13–17.

Nathanson, D. L. (1986), The empathic wall and the ecology of affect. *The Psychoanalytic Study of the Child*, 41:171–187. New York: International Universities Press.

———— (1992), *Shame and Pride.* New York: Norton.

———— (1994), Shame, compassion, and the "borderline" personality. *Psychiat. Clin. North Amer.*, 17:785–810.

Rank, O. (1952), *The Trauma of Birth.* New York: Brunner.

Sartre, J.-P. (1948), *The Emotions.* New York: Philosophical Library.

Stoller, R. J. (1987), Pornography: Daydreams to cure humiliation. In: *The Many Faces of Shame*, ed. D. L. Nathanson. New York: Guilford, pp. 292–307.

Tomkins, S. S. (1962), *Affect Imagery Consciousness. Vol. I.* New York: Springer.

———— (1992), *Affect Imagery Consciousness. Vol. IV.* New York: Springer.

Wurmser, L. (1981), *The Mask of Shame.* Baltimore, MD: Johns Hopkins University Press.

16

DONALD L. NATHANSON

Attentional Disorders and the Compass of Shame

The importance of this volume is implicit in its title. Until the small band that Helen Block Lewis called "shamnicks" began to study what Rycroft (1968) called "the ignored emotion," practitioners tended to view shame from the standpoint of their own highly personal experience. Lewis's (1971) landmark differentiation between shame and guilt, Wurmser's (1981) demonstration of the depth and power of shame-based psychopathology, the links to self psychology provided by Morrison (1987, 1989), and the powerful investigations of Lansky (1984, 1987) showing the role of shame in intrafamilial violence have made clear the importance of this emotion in all aspects of human life. In a series of books and papers (Nathanson, 1987b, 1992, 1994; this volume, chapters 4 and 15) I have elaborated on the view of shame offered by Silvan Tomkins (1962, 1963). We have come to understand that shame is a realm rather than a point within it, a range of emotional experience far more extensive than was understood at any previous time in our history. In this brief chapter, I suggest that Attention Deficit Disorder and Attention Deficit Hyperactivity Disorder (ADD/ADHD) are clinical conditions caused by aberrations of affect mechanisms rather than matters of pathological cognition arising in response to disorders of neocortical function. I shall demonstrate that all the symptoms noted and treatments offered by those who have studied this cluster of illnesses may be understood in terms of the Compass of Shame (Nathanson, 1992; see also chapter 4, this volume).

Clinicians trained in modern affect and script theory approach patients in a manner unique to that discipline. Psychoanalysts tend to think in terms of ego mechanisms and intrapsychic conflict; cognitive therapists look for skeins of thought hovering at the edge of consciousness; couples or family therapists seize on sources of interpersonal conflict; and psychopharmacologists work with patterns of symptoms that suggest the dysfunction in one or another neurotransmitter system. The system of therapy based on the affect and script theories of Tomkins (1962, 1963, 1991, 1992) and moved into neurobiology and psychotherapy by Nathanson (1988, 1992, 1994) offers a different template. As we listen to and observe the individual, couple, family, or community brought to our attention, we think about and look for each of the nine innate affects in an attempt to identify the specific affect that has precipitated the need for treatment. Then we make some judgment about whether that affect has been produced or maintained by an aberration of hardware, firmware, or software. The story or context brought to us is appraised constantly to see in what way the six basic affects (interest-excitement, enjoyment-joy, surprise-startle, fear-terror, distress-anguish, and anger-rage) were triggered by conditions of stimulus increase, stimulus decrease, or stimulus level; the two drive auxiliaries of dissmell and disgust triggered to produce interpersonal distance; and the affect auxiliary of shame-humiliation triggered in response to interest-excitement or enjoyment-joy that has been impeded but not stopped entirely.

Within affect theory, it is taken for granted that no stimulus or source can become the subject of attention unless and until it has triggered an affect; indeed, attention itself is defined as the mental state produced by affect. The nine innate affects produce nine highly specific forms of attention. We view the affect system as analogous to a collection of spotlights, each a different color, each capable of motivating us in a different manner, each turned on by its specific trigger and turned off when the individual begins to pay attention to the triggering source. When an affect lasts a long time and causes enough discomfort to produce a request for therapeutic assistance, we try to define the scripts—the systems of affect management—within which that affect has been nested.

It seems only reasonable, then, to extend this reasoning to suggest that whenever a person presents a problem with the initiation or maintenance of attention, we look to the affect system for an explanation. With this approach in mind, I visited a seven-year-old boy who had been evaluated for ADD/ADHD by a number of highly regarded child psychiatrists and been seen at a nationally known children's clinic. All these experts concurred that Jeremy was severely afflicted with this disorder and that his response to medication and psychotherapy had been gratifying but less than perfect. Although I will report in some detail about this specific child, I have confirmed these observations on several occasions by studying other similarly diagnosed children in the company of their parents, their therapists, or both.

There is quite a difference between idea and execution. Once it became clear that Jeremy had accepted my presence, his entire family disappeared, deserting me and celebrating their relatively brief freedom from responsibility for him. Several months later, when I had recovered fully from the two hours I spent in his presence, I accepted with amusement their politely covered glee at this brief opportunity to escape from responsibility for their almost inaccessible offspring. The idea of science usually carries with it some concept of a controlled workplace; it would have been far easier to observe him through a one-way mirror, for every minute spent with Jeremy was hard work. Like a shipwrecked sailor stranded on a tropical island with every possible creature comfort, I wandered helplessly through the basement recreation room outfitted by wealthy parents for their seven-year-old son. A plastic basketball court, its hoop at just the right height for the whirling dervish who ruled there. Electronic games everywhere, from small hand-held units to a personal computer with keyboard and screen. Things to throw, soft things to catch, plastic weapons of war designed for conflicts through the ages from stone age clubs through medieval helmets to Renaissance swords, a wide range of modern firearms, and tools heralding future deadly confrontation.

Children at play offer one of the best theaters at which to study innate affect, and it was my curiosity about Jeremy's affective life that had drawn me into his gilded cage. All disorders of attention must involve the affect system simply because there is no way to pay attention to anything unless an affect has made it salient.

DISORDERS OF ATTENTION

Jeremy's father led me into the playroom, the cave of pleasures within which this difficult child seemed most comfortable. We picked up a basketball and practiced foul shots. The first time he missed, Jeremy left the plastic court and turned away from us. "That's what he does in the classroom, according to his teacher," said his father, looking daggers at his inept child. "Play with me, Daddy," Jeremy responded somewhat helplessly; but in a moment he was working with the punching bag. Father and son sat down at the computer to play a game designed to teach children how to type; words floated slowly across the screen as the player tried to match one letter after another from the keyboard. When he chose the correct letter, a missile rocketed from the ground to shatter its floating equivalent. Jeremy's success at shooting down "house," "you," and "them" kept him focused on these tasks to the extent that his father could retreat quietly and leave us alone.

Novelty gave way to boredom, lessened interest, and an increasing frequency of failure. All at once, Jeremy, abandoning the typing game for a sword and helmet, rushed over to these weapons with a yell. He stood on a chair, leapt into the air chasing an imaginary dragon, and crashed to the ground. For a couple of moments he sat on the ground with me as I asked him to tell the story of the dragon, but then he began to squirm, rolled away on the floor, and jumped up to swat a tethered ball with a yellow plastic baseball bat. Skinny as a rail (for treatment with methylphenidate and the amphetamines had reduced his appetite severely), he literally whirled from the baseball encampment to look at me for a few seconds. Experimentally, I grabbed him and we tussled for a little while. His expression varied rapidly from fear to excitement to anger to fear and anger again as it turned out that I was neither a pushover nor a monster and that he was allowed to play as he wanted. But he lost interest in that, too, looking down and turning away.

Pause, for a moment, and review the scenes I have just described. Most of us have had some experience shooting fouls on a basketball court. No one gets the ball in the basket every time; professional players are rated on the percentage of success at this task, and we take for granted that there is no level of skill that guarantees perfection. We have been brought up to work at the foul line to improve this skill, to sharpen our technique so that the percentage of successful shots rises; information derived from the missed shots informs subsequent attempts. Wurmser (1981) pointed out that the degree and intensity of shame is directly proportional to the gap between the idealized self and the self revealed in the moment; healthy pride (Nathanson, 1992) involves efficacy within the context of positive affect. The ordinary person expects to miss a great many shots and is pleased to miss only a few. Jeremy was willing to play only until he missed, at which time he left the game. Such a "lack of tolerance for frustration" suggests an exaggerated sense of shame at failure, rather than a primary failure of his ability to pay attention to the task. This represents the *withdrawal* pole of the Compass of Shame (see chapter 4, Figure 1).

Yet just as Jeremy withdrew from the basketball court, he looked to his father for confirmation that he was loved. Wurmser (1981) suggests that at the heart of shame is the feeling that one is unlovable; I (Nathanson, 1992) define love in terms of sequences of positive and negative affect, explaining Wurmser's observation as one of the ideoaffective complexes encrypted within the development of shame as it moves from an innate affect to a variegated mature emotion. When Jeremy looked toward his father for solace, he was rewarded with a moment of contempt, to which he responded with more shame, which this time was expressed at the punching bag as the *attack other* pole of the Compass of Shame.

Moments later, father and son linked again at the game called "Type Attack," through which Jeremy could launch missiles with pride. Although his father's presence at that time might have operated as a selfobject function, mirroring and modulating Jeremy's excitement about the game and holding it within the limits needed for competent performance, Jeremy's attention to Type Attack was so fixed that he barely noticed that his father had left. As novelty decreased (and with it the degree of interest-excitement triggered by this task), failure triggered shame of a degree unacceptable to the child, who left the game for another sequence of *attack other* fantasies.

Only one activity held his interest for more than a couple of minutes, and within its grasp he was so spellbound that it was all I could do to pull him away from it to relieve my own boredom at feeling locked in his cave with nothing to do and no purpose to fulfil save that of terribly passive and utterly bored behavior. Jeremy's rapt and steady attention to the "action" genre of computer games was so stable and consistent, his affective involvement in them so intense, that it is important for us to examine them closely,

COMPUTER GAMES

"Computer games" involve the player in several types of interaction. The most primitive are pure games of skill in which steady improvement in hand-eye coordination is rewarded by colorful displays of point scores as indications of prowess. From the standpoint of innate affect, they offer sequences of interest-excitement and enjoyment-joy. The more sophisticated games dig more deeply into the affective life of the child and involve carefully contrived scripts within which individual scenes trigger excitement, fear, shame, and anger. Jeremy was a whiz at Nintendo. He played games in which he could swat, batter, shoot, and otherwise destroy a host of opponents with a wide range of disgusting or unlovable characteristics.

Excitement in computer games, of course, is produced by events and accompanying music that take place at a steadily rising tide of stimulation; success at the requested tasks triggers pride as a coassembly of efficacy and enjoyment-joy. With this success comes a new, programmed level of the game, at which point events begin to occur more quickly but still within the processing skill of the player. Eventually, this efficacy leads the computer to adjust the game so that things happen "too quickly." There is a rate of data acquisition at the range between that which triggers interest-excitement and that which triggers fear-terror, and we tend to describe things that happen in this realm as "thrilling." Eventually the game speeds up to the level at which the beginning player is momentarily frightened, experiences a decrease in processing skill (the shaking paralysis of the innate fear mechanism is not a particularly useful moiety of this affect in our era of sudden and cascading overmuch; all of the affects evolved much earlier in our history!), and then fails in an embarrassing manner (dumped into a pool of mud, eaten by a cartoon crocodile, evaporated by a ray gun). To this embarrassment the child tends to respond by starting over, for shame is a good teacher; we want to acquire skills that prevent it, especially those skills that provide good helpings of interest-excitement and enjoyment-joy. As is obvious from the inherent circuitry postulated for the innate affects by Tomkins (1962, 1963), the mild experience of shame (in response to an impediment to positive affect) may be diminished by increasing our level of excitement. A game is discarded when the player hits a wall by finding the limit of skill possible for himself, making the outcome entirely predictable and therefore neither a source of novelty nor one of enjoyment, which now will come only from a new game of similar design.

As any child will tell you, those games are only for kids. The real games, the ones that have built an empire for a few corporations of computer wizards who understand this peculiar psychology, involve the same sort of stimulus-affect-response sequence that make action movies so successful. In these games, the hapless victim is pummeled, trounced, beaten up, and roundly humiliated by the villain, who can be defeated only when the player learns specific skills that then allow the tables to be turned on the villain, for whom no one has any sympathy. These are games about shame and redress of humiliation through fantasized scripts that carry the *attack other* methodology to levels previously undreamed of in our culture. Every child who plays these games is receiving instruction about the management of shame. Failure leads to shame that cannot be abided but must be avenged through violent and deadly attack on the perpetrator. Limitations of space preclude my discussing the social consequences of such training, but the reader can intuit a connection between the current trend toward violence throughout our culture and "innocent games" that teach a response to shame precluding sober analysis of failure and the development of techniques for negotiation.

Even if you do not believe that such computer games are a *primary* source of training for the stimulus-affect-response sequence that leads to public and private violence, at least you must accept that these games parallel the current adult trend toward the experience of shame as insult worthy only of explosive attack and, as analogues of this trend played over and over with large dollops of rewarding positive affect, are magnifiers of it. Tomkins (1962) stated that

> the complete, sudden reduction of intense, enduring shame activates joy; the incomplete reduction of intense, enduring shame activates enjoyment. . . Achievement motivation which is powered by shame is enormously strengthened by the incremental rewards of joy which are released by the sudden reduction of shame when success attends protracted effort toward the solution of a problem or the attainment of a goal [p. 293].

The effect of computer games on our children is important, serious, and addressed only by helpless handwringing by those who do not know enough about affect theory to make their point with any vigor.

Although much attention has been paid anxiety as the negative affect most important in child development, I believe shame to be of far greater importance. Growth and development bring new powers that can be used with skill only after embarrassing periods of trial and error. The changing attributes of a growing child will always invite comparison with those of others, as the result of which that child will be placed somewhere on the shame–pride axis (Nathanson, 1987). Pride in accomplishment and shame at failure are the primary colors of normal childhood; this balance of rewards and punishments is magnified in computer games. Clinical experience leads me to believe that the children most susceptible to the lure of the more advanced computer games are those for whom the *avoidance* and *attack other* poles of the Compass of Shame have become most salient. I do not believe that children with healthy self-esteem invest much of their time playing these counter-shame games in arcade or home entertainment centers. More to the point of this essay, I believe that computer games have evolved as perfect lures for children and adults with ADD/ADHD and that whoever seems "addicted" to this realm of entertainment warrants evaluation for a disorder involving shame.

SHAME AND ADD/ADHD

The phenomonology of shame in ADD/ADHD seems clear enough. In these children I observe primary shame—attempts to focus on novel stimuli, accompanied by the facies of interest-excitement that is maintained for no more than a few seconds before the eyes turn down and away from the previously interesting source, the head droops, the entire posture sags momentarily. At other times, the same child will use the language of the *attack self* pole and say out loud, "You're so stupid. Bad." Then, looking right at me for a moment, "Dumb kid." More often, though, the child, showing off in the characteristic manner of the *avoidance* pole, will move quickly to some other activity at which more proficiency may be expected. Yet of all the activities likely to sustain interest, what works best for these children is the sort of game at which they can bash someone or something that for the moment is the designated inferior in that moment of self-esteem raising we call *attack other* behavior. None of this shame psychology would have been ignored by our field had observers paid attention to the face, the evolved display board of the affect system, or been aware that shame is an affect long before it is a complex emotion.

There is also a great deal of secondary shame in such children (and later when they reach adulthood) as they come to understand that they are less than their peers. Their lives feature constant failure at tasks that seem easy for everyone else, an inability to sit still (shame affect, like all the affects, is painful and makes us want to do something to get rid of it; activity helps when the affect makes you feel helpless and passive), the red-faced shame that comes when the teacher singles you out for bad behavior that you cannot seem to alter, the heightened sense that you are defective, the growing difficulty playing games with others especially when these games require long periods of attentive waiting. The list of failures and deficiencies is great, the solace available from others minimal, and from self slight, save for the momentary feelings of triumph allowed by *attack other* scripts that become increasingly important to self-esteem.

I understand the cluster of conditions known as ADD/ADHD to involve one or many types of inborn error in the regulation and maintenance of the affect interest-excitement. The sequence of events seems to involve normal attention to a novel source, followed by normal interest-excitement that is interrupted very quickly despite the continued presence of the initial trigger for interest. Within affect theory, this is the postulated (normal) trigger for shame affect that then registers immediately on the face of the person and is experienced as a cognitive shock and consequent inability to remain focused on the previously important source. That the moment of shame is handled through the mechanisms of the Compass of Shame is obvious. Given our present technology (or my limited understanding of and access to it), there seems to be no way to determine whether the lesion involves the affect protocol for interest-excitement as a primary error in its inherited affect script, or a neurological mechanism (external to that specific subcortical location) responsible for rapid, nearly immediate interruption in ongoing interest-excitement that must then trigger shame affect as its scripted analogue.

Let us consider the effects of medication and drugs of abuse in terms of affect theory. I have outlined in detail (Nathanson, 1992; Nathanson and Pfrommer, 1996) the hypothesis that exogenous substances are capable of influencing emotions only when they cause things to happen at the sites of action normally activated by the affect system. It is the gestalt of such activity that is registered as a pattern by the organism, as when the facial muscles are contracted and relaxed by one or another affect program. In the now-classic experiment by Ekman, Levenson, and Friesen (1983), when actors were asked to adjust their facial muscles in the patterns known to accompany certain innate affects, pulse and respiration also increased or decreased to fit the remainder of the normal affect display. The rauwolfia alkaloid reserpine sets off enough receptors to produce the experience of guilt in many people, just as ethyl alcohol reduces shame and fear.

Every treatment modality so far developed for this cluster of disorders known as ADD/ADHD confirms my hypothesis that these syndromes may be described or understood as lesions in the biology of interest-excitement. I see these illnesses as malfunctions in the firmware for the maintenance of interest-excitement, the failure to maintain attention thus triggering shame affect; or as a malfunction that produces a relatively sudden interruption in the operation of interest-excitement and thus triggering shame affect as an amplification of that impediment. Intrinsic to shame affect, as I have noted elsewhere (chapter 15, this volume) is the cognitive shock that

accompanies the sudden inability to remain focused on the previously interesting source and, clinically, as significant interference with
the mutualization of interest-excitement required for normal social
interaction.

Methylphenidate and the amphetamines cause increases in
excitement that seem to reduce the frequency of interruption or at
least make available enough excitement that attention to the desired
source may be maintained. This is a pharmacologic equivalent of the
psychosocial techniques through which all us learn to increase the
level of ambient excitement so that moderate degrees of interference
are less likely to trigger shame affect. In clinical practice I have noted
that, unless they have been in a more or less constant state of shame,
previously addicted patients find these drugs unpleasant. The term
depression is actually a collective noun within which clinicians
assemble a pleomorphic cluster of dysphorias characterized by
prolonged experiences of any one or more of the six negative affects.
For some years I have maintained (Nathanson, 1987b, 1992, 1994)
that medications that increase the amount of serotonin available in
the interneuronal cleft (SSRIS, including fluoxetine, paroxetine,
sertraline, and other new agents) offer excellent relief from the many
biological disorders of shame affect known as "the atypical depressions." Finally, agitated children are often treated with antimanic
agents like Lithium salts and divalproex; it is clear and obvious
(Nathanson, 1987, 1992) that the heterogeneous conditions known
as bipolar and unipolar affective disorder also involve lesions of the
affect interest-excitement (wild increases in the manic phase, painful
inability to become interested in anything during the "depressed"
phase). All these medications have found use in ADD/ADHD, and their
efficacy seems to offer confirmation of the biological scheme I
suggest here. I believe that the SSRIS help both the secondary shame
produced as children grow up with failure as their constant reality
and the primary shame associated with what I postulate as the
underlying problem. Finally, just as there seem to be many different
causes for the symptom complex known as the cyclic mood
disorders, I am certain that there are many pathways to any attentional disorder requiring that the therapist vary treatment frequently.

CONCLUSION

Clinicians and scientists tend to see what they understand, and to
discuss only that data for which they have language. This chapter is
an attempt to shift the attention of the psychotherapy community

away from the idea that attentional disorders are caused by a primary malfunction of neocortical structures and toward the relation between the positive affect called interest-excitement and shame-humiliation as the amplification of any impediment to that affect. All the stimulus-affect-response sequences that I have defined for shame-humiliation may be subsumed under the rubric of the Compass of Shame, a quartet of behavioral scripts engaged when the affect is triggered as an analogue of any impediment to ongoing positive affect or by neurobiological errors that can both cause and masquerade as psychosocial problems.

REFERENCES

Ekman, P., Levenson, R. W. & Friesen, W. V. (1983), Autonomic nervous system activity distinguishes among emotion. *Science*, 221:1208–1210.

Lansky, M. R. (1984), Violence, shame, and the family. *Internat. J. Family Psychiat.*, 5:21–40.

———— (1987), Shame and domestic violence. In: *The Many Faces of Shame*, ed. D. L. Nathanson. New York: Guilford.

Lewis, H. B. (1971), *Shame and Guilt in Neurosis*. New York: International Universities Press.

Morrison, A. P. (1987), The eye turned inward: Shame and the self. In: *The Many Faces of Shame*, ed. D. L. Nathanson. New York: Guilford. pp. 271–291.

———— (1989), *Shame.* Hillsdale, NJ: The Analytic Press.

Nathanson, D. L. (1987a), The shame/pride axis. In: *The Role of Shame in Symptom Formation*. ed. H. B. Lewis, Hillsdale, NJ: Lawrence Erlbaum Associates, pp. 183–205.

———— (1987), *The Many Faces of Shame.* New York: Guilford.

———— (1988), Affect, affective resonance, and a new theory for hypnosis. *Psychopathol.*, 21:126–137.

———— (1992), *Shame and Pride.* New York: Norton.

———— (1994), The case against depression. *Bull. Tomkins Instit.*, 1:1–4.

———— & Pfrommer, J. M. (1996), Affect theory and psychopharmacology. In: *Knowing Feeling*, ed. D. L. Nathanson. New York: Norton, pp. 177–190.

Rycroft, C. (1968), *A Critical Dictionary of Psychoanalysis.* New York: Basic Books.

Tomkins, S. S. (1962), *Affect Imagery Consciousness, Vol. I.* New York: Springer.

———— (1963), *Affect Imagery Consciousness, Vol. II*. New York: Springer.

———— (1991), *Affect Imagery Consciousness, Vol. III*. New York: Springer.

———— (1992), *Affect Imagery Consciousness, Vol. IV*. New York: Springer.

Wurmser, L. (1981), *The Mask of Shame*. Baltimore, MD: Johns Hopkins University Press.

17

LÉON WURMSER

The Shame About Existing: A Comment About the Analysis of "Moral" Masochism

For a long time, partly in conjunction with my work on shame as well as with that on the addictions, I have been struck by the extent to which problems of masochism permeate most treatments in one form or another (Wurmser, 1987, 1989, 1993). I believe that an in-depth understanding of the dynamics underlying masochism can elucidate much of what is most recalcitrant in the treatment of the "severe neuroses," those usually subsumed under the catchall diagnosis of "borderline." In fact, I have become more and more certain that the study of superego problems, especially issues of shame and guilt, of resentment and loyalty, are but one side of the coin; studying the dynamics underlying masochism is the other side.

The term masochism is purely descriptive; by itself it does not explain anything. The work begins with it; it does not end with it. The phenomena so described are the result of complex inner processes at all developmental strata (Maleson, 1984; Grossman, 1986, 1991; Meyers, 1988).

Briefly and provisionally stated, *masochism is the need to seek suffering, pain, or humiliation in order to obtain love and respect and to sabotage one's chances and success.* "The term masochism will be most usefully and understandably applied to *those activities organized by fantasies involving the obligatory combination of pleasure and unpleasure, or to the fantasies themselves*" (Grossman, 1986, p. 408, Italics added).

I have found it useful to differentiate the following four forms of masochistic pathology:

1) *Outer masochism*: The main relationships with others seem to reflect an incessant search for and clinging to tormenting and humiliating partners, a need to end up as the victim.

2) *Inner or moral masochism*: Tormenting, berating, and shaming are mostly carried by the conscience and directed against the self.

3) *Sexual masochism, masochistic perversion*: Sexual gratification is bound to symbolic or concrete pain and humiliation.

4) *Masochism covered by a sadistic-narcissistic façade*: What appears as outwardly directed cruelty and selfishness has to hide the acting out of a masochistic core fantasy.

These four forms of manifest pathology are not sharply separated from each other. In reality they usually coexist, albeit in different strength. Dynamically they form *one* connection, *one* texture with varied patterns. These patterns themselves are universal. They are pathological only insofar as they have a compulsive quality. There is just as much normal masochism as there is normal narcissism or normal aggression. The distinction between normalcy and pathology follows separate criteria (see Brenner, 1959, p. 206).

These four forms are hierarchically arrayed: the core is not found in the perversion that originally gave its name to the entire complex of issues. Rather, it seems that the perversion itself, as a manifest pattern of behavior (in contrast to the role of sexualization as defense, that is, as a deep, dynamic aspect), serves as a kind of grandiose defensive structure against the superego problems. The obligatory conditioning of sexual gratification with humiliation and torment, which is playfully enacted rather than earnestly lived out, serves as a protection against the severity and complexity of moral masochism. The massiveness and gravity of such superego pressure, however, is particularly an expression of conflicts *within* the superego, in the form of shame–guilt dilemmas, loyalty conflicts, or, more generally, deep value conflicts.

I agree with Berliner (1947) that "the analogy with the sexual perversions obscured the fact that *moral masochism is the general and basic form that furnishes the ground* upon which, in a minority of persons and under certain circumstances in psychosexual development, the perversion may evolve" (p. 459). It is my impression that the masochistic character neurosis (in the sense of external and moral masochism) is far more widespread than the perversion and is fundamental to its understanding. In fact, the *manifest perversion represents a reexternalization of complex intrapsychic and interpersonal dynamics*, not its basic layer. Accordingly, the causal constellation of an analyzed perversion is in no way any less complex, or any more basic and primary, than that of "merely neurotic" cases; rather, the opposite is true.

The same holds true for outer masochism: the unconscious, but painfully compulsive and repetitive, search for tormenting partners or for situations of anguish and unsolvable conflict in intimate relations is not so much an automatic repetition of older object relations as it is the result of reexternalization of an inner conflict, especially of a tormenting superego pressure (and only indirectly reflection of archaic object relationships, i.e., of external conflict). Thus outer and sexual masochism both resemble vast defensive glacis put up in front of moral masochism.

The fourth form, countermasochism, often the almost impenetrable sadistic-narcissistic façade, hides the other three forms (Berliner, 1947; Cooper, 1988).

The really important problem for us as analysts is not only how to understand dynamically what underlies these varied forms and layerings of clinical masochism, but how to bring about long-term, in-depth alterations of the masochistic character structure. The link between these two is not always automatic and simple. The need for self-punishment, and with that the incessantly repeated "negative therapeutic reaction," make for particularly prolonged, particularly difficult, particularly exasperating psychoanalytic work. The transference–countertransference problems are especially difficult and insidious; the patience required of us, and with that the technical obstacles, especially great. Also, in the light of the dynamic complexity, the presentation of such cases appears to me quite daunting.

Yet, as Brenner (1959) observed, these patients are analyzable, although the duration of treatment may seem frighteningly long. In this context, the central dynamics of shame in this work are to be particularly stressed.

CASE EXAMPLE

The following case illustration reveals three of the most important mutative insights from the analysis of an especially difficult case, which was only successfully terminated after more than nine years, 1550 hours.[1] The patient prominently showed "external" and "moral" masochism.

---

[1] For a very detailed study of this case, see Wurmser, 1993, ch. 6.

Thomas, a physician who was at the time 35 years old, was referred to me because of problems of chronic, low-level depression and anxiety, His problems had, for many years, been interfering with his enjoyment of life, the attainment of his professional potential, his ability to make decisions, and the possibility of his engaging successfully and with inner commitment in close human relationships. He had been unable to establish a satisfactory heterosexual relationship after his first marriage ended in severe strife and failure. He was increasingly concerned about the severity of symptomatic acts of a self-destructive, self-sabotaging nature that repeatedly and seriously jeopardized his own safety and that of others. He also complained about marked episodes of depersonalization, pervasive anhedonia, some transient minor psychosomatic symptoms, and unexplainable mood swings, especially of intense sadness or violent rage. His relationships showed persistent tendencies to turn into masochistic bonds where he was the victim of some injustice or where he, in fact, was taken advantage of or deceived. His social anxiety assumed paralyzing proportions, and such attacks of panic were frequently followed by frantic attempts to find sexual gratification by viewing pornographic shows; in his adolescence he had been actively voyeuristic and had prowled the streets to observe nude women through windows.

These symptoms have to be seen against a severely traumatic history. The mother appears to have been a severely phobic and obsessive–compulsive woman who dominated the household with her temper tantrums. After giving up a successful career as a civil service employee to take care of her children, she showed a chronically depressive, angry scowl to the world. The father, a weak and meek man entirely under the thumb of his wife, suffered from a congenital severe impediment of vision that left him legally blind and able to perform only subordinate types of work. Especially during Thomas's later childhood and with the advent of more children, the father too became very irascible and abused the children physically.

The parents evinced a terrifying blindness to the individuality of their five children (see Brouček, 1991). In an entirely one-sided and obstinate, ruthless way, they forced Thomas and his three brothers, from early childhood on, to direct all their activities toward the singular goal of becoming physicians—with the expectation that they would cure their father's blindness. The fixity and violence with which this choice of career and other prejudices were imposed on the children had a nearly delusional quality and had, for some of them, catastrophic consequences.

The first of the central insights in the analysis was how in the patient's experience, from earliest time on, every wish and every expression of his own will had been treated as evil, especially by his mother. Willfulness itself he equated with the killing of his parents: "That was the only choice I had: either to comply completely or to rebel totally." At the same time, his shame about his dependency on his mother was very deep. He professed his inability to do much of his homework for school during his growing up, and she had stayed up through the night to do it for him. Thus, of course, she, among other things, avoided the marital bed and ascribed her chronic insomnia to these tasks. All the work he did on his own was devalued. In school he knew he was a cheat and feared humiliating exposure that the work had not been done by him. Then, and even now, the more ashamed he is, the more awkward he feels and the more he has to direct the anger against himself.

"I felt I didn't exist. As if I had lost most of what I really am, and that everything had been put on me from the outside." Hence the lifelong deep sense of loss—loss of the self, of his identity. The obsessive thought that he would lose his children represented the death of his personality. There was a deep grief in him for "the self I had never been allowed to be." He often stressed the "immense sadness" within; there were only a few sessions when he was not in tears at some point. *His shame about being* was all pervasive. Even at the end of his analysis, his thoughts, feelings, wishes, and decisions do not count for anything with his parents.

"Shame about not having a self—guilt about wanting to assert myself, about saying no, resisting, because it is murderous," he says. "Being myself, standing up for myself, is murderous and brings the severest retaliation." To appear in public, as a lecturer or discussant, even to talk to others under social conditions, causes an anxiety attack.

This brings us to the two equations important in his dynamics, but also relevant generally. Separateness, being an individual with his own will, is absolutely evil: *success = separating himself = injuring and killing the other = dying = immense guilt*. Every self-affirmation is, in and by itself, an act of defiance and thus something very bad. In turn, *submitting = passivity = dependency and weakness = loss of oneself = shame and humiliation*. Feeling ashamed is the price to be paid for being loved. These two equations mean the radical and absolute nature of the conflict between separation guilt and dependency shame.

Thomas's pervasive shame hides a great complexity of conflicts and, among other things, veils profound competitiveness, murderous wishes and revenge for what can only be described as the soul-blindness and soul-murder inflicted on him over a lifetime—his sense of having always been treated as an object rather than as an individual in his own right with his own subjectivity. His shame hides his deep sense of self-loss. It hides all the yearnings for a redeeming union, the defiant wishes to rescue a little core of self and to discard the "peels of the onion" once and for all; it hides the reparative excitement.

Thomas's is a double shame: "The shame that I am alone and have no relationships, and the shame about being empty, a mere shell, and therefore cannot have any meaningful relationships . . . I got that crazy double message: in order to have a relationship, I have to empty myself. But by doing so, I destroyed the ability to have any relationship."

A second decisive insight during Thomas's treatment came in form of an anxious fantasy from his early childhood. His fear was that his "sperm," in the form of a little pea (a little child of his own), had left his penis and was being flushed down the toilet. Frantically he had tried to retrieve "the pea": "It was me," he said. "I, myself, the essence of me. I lose everything because I am nothing" (when he compares himself with his competitors—all those big fathers and mothers).

I said, "Either you had a self, but no love and no relationship to your mother, or you renounced your own self, were being flushed down like the little pea, were crap, a nothing, but had the relationship to your mother."

"With pain," he answered. "To be a shell and a façade—that is how I lived and how I still live."

I responded, "The pain is the only reality of relationship—the rest is nothing. And the constant complaint about the nothingness here and the pain repeats the ancient relationship to your mother . . . Better to be nothing and to have mother—than to be something but have nothing."

He could live only with a "false self"[2] with his parents, while his "true self" had to be wiped out. And when he was separated from his parents or rejected by them, he felt terribly ashamed for being just a shell, a person without substance.

---

[2] The concept of the "false self" is usually attributed to Winnicott. In fact, it was first used by Erich Fromm (1941) in the formulation of the "pseudo self" (pp. 229-230).

"I can never get rid of this feeling of sadness," he said. "It is the importance of pain and sadness as a symbol for the lost relationship. The pain and the sadness–they were the substitute for mother."[3]

As a consequence, his self and his world had to be split: He had to live constantly in a double reality: the reality of reason, of social functioning, of external adaptation and achievement; and the reality of a world that was irrational, "crazy," bizarre, subject to the totalitarian pressure of authority, exaggerated expectations, and threats. In theoretical terms, this doubleness of inner and outer reality is that of an ego-determined reality versus a reality entirely dominated by an archaic, anal-sadistic superego. The outcome of this double reality (really an intrasystemic conflict both in ego and superego) is his *shell existence*, the feeling of having no self, no identity–shame generating depersonalization; depersonalization, in turn, generating more shame. When Thomas states that the double anxiety, the dilemma, was between *shame* (submission) and *death* (separation), he is referring to the result of *soul murder* (Shengold, 1989): With either solution–*adaptation to the social world* or *submission to totalitarian authority*–he felt deprived of his substance; his self was crushed, and he became a nothing, a shell. Only forceful breaking out would give him the hope of finding himself, of feeling himself; yet doing so would also entail a break with his mother, expulsion from his family (as had, in fact, happened to his sister). And separation too would be intolerable, deadly, murderous.

The third major insight is the *anxiety of envy,* which blocks him. "The envy makes me smaller and exaggerates what I see as my lack . . . *The envy is all-pervasive*; I feel it constantly, in every interaction with others, even within myself: always I have to compare myself. I never live up to the ideal, and the shame is paralyzing."

This fear has a clear family dynamic background. It was very important for his parents that their children be better than everybody else, especially in comparison with the children of their own siblings. It was vital that the parents be envied by others instead of their envying others. "So it goes through the entire family: to make others envious, in order not to be envious oneself."

---

[3] See Valenstein's (1973) concept of "attachment to painful affect": pain, grief and other negative affects come to stand for the lost object. See also Blos (1991) and Bach (1991).

But his envy leads immediately to another huge danger. Since he knows how destructive, how frightening and murderous it is, his anxiety about being envied by others must be immense. At the same time, he has to strive, in accordance with the imperative at home, to do everything in his power to make the others envious of him, thus attaining the reversal of his own envy: "Because it is the content of my envy: to replace the other or to kill him (the envied rival)." Yet, this means, of course, deadly danger to him. The manifest shame and panic, his "social anxiety," hides the entire drama of envy: he has to be "empty" for fear of his own envy.

The fear of his own envy was the core of the neurosis. This conflict about envy was strongest in regard to his mother, in the form of envy of her breasts, her womb, her pregnancies, and thus of femininity in general. But it also pertained to her physical and mental creativity and articulateness. Some of this envy was lived out in the perverse compulsions to look and to show. Most relevant for his masochism was what could partly be seen as a projection of his own envy: his fear of the envy of others, most of all of the devouring, castrating envy of his mother.

This third major insight provided the solution for his masochism. As carrier of the ambition of his mother, he had to be successful for her, to outshine all the others, and thus to satisfy her envy toward the world. At the same time, he was not allowed to be successful in her eyes, because his self-assertion, his autonomy (e.g., his own creativity in his homework) aroused her envy of him and her competitiveness, and thus was mercilessly destroyed. Parallel to the issue of envy, it was expected that he would become the healer of his father, that he would cure not only his blindness but also his low social standing and shame and would become a great star, a rich doctor, a Nobel prize winner. Yet, like the mother's envy, the father's resentment did not allow Thomas to have any strength, to achieve any success, to have any existence as himself. This was an incurable, almost untreatable dilemma from which seemingly only failure, suffering, and weakness offered a way out. In such failure he could identify with his shame-ridden father and could be close to his power-greedy mother. *The masochism was a necessary compromise formation.*

THE VICIOUS CIRCLE IN MASOCHISM

The dynamics underlying masochism can be ordered–(re)constructed–into a kind of circular sequence that is typical both for the present and for the genesis (Gray, 1994). It can be seen as a sequence of ego states, in the here-and-now of the transference and of current interpersonal interactions; it can be seen as a developmental sequence, as a kind of layering of the "instinctual vicissitudes" of "aggression" and "narcissism"—in the sense of recurrent inner events.

Narcissistic Crisis

At issue is a high or, more typically, much exaggerated, expectation, especially in form of *grandiosity*, of *"perfection,"* of the patient's capability to heal the unhappiness of the family and to reconcile the adversaries as well as the opposite values. Because reality can never come close to this grandiose expectation, there is an abrupt collapse of the patient's brittle self-esteem into overwhelming shame. This phase of the process we may call the *narcissistic crisis*.

The narcissistic crisis reflects, even repeats, the original, lifelong *traumatization* (Berliner, 1940; Glenn, 1984). In Thomas's case, the traumata are "soul blindness" and "soul murder"—invisibility of the personal needs and emotions of the child and constantly oscillating overstimulation in the form of seductiveness and verbal violence and abuse (Shengold, 1989). Not being "seen," not being acknowledged as a person with his own autonomy and feelings means pervasive, archaic shame.

Affect Regression and Attachment to Pain

The next step, affect regression, consists in the dedifferentiation, deverbalization, and resomatization of affects, mostly as uncontrollable eruptions of rage, shame, and despair (Krystal, 1974, 1975). It is a breakdown of the affect defense. Often the affect itself may disappear and be replaced by a vague but intolerable tension, perhaps a longing or "craving" for "fun," a hectic search for pleasurable excitement and relief, a mood of aimless but intolerable restlessness. Being helplessly flooded by emotions, especially by such archaic feelings, is itself an extremely powerful wellspring of shame.

Complementary to affect regression is the attachment to the painful affect: the intensely held feeling of pain, shame, guilt, or despair, often of pre- or nonverbal intensity, represents the lost object (especially the depressive, emotionally absent mother; see Valenstein, 1973). It culminates in the character-based appeal: *"Torture me, but don't abandon me"* (see Bach, 1991).

Sexualization

Simultaneous with affect regression is a translation of its global affect into sexual tension. Sexualization is reflected in the following archaic equation: sexuality and *sexual excitement* = *violence*, cruelty, explosive bursting = *painful, intolerable tension* = *overwhelming, unbearable feelings* (Freud, 1924; Coen, 1988; Grossman, 1991). This sexualization too, is so embarrassing that it needs to be forcefully repressed.

Reversal, Fantasy of Omnipotence, and Double Self

Reversal is a turning of passive into active, ego-psychologically speaking an identification with the aggressor or with the trauma. Reversal may take the form of rage and indignation directed against another person or the surround; it may be a vain attempt to change suffering into action or at least a provocation, or it may take the form of very intense envy and jealousy.

Central is the split into an omnipotent self and a shame self: grandiose self-expectations and self-images coexist with a pathetic, vulnerable, weak self and are often experienced simultaneously (Novick and Novick, 1987, 1991). The fantasy of omnipotence is a particularly powerful defense against overwhelming anxiety and shame (Morrison, 1989). As one patient said during the recital of a fantasied orgy of torturing and mutilating his victim: "I am thrilled at torturing somebody, not simply killing him. But it's an excruciating torture where he is helpless. It is the manifestation of my desire for frenzied power. The man is helpless, bound. I can do what I want to do. My fury to humiliate the man goes to the maximum, grips me beyond any emotion."[4]

Part of this omnipotent turning of passive into active is the active dehumanization of the other: the patient uses others as tools and part objects in the same way as he had been used—objectified, dehumanized, manipulated, depersonalized. In general, *perversion is dehumanized sexuality or sexualized dehumanization* (Kernberg, 1988; Cooper, 1991).

The result is a *doubling of the self* with the aim that protection can be obtained and anxiety and particularly shame can be transcended.

---

[4] From the analysis of the case Albert (hour 471) (Wurmser, 1993, ch. 7).

Through this magical transformation, the "true self" is split off from its masks; it can be hidden, abducted, removed to some other, strange place, eventually to reemerge in powerful disguise. This type of fantasy and much of the doubleness of many patients with "multiple personalities" are important protective fantasies in the face of overwhelming traumatization: "It is not me who suffers something so horrible. It is my 'alter ego,' my body, my 'shell.' In reality I am somewhere else and am somebody different."

This splitting or doubling requires a massive denial of inner reality, mostly by blocking overwhelming affects and the extensive formation of a false self. Such denial is supported by an invalidation fantasy set up to make the perception of reality inoperative.

Introjection

The next station or layer is introjection, or the internalization of the trauma: the cruelty of trauma and abuse becomes part of the superego—parallel to the turning of the rage, the envy, and the contempt against the self.

This "inner judge" reflects (as we know from Freud) not only the aggression of the traumatizing object, but the aggression of the subject to be contained by this inner authority.

Conflict in the Superego

The sixth station, conflict within the superego, is an elaboration of introjection.

What is crucially important here, however, is the intrinsically contradictory, split nature of the values enforced by the inner judge (see Hartmann and Loewenstein, 1962; Rangell, 1963a, b; Wurmser, 1981, 1987, 1989, 1993). It is as if "he," the inner judge, were following opposite laws, opposite values, which nevertheless demand absolute adherence. Several such conflicts are possible. I stress two types: the opposition between different loyalties and the conflict I have described as the shame-guilt dilemma. The shame-guilt dilemma poses the values of strength, power, self-assertion, and self-realization against the values of belonging, love, community, and consideration for others. Violation of the former evokes shame; violation of the latter, guilt. The excessive, even global character of both affects leaves virtually no room in between. It makes of life a walk on a very thin crest—abyss to the left, abyss to the right.

Again in both regards—the absolute, but opposite claims for loyalty and the total quality of shame and guilt—I am talking about intrapsychic processes, not about object relations. Still, this entire intensification of superego aggression can be understood as a move to protect the object and the object relation from outward aggression, especially in form of the internalized "attachment to pain."

Envy and especially resentment vested in the superego mean that no pleasure or success can be granted to the self, just as it cannot be granted to the other.

Absoluteness—The Narcissistic Stigma

In the light of the globality and absoluteness of the previous stations, responsibility and self-ideal assume a similar totality. Thus, we find a grandiose ego-ideal as pendant to the cruel conscience-judge-superego, a fantasy of omnipotence connecting (in the view of the Novicks, 1987, 1991) all the developmental points. It is a *totalitarian superego* (in Fromm's word, *authoritarian*), often with opposite demands of irreconcilable totality.

Generally, narcissistic fantasies serve in traumatic situations, as we saw before, as protection against helplessness. There exists, however, a particularly important version of such protective omnipotence, a fantasy, almost a delusion: the omnipotence of responsibility, as if to say, "If I only were strong and good enough, all these awful things would not happen. Whatever abuse occurs, it is all my fault." At the price of enormous guilt, the patient protects herself (or himself) against the even more frightening helplessness.

Part of the fantasy of omnipotence is the *rescue mission*: in order not to be helpless anymore one prefers to assume the guilt for the horrors witnessed and sees one's task as being a savior. In that connection, it is striking how the internalized expectations of the parents are the carriers of such grandiosity, carriers precisely of a grandiosity that speaks for the depth of the parents' envy. Thus it is less one's own grandiosity than the exaggerated demand imposed that presents the major problem of narcissism.

Almost all strongly masochistic patients show a splitting, a "doubling" of their sense of reality. On one side, it is the world as perceived by others, consensually validated, confirmed by the ego. On the other side, either it is a reality that is being built up so that traumatization can be denied, that is, a reality built upon fantasies woven around denial; or it is a reality shaped and twisted by a totalitarian superego. It is in particular the conflict between the perceived reality and the superego-reality, that leads to an often dramatic cleavage between self and world, with all its consequences.

Reexternalization of the Cruel Conscience

With reexternalization, others are treated with the same scorn as the patient and are punished with the same pitiless harshness, as the "inner judge" deals with everything one does and feels. Thus one becomes the cruel judge of others: *sadism disguised as morality.* Simultaneously with this turning of the superego's aggression against the outside world, we encounter the narcissistic attitude of entitlement. The recognition of the consistent defense of masochism by cruelty and arrogance against the external world ("countermasochism," see Berliner, 1947; Cooper, 1988), specifically in regard to superego aspects, and reenacted in the transference has become for me one of the most important technical tools in the treatment of the severe neuroses and one of the most valuable insights into the genesis of aggression altogether.

Provoked Victimization

In a clinically (though not socially or culturally) much more prominent alternative to reexternalization, the patient ends up, again and again, in the position of the victim. This is the masochistic side dominating the surface appearance and marking the symptomatology. The masochistic core fantasies relive traumatic experiences in staged scenarios of managed suffering and shame, with the primacy not of the mechanisms of perverse sexuality, but of fantasy equations of sexualization of violence (Coen, 1988), centrally repeated in the submission to the tormenting, rigidly judgmental, anal-sadistic superego. The aim of the masochistic phenomena consists in a series of magical, "omnipotent" transformations, hidden within the masochistic beating fantasy (Freud, 1919). Through suffering and humiliation, the patient tries to achieve love and respect on many developmental levels: "Only through pain is it possible for me to preserve attachment, love and sensuality" (Wurmser, 1993, p. 300). Most poignantly, the patient tries to alter reality magically and omnipotently and bring about a series of massive denials and reversals:

> By the suffering provoked, brought about, reenacted by me I transform passively endured pain into pleasure, anxiety into sexual

excitement, hatred into love, separation into fusion, helplessness into power and revenge, guilt into forgiveness, shame into triumph and most of all passivity into activity. . . . in "*the alchemist's dream*" [Wurmser, p. 311].

Masochism is understandable on the basis of the premise of *power through suffering*. Yet this aim remains unconscious, remains self-defeating. The end is suffering and often catastrophe. The vicious circle is closed.

REFERENCES

Bach, S, (1991), On sadomasochistic object relations. In: *Perversions and Near-Perversions in Clinical Practice*, ed. G. I. Fogel & W. A. Myers. New Haven, CT: Yale University Press, pp. 75–92.

Berliner, B. (1940), Libido and reality in masochism, *Psychoanal. Quart.*, 9:322–333.

——— (1947), On some psychodynamics of masochism. *Psychoanal. Quart.*, 16:459–471.

Blos, P. Jr. (1991), Sadomasochism and the defense against recall of painful affect. *J. Amer. Psychoanal. Assn.*, 39:417–430.

Brenner, C. (1959), The masochistic character: Genesis and treatment. *J. Amer. Psychoanal. Assn.*, 7:197–226.

Brouček, F. J. (1991), *Shame and the Self*. New York: Guilford Press.

Coen, S. J. (1988), Sadomasochistic excitement: Character disorder and perversion. In: *Masochism,* ed. R. A. Glick & D. I. Meyers. Hillsdale, NJ: The Analytic Press, pp. 43–60.

Cooper, A. M. (1988), The narcissistic-masochistic character. In: *Masochism,* ed. R. A. Glick & D. I. Meyers. Hillsdale, NJ: The Analytic Press, pp. 117–139.

——— (1991), The unconscious core of perversion. In: *Perversions and Near-Perversions in Clinical Practice*, ed. G. I. Fogel & W. A. Myers. New Haven, CT: Yale University Press, pp. 17–35.

Freud, S. (1919), A child is being beaten, *Standard Edition,* 17:175–204. London: Hogarth Press, 1955.

——— (1924), The economic problem of masochism. *Standard Edition*, 19:157–172. London: Hogarth Press, 1961.

Fromm, E. (1941), *Escape from Freedom*. New York: Avon/Discus, 1968.

Glenn, J. (1984), Psychic trauma and masochism, *J. Amer.Psychoanal. Assn.*, 32:357–386.

Gray, P. (1994), *The Ego and Analysis of Defense.* Northvale, NJ: Aronson.

Grossman, W. I. (1986), Notes on masochism: A discussion of the history and development of a psychoanalytic concept. *Psychoanal. Quart.*, 55:379–413.

––––––– (1991), Pain, aggression, fantasy, and concepts of sadomasochism. *Psychoanal. Quart.*, 60:22–52.

Hartmann, H. & Loewenstein, R. M. (1962), Notes on the superego. *The Psychoanalytic Study of the Child,* 17:42–81. New Haven, CT: Yale University Press.

Kernberg, O. F. (1988), Clinical dimensions of masochism. In: *Masochism,* ed. R. A. Glick & D. I. Meyers. Hillsdale, NJ: The Analytic Press, pp. 61–80.

Krystal, H. (1974), The genetic development of affects and affect regression. *The Annual of Psychoanalysis,* 2:98–126. New York: International Universities Press.

––––––– (1975), Affect tolerance. *The Annual of Psychoanalysis,* 3:179–219. New York: International Universities Press.

Maleson, F. G. (1984), The multiple meanings of masochism in psychoanalytic discourse, *J. Amer. Psychoanal. Assn.*, 32:325–356.

Meyers, H. C. (1988), A consideration of treatment techniques in relation to the functions of masochism. In: *Masochism,* ed. R. A. Glick & D.I. Meyers. Hillsdale, NJ: The Analytic Press, pp. 175–188.

Morrison, A. F. (1989), *Shame.* Hillsdale, NJ: The Analytic Press.

Novick, K. K. & Novick, J. (1987), The essence of masochism. *The Psychoanalytic Study of the Child,* 42:353–384. New Haven, CT: Yale University Press.

––––––– & ––––––– (1991), Some comments on masochism and the delusion of omnipotence from a developmental perspective. *J. Amer. Psychoanal. Assn,* 39:307–331.

Rangell, L. (1963a), The scope of intrapsychic conflict: Microscopic and macroscopic considerations. *The Psychoanalytic Study of the Child,* 18:75–102. New Haven, CT: Yale University Press.

––––––– (1963b), Structural problems in intrapsychic conflict. *The Psychoanalytic Study of the Child,* 18:103–138. New Haven, CT: Yale University Press.

Shengold, L. (1989), *Soul Murder.* New Haven, CT: Yale University Press.

Valenstein, A. F. (1973), On attachment to painful feelings and the negative therapeutic reaction. *The Psychoanalytic Study of the Child,* 28:365–392. New Haven, CT: Yale University Press.

Wurmser, L. (1981), *The Mask of Shame.* Baltimore, MD: Johns Hopkins Press.

———— (1987), *Flucht vor dem Gewissen.* [Flight from Conscience]. Heidelberg: Springer.

———— (1988), *Die zerbrochene Wirklichkeit.* [Broken Reality]. Heidelberg: Springer.

———— (1993), *Das Rätsel des Masochismus.* [The Riddle of Masochism]. Heidelberg: Springer

18

AARON LAZARE

Shame, Humiliation, and Stigma in the Medical Interview

This chapter explores the importance of shame and humiliation in the clinical encounter. The experience of shame and humiliation in medical encounters seems natural when one considers that patients commonly perceive their diseases as defects, inadequacies, or shortcomings and that they must expose their bodies and minds to strangers to receive the desired help. The subject of shame and humiliation in the medical care of patients, however, is seldom discussed, studied, or written about.

SEMANTICS, PHENOMENOLOGY, AND GENERAL PSYCHOLOGY

Shame, humiliation, and related states refer to painful thoughts and feelings resulting from perceptions of oneself as less than one has thought or hoped for. In this state, we feel or believe that we have been acutely exposed (to others or to ourselves) as not measuring up to ideals or standards that we have set and accepted for ourselves (Lewis, 1971; Lynd, 1958; Wurmser, 1981; Miller, 1985). The acute shame reaction is usually sudden; may be experienced as a blow, a jolt, or a sting; and may be accompanied by autonomic reactions of blushing, fainting, sweating, burning, freezing, or weakness. On a cognitive level, there is a painful awareness of being defeated, deficient, exposed, a failure, inadequate, wanting, worthless, or wounded. The deficiency seems pervasive. The very essence of the self feels wrong.

One can list hundreds of words that express these emotions. They include expressions that emphasize visual exposure (exposed, naked, red-faced, scarred, shamefaced, stigmatized); reduction in size (belittled, diminished, humbled, put down, slighted, taken down a peg); overall deficiency (degraded, dehumanized, devalued, dishonored, insignificant); being tortured or murdered (whipped, nailed to the cross, trashed, devastated, demolished, destroyed, assassinated); and avoidance responses (disappearing from the face of the earth, hiding one's face in shame, hiding under the rug, sinking into the ground) (Lynd, 1958; Lewis, 1971; Wurmser, 1981; Miller, 1985). Humiliation differs from shame in that it is not so much an exposure of the self (with or without the involvement of another) as a lowering, debasement, or degrading of the self by another.

Before exploring the significance of shame in medical settings, it is important to comment on the value of shame in human experience. Our ability to experience shame is healthy. It means that we have ideals and a sense of pride and that we are social beings who care what others think about us. All of this is necessary for meaningful social interaction. The adaptive–maladaptive polarity of shame may be likened to blood pressure, which is necessary for physical existence; too high or too low blood pressure is pathologic. A normal range of blood pressure depends on finely regulated homeostatic mechanisms.

THE DETERMINANTS OF SHAME

For the purpose of exposition, I propose that any experience of shame can be understood as resulting from the interaction of three factors: the shame-inducing event; the vulnerability of the subject; and the social context, which includes the roles of people involved. These factors are a part of any shame experience, and their contributions are usually additive or complementary, yet any one may be so powerful in a particular situation that it alone can dominate the experience.

The Shame-Inducing Event

In medical settings, patients may experience physical or psychological limitations as defects, inadequacies, or shortcomings that assault various treasured images of the self: youth, beauty, strength, stamina, dexterity, self-control, independence, and mental competence. This sense of inadequacy further jeopardizes social roles that give meaning to patients' lives, such as the roles of student, teacher, physician, parent, sexual partner, and provider. Treatments and their side effects—for example, mastectomies, the loss of hair, and impotence—may be potential sources of further shame and humiliation. In psychotherapy, interpretations are potentially humiliating when patients are told truths about themselves that they previously have kept out of consciousness. (Whether or not the interpretation is perceived as a humiliation depends largely on the nature of the therapist–patient relationship.)

For some patients in certain clinical situations, death is preferable to disfiguring treatment. The issue of dignity in dying was illustrated by Peter Noll (1989) who began a diary after learning he had cancer of the bladder. He was informed that he needed surgery, which he understood would result in removal of the entire bladder, the placement of a plastic urine pouch on his abdomen, and permanent impotence. He refused surgery with the following comments:

> Perhaps my decision to refuse surgery is motivated by too much pride and arrogance. . . . I can't bring myself to submit to surgery that leaves me hollowed out, like a dugout canoe that floats along with no one in control . . . diminished and mutilated. . . . The urge to survive must never be allowed to become so absolutely overpowering that one submits to all of these indignities [p. 8-99].

When patients discuss the importance of dying with dignity, the indignities they refer to are damaged body image (edema, emaciation, deformities, etc.), diminished awareness, loss of control (incontinence), loss of independence (the need to be washed and fed, to ask or beg for medicine to relieve pain, to ask for a bed pan, to be cleaned after defecation), and the perceived loss of meaningful social roles and social value. In general, there is the loss of distortion of one's self-image. Many patients who are dying prefer privacy so that their prior image as a vital and healthy person is maintained to others. A friendly visit, in such situations, may be experienced as a humiliation.

SHAME IN DIFFERENT MEDICAL SPECIALTIES

In each medical specialty there is a different set of events and issues that evoke shame responses. In pediatrics, parents experience shame for their perceived genetic contributions to a child's disease or for their perceived failure to provide adequate care. In dermatology, the disease is often visible for the patient and others to see. John Updike (1980) eloquently describes his feelings about his psoriasis:

I am silvery, scaly. Puddles of flakes form wherever I rest my
flesh. . . . My torture is skin deep: there is no pain, not even itching;
we lepers live a long time, and are ironically healthy in other
respects. Lusty, though we are loathsome to love. Keen sighted,
though we hate to look upon ourselves. The name of the disease,
spiritually speaking, is "Humiliation" [p. 181].

In the field of obstetrics/gynecology, a patient may perceive her
sexuality as promiscuity or her lack of sexuality (or lack of pleasure
in sexuality) as incompetence. Inability to conceive or deliver a
normal fetus is further failure. Conceiving too many children or
children out of wedlock is considered socially irresponsible. Venereal
disease is seen as a sign of moral failure. Even when there is no
pathology, the examination requires undressing, exposing, and
penetrating the most private parts of the body. In the field of
gastroenterology, some diseases are believed to be stress related with
the implication of psychological weakness (peptic ulcers, ulcerative
colitis, irritable colon, Crohn's disease). Surgery for certain diseases
requires ileostomies and experiences of odors, deformities, and
incompetence.

NAMES OF DISEASES

As if the humiliation of disease, treatment, and dying were not
enough, there are medical and lay terms assigned to various diseases
that may be intrinsically shaming. In cardiology, there is cardiac
embarrassment, heart failure, coronary insufficiency, hypertension,
and inferior infarction. In reproductive medicine, one may be barren,
sterile, or suffering from an incompetent cervix. Personality disorders
in psychiatry include the narcissistic, histrionic, and borderline. In
infectious disease, AIDS is a deficiency disease. In orthopedics, there
is osteogenesis imperfecta and various degenerative diseases. All
cancers, even the curable ones, are malignancies. Patients with
certain physical limitations are referred to as in-valid. This list has
more than academic interest—patients are troubled by and resentful
of these labels.

STIGMA

In addition to the physical and psychological limitations caused by
the disease, patients may also feel stigmatized; that is, they are
socially discredited or branded, anticipating unfavorable reactions by

others. The subtitle of Goffman's (1963) book, *Stigma*, is particulary poignant: *Notes on the Management of Spoiled Identity*. Diseases that are stigmatizing may be categorized in the following ways: they offend others through their sight, odor, contagion, and the possibility of physical violence (e.g., leprosy, other dermatologic conditions, gross body deformities, contagious diseases, mental disorder, epilepsy); they are associated with low social station or poor living conditions (e.g., tuberculosis, lice, and gross dental neglect); they involve sexual or excretory organs (e.g., venereal disease, cancer of the rectum); they are believed to be caused by behaviors that are perceived by others as weak, stupid, immoral, or manifestations of personal failure (alcoholism, mental disorders, obesity, venereal disease, and AIDS). Given our current knowledge about the prevention of disease, many persons who become ill feel ashamed over their failure to behave in a prudent manner—by overeating, smoking, or failing to exercise. Similarly, patients who develop diseases that are believed, at least by the lay public, to be caused by stress or personality defects may feel a sense of inadequacy or personal failure. Such diseases include peptic ulcer, ulcerative colitis, rheumatoid arthritis, asthma, migraine headache, cancer, coronary artery disease, and essential hypertension.

There are exceptions to the principles I have described. To some persons, peptic ulcer or myocardial infarction is a badge of courage, evidence of hard work and success. In the 19th century, tuberculosis was associated with sensitivity and creativity. The stigma of epilepsy, tuberculosis, mental illness, and cancer has diminished over time as more has become known about their causes and as treatment has become more effective.

The Vulnerability to Shame

Attempts have been made to categorize issues over which people may be vulnerable to shame (Wurmser, 1981). These include the need to be loved and taken care of, not rejected; to be strong and powerful, not weak; to succeed or win, not fail or lose; to be clean and tidy, not messy and disgusting; to be good, not bad; to be whole and complete in physical and mental makeup, not defective; to be in control of bodily functions and feelings, not incontinent and out of control. A multitude of day-to-day issues involving self-esteem may be subsumed under these categories. The vulnerability to one or a combination of these issues varies from person to person, and the wide range of issues over which a person may be vulnerable makes it difficult to predict how that person will respond to a particular event.

In the medical setting, it is evident from clinical experience that self-esteem may be associated with physical attractiveness, strength, dexterity, intellectual acuity, sight, hearing, other physical or psychological attributes. One can make no iron-clad assumptions in advance that a given patient will or will not be humiliated over a given symptom or disease. Adolescents, in general, are more prone to shame than are people in other age groups; this vulnerability may be attributed to the rapid changes that are occurring in their bodies and identities. Physicians, many of whom enter the profession to conquer, master, or control disease and who are expected to know more about disease and its prevention than lay people, may be particularly shamed by their own illness (Pinner and Miller, 1952; Groves, 1986-87; Mandell and Spiro, 1987). This vulnerabilty to shame may explain, in part, why physicians delay seeking help for their own symptoms.

The Social Context of Shame

In the medical setting, a shame-inducing event (the perceived disease) and personal vulnerability ultimately interact with a social context when the patient seeks professional help. Patients who visit urban hospitals for the first time often brave unfamiliar traffic, search frantically for a parking space in high-priced lots, and, making their way through a labyrinth of buildings, pass busy and seemingly indifferent hospital employees as they search for the doctor's office. In the elevator, they hear white-suited house officers openly discuss patients. They hope they do not meet any acquaintances who may ask, "What are you doing here?" These patients may understandably feel bewildered, harassed, exposed, insignificant, and incompetent. They are not quite sure at that moment what preoccupies them most—their disease, their insignificance, or arriving late. In the waiting room, privacy is further eroded. Patients are noticed by other patients and labeled as people who belong in this office or clinic—oncology, hypertension, arthritis, psychiatry. In the waiting room they may be acutely aware of telephone communications in which other patients' names are mentioned within earshot of strangers. Eventually they are acknowledged by the secretary or other office personnel.

Once in the examining room, patients must reveal personal information (often about their weaknesses), expose their bodies, place themselves in undignified postures, and accept handling of their bodies, including intrusions into orifices. In normal socialization, we learn that such behaviors are shameful. On admission to the hospital, they must give up everyday clothes, valuables, freedom, and privacy. For certain diagnostic and treatment procedures, there is the further surrender of glasses, dentures, and hearing aids. In providing detailed histories, patients may be expected to describe their perspectives on their illness. They must tell of previous attempts to find lay and professional help, use of home remedies, theories about the cause and pathophysiology of the disease, fears about what is wrong with them, the reason for deciding to come for help at this time, goals of treatment, and desired methods of treatment. In anticipating such an inquiry, many patients fear they will be laughed at or criticized for their ideas about the nature of the disease, for causing or aggravating the disease, for waiting too long before seeking medical attention, or for coming too soon with such trivial complaints and so wasting the doctor's time. Patients may be further humiliated by the physician's pursuit of historical data about the possibility of such diseases as AIDS and venereal diseases. In communicating the diagnosis to the patient, physicians may become the messengers who carry the news of the humiliating event, that the patient has coronary insufficiency, heart failure, alcoholism, or syphilis. In effect, the physician or nurse may humiliate the patient by communicating the diagnosis.

Emergency-room visits are particularly humiliating because patients are apt to be frightened and privacy is often inadequate, particularly as they wait unattended in corridors for their X-rays or sit or walk about in "johnnies" flapping open at the rear. The curtain that covers the cubicle in the emergency room is seldom wide enough to provide adequate privacy.

REACTIONS TO SHAME

There is a wide variety of adaptive and maladaptive reactions to shame and humiliation (Lynd, 1958; Lewis, 1971; Wurmser, 1981). One adaptive response is to overcome one's weakness. For example, the desire to avoid shame may help the patient lose weight and maintain an exercise program. Three common maladaptive responses are depression, hiding/avoidance, and anger. The depressive response is understandable because depression and the low self-esteem of shame are so intertwined. In medical settings, the response of hiding or avoidance takes the form of lying to the physician about the severity of the symptoms, failure to comply with the prescribed treatment, self-treatment, breaking appointments, or generally avoiding the physician. ("I will see the doctor after I have lost weight." "I will make an appointment when my blood pressure is down." "I will see the dentist after I get my gums in better shape.") The most maladaptive forms of hiding are suicide and the denial of illness.

An angry response is a manifestation of humiliated rage. Such anger is particularly dangerous because it may lead to long-standing grudges and acts of revenge. Patients respond to humiliated rage by expressing anger indirectly through criticism of other employees in the office or hospital ward, changing physicians, complaining about the medical profession, filing a formal complaint with the patient care office, or suing.

I believe that most patients who are angry at their physicians or nurses are responding to perceived experiences of shame. The specific complaints are not that the doctor makes mistakes, misses the diagnosis, causes too much pain, or charges too much. The complaints are that "the doctor seems too busy for me," "the doctor tells me I am too fat," "the doctor treats me like a piece of meat," "the doctor is sexist," "the doctor insults my intelligence," "the doctor thinks my problem is all in my head." Underlying these complaints are expressions of shame and humiliation.

SHAME AND HUMILIATION IN PHYSICIANS

Physicians are particularly prone to shame because of their perfectionistic personality traits, their concern over the life-and-death issues of everyday practice, their fear of ignorance in the face of overwhelming information, and the changing nature of the doctor–patient relationship, which diminishes their authority.

During the past several years, I have lectured to physicians and nurses on the general subject of shame and humiliation in medical encounters. At the end of the lecture I have asked the audience to respond on a blank sheet of paper to the following directions: "Please describe the most shameful or humiliating experience of your professional career." Approximately 20% of the audience completes the form. The responses can be organized into five categories. The first includes experiences related to humiliations during student or house officer training. The second includes experiences with the person's own illness or illness of a family member; third, experiences related to feelings of incompetence regarding professional functioning;

fourth, reactions to criticism by fellow professionals; fifth, reactions to criticism by patients. Most striking about the responses are the detailed descriptions of painful experiences, many of which occurred many years before.

THERAPEUTIC IMPLICATIONS

Shame is a common source of suffering. To manage shame optimally in medical encounters, clinicians should assume that any disease (and treatment) can be a shame-inducing event, which then interacts with a patient's individual vulnerabilities. With this heightened awareness, clinicians can then use their skills to manage the social context of the medical encounter. In this role, clinicians attend to three interrelated tasks: (1) diminishing the patient's shame; (2) avoiding exacerbating the patient's shame; and (3) recognizing and managing their own shame.

To accomplish these goals, physicians and nurses should attempt to develop relationships in which the patient allows them to come inside the protective boundaries erected to avoid shame. Ideally, patients should come to believe that their exposure to physical and emotional weaknessess will be respected. From this perspective, there are common elements in patients' relationships to their physicians and to those they love. Patients' lonely anguish over their illnesses and the physicians' socially defined roles as nonjudgmental healers make such relationships both possible and desirable. The betrayal of such a trust will lead to humiliation, usually beyond repair.

What follows are several observations and suggestions on the management of shame based on discussions with patients and experienced clinicians.

The Ambience of the Hospital and Office

Physicians have the ability and responsibility to influence patients' experiences in the hospital and office, including the admission procedure, emergency attendance, X-rays, and blood drawing. Patients commonly feel frightened, depersonalized, and dehumanized and feel that their presence and needs are an imposition on the complex bureaucracy rather than the reason for its existence. Physicians and nurses need to work with administrators to create an atmosphere in which patients feel welcome, cared for, and respected.

Waiting for the Physician

It is important for the physician to see patients with minimal delay. Long waits after the designated appointment time or interruptions during the visit devalue the importance of patients' time and worries. A simple apology for significant lateness or unavoidable interruptions acknowledges that the delay or interruption is the physician's problem or a result of unavoidable circumstances and not an indication of the patient's lesser status.

The Use of Surnames

Professionals seeing adult patients for the first time should refer to them by their proper titles and last names. Calling new patients by their first names forces a level of intimacy to which the patient has not agreed. It also assigns to patients a lesser status, since they are generally not expected to refer to the physician by his or her first name. Asking patients how they would like to be addressed puts the burden on them to anticipate what the professional would like to hear. Changes in the way professional and patient address each other should be initiated by the patient or negotiated as the relationship evolves.

Supporting the Patient's Self-Concept

A patient's self-concept is placed in jeopardy by feeling sick, by assuming the patient role, and by specific medical procedures (removing clothes and other personal belongings). Patients attempt to strengthen their self-concept by bringing personal possessions, such as photographs, to the bedside and by sharing personal stories that emphasize the nonpatient role. Professionals should support these attempts.

Attention to Privacy

Professionals communicate respect and dignity to patients by attending to the privacy of their body parts, verbal disclosures, and records.

The Professional's Self-Exposure

The professionals' self-exposure, carefully thought out, can help diminish the patient's shame and humiliation. ("I broke my leg skiing. The recuperation can be dreadful, having to ask people for help all the time.") There are at least three pitfalls in the use of self-exposure. First, patients may feel the professional is burdening them with his or her problems. Second, patients may experience the professional as superior and condescending, because they have already solved similar problems. Third, patients may experience the professional as offering insincere support ("I know how you feel").

Shaming the Patient

Shaming the patient can be effective when it is done out of a sense of caring by a professional whose relationship with the patient is positive and secure. Otherwise, the shaming will damage and possibly terminate the relationship. "John, I've known you and your family for 20 years. You just have to stop smoking."

Acknowledging the Patient's Shame and Humiliation

When professionals suspect that shame and humiliation are important aspects of the patients' experience, they may engage patients by empathically commenting on their distress without referring specifically to shame. For example: "It is not easy to come and see a physician" or "This disease can place enormous stress on a person" or "What does this illness mean to you?" Such comments or questions invite patients ultimately to share more specific aspects of the stress, including feelings of shame and humiliation. Helping the patient identify these emotions helps dissipate some of the suffering.

Validating and Praising the Patient

It is often helpful to support a patient's decision to see a professional ("It was wise of you to come today; change in pigmentation of a mole, like you have, can be quite a source of worry"). Such a response diminishes patients' concerns that their worries are trivial or foolish and that they are wasting the physician's time. It may be equally helpful to praise patients on the management of their disease. In the lonely struggle with chronic or deteriorating disease, patients often feel that they are failures. Their families may feel helpless, discouraged, and angry. The physician may be the only one who can see courage and heroism in the patient's coping behavior.

Clarifying the Patient's Perspective on the Problem

Professionals may be able to diminish patients' shame and humiliation by eliciting and responding to the patients' perspective on the illness—their definition of the problem, including their theories about the nature of the illness; their goals of treatment; and their requests for particular methods of treatment. It is common for professionals to discover through this inquiry a set of unrealistic beliefs that support shame-based views of the disease—that the patient is to blame for the disease, that the infectious disease is contagious, that the patient is morally or physically weak, or that the disease is a source of stigma. Such an inquiry affords the professional the opportunity to discuss and refute such beliefs and to provide alternative explanatory models.

The Use of Support Groups

Certain patients and families of patients with humiliating conditions make good use of support groups made up of people with similar disorders. Obese people, alcoholics, families of alcoholics, families of brain-injured patients, women who have undergone radical mastectomies, families whose infants died of sudden infant death syndrome, infertile couples, and families of the mentally ill have all organized self-help groups.

Responses to Patients Who Fail to Accept Medical Advice

With patients who are obese, who smoke, or who engage in other behaviors that obviously impair health, the professional runs the risk of causing humiliation with lectures or confrontations during each visit. One solution to this problem is to educate such patients about their illness during a visit and then assure them that this will be the last such lecture until and unless the patient initiates the discussion. Another method of responding to such diseases is to encourage the patient to define the problem: "Are there any other problems that you would like me to help you work on?" Patients who acknowledge their own problems are more apt to maintain their dignity than are those who are confronted by others with their weaknesses.

Professionals' Management of Their Own Shame

One of the most difficult but important tasks for physicians in the clinical encounter is the recognition and management of their own shame. A clue to this situation is the professional's anger at the patient, inadvertent humiliation of the patient, or a wish not to see the patient again. By attending to any of these signals, professionals can explore whether they feel shamed or humiliated by the patient. They can then analyze the dynamics of the relationship and plan a therapeutic response. For example, a frustrated and embarrassed physician whose patient is not responding to treatment asks the patient: "Are you sure you are taking the medications I have prescribed?" The patient, feeling insulted that his integrity has been questioned, says, "I do not think we are getting anywhere. Perhaps I should consult with another doctor." The physician, further humiliated by the patient's request, might continue the downhill spiral of counterhumiliation by encouraging the patient to leave. Alternatively, the physician can return to the critical juncture and address the insult: "I did not mean to offend you by my question about your taking the medicine. I apologize." In another example, a 55-year-old woman consults a physician for her high blood pressure. He performs the proper examinations, confirms the diagnosis, and recommends that the patient lose weight, lower her salt intake, take antihypertensive medications, and return in three weeks. The patient returns in five weeks and informs the physician that she is a religious woman and that God has told her that she does not need to lose weight, lower her salt intake, or take pills. The physician, feeling humiliated that his carefully thought-out recommendations were not heeded, humiliates the woman and her religious beliefs by saying: "Did your God tell you who your next doctor will be?" Had the physician been aware of his own feelings and response, he could have made one of many nonhumiliating responses, such as, "Is there some way in which you would like me to help?" After all, the patient did return.

Physicians can also gain some mastery over their humiliation by creating an atmosphere among their peers where these feelings can be openly discussed instead of avoided for fear of seeming weak or unprofessional. Such discussions and labeling of emotions diminish the psychological need for counterhumiliation on the part of physicians and provide profound insights into the suffering of patients.

CONCLUDING REMARKS

It is curious that experiences of shame and humiliation are generally ignored in the medical and nursing literature. There are three possible explanations for this omission. First, even as physicians and nurses treat patients with the greatest sensitivity, respect, and decorum, it has not been part of the medical tradition to inquire about the subjective experience of the patient. Second, in our concern as physicians and nurses to do no harm, it is difficult for us to contemplate how we inevitably contribute to the suffering of shame in patients. Finally, neither patients nor medical practitioners like to acknowledge or discuss their own shame and humiliation. It is shameful even to admit that one feels ashamed.

REFERENCES

Goffman, E. (1963), *Stigma*. New York: Simon & Schuster.
Groves, J. (1986-1987), *Physician Sketch Thyself*. Harvard Medical Alumni Bulletin. 60:36-38.
Lewis, H. (1971), *Shame and Guilt in Neurosis*. New York: International Universities Press.
Lynd, H. M. (1958), *On Shame and the Search for Identity*. New York: Harcourt Brace & World.
Mandell, H. & Spiro, H., eds. ((1987), *When Doctors Get Sick*. New York: Plenum Press.
Miller, S. (1985), *The Shame Experience*. Hillsdale, NJ: The Analytic Press.
Noll, P. (1989), *In the Face of Death*. New York: Viking Press.
Pinner, M. & Miller, B. F., eds. (1952), *When Doctors Are Patients*. New York: Norton.
Updike, J. (1980), *Problems and Other Stories*. New York: Knopf.
Wurmser, L. (1981), *The Mask of Shame*. Baltimore, MD: Johns Hopkins University Press.

19

MICHAEL J. BADER

Shame and the Resistance to Jewish Renewal

A 30-year-old man—I'll call him Robert—has been in psychotherapy with me for two years. Our work has been enormously productive. As a result of working through a number of conflicts, Robert has made profound changes in his life, including freeing up his professional ambitions and finally getting into a long-term and loving relationship with a woman. One of the unexpected byproducts of his therapeutic work was his decision to return to and renew his connection to Judaism. I therefore have had a unique opportunity to observe how working through specific psychological conflicts seemed to enable Robert to seek out a deeper experience of Jewish spirituality.

Robert's conflicts primarily involved his intense feelings of shame and embarrassment when he was faced with or drawn to situations that seemed to invite an experience of awe, surrender, or love. Prayer and faith—even if defined within a progressive context—were just such situations. Relational configurations that invited Robert to open himself to love and being loved, to "let go" of his customary cynical caution and surrender to a dyadic or group intimacy, tended to trigger intense feelings of shame that invariably led him to retreat.

The issues that Robert's idiosyncratic struggles with shame brought into bold relief resonated with conflicts of my own that emerged when I decided to convert to Judaism. Belonging to a

---

The Editors wish to thank Stanley Goodman, M.D. for drawing their attention to this essay.

group, ritualized devotion, the "God" word, openness to nonrational experience, recognizing the limits of human agency, all had personal meanings that both drew and repelled me. Although my formulations about Robert were highly case specific, there were ways that his struggles felt familiar to me. Furthermore, as I talked with other Jews about our resistances to the spiritual aspects of Judaism, these shame-based reflexes seemed to emerge frequently. Thus, an analysis of Robert's unique ways of associating spiritual surrender, love, embarrassment, and cynicism can highlight a more generic problem many of us face in connecting with a spiritually meaningful Judaism.

During the course of our work, Robert discovered the extent to which he had grown up highly sensitive and vulnerable to feelings of shame. One particular memory highlighted some of the central meanings of embarrassment in Robert's development. He remembered that when he was a young child a neighboring family used to spend Sundays together, barbecuing, playing games, singing. Robert's father was openly contemptuous of their neighbors and frequently mocked them for being like "the Cleavers." Robert inferred that his father felt it was pathetic to be so insular, that there was something shameful about the neighbors' apparent "need" to "glom" onto each other. He felt embarrassed about and for them.

Years later, talking to me about it, Robert realized that he had come to view familial togetherness itself as weak, pathetic, and embarrassing, while idealizing its opposite—his own family's experience, which was one of isolation, alienation, and disconnection. His own parents were alcoholics, his father a cynical and stoic intellectual, a "loner." Robert idealized his father and, therefore, his father's model of relatedness in which love, tenderness, and dependence were implicitly devalued and shameful. Because Robert, like all of us, continued to experience desires for affiliation and loving connection, he was always vulnerable to feeling embarrassed. If he loved someone too tenderly or too openly, he fell victim to the same contempt from his conscience that he had once experienced from his father.

How do love and shame come to feel connected? What is the structure of the inner experience of someone, like Robert, who feels—or fears feeling—this way. Perhaps if we could unpack this state and make it "talk," it might say something like this: "I openly declare that I love you and need you to love me. I experience you as rejecting or ignoring my declaration. At this hypothetical moment, I feel as I did as a child, that I'm not *supposed* to be loved or have my love accepted. It is not *you* who are impaired or sadistic and unable to enjoy giving and receiving love, but it is I who am not offering or deserving good things. Rather than having just revealed to myself and you what is most wonderful about me, I have just disclosed something bad about me that accounts for your negative or absent response." The experience of involuntary exposure of something that is precious to me but bad or unimportant to you is what becomes internalized in the feeling of shame.

Feelings of shame and embarrassment can enforce our unconscious loyalty to our parents and, later, to an internalized authority who prohibits certain feeling states and demands compliance to other ones. Given our dependency on them, our parents have an awesome power to shape our core identities. As children, we experience *what is*—the affective realities of family—with *what is supposed to be*. Reality is also morality. Because Robert's family tended to be cynical, isolated, and joyless, he sensed that he—and the world—were fated to be cynical and joyless as well. To be cynical might be painful, but it was familiar and made "sense." For Robert to have been optimistic, idealistic, and joyful, for instance, would potentially pose any number of threats. He might have lost his connection to his family or exposed himself to the ridicule of his father; he might have felt guilty for having a better life than his cynical father or alcoholic mother had; he might have felt tormented by pity.

Joseph Weiss (1993) has termed the kinds of belief structures about love that Robert developed as "pathogenic beliefs." Weiss argues that, as children, we all continually construct theories about cause and effect, infer various rules that appear to govern relationships, and ascribe meanings about who we are from our affective exchanges with our caretakers and significant others. We are highly motivated to do so in order to maintain safe and gratifying connections to these caretakers. Robert's pathogenic belief was that tender love and familial intimacy were pathetic, that it was shameful and weak to desire these things, and that the ability to "go it alone" stoically and cynically was admirable and a sign of strength. This unconscious belief enabled him, by way of identification, to maintain a connection to his father, ward off his father's contempt, avoid guilt over having a better life than this father, and maintain the comforting illusion that his father was strong, not disappointingly and frighteningly weak (which, of course, the father actually was).

Over time, Robert came to see that his defensive idealization of his father's cynicism included the father's defiant and contemptuous secularism. Robert's father had himself been raised in a politically conservative, Orthodox family. He had rebelled against an autocratic father by moving away geographically (to the opposite coast),

politically (becoming a leftist), and religiously (rejecting all religiosi-
ty). Robert's father had spurned all of the spiritual trappings of his
family's authoritarian Judaism, by becoming a secular, hyperintellec-
tual, politically cynical adult. He had allowed Robert to become a bar
mitzvah because of his wife's insistence and some residual guilt
toward his own parents, but he had strongly conveyed to his son his
scorn and skepticism of religious ritual and belief.

In his desperate attempts to maintain a connection to the father,
Robert thus identified with the parent's hyperrational and cynical
secularism. Unconsciously, Robert associated a spiritual experience
of Judaism with the other affects that seemed to make his father
uncomfortable and critical. Robert unconsciously found security and
the illusion of belonging by internalizing his father's character in all
its manifestations.

Unfortunately, for Robert these unconscious benefits were
purchased at the cost not only of a connection to Judaism but also of
his ability to love and tolerate intimacy, states he associated with
shame. When Robert got too close to gratifying his longing to belong
and experience a loving connection, he would begin to feel mildly
embarrassed. He would then unconsciously begin to take evasive
measures to nip this painful state in the bud. He would pull back,
intellectualize, make a joke, become sarcastic and cynical. To further
reinforce his defenses against being "seduced" down a slippery slope
of intimacy, he would choose friends and partners who themselves
were embarrassed about vulnerability or love.

Robert even found a way to collude with his first psychotherapist
in his shame-based battle with feelings of love, idealization, and
surrender. The therapist frequently interpreted Robert's love for him
in terms of transference; he would point out that Robert was
idealizing him in order both to express and to avoid certain childhood conflicts involving his disappointment, hostility, and competitiveness with his father. Although partially correct, by focusing only
on the conflictual and infantile meanings of Robert's loving idealization, the therapist unwittingly confirmed the patient's view that there
was something irrational and even unseemly about these feelings.
Ironically, the patient was grateful for and relieved at the subtle push
to distance himself from these embarrassing feelings, a push that
unfortunately enabled Robert to avoid dealing with the conflicts that
these feelings evoked.

Robert's battle with shame was not limited to experiences of
love. For instance, he remembered that when he was 11 years old,
he bought a pair of iridescent pants that he hoped would boost his
seventh-grade social life. On the first day of school, the prettiest girl

in the class sarcastically commented, "Look at that—Robert think he's so cool with his new pants!" He almost died from embarrassment. This incident was the tip of an iceberg of shame over another set of feelings that also went back into Robert's earlier childhood. Showing-off, being proud, feeling sexy, exuberant, and cocky formed a complex of affective states that Robert had inferred (à la Joseph Weiss) would elicit a negative response or rejection, cause harm, disrupt a connection, or, at least, not be mirrored. The sword of Damocles that hung over his head when he began to express these strivings was the traumatic experience of shame.

If one searches one's own past honestly, experiences of shame can often be found to have shaped one's personality. I remember experiences of being ridiculed, usually by peers, for being a "teacher's pet." I later understood that I had a desperate need to attach myself to a strong authority with whom I could have a "mutual admiration society." This need had to do with conflicts and deficiencies in my own family. I came to feel embarrassed about my (healthy, I now believe in retrospect) desire to find someone to idealize and who would recognize and love me in return. It is easy to see how shame over being a "teacher's pet" might have extended to embarrassment over having any kind of special relationship to the divine!

As Robert and I analyzed these shame-based conflicts, he began to allow himself to experiment with more intimate and less cynical relationships. He found a partner who seemed unembarrassed about giving and receiving love. I was able to help him accept his love for me and understand that his need to see it as "transference" and not *real* was a compliance with his father's—and former therapist's—perceived inability to tolerate love. In the course of Robert's growth, he became aware of desires to reconnect with Judaism, to "belong" to the Jewish community, and to explore its spiritual rituals and meanings with a more open mind. He sought out private and group teaching from both a Jewish renewal rabbi and a Conservative rabbi and, looking for the right "fit," attended services in a variety of congregations. He began to observe Shabbat and sought to find ways to pray that he could intellectually accept.

Robert's spiritual renewal seemed to flow directly from his new-found freedom from the inhibitions that his shame had imposed. The threat of embarrassment had somehow helped him cut off his positive feelings about Judaism, and he felt a resurgence of these feelings when he worked through some of his shame-based psychological conflicts. His deepening encounters with Judaism continually stirred up all these earlier conflicts, although now he could attempt to confront and work through them.

This process helped me understand how certain aspects of the spiritual experience have a quintessential power to evoke shame and a defensive resistance. I saw it clearly in Robert, in myself, and in some of my friends. I believe that we can generalize from Robert's experience to get a better understanding of why many Jews—whether they be converts like myself or secular Jews—might have difficulties embracing the spiritual dimension of their religion.

How did Robert's attempt to return to Judaism evoke signals or full-fledged experiences of embarrassment? The notion of God embarrassed him a little. He could not escape images of a paternalistic reified God toward whom he felt pressed irrationally to submit, a relationship he found throughout the *Siddur* (prayer book). It embarrassed him to express love and gratitude to this God. At first, the problem seemed "rational"—after all, Robert did have rational and healthy grounds for viewing this kind of expression as a naive and hypocritical submission to an empty or hierarchical concept. So why not look for a different understanding of God? He had a hard time finding one that didn't seem too abstract or somehow "gimmicky." He became aware, however, that his discomfort stemmed from more than a set of reasonable intellectual objections. Even when he found certain conceptualizations about God to be pleasing, he had a hard time praying, or even meditating, in any way that felt spiritual to him. There was something in the stance of worship itself that triggered shame signals.

The Jewish renewal congregations he looked into were better in some ways but worse in others. One of them, for instance, seemed to have a high level of creative spiritual energy, but Robert felt distracted and embarrassed by many of its New Age elements. For instance, one meditation exercise involved each member's being greeted by the group chanting the *Sh'ma*,[1] but replacing "Israel" with the individual's first name. On another occasion, the group was encouraged to pretend they were at Sinai or to creatively visualize a conversation with Abraham.

Robert recognized the potential value of these exercises, aimed as they were at helping people develop their own personal and unique spiritual relationship to God, to prayer, and to the Jewish community. But he still felt uneasy, felt the familiar upsurge of embarrassment and cynicism. He had always felt cynical about "New

---

[1]The *Sh'ma* is the cornerstone of Jewish belief, that is, the belief in only one God.

Agey" techniques designed to foster greater self-awareness and intimacy: he saw them as artificial and intrusive. Robert sensed, however, that there was more to his current discomfort, since he knew that the people involved were actually quite sincere and respectful. In fact, he realized that the absence of cynicism and intellectual distance in these groups made him anxious and embarrassed, almost as if he were being asked to disrobe or open his heart. He was aware of reflex reactions of contempt, distancing himself from the group with rationalizations (partly true) about the problems of New Age psychology. Robert was familiar with these reflexes, having analyzed them extensively in relation to other interpersonal situations, and thus he understood that his principled objections to the "gimmicky" conventions of the Jewish renewal minyans he visited were also fueled by more personal and neurotic issues.

What are the particular meanings associated with spiritual experience that, for some people, evoke strong signals of embarrassment? One such meaning involves the quality of surrender and awe and its association with infantile dependence.The feeling of "awe" that often accompanies spiritual experience is a state of being that, in our culture, characterizes the child's world view much more than the average adult's. It arises in the context of the child's experience of his or her smallness and helplessness in relation to powerful and idealized parents. Within the context of this asymmetrical relationship, the child's love for the parent is marked by a powerful experience of the parent's power and perfection and a wish to draw from this power through association, dependence, and identification. Idealization and the wish to surrender to and identify with the parents' perfection are normal and healthy in children and, despite the prevailing cultural celebration of autonomy and personal freedom, remain crucial components of healthy adult relationships.

Several factors often intervene to make this feeling state highly conflicted. First, there are various forms of distortion or breakdown within the parent–child relationship. The parent might feel unworthy of the child's idealization and admiration because of his or her own low self-esteem or anxiety about being loved in this way. Sensing that the parent doesn't enjoy or cannot tolerate his admiration, the child is unable to enjoy admiring the parent. Or the parent might actually be profoundly impaired or otherwise disappointing, thus frustrating the child's need for a hero. The child might pretend that the parent is not flawed, but harbors a deep cynicism nevertheless. Or the parent exploits the child's idealization by narcissistically requiring it, thereby increasing the child's feelings of helplessness. Awe, then, comes to be associated in this instance with submission. In any case, the capacity to experience awe and wonder is associated with disappointment and some form of humiliation.

The experience of love in which one surrenders to an idealized other can threaten to evoke a traumatic sense of deflation or rejection and thus must be disguised or otherwise warded off. This kind of defensive activity can take many forms. A person might develop a certain cynicism about the possibilities of love. She or he might be vigilant about not appearing to admire or idealize anyone or anything too much. One might develop a sarcastic manner or personality style or be the first to be "realistic" whenever an idealistic venture is being discussed.

The spiritual experience contains meanings that function as the quintessential triggers for these intrapsychic conflicts. The person who is praying is expressing his or her love for and belief in something greater than the self. It is a state of voluntary surrender. It is saying, "I love you and am loved by you," however the divine "you" is conceptualized or represented. This is a state of potential humiliation for many people. All the disappointments, rejections, and prohibitions against experiencing the vicissitudes of this state are brought into play within the person approaching this state, and with all of the concomitant defensive resistances. Many—if not most—conceptions of God, for instance, within the Jewish liturgy and practice can become the lightning rod for this conflict. Whether it be declarations of love for the Sabbath "Bride," the flat-out celebration and awe of God in the Psalms, or the images of humble self-efface-ment in the morning prayer (*Ribon Kol Ha-Olamim*), Jewish rituals and prayers that describe the special relationship between Israel and God as one of loving idealization, awe, and surrender can tap into our reservoirs of shame. And even if we discount the manifest and literal meanings of the words and introduce feminine images of God, or views of God as a force moving us toward transformation and healing, we are still faced with the latent shameful meanings that are attached to the very stance of spiritual devotion, awe, and love.

Depending upon one's idiosyncratic history as well as certain modern cultural norms, this stance of religious observance or worship is unconsciously equated with a naive, vulnerable, and childish position and thus triggers signals of embarrassment. Believing in God, then, not only is problematic on scientific/rational grounds, but also is associated with several levels of shameful experience. First, the "God" of one's childhood was probably a personified presence, empty of meaning, with whom everyone around you had a hypocritical, sterile, obsequious, or irrelevant relationship. Having grown up, become "enlightened," and freed yourself of much of the pathogenic baggage of the past, you see the prospect of relating to this flat God-image of your childhood as a humiliating retreat or self-defeating identification with role models long since discarded.

Second, we all, of necessity, adapt to the disappointment in and corruption of important authorities in our lives, and any notion of a divine authority, however broadly defined, threatens to re-expose us to psychological trauma. We defensively identify with that aspect of our parents which has given up hope, accepted compromise, become resigned to failure, sunk into cynicism. As children we all sought to connect with our parents in any way that provided us with security. Loving or believing in a divine force that offers up hope and the possibility of transformation, of goodness, can become unconsciously equated with thumbing one's nose at the cynical morality of one's family and facing the extent to which they have disappointed and failed us. To abandon oneself to any kind of transcendental spiritual experience breaks or defies these familial identifications and creates intense anxieties and fears of retribution. The form this punishment often takes is the prospect of being deeply shamed or humiliated.

Historically, psychoanalysis has understood the experience of worship in pathological terms—as a passive and infantile love for the father and a sexualized surrender to or merger with his power. I suggest that this is not only a deep distortion of Judaism but a pathogenic psychological belief, a belief that equates surrender with submission, idealization of the other with self-effacement, and love with weakness. In fact, as I have argued, awe, surrender, and idealization are naturally occurring states of being in healthy development, dialectically in tension with other states of self-control and egoistic mastery. The capacity not only to objectively recognize forces we cannot control but to relax our controls at certain times and be swept away by these forces without fear of identity diffusion or humiliation requires that we achieve certain developmental skills and acquire a certain self-confidence and basic trust. One could even say that the inability to "let go" to some experience or relationship that is "greater" than we reflects an impairment and significant inhibition and reveals the workings of various pathogenic beliefs.

It is important that I be clear that I am describing one factor— shame, psychodynamically understood—that contributes to the resistance to spiritual involvement among many modern Jews. Obviously, there are a host of other meanings associated with awe, surrender, and worship that lead people to pull away from the experience. To the extent that surrender, in fact, is associated with submission, it will evoke all the unacceptable memories and situations that we correctly oppose. Whether it be women's submission to male authority, submission to self-serving social and political authority, or the daily pressure to comply with pathological familial situations while we were growing up, many of us have both deep-seated and healthy resistances to bowing down before anything "greater" than ourselves. In addition, there are all the complex ways in which, throughout the social history of Jews as well as the personal experience that many Jews have had with the religious authorities of their childhood, the experience of worship was empty of meaning, autocratic and repressive, sanitized by assimilationist forces anxiously seeking public acceptance, or otherwise hypocritical and dead. And my own experience reminded me that this spiritual emptiness and resulting embarrassment is common among non-Jews as well. But the relevant issue in my current argument is that many Jews have been left with deep visceral reflexes against spiritual experience at all, much less one involving themes of awe, mystery, or connecting to some ineffable "energy" over which one has little or no control.

These reflexes can indeed be rational and healthy and are not intrinsically reducible to irrational psychodynamic conflicts. My interest, however, is in looking at how the irrational psychodynamic conflicts that do exist contribute to a rejection of conventional forms of Jewish spirituality as well as more contemporary, progressive attempts at Jewish renewal. There is an interplay, in other words, between the rational and the irrational forces at work, and it behooves us to recognize both. To the extent that our resistances are based on irrational dispositions to shame, then even the best attempts to humanize and radicalize Judaism will incur a reflex opposition.

Finally, I believe that it is easy to see how political resignation and a culture of cynicism and self-interest fits into this characterological inhibition. If everyone is out for himself or herself, why should I open myself up by believing in some pie-in-the-sky future or have idealistic hopes for anything? Protecting and expanding one's own turf, not being taken for a fool, guarding against being exploited, firming up one's capacity to act autonomously, being sure not to get one's hopes up, being "realistic"—these are all adaptive, albeit defensive, responses to the kind of market-oriented culture of individualism that we live in today. These socially conservative reflexes harmonize with the intrapsychic reflexes that I have been describing. And, similarly, they are also all intended to ward off the shame and embarrassment of believing in something greater than the self—in this case, that "something" is political transformation and the possibility of a society built on compassion and love. In this sense, then, the contemptuous attitude of Robert's father toward his neighbors' enjoying a family barbecue is intimately related to the media's contemptuous dismissal of Hillary Clinton's attempts to talk about spirituality and meaning in politics; And all of this is related to the embarrassment of someone invited to share a spiritual experience at a Jewish Renewal minyan. They are linked in their insistence that belief in the transcendent power of love is, ultimately, foolish, sophomoric, and shameful.

An understanding of the dynamics of shame can thus be used to illuminate the resistance to spiritual experience within any religious paradigm. There is nothing especially embarrassing about Jewish versions of prayer, God, or religious ritual and observance. In fact, as I mentioned earlier, the dynamics I am analyzing apply to the popular cynicism about nonreligious experiences as well, for example, advocacy of a politics of meaning community, or an idealistic vision of social change. For those of us committed to helping people connect with a Jewish spiritual practice, however, the ways that this practice acquires meanings that trigger shame and avoidance is obviously crucial to understand and somehow address.

How do we help ourselves and others feel less embarrassed? I cannot help but try to import certain paradigms that seem to work in psychotherapy. In general, as a therapist, I try to make it safe for the patient to expose shameful aspects of herself or himself, identify the pathogenic beliefs that produce the shame, and provide experiential evidence in the form of actions, explanations, and attitudes that disconfirm these beliefs and expectations. Successful therapy depends on unconscious, as well as conscious, learning. For instance, with a patient such as Robert who has identified with a cynical father and is contemptuous of his own tenderness or wish for love, I might repeatedly explain to him at moments of emerging shame why he feels that way; explain how it makes "sense" given his familial experience; help him see how it is now highly self-defeating and maladaptive; and articulate a healthier vision of love and mutuality to provide a therapeutic reference point. In addition, I would not hesitate to model or otherwise reveal attitudes of robust and self-confident tenderness and unembarrassed expressions of warmth. I would not, however, get too far ahead of the patient If he tended to use humor, sarcasm, or intellectualization, I would respect his defenses and would "join-in" to some extent, all the while attempting to push the envelope of his ability to tolerate a more serious mutuality by talking to him about his underlying pathogenic beliefs. As Stephen Mitchell (1993) put it, it is as if the patient had

asked you, the therapist, to dance but only knows one step. You
don't condemn the patient for this limitation or refuse to dance. You
accept the invitation and gently suggest some new steps.

Likewise, on a social or community level, we might try to find
ways to talk about how spiritual experience can be embarrassing. We
might confront our self-consciousness about collective spiritual
experience, self-disclosure, and anything that smacks of spiritual
surrender. We should be explicit that it is healthy and good for
people to pray and spiritually connect in their own way, however
imperfect, so that everyone feels that whatever they do is O.K. and
better than doing nothing. We should continue, as Michael Lerner
(1994) has done, to generate images of God that people can hook
into without shame. We need to talk to each other about how we
can surrender and feel awe without submission. We need to redefine
strength and weakness in our religious traditions, as well as in the
broader struggle to develop a politics of meaning. The challenge is
to find ways of talking about surrender, awe, and idealization in a
context of strength—now reconceptualized as deriving from love,
interconnectedness, and a sense of being part of a larger historical
religious tradition and movement. These attempts at redefinition can
help make it safer for those Jews and others vulnerable to spiritual
embarrassment to reengage with religious rituals and experience.
Understanding the underlying fear and pain that lead to cynicism
about spiritual experience can help us develop a greater openness to
and tolerance of each other—our imperfections as well as the unique
way that each of us relates to the divine.

REFERENCES

Lerner, M. (1994), *Jewish Renewal*. New York: Addison-Wesley.
Mitchell, S. (1993), *Hope and Dread in Psychoanalysis*. New York:
    Basic Books.
Weiss, J. (1993), *How Psychotherapy Works*. New York: Guilford
    Press.

Index

A

Absoluteness, in moral masochism, 378–379
Abstemiousness, stance of, 36
Abstractness, 114, 119
Acceleration, 121–122
Acceptability, 13, 99
Acceptance, 205
Acknowledgment, Nietzsche's view on, 197
Action, 49, 166, 167
Adam and Eve, shame and, 173, 174, 206–207, 233
Adamson, L., 49, *62*
Adler, A., 66, *84,* 140, 149, 150, *153,* 220, *228,* 314, *322,* 336, *337*
  Freud's discussion of, 15
  shame and, 66
  view on pathological shame, 150
Adolescents, shame in, 388
Adult, affect production in, 339
Affect, 36, 45, 46, 89, 111–112
  ability to tolerate, arrest in, 277
  activation of, 112, 113, 114, 261
  activators of, 113
  amplification, 125
  amplification of sex drive by, 115
  as analog amplifier, 122, 262
  Basch's view on, 342
  basic, 121
  biological systems for, 110
  cause and effect relationship, 51n
  density, 128

differentiated from emotion, 134
drives and, 111
experience of, 79, 119, 132, 133t, 344
innate, 115, 116, 117, 123, 131, 133, 136, 356
  shame as, 46, 47
  Tomkins's view on, 120
integration, 78, 79
interaffectivity, 344, 345
within intersubjective system, 79–80
learned triggers for, 128
magnification, 125
management, 356
match and mismatch with other mechanisms, 119
mechanism, 119
motivational primacy of, 78
mutualization of, 348
negative, 45, 56, 112, 126
  hierarchy of, 123–124
  shame as, 124
object of, 119
painful, attachment to, 373n
positive, 45, 112, 122, 124, 126, 127–128, 347
  impediment to, 130, 348, 360
  incomplete reduction of, 46, 124
  shame and, 46
primary, 128, 130–131
rejection of, 128
in relation to self and object, vii

409

Stierlin, H., 5, *40*
Stigma, in medical setting, 386–389
"Still-face" experiments, 49
Stimulus
    acquisition, 122
    analogue of, affect as, 122
    response to, 349
Stimulus-affect-response sequence
        (SAR triplets), 116, 131, 360,
        361
Stimulus decrease, 45, 113, 115, 121,
        122, 356
Stimulus density, 115, 343
Stimulus gradient, 343
Stimulus increase, 45, 113, 115, 121,
        122, 356
Stimulus level, 45, 113, 115, 121,
        122, 356
Stimulus-response (S-R) pairs, 116,
        131
    language of, 349
Stiver, I., 317, *322*
Stoller, R. J., 350, *354*
Stolorow, R. D., 44, 74, 75, 77, 78,
        79, 81, 82, *84, 87,* 102, *104*
    description of Kohut's idea of
        vertical split, 103
    view on narcissism and intersub-
        jectivity, 93
    view on shame, 89, 99
Strachey, J., 34, *40*
Strength, 183
Student, university, instances of
        shame in, 233, 234
Studies on Hysteria (Breuer &
        Freud), 7, 9
Subgroup, as sacred community, 239
Subject
    bond with object, 13
    as isolated, 92
Submission, 405
Sudnow, D., 257n, *260*
Suffering, shame entailing, 166
Suicide, 73
    avoiding shame by, 241–242
    Durkheim's view on, 223
Superego, 66, 90, 140
    aggression against outside world,
        379
    conflict in, 185, 373, 377–378
    constricted sense of, 24

envy and resentment vested in,
        378
    Freud's view on, 23–26
    Nietzsche's view on, 201
    postoedipal, 26
    problems, 367, 368
    projecting onto analyst as leader
        or parental figure, 34
    totalitarian, 378
Superego anxiety, shame as, 25
Superego phenomena, types of,
        Freud's view on, 29
Superman, *See also* Overman
    audacity of, 188
Support groups, use of, 394
Supportive social structure, people
        cut off from, 68
Surnames, use of, in physician's
        office, 392
Surprise, 112, 343
Surprise-startle, 121, 356
Surrender, 400
Surrey, J., 317, *322*
Sussman, H., 316, *323*
"Switching on" experiments, 52

T

Tangney, J., 145, *154*
Tavuchis, N., 148, *154*
    view on genuine apology, 148
Taylor, G., 209, *230*
Teasing, sadistic, 58
Tension, ego-syntonic avoidance of,
        277–278
Terror, 123, 125, *See also* Fear-terror
    intense state of, 125
    pulse and respirations in, 342
Thanatos, 24, 25, 334
Theoretical claim, 185
Theoretical construct, shame as, 118
Therapeutic situation
    impasse, in, as antecedent to
        shame, vii
Therapist
    patient's love for, 400, 401
    perfect emotional equilibrium of,
        332
    responsiveness, addiction to, 81
    unawareness of pride and shame
        in therapy, 221